Mr. Basketball

MR. BASKETBALL

George Mikan, the Minneapolis Lakers,
and the Birth of the NBA

MICHAEL SCHUMACHER

BLOOMSBURY

Published by Bloomsbury USA, New York
Distributed to the trade by Holtzbrinck Publishers

All papers used by Bloomsbury USA are natural,
recyclable products made from wood grown in well-managed forests.
The manufacturing processes conform to the environmental
regulations of the country of origin.

LIBRARY OF CONGRESS CATALOGING-IN-PUBLICATION DATA

Schumacher, Michael.
Mr. Basketball : George Mikan, the Minneapolis Lakers, and the
birth of the NBA / by Michael Schumacher.—1st U.S. ed.
p. cm.
ISBN-13: 978-1-59691-213-7
ISBN-10: 1-59691-213-8
1. Mikan, George, 1924–2005. 2. Basketball players—United States—Biography.
3. Minneapolis Lakers (Basketball team)—History. I. Title. II. Title: George Mikan,
the Minneapolis Lakers, and the birth of the NBA.

GV884.M54S38 2007
796.323092—dc22
[B]
2007009066

First U.S. Edition 2007

1 3 5 7 9 10 8 6 4 2

Typeset by Westchester Book Group
Printed in the United States of America by Quebecor World Fairfield

For my brothers and sisters:
Gary, Mark, Anne, Sue, Jim, Mary Kay, and Teresa,
and their families

(I can't do one for each of you, so this will have to do.)

*George Mikan is 6 feet 10 inches tall, but he could not be greater
if he were 10 feet 6 inches tall.*
—Oscar Fraley, United Press International

*A little guy with an Uzi came over. He said, "That's George Mikan.
I saw him play at the Garden."*
—George Mikan, remembering an incident
at a security checkpoint in Tel Aviv

CONTENTS

PROLOGUE

Wednesday, December 14, 1949

NEW YORK CITY is decorated in greens and reds for the upcoming holiday season. It's business as usual, as the country's largest city prepares for its annual festivities. The Rockettes are high-kicking before sold-out audiences at Radio City Music Hall, holiday movies are playing in theaters all over Manhattan, and Christmas trees are being sold on sidewalk lots. Storefront windows are decked out in seasonal décor.

At Madison Square Garden, a different kind of decorating is taking place on the marquee overhanging the sidewalk outside the main entrance.

Basketball's Minneapolis Lakers are in town to play the New York Knickerbockers at the Garden, but since the game is being staged in the middle of the week, the folks at Madison Square Garden want to make certain that everyone knows that the NBA's premier attraction is in town. After all, the National Basketball Association is a new league, competing with boxing and college basketball for the sports fan's dollar, and the other two sports draw much better than pro basketball. They'll pack the Garden in a couple of nights, when the popular "Friday Night Fights" take place.

Between now and then, fans need to know there's a game on, and not just any game.

The Lakers might be the reigning world champs, but George Mikan, the team's star center, is the NBA's meal ticket. He's the Babe Ruth of basketball, the main reason people in small towns in the Midwest leave the warmth of their homes to slosh through nasty weather to attend a game that's still a mystery to most of the country. Mikan only comes to New York City a few times a year, and even then, the chances are good that he'll be playing in the old 69th Regiment Armory rather than the Garden.

One by one, large letters are affixed to the theater-style Madison Square Garden marquee until the message is spelled out: GEO MIKAN v/s KNICKS.

Mikan arrives at the Garden at the appointed time, well before the game is scheduled to begin. He's to take part in a newspaper photo shoot. The setup is simple: Mikan is to climb up a tall ladder and, once he's reached the marquee, polish the letters of his name with a rag while a photographer snaps away.

As soon as he sees the sign, Mikan knows he's in for some serious ribbing from his teammates. Four of the Laker starters—Mikan, Jim Pollard, Slater Martin, and Vern Mikkelsen—will be Hall of Famers someday, and Pollard in particular is likely to take exception to the notion of Mikan's being a one-man team. Pollard would be the main man on any other club in basketball, but with the Lakers he's running a distant second to Mikan, at least in the eyes of the fans and the media.

Mikan knows that he's being used—by the Knicks, Lakers, and NBA—to publicize a league in dire need of promotion. It's not uncommon for him to travel to an opposing team's city a day or two in advance of his teammates. He'll meet with the press, pose for photos, schmooze with the bigwigs—anything to let the people in town know that there's an upcoming game. He complains about it privately from time to time, but when the flashbulbs go off or the microphones are switched on, he's all smiles.

"George was good-natured about it," Harry "Bud" Grant would remember many years later. Grant, a backup forward with the Lakers, would eventually earn his Hall of Fame credentials in football, first as a player, then as coach of the Minnesota Vikings. According to Grant, "[Mikan] would bitch and moan sometimes about the imposition they put on him, but he always did it. He enjoyed being George Mikan. Nobody enjoyed [the publicity] more than he did."

He's a natural at it. With his black horn-rimmed glasses and Hollywood grin, he's got a Clark Kent look to him, and, like the DC Comics character, he knows he'll turn into someone almost invincible once he trades his suit and tie for the uniform that made him his name. He has a friendly midwestern air about him—a personality that contradicts the ferocious competitor he becomes when he's on the court—and he's bright enough to anticipate and deliver what the press and basketball fans are looking for.

He's up on the ladder, polishing away at the lettering, when Vern Mikkelsen walks up. Mik has heard from a reporter that the Garden had a publicity stunt like this in the works, and rather than use the players' entrance to the building, he's decided to walk around the building and inspect the marquee firsthand.

What he finds is the Lakers' most valuable player, dressed in a tent-sized overcoat, hovering over the sidewalk on a ladder that might or might not bear up under his weight.

Mikkelsen is amused by the whole thing, but he's also a little uneasy about it.

"George," he scolds when Mikan finally makes his way back down the ladder, "what in the heck are you doing? You could have slipped on one of those steps, or that stepladder could have crashed down and you could have been done."

Mikkelsen has a way of being serious even when he's kidding around. Like Mikan, he's a brute force on the Lakers' front line, a total mauler on the boards, but this son of a preacher rarely swears, and he has a quiet, direct demeanor that seems to add weight to anything he says.

"I didn't even think of that," Mikan allows.

"Well, just keep that in mind next time."

The two head for the visitors' locker room. Some of the other Laker players are already there, but nobody's in any rush to dress for the game. Mikan thinks nothing of it. He finds his locker, takes off his glasses and places them safely above the locker, and begins his nightly ritual of preparing for the game. The process takes a while, often up to a half hour, since the Lakers don't travel with a trainer and he has to tape his own ankles. While he dresses, he listens to his teammates carrying on with their usual locker-room conversation and banter.

Unbeknownst to Mikan, Slater Martin, the Lakers' scrappy little guard and locker-room leader, has set him up for a practical joke. Mikan is a little gullible to begin with; and that, along with the fierce intensity that he brings to every game, makes him a natural target for pranks. The Madison Square Garden marquee has given Martin an idea. "Pretend you're getting dressed for the game, but keep your regular clothes on," he's instructed the others. "I'll take care of it."

Mikan is half-blind without his glasses. Everything in the room is a blur, and he has no idea that his mates aren't getting ready for the game. He only notices them in their street clothes after he's slipped on his game glasses.

"What are you guys doing?" he asks.

Martin steps forward and answers without a trace of humor.

"It says on the marquee that it's Mikan versus the Knicks," he declares. "You get 'em. Go ahead and play them. Good luck to you."

At first, Mikan doesn't realize that Martin is joking. He cusses at his teammates and orders them to get dressed. Then a few of the guys laugh and Mikan finally understands that he's been had. He also knows that it won't end now. They'll be giving him the business about this for weeks to come.

It's different when the Lakers take the floor. The players are all business, focused on what's sure to be a very tough game ahead. Winning on the road is always a challenge, regardless of where you're playing, and the Knicks are murder in the Garden. The New York team is hot, winners of eleven of its last twelve games. The Knicks have all kinds of talent, including four or five players who can light up the scoreboard on any given night. "Tricky" Dick McGuire, the Knicks' superb playmaking guard, has the uncanny ability of seeing that the ball gets distributed to whoever has the hot hand.

Trying to beat this team on their home court is a tall order.

Opposing teams' fans can be disruptive at best, violent at worst, but Mikan enjoys the Knicks' fans. He can't stand their cigarette and cigar smoke, which creates a haze in the building and bothers his allergies, and he's been unnerved by an occasional remark; but as a rule, the Knicks' fans know their basketball and will applaud a good effort, even when it's coming from an opponent. If they give him all kinds of verbal grief over the course of a game, at least it's not as nasty as it is in Rochester or Syracuse, where the fans truly hate his guts. As far as Mikan's concerned, it's all part of the price of stardom.

He wouldn't have been able to predict any of this six or seven years ago, when he was just starting out at DePaul University. He'd always been a lot taller than the average guy—reason enough for the Chicago school to hazard a look at him—but it had taken a lot of hard work for him to really learn the game. Once he did, he was unstoppable. His skills had improved with each passing season, first in college and then in the pros, until he'd reached a level of play that literally found the game changing its rules in order to stop him. So far, nobody had succeeded.

Slater Martin dribbles the ball up the floor. Once in the forecourt, he fires a pass in to Jim Pollard on the left wing. Pollard squares up for a shot, but he has a man on him. Mikan moves up near the basket, and he holds up his arm, calling for the ball. It's always a good idea to get the ball to Big George when he calls for it.

When Pollard and Mikan are in sync, they can take the air out of a room. Pollard has a bounce pass with some real English on it: it'll actually spin away from a defender playing behind Mikan, giving the Minneapolis center the chance to use his long reach to bring in the pass. At this point, things can get interesting. Pollard has amazing quickness, and if a defender isn't careful, Pollard will cut past him, take a return pass from Mikan, and score an easy layup. Or, if he chooses, Mikan will take the shot himself.

It's a play that Coach John Kundla drew up for the two, and, so far, no team has an answer for it. In time, it will be a standard play for all levels of basketball, from playground to pros, but this is the era of freelance basketball, when very few plays are designed, practiced, or used in a game. Most teams have a few plays they might try after a time-out; the Lakers have them for all occasions.

Mikan takes Pollard's pass and, without putting the ball on the floor, turns toward the basket. In the future, tall, athletic centers and forwards will move with a grace that will prompt sportswriters to drag the word "ballet" into some of their game descriptions. That will never be the case with George Mikan. His move to the basket, strong and violent, carries a whole lot of force and very little grace. He swings his left arm out and slams it into his Knick defender, who, by instinct, has moved in closer to block his path to the basket. Mikan's arm catches the defender and knocks him silly. With his right hand, Mikan launches a hook shot that will influence generations of future centers. The ball drops through the cylinder for two points.

He could do this in his sleep.

The jury is still out on the new league calling itself the National Basketball Association. It's only been a matter of weeks since the NBA opened its inaugural season, after combining teams from the Basketball Association of America and the old National Basketball League to form the new league, and the fans are just getting used to it. New Yorkers have to pull out their atlases to find Fort Wayne, Waterloo, Sheboygan, and Anderson. All have teams in the NBA.

Mikan knows where all these cities are, and then some. Although he's only beginning his fourth year as a pro, he's already played in the National Basketball League, the Basketball Association of America, and, for a very brief time, a doomed pro league called the Professional Basketball League of America. He's played pro games everywhere, it seems, from Oshkosh to Moline—and that doesn't even include the barnstorming adventures that have found him playing in every Godforsaken city in the midwestern and plains states. He's played in high school gyms and dance halls, in state fairgrounds and makeshift courts. One thing has always remained the same: no matter where he's turned up, he's the main attraction.

He's also the game's highest-paid player.

But on this night, in front of 9,500 in the Garden, he isn't going to beat the Knicks singlehandedly. Dick McGuire has an outstanding night and the Knicks take the contest, 94–84. The New York Times *will call the game a thriller; Mikan will call it a loss. It doesn't happen all that often to the Lakers—they'll only lose seventeen games during the season—but Mikan doesn't take well to losing at all.*

So far, every pro team that he's played for has won its league championship. This year's team will be no exception. And, when the season ends, he'll be given the greatest honor of his career when he's named the greatest player of the first half of the twentieth century. With that honor will come the nickname that he'll carry with him for the rest of his career: Mr. Basketball.

One

Awkward Kid with Glasses

GEORGE MIKAN WOULD always remember an incident that occurred in his family's tavern when he was a college student at DePaul University. Many nights, after classes and basketball practice, he'd return home to Joliet, a southwestern suburb of Chicago, and spend the evening behind the bar, serving *kannuppers*—shots of liquor—to the bar's working class clientele.

One evening, two strangers walked into the place, approached Mikan, and informed him that they were the new neighborhood "protection." Mikan's Tavern, they said, would be paying them protection money in the future.

Several of the bar's regulars, witnessing the confrontation, broke beer bottles and, brandishing their jagged remains, ordered the intruders out of the bar, lest they need protection of their own.

And that was the end of that.

Mikan never said whether the next round was on the house, but he never forgot the lesson.

Or any of the others that made him the man he would become.

Carl Sandburg didn't give Chicago big shoulders because he needed a catchy personification for one of his poems. The city earned its reputation. This was the hub of the Midwest, the base of Lake Michigan. People from the East, moving westward across land in pursuit of American fortune, stopped there for a rest and stayed for a lifetime. There was always work in building and shipping, or in the stockyards, the railroad yards, the factories, or, if you were really ambitious, your own business. Even in its youth, Chicago had an old soul.

Chicago grew, neighborhoods expanded. The ethnic cells of the city divided. Bordering towns sprang up and developed into their own distinct enclaves, each with distinctive personalities. More and more smokestacks poked into the sky. Families nursed at the teat of heavy industry. Chicago and its neighboring suburbs were no places for pretension or people with unfocused hearts. You worked hard, you said what you meant; your identity was forged by a work ethic that demanded that you keep things simple and clean—unless, of course, you were a politician. The city's politics could be as corrupt as rust eating through iron pipe; but when it attached itself to the average working man, he preferred to look the other way. Chicago, as the saying went, was a city that worked, even when the law was interpreted by the person most likely to benefit from it.

Two of the city's great writers, Studs Terkel and Mike Royko, recognized all this and devoted their careers to giving voice to the working stiff. Both learned the ropes growing up in tough, adult-filled environments. Terkel, who appropriated his nickname from James T. Farrell's Studs Lonigan character, grew up in rooming houses run by his family, in places called home by some of the neighborhoods' more colorful figures. Terkel learned to listen for the humanity bleeding into the words of the underdog, the downtrodden, the soapbox preachers of Bughouse Square, the battered spirits of the day-to-day survivors. He knew instinctively that their stories carried at least as much clout—and a lot more salt—than the voices shouting off the front pages of the *Chicago Tribune*. In time, their voices, or voices like theirs, were immortalized first on Terkel's radio programs, and then in such works as *Division Street: America*, *Hard Times*, and *Working*.

"Sparrows, as always, are the most abundant of our city birds," Terkel wrote poignantly. "It is never glory time for them. As always, they do the best they can. Which isn't very much. They forever peck away and, in some cock-eyed fashion, survive the day. Others—well, who said life was fair?"

Royko celebrated similar individuals in his newspaper columns, his disdain for the high and mighty translated into the language of sarcasm, his innermost feelings given voice through a blue-collar alter-ego named Slats Grobnik. Royko, who spent his early years living above a tavern, received his education on the ways of the world on a bar stool throne, where truth was usually assisted by alcohol and scores occasionally settled on the spot.

Even after he'd received celebrity status from his syndicated column, Royko preferred to knock back a few with the guys who ran the printing presses rather than fellow writers, more often than not in an establishment called "Billy Goats," run by an Old Countryman named Sam Sianis, whose shouts for "cheez-borkers" became part of the public consciousness in the renowned *Saturday Night Live* comedy skits.

George Mikan spent his youth among such people. He would readily admit, as he did in the opening passage of his autobiography, that he was a simple man, not given to flowery words or grandiose actions. What you saw was what you got. He grew up in a neighborhood populated by Croatians, Italians, Serbs, and Slovaks—people with neither the time nor patience for anything artificial.

Nor, for as long as he lived, did Mikan.

George Lawrence Mikan was born on June 18, 1924, the second of four children in a working-class family from Joliet. Mikan was named after his paternal grandfather, known in the family as Gramps or Grandpa George. The elder Mikan had been born and raised in Eastern Europe, in what is now Croatia. He'd met his wife, Mary, always called Blondie by friends and family, and the two had eventually made their way to the United States. They settled in Pittsburgh, where George worked in a steel mill, and he and Blondie raised their son, Joseph.

Gramps and Blondie moved to the outskirts of Joliet and opened Mikan's Tavern, a popular watering hole among the city's blue-collar workers, located on the corner of Elsie Avenue and North Broadway. The entire Mikan clan lived and worked there. For the Mikans, living and working were virtually synonymous. The Mikans lived in a house connected to the bar, so they were never too far removed from all the reminders of work.

When Joe grew up and married, he and his wife, Minnie, stayed with Joe's parents in the 101 Elsie Avenue house. The extended family continued to grow with the addition of Joe and Minnie's children, each of whom was expected to contribute to the family enterprise. Gramps and Joe ran the tavern, Blondie raised the kids, and Minnie supplied the delicious home-cooked meals that gave the tavern its reputation. The children—Joe, George, Eddie, and Marie—helped around the kitchen or the bar. Mikan's Tavern was, in every sense, a mom 'n' pop operation.

The younger George would always remember his family as being extremely tight-knit. He grew up to the sounds of his grandparents' speaking Croatian, the smells of his mother's fried chicken, and the sight of his grandfather standing behind the bar, pouring drafts of ice-cold beer for local characters with such unlikely names as the Crazy Serbian or Monkey Joe, tavern regulars who held down bar stools and saw that there was always a rattle in the cash register drawer whenever it was slammed shut.

Minnie made some of the best fried chicken in the Chicagoland area, and for thirty-five cents, customers could eat their fill. The Mikans were a tall, big-boned group—Joe was six-one and Minnie, five-eleven—and with three growing boys, they expected hefty appetites. George's friends and teammates would remember their visits to the Mikan house, where they would be fed until they thought they would burst.

"They were all Croatian, from the Old Country, and they were up at six o'clock in the morning, cooking chicken," Gene Stump, one of Mikan's DePaul teammates, recalled. "They'd bring out a platter, and it'd be enough for a whole table, but that was just yours."

"It was an experience, staying overnight at his house," Charlie Butler, a teammate on the Chicago Gears, pointed out. "His mother was a good cook, and she made sure there was ample food on the table. The three boys were big guys, and they were always saying, 'Eat more, eat more, eat more.'"

Mikan's Tavern also featured a weekly fish fry, and Joe, George, and, later, Eddie grew to hate Fridays, when they'd spend much of the day scaling, cleaning, and salting fish until they could no longer stand the sight or smell of Lake Michigan perch. The huge meals, however, served a greater purpose than simply earning a family its livelihood: in Depression and post-Depression Joliet, day-to-day life could be tough, and the Mikans, who lived two blocks from the edge of town, saw the gray faces of those sweating out livings in the nearby refineries, paper mills, and factories. They only had to look out their window to see the brickyard across the street, or, at night, with the smells of American industry still hanging in the humid air, they could listen to a train passing nearby, moving cargo to places a bit more hopeful. A platter of fried chicken or a decent fish fry might not have meant much to the people living on Chicago's Gold Coast, but they meant comfort to the working stiffs of Joliet, and if a soul stumbled in without the wherewithal for a home-cooked meal or glass of beer, the Mikans would see that they were taken care of in any event.

George Mikan's father had a saying that stuck with his son throughout his life: "Do the best you can," the elder Mikan advised his son, "and so be judged."

When they weren't sweeping the barroom floor, doing dishes, scaling and cleaning fish, waiting tables, doing odd jobs around the house, or, nine months a year, attending classes at St. Mary's Croatian School, the Mikan boys might be found playing in neighborhood pickup games or skating at the roller rink next door. All were very athletic, and they had each other's back if things got rough.

Charlie Butler recalled a time, when the Mikan boys were older, when he got to see the Mikans in action. George had just purchased a car and, on the way home, he inadvertently cut off a Chicago cab driver. The cabbie responded with a Windy City salute.

"The cab driver rolled down his window and let out the biggest string of swear words you've ever heard," Butler recalled. "And, with that, three doors opened. George, his brother Ed, and his older brother Joe—all got out of the car. I wish I had a picture of that cab driver, rolling up the window. He couldn't have picked another car where three bigger guys were sitting at the door."

It wasn't all sports, though. George took piano lessons, and while no one would ever mistake him for Horowitz, he was a skilled player. (He'd later claim that eight years of piano lessons, although not welcome at the time because they took him away from other activities, helped build the soft hands and strong fingers that came in so handy in his basketball career.)

Then there were the neighborhood marbles games: Joe and George Mikan were the best around—George boasted that he shot so accurately that he could "dot the i in my name at forty paces" with his shooter—and a Will County marbles tournament, sponsored by the *Herald-News*, gave George his fondest childhood memory.

He'd just turned ten, and he'd beaten all comers, including his brother Joe, in the tournament. The first-place prize was a trip to Comiskey Park for a White Sox game, but it wasn't just any baseball game: the Sox were playing the New York Yankees; and before the game, Mikan and the other counties' champs were taken to the field to meet Babe Ruth. Mikan shook hands with

Ruth, and the two talked briefly about the tournament. Ruth promised to hit a home run for Mikan and, to the young boy's delight, he did.

"For a moment," he'd joke, years later, "I thought he could perform on command."

After the game, the boys were again taken to the field, this time to pose with Ruth for pictures for the paper. The fan who had caught the home run ball was also there, and he asked Ruth to sign it for him. Ruth signed the ball but, rather than return it to the fan, he palmed it and gave him one of the balls he'd autographed for the boys. After the fan had left, Ruth handed the home run ball to Mikan.

About that time, Mikan began playing basketball, albeit a crude form of it. Joe and George Mikan were shooting up in height—the photo of George with Ruth shows George to be almost Ruth's height—and Joe, wanting to play on his school's team, fashioned a homemade backboard and basket out of an old board and a barrel rim. For a basketball, the boys used a beach ball with its valve taped down. Neither knew the first thing about the rules, but that didn't prevent them from playing one-on-one for hours on end. Blondie settled their occasional disputes, usually with a broom that she was happy to use on an offending party. She knew no more about the rules than either of the two boys, but she had a pretty good notion about what was fair.

For a while, it looked as if a couple of childhood mishaps might have conspired to prevent Mikan from playing the game he loved.

The first incident occurred when Mikan was twelve years old. He was sitting in the tavern's kitchen, watching his older brother whittle a piece of wood with a butcher knife. Whittling had become one of Joe's obsessions, and George loved to watch him fashion slingshots out of forked branches or little toy boats out of small, flat scraps of wood. On this occasion, Joe dug the knife blade too deep in the wood and the knife blade stuck. Joe struggled with the knife to pry the blade loose, and when a sliver of wood finally tore free, it flew up and caught George in the corner of his left eye, next to his nose. As George would later recall, there was a lot of screaming and bleeding, and his parents rushed him to the family doctor, who stitched the cut and told them George had suffered some nerve damage to his eye. From that point on—or so it seemed to the family—George's eyesight weakened until he eventually had to get eyeglasses with a strong prescription. Whether the accident was responsible for George's needing glasses, as Joe feared, was debatable. George's father had very weak eyes and wore glasses and, in all likelihood, his son wore glasses more as a result of heredity than as the result of an accident.

Whatever the reason, the thick-lensed glasses became a lifetime trademark. Mikan hated wearing them, as most kids do, and later, at a time before contact lenses became affordable and popular, he would play basketball with his glasses taped to his head, or held on by a thick strap that connected the stems at the back of his head. His coaches carried extra pairs of glasses in case his regular game glasses were broken, which they occasionally were. Elbows would send the glasses flying or would drive them into Mikan's face, cutting him and causing a stoppage of play. His glasses would fog over or get drippy from sweat, and opposing coaches would complain that Mikan's teams were actually taking a time-out when they (or George) would ask for a moment for him to wipe his glasses. There was never a question about whether he needed them to play: without the glasses, he'd say, his vision was similar to trying to look through a car's windshield during a rainstorm when the car had no wipers.

The extent to which Mikan's poor eyesight affected his play is debatable, but at least one of his foes believed it was significant. Bob Kurland, a star college player at Oklahoma A&M and a Mikan nemesis throughout his college career, felt that Mikan's ability to see all of the court might have been impaired by his weak vision.

"I believe that if he had any weaknesses, it was the fact that he had to wear glasses," Kurland said. "His peripheral vision wasn't probably as good as it might have been, had he not worn glasses. They cut down on his seeing the movement of players on the outside part of the court. He could always turn his head, but if you could see the guy more and not give away the fact that you saw him, you had a better chance of deceiving his opponent, in terms of where you threw the ball."

When he first started wearing glasses and his eyes weren't as weak as they would become, Mikan tried going without them. His classmates teased him about them and he was already taking enough guff about his height. When he tried out for basketball as a freshman at Joliet Catholic High School, he did so without his glasses. Despite his lack of experience—and probably because of his height—he escaped cut after cut, lasting until the day before Joliet Catholic's first game, when the coach had to cut the team from fourteen players to twelve.

After the final practice, Father Gilbert Burns, the priest coaching Joliet Catholic's team, caught Mikan squinting while he was delivering a pep talk to the team.

"What are you squinting at?" he demanded.

Mikan muttered something about the light's bothering his eyes, but the coach wouldn't accept the explanation. Nobody else, he pointed out, seemed to be bothered by the light.

Mikan had no choice but to come clean.

"I guess it's because I'm not wearing my glasses," he confessed.

Father Burns's decision was instant and final. He told Mikan to turn in his uniform.

"You just can't play basketball with glasses on," he declared.

At least that's the way Mikan would tell the story later. The glasses were probably a convenient excuse, a way to help the coach make a difficult decision. As Ray Meyer would discover a few years later, Mikan was a smart, willing athlete; but apart from his height, he had little to distinguish him from other players. He still needed a lot of work.

It was a difficult, confusing time for the young teenager. He was growing like a weed, but he couldn't play basketball for the school team because he wore glasses. He was bored with his piano practicing and lessons, which cut into what little time he had after attending classes, doing homework, or helping around the house or tavern. For most of his boyhood, he'd figured he would be a doctor when he grew up, but even those aspirations faded after he and Blondie visited a parish priest laid up in the hospital. The priest suggested that Mikan might make an excellent Catholic priest, and he encouraged George to attend the seminary. Mikan wasn't so sure about the vocation, but he did know that, after the basketball fiasco, he was through with Joliet Catholic. When the priest set up a parish scholarship fund to help defray the expenses of his attending the seminary, Mikan decided to give it a shot.

Commuting to Quigley Preparatory Seminary required some effort. The school was located on Chicago's far north side; to get there from Joliet, Mikan had to catch, first, a bus to a nearby railroad station, then a train to downtown Chicago, and finally a streetcar to the school. The trip, including all the transfers, took more than two hours. Mikan traveled to the school every day with two friends also studying for the priesthood, and after taking the long way to Quigley for a few weeks, the boys were able to persuade the Joliet Bluebird Bus Lines to take them straight from Joliet to Chicago, which cut the travel time by more than a half hour.

Mikan was too busy with his schoolwork to even consider playing any basketball other than an occasional intramural game, but the Joliet Catholic experience, as depressing as it was, failed to totally extinguish his enthusiasm for the sport. Mikan would never accept defeat—or even the suggestion that there was something he couldn't do, once he applied himself to it—and at the beginning of his second year at Quigley, he joined a Catholic Youth Organization (CYO) league. Joe and George Mikan played on the same team, and their height made them a formidable center and forward combination.

It was during his stint in CYO basketball that Mikan had to deal with his second serious basketball-threatening injury. His team had driven to Waukegan, a city about a half hour north of Chicago, to play a rare road game against the St. Anne's CYO team. The game had just started when Mikan, wearing new gym shoes, tried to move around his opponent and the sole of one of his new shoes stuck to the floor like a suction cup. Mikan stopped suddenly, twisting awkwardly, and his opponent ran into his leg. Mikan went down in a heap, his leg badly broken—a compound fracture. Mikan was loaded into the team's car, a converted hearse, and was driven around until someone could find a doctor to apply a temporary cast.

The hearse pulled up to the Mikan residence around midnight, and Joe dashed into the house to awaken his parents. Minnie Mikan fainted at the sight of her son in the back of the car, but the Mikans managed to get George in the house for the rest of the night. The following morning, he was taken to a hospital, where he would remain for the next eighteen days.

Months of rehabilitation followed. Ironically, Mikan went through a tremendous growing spurt while his leg was healing. At the time of the accident, Mikan stood five-eleven; by the time he was finally off crutches six months later, he had grown a half a foot.

He was now six-five, and still only fourteen years old.

It was inevitable that, sooner or later, George Mikan would be invited to play for the Quigley Prep basketball team, and the opportunity arose shortly after his return to the school following his long period of recovery from his leg injury.

The Quigley Prep coach, naturally interested in the much-taller-than-average seminarian he'd seen walking through the halls, approached Mikan about playing on the team. Mikan responded that he might be interested, but informed the coach that he had to wear glasses when he played. The coach wasn't concerned.

Mikan couldn't consider anything soon. He had fallen behind in his schoolwork while he was recovering from the broken leg, and he was scurrying to catch up. Besides, his leg was still too sore and weak to withstand any kind of strenuous activity. Coach and player agreed to meet again the following fall, at the beginning of Mikan's junior year.

Mikan never did play basketball during his junior year. His leg wasn't yet at full strength, and that, along with his schedule at school and at home, kept him from suiting up for the team. Starting at age fourteen, he'd taken a series of jobs, some in the summer, some year-round, to help supplement the family income. The first was with a railroad company, a job that involved his carrying heavy cross-ties, laying them out, and spiking them into place with a sledgehammer. The next year, he took a job with Joliet Rubberoid, loading skids and, eventually, stacking sheets of roofing. He built his strength through the physical jobs, but they also interfered with the practicing he needed for basketball.

He finally played for Quigley Prep during his fourth year at the school, although on a very limited basis. His size and strength gave him a huge advantage over his opponents, but his other obligations and the long commute to and from school prohibited him from playing except on Wednesdays and Saturdays. Quigley Prep didn't belong to a conference, so the school played a grab-bag of games, some against strong schools, many against weaker opponents.

Charlie Butler, a teammate of Mikan's as a professional, played high-school ball against Quigley Prep. The team, as he recalled it, was undisciplined and poorly trained.

"We used to go to their bandbox at Quigley and I was scared to death," he said. "I was never a very husky person, and when you played against five guys who really didn't know what they were doing, you could get killed very easily. They were all tough kids, but they didn't work together."

St. Leo's was one of the strongest teams Quigley played, and Mikan scored 24 points against the Chicago school. After the game, Mikan was approached by Paul Mattei, the athletic director at DePaul University. Mattei had been scouting one of the St. Leo's players, but he had his head turned by Mikan's performance.

"If you ever want to go to college," he told Mikan, "come to DePaul and we'll give you a scholarship."

When Mikan decided to attend DePaul, he enrolled without telling his parents. He wasn't sure how they—or Blondie, for that matter—would react to his decision to abandon his studies for the priesthood, so he reasoned that they wouldn't need to know—not right away, at least. The costs of his tuition and books were being covered by his scholarship to DePaul, so who knew how long he could maintain the ruse of his still attending the seminary?

The answer: until he got his name in the paper.

His father happened to be reading the sports pages of the *Chicago Tribune* one morning in the fall of 1941 when he spotted an item that caught his attention. He called George into the kitchen and showed him the article.

"I never knew we had relations in Chicago," he said, "but there's a George Mikan playing for DePaul University."

George told his father the truth. He filled him in on the scholarship offer and his decision to leave Quigley Prep, and how he was now thinking about becoming a lawyer. He hadn't wanted to disappoint everyone, he said, so he'd just said nothing about transferring to DePaul.

Fortunately, his father was more amused than upset by the disclosures. DePaul was a good Catholic school with a solid reputation for its academics, and if the priesthood wasn't George's calling, a job as an attorney would be plenty respectable. George would be attending classes near home, which meant he'd be able to tend bar in the evenings in the tavern.

Playing for the DePaul freshman team proved to be nothing special. The freshman team was essentially a practice squad for the varsity, and Mikan and his teammates were, in Mikan's words, "guinea pigs" on which the varsity experimented with new plays. The freshmen occasionally scrimmaged with another school, but for someone like Mikan, who needed instruction in his continued development as a player, the freshman squad was barely adequate. He was, however, getting quite a bit of basketball from all the games he played for CYO and City League teams. He and Joe were still teammates, but now they'd been joined by Eddie, who, like his older brothers, had grown to well over six feet and was showing great promise of his own.

The attack on Pearl Harbor and the United States' entry into World War II changed the face of college basketball. The war meant a sudden loss of talent, as young men everywhere, caught up in the patriotic fervor immediately following Pearl Harbor, enlisted in the service. Ironically, some of the best basketball teams in America could now be found on some of the armed forces bases, which, over the next five years, would assemble teams that competed with other units and colleges. Organized professional and amateur leagues, such as the National Basketball League and Amateur Athletic Union, were affected as well.

Nothing changed for Mikan. Every morning, he'd be up early to catch the Bluebird bus to Chicago. He'd attend classes until 1:00, and then it would be basketball practice. He'd be home by 5:30 in the late afternoon. He managed to complete most of his homework on his bus trips into and out of the city, although there were times when the bus was full and he'd have to stand for most of the trip. On some of those trips, he'd joke later, he managed to catch a catnap while hanging from the bus strap.

One day in December 1941, after a vigorous scrimmage against the varsity, Mikan was pulled aside by Frank Gaglioni, a Notre Dame alumnus and the present coach of Joliet Catholic, Mikan's old school.

"George," Gaglioni began, "why don't you go to a school that's known for basketball? Why don't you go to Notre Dame?"

Mikan wasn't immediately interested. He told Gaglioni that he was happy at DePaul, where he had a full scholarship and was living close to home. Notre Dame had a terrific basketball program, but he wasn't sure he'd fit in.

Gaglioni explained that he could set up a tryout. Notre Dame offered scholarships to those making the team, and with a little guidance from a good coach—someone like Notre Dame's highly regarded George Keogan—Mikan might develop into an outstanding player. After all,

Mikan already possessed one quality that others couldn't gain through hard work: height.

"I'm going up during Christmas vacation," he continued. "Why don't you run along up there with me and meet George Keogan?"

Mikan thought it over. He had nothing to lose by going to South Bend, and maybe there might also be a place on the team for his brother Joe. Mikan finally agreed, on the condition that Joe could tag along.

"We were going to give them a package deal," Mikan remembered.

At Notre Dame, Mikan met Keogan and his assistant, Ray Meyer. During the tryout, Mikan played with Notre Dame's freshman team against the varsity, and he fared no better than he did when DePaul's freshman team went up against the more experienced players on the varsity. Mikan had a difficult time keeping up with the quicker players, and he looked clumsy. To make matters worse, he had injured his right foot during a recent DePaul practice, and his movement was badly hindered.

Keogan had seen enough. Practice ended and he pulled Mikan aside. He told Mikan he wasn't sure he was basketball material; he might be better served, Keogan suggested, if he returned to Chicago and hit the books, maybe make his way via the academic route. In any event, he wasn't a good Notre Dame candidate. If he really had his heart set on basketball, he'd have to look elsewhere.

"Go to a school," Keogan advised him, "a little school where they have a lot of time to spend with you."

Neither Mikan brother would be playing for Notre Dame, but George, never one to admit defeat, wasn't about to listen to Keogan's telling him that he was a scholar, not a basketball player.

"You'd be wrong on two counts," he told the coach.

After the tryout, Notre Dame's trainer took a look at Mikan's foot and told him he had a broken arch. Mikan would always blame the injury for his failure to make the Notre Dame team, and while there may have been a good deal of truth to it, it was probably more a case of his finding a convenient excuse. Throughout his basketball career in college and the pros, Mikan would suffer from bad feet. His arches were shot from the beginning, to such an extent that he had special shoes and arch supports made for him. Anyway, even if his feet had been in perfect health, Mikan might not have made the team.

Not that it mattered: he was comfortable at DePaul, and he'd earn his reputation at the Chicago school.

Or so he thought, until the first day of practice in the fall of 1942. DePaul had a new coach named Ray Meyer, the same Ray Meyer whom Mikan had seen standing at George Keogan's side in South Bend.

Mikan figured it might be time to look for another school.

Two

THE PROJECT

R AY MEYER, DEPAUL University's first-year basketball coach, took one look at George Mikan out on the practice floor and thought, "This big guy is my future."

In a sport populated by tall, slender men, Mikan towered over everyone around him, and he was broad enough through the shoulders to make going through a doorway a tight squeeze.

And he was still growing.

An old basketball cliché says you can't teach height, but Meyer had an observation of his own: A big man could score more points by accident than a short player could get through hard work. Now, if only he could find a way to teach this big kid some coordination and basketball . . .

Meyer remembered Mikan from his disastrous tryout with Notre Dame a few months earlier. He'd watched Mikan walk away, and, as far as he knew, he would never see him again. Then, only a few weeks later, DePaul Coach Willie Wendt resigned. The team had lost eleven of its last fourteen games, finishing with a 10–12 record in what had started out as a promising season. DePaul hired Meyer as his replacement, and Meyer inherited a team that, by all indications, had underachieved during the previous season, largely due to a lack of discipline. Not even certain that he wanted the job, Meyer had insisted on a one-year contract. DePaul would have to improve in a hurry or he'd wind up regretting his decision to leave the security of Notre Dame.

Meyer called his first spring practice on April 1. The Mikan kid was there, standing head and shoulders above the rest of the players assembled before him.

"There are no positions filled on the team," Meyer began, "and if any-body here doesn't want to work hard at basketball, he may as well not even bother us."

That said, Meyer removed his navy-blue sport coat, loosened his tie, and began practice in earnest. He ran his team through the old, familiar drills and added a few new ones. He encouraged some of the players and chewed out others; he even dismissed one for not giving enough effort. There would be no loafing on this team.

Through it all, he kept a close eye on Mikan. The big guy was clumsy as hell, but he also showed plenty of raw talent. Best of all, he worked harder than any two or three other guys combined. He'd probably make a pretty good player, Meyer thought, but they'd have to start from scratch.

Meyer called Mikan over for a brief word.

"You see this round ball?" he asked, handing Mikan a basketball. "You take this and put it in that basket over there. That's the object of this game."

At a later time, the sports media would call a kid like George Mikan a "project," meaning that he had a whole lot of natural talent and potential, but he'd need a boatload of work and coaching if he ever expected to amount to anything.

To Ray Meyer, George Mikan was a project—and then some.

Mikan had played a little ball for DePaul's freshman team the year be-fore, but, other than that, he'd had precious little experience in tough, competitive basketball. CYO and City League ball didn't count. NCAA basketball was an entirely different game, and Mikan would have to sub-stantially elevate his game if he ever hoped to play for the Blue Demons. Mikan's footwork, if one were being kind, was marginal, and his size and bulk, which should have been an advantage, worked against him. He'd run into anyone or anything, which would only translate into a flurry of fouls when it came time to play a regular game. He had a passable right-handed hook shot, but not much else; defensive players would be able to stop him by blocking his movements to his right. He could run all right for someone six-seven, and he could jump just enough to be a rebounding threat.

A project.

But this project had qualities you could nurture.

"George was a very intelligent man," Meyer recalled years later. "I learned from him that it's easier to coach an intelligent person than it is to coach a dumb one. You tell an intelligent person what to do and he does it; a dumb one learns by repetition."

Meyer wasn't afraid to work overtime with his new protégé. To sharpen Mikan's physical skills and coordination, Meyer employed every kind of exercise he could think of, including some unorthodox drills not usually associated with basketball. DePaul had a boxing team, and Meyer had Mikan jumping rope with the boxers and working on a speed bag to sharpen his coordination and quickness. To improve his rhythm and grace, Meyer hired a short co-ed to teach him to dance. There seemed to be no end to Meyer's creative ways of goosing Mikan's motor skills.

"We even had a kid who stood about five-five run around the court so George could chase him," Meyer remembered.

The "kid," guard Billy Donato, ran Mikan all over the floor.

"Billy used to take him to the top of the circle and they'd go one on one," Meyer said. "Billy would go by him, and it looked like an elephant chasing a fly. But after a couple of weeks, George would get him, and if he didn't get him in front, he'd get him from behind. He was so determined."

Mikan was not only Meyer's pet project; he was his *only* project. After running his team through its initial practice, Meyer dismissed the players for the summer, choosing to focus all his attention on the kid he hoped would be his future starting center. He worked with him for six weeks, day in and day out, and, to his delight, Mikan was a quick learner. As a rule, you only had to show him something once, and then it would be a matter of perfecting through repetition.

"He couldn't do anything with his left hand, so I made him shoot about three hundred shots a day with his left hand," Meyer explained. "Then I'd stand him outside the basket, and I'd throw the ball up and make him re-bound. I'd hit it so it would come close to the basket and hit the board so it would come off the front and he'd have to use his other hand. I wanted him to learn to tip with one hand. For timing, I'd go to the top of the cir-cle, shoot the ball at the basket, and make him go up and bat it away; little did I know we'd ever use that in a game. He wasn't getting off the floor with his hook shots, so we put a bench [near the basket] and he had to jump over the bench to hit his hook shot."

Of all his creations, Meyer would be most remembered for what simply came to be known as the "Mikan Drill"—a drill that high school and college coaches would use for decades, long after Mikan's days at DePaul. The exhausting exercise, designed to combine quickness, coordination, and shooting skills, began with Meyer tossing Mikan the ball on the left side of the basket. Mikan would catch the ball with his left hand, move under the basket, and put up a right-handed shot; he would then catch the ball as it came through the net, move to the other side of the basket, and put up a left-handed shot. The exercise was repeated, over and over and over and over, with Mikan moving in a figure-eight pattern, until Mikan thought he would drop. The overall effect? Mikan learned to effectively shoot with both hands, which, combined with his massive size, made him almost unstoppable around the basket.

Even after Meyer dismissed Mikan for the summer, the personalized attention was only beginning. In the fall, when the entire DePaul squad assembled for regular practices, Mikan would stay after practice and work with his coach. The crash course produced steady improvement. Mikan was still a long way from becoming the dominating presence he'd become in the pivot, but he was light years ahead of the player he'd been when Meyer saw him that first practice, when size and bulk were his only real weapons.

Long after they had retired from their respective careers and were living the good lives that sports legends lead—being called for quotes on anniversary dates or whenever something important happened in their sports, being given lifetime achievement awards and having streets named after them, being asked to attend the big games at their alma maters, etc.— George Mikan and Ray Meyer would remain close, each crediting the other for his success. "I saw George Mikan and I saw my future," Meyer said in what would become one of his most often-quoted statements—a statement with a number of variations but always the same point—and Mikan responded by saying that he never would have been the player he became without Meyer's guidance. "One of the luckiest days of my life [was] when DePaul hired Ray Meyer to be the coach," he'd say. "Everything I learned, I learned from him."

If the two seemed tethered together by fate and circumstance, they also shared experiences and crisscrossed paths enough to make one wonder about destiny and the way it dusted their individual lives.

Like Mikan, Ray Meyer was a deeply religious man who once considered the priesthood, and, like Mikan, he attended Quigley Preparatory Seminary, although he lasted two years at the school as opposed to Mikan's four. Like Mikan, Meyer gave up his pursuit of the ministry because he was interested in basketball. Ironically, Meyer had been offered the coaching job at Joliet Catholic High School in 1940, several years after Mikan had attended the school, but he walked away from the job because he and the school were one hundred dollars apart in their differences over his annual salary. And, despite Mikan's fears about what Meyer had thought of him during his miserable tryout with Notre Dame, Meyer thought favorably of the young center when he watched him.

"I played with Paul Nowak, who was about six-six, and he was bigger than all the other players and he dominated them," he explained. "When I saw Mikan out there, I thought, 'Boy, oh, boy, if I had a center like that guy, we'd be a winner.'"

Meyer, the youngest of nine children, had grown up in Chicago, and, again like Mikan, he knew something about the hardscrabble life and the value of a strong work ethic. His father died from complications of diabetes—a Mikan family affliction—when Ray was only thirteen, and the Meyer family, supported by Ray's two oldest brothers, struggled to get by. Ray loved sports, particularly baseball, but he would distinguish himself in basketball, first when his high school team, St. Patrick's, won the National Catholic Interscholastic Basketball Tournament in 1932, and, a few years later, when he starred at Notre Dame. He had been the team's captain during his junior and senior seasons, and he developed a very close relationship with George Keogan. After Keogan suffered a heart attack in 1940, Meyer took a job as his assistant, and, at times when Keogan was too ill to coach, his replacement. Meyer and his wife, Marge, lived with the Keogans during Meyer's brief tenure on the Notre Dame coaching staff, and when DePaul called with a coaching offer, Keogan encouraged him to take the job.

The team Meyer inherited needed guidance, and Meyer was the right man for the job. Known as a generous, kind-hearted man when he was away from the court or locker room, he could be a fierce, almost tyrannical perfectionist when running operations in the "Old Barn," the aging theater building where DePaul practiced and played a good number of their games. Meyer was a teaching coach, as he proved with Mikan and scores of other raw recruits who he converted into solid performers during his long coaching career, but he wasn't one to suffer stupidity, low effort, or poor play. Meyer expected no less from his players than he'd given when he played for Notre Dame, and he could be very vocal about it. During the halftimes of DePaul's games, opposing players would often hear Meyer giving his team a good chewing out, the sounds of his tongue-lashings penetrating the walls of the visitor's locker room.

"He [could] get a team so high the players [would] want to climb the walls," noted Tony Kelly, a starting guard and team captain during Meyer's first year at DePaul. "Somebody told me he saw Ray so upset he pulled four iron coat hangers out of the wall during a halftime intermission before he could talk to the team."

Meyer directed that same high energy and passion at officials when he felt they weren't doing their jobs—to the extent that he nearly forfeited his seventh game as DePaul's coach. DePaul was playing a road game against the University of Toledo, and near the end of the first half, a Toledo player held on to a DePaul player's ankles to prevent a Blue Demon fast break. Meyer flipped out when the referee called for a jump ball. When he made no headway in the ensuing argument, Meyer pulled his team from the court. Toledo's business manager threatened to withhold DePaul's share of the game's earnings unless Meyer finished the game, but Meyer refused to budge. The president of the university finally interceded, promising a fair game, and only then did Meyer back down.

"I would have been in deep trouble if I'd refused to continue and gone back to DePaul from my first road trip without any money from Toledo," Meyer admitted. "But I never thought about that. I was angry, feisty, and young."

That was the fire he wanted to ignite in his players—a passion the team had lacked the year before he arrived.

Fortunately, that competitive drive was another trait that he shared with George Mikan, and that passion would elevate both to a level of success that neither would have imagined when they were attending Quigley Prep and contemplating their future lives as priests.

*   *   *

By the time DePaul played its first game against Chicago's Navy Pier on December 2, 1942, Mikan had shown remarkable growth as a basketball player, but not enough to persuade Meyer to start him in the center position.

"He wasn't ready," Meyer recalled. "I had a kid by the name of [Johnny] Jorgenson, who I played at the pivot, and I played George as a forward. After about six games, I thought, 'Oh, the hell with this' and I put him under the basket. He [became] a fixture under there."

DePaul manhandled Navy Pier in Mikan's first collegiate appearance, with Mikan scoring 10 points, considerably less than the 18.7 he'd average per game by the end of the year, but nevertheless a good start. The Blue Demons went on to win their next three games by lopsided scores, including a 40–16 pasting of Chicago Teachers College and a 73–32 rematch against Navy Pier.

The wins were great confidence-boosters, even if the competition was less than sterling. The fifth and sixth games, though, tested DePaul to a much greater degree. Both were held at Chicago Stadium, DePaul's home court against bigger, better opponents. Meyer had played every member of his roster during the first four games, but when Purdue came calling for game five, Meyer settled into a coaching pattern that he'd maintain throughout his career: unless a game was totally lopsided, Meyer played his starters for most of the game, with only two or three substitutes giving them brief spells on the bench. Not all of the players liked it, of course, and Meyer would even catch some flak from sportswriters for not using his bench more, but, as he argued, his system won games.

The Purdue game was a tussle, with the Blue Demons pulling out a 45–37 win. Mikan caught an earful from Purdue coach Ward "Piggy" Lambert, who would go on to act as the commissioner of the National Basketball League. In the future, Mikan would hear plenty from coaches and players trying to get inside his head and throw off his game, but George, who scored 16 points in the Purdue game while playing almost the entire contest, wasn't bothered. At one point, he had a word or two himself for Purdue's coach. Just before putting up a free throw by the basket near the Purdue bench, Mikan, who never kept his self-confidence locked away and out of sight, even when he was first starting out, turned to Lambert and declared, "This one's for you, Piggy." Then he sank the free throw.

Mikan's size and strength gave him a noticeable advantage in his first handful of collegiate games, but he bumped into his match when DePaul hosted Southern California in its next game. Alex Hannum, who would go on to enjoy a Hall of Fame career as a player and coach, played a much more physical brand of basketball than Mikan had seen in the previous five games, and their banging under the baskets gave Mikan a strong preview of the kind of rough, physical basketball he'd be playing in years to come. DePaul took the game, 49–47, keeping its season's record perfect.

The Blue Demons won seven of their next eight games, losing only to Duquesne in a game that Ray Meyer dismissed as a "farce." The Pittsburgh school had a tiny gym, and Meyer felt that the seating, with spectators placed very close to the playing area, was dangerous to his players. In addition, he complained that the floor was damp and hazardous. His first loss as a coach left him in a foul frame of mind.

In winning fourteen of its first fifteen games, including contests against Marquette and Michigan State, DePaul had established itself as one of the better teams in the Midwest. Mikan was improving with each game, and opposing coaches puzzled over how to neutralize his obvious superiority around the basket. He was almost unstoppable at close range, and when he was defending the basket, players had to alter their usual shooting styles just to get the ball over his outstretched arms. It didn't help the opponents, either, that he had a strong supporting cast around him.

One of the season's most pleasant surprises was junior Dick Triptow, who had played high school baseball and basketball at Lane Tech, Chicago's sports factory. Tall and athletic enough to play forward but also quick enough and skilled enough a ballhandler to play guard, Triptow could run all night, and his speed amazed his teammates to such an extent that, later on, when he was playing professionally for the Chicago Gears, his teammates would wager on whether he could outrun a taxi to their hotel.

"We'd get into the train station," Triptow remembered, "and we'd get a cab. Bob Calihan would say, 'All right, Trip. We've got the cab. You run to the hotel and we'll see who gets there first.' They were always giving me the business about that."

No one took DePaul's early success for granted. The previous year's team had started out with a 7–1 record, only to tailspin and finish at 10–12.

The Blue Demons still had games scheduled against Notre Dame and Kentucky, two college powerhouses. The country's sportswriters were beginning to take notice of George Mikan and DePaul, but Meyer didn't want his team to take anything for granted. Each game, he told his players, started with a 00–00 score, and it was always wise to stay focused on the present opponent. There was still a lot of season ahead.

January 30, 1943

The epicenter of college basketball might be New York City, but for one night, the eyes of the country are on Chicago, where Notre Dame is meeting DePaul in one of the biggest college showdowns of the year. It's the first game of a scheduled double-header at Chicago Stadium, with Marquette taking on rival Bradley in the nightcap. You couldn't ask for much better.

The Fighting Irish have lost only one of their first eight games and, with only the road loss to Duquesne to blemish his record, Ray Meyer has his team ranked Number One in the Dunkel ratings. But rankings mean nothing. He's now up against the man who gave him his basic training in college coaching. The game, he decides, will be a contest between DePaul's superior size and Notre Dame's quickness and experience.

Mikan wants this game as badly as he's wanted to win any game he's played to this point. It's only been a little more than a year since George Keogan rejected him at Notre Dame, and Mikan is not the kind of guy who easily forgives or forgets a transgression. He'd love nothing more than to make the Notre Dame coach eat his words—slowly, and one at a time—in front of the Chicago fans.

The game is a hard-fought, punishing contest. Both coaches preach hard-nosed defense as the key component to winning basketball, and the players on both teams respond with tight, physical coverage that keeps the officials busy. Before the night's over, officials will have called 40 fouls, and important players for both sides, including both of DePaul's centers, will be sitting on the bench, victims of their aggressive play.

Notre Dame collapses on Mikan every time he touches the ball. The players slap at the ball, trying to dislodge it from the big center's grip. They play in tight, hoping to draw charging fouls. Mikan stays close to the basket, hoping to score off short hook shots and layups, but, as often as not, he finds himself blanketed by defenders and dumps the ball off to an open man. Jimmy Cominsky and Johnny Jorgenson are hitting their shots, though they struggle with their free throws. Notre Dame, on the other hand, has no such trouble at the line, and their free throws compensate for their poor shooting percentage from the field.

The game stays unbelievably close. The score is tied six times in the first half, including a 19–19 halftime score. Ray Meyer, who secretly wondered how his team would stack up against the Fighting Irish, goes into the locker room content. He's battled his mentor to a draw. Mikan's doing nothing in terms of scoring, but that will probably change. If he can stay out of foul trouble, he could be the difference in a close game.

Mikan is frustrated. Notre Dame is not only doing an admirable job of denying him the ball; when he does get a pass, the Irish seem content to hack him and force him to earn his points from the free throw line. Mikan will convert six of eight charity tosses over the course of the game, but that's not the real issue. The problem for Mikan is in controlling his emotions and not committing foolish retaliatory fouls.

The Blue Demons come out after the intermission and take control of the game, outscoring Notre Dame 8–2 in the early going for a 27–21 lead. Mikan's shots won't fall, but Jorgenson, who will wind up leading DePaul scorers with 14 points, picks him up. Fortunately for DePaul, Notre Dame is shooting as poorly as the Blue Demons, neither team connecting on more than one third of its shots.

The game gets rougher, leading Wilfrid Smith, the Chicago Tribune's *basketball writer, to comment later that "the 9,000 spectators [were] uncertain whether they were seeing basketball or football." The officials call a close game, and Mikan's night ends early with a disappointing 10 points—six from the free-throw line. Frank Wiscons, DePaul's backup center, fouls out a short time later. Without a big center in the way, Notre Dame takes over. Charlie Butler and Bob Rensberger, two of Mikan's future teammates in the pros, torment the Blue Demons with a variety of layups and long-range bombs. Notre Dame builds a decent lead before withstanding a final DePaul charge, winning a squeaker, 50–47. When the final numbers are tallied, DePaul has outscored Notre Dame from the field, the final difference determined by the Blue Demons' miserable 13-for-24 free-throw shooting.*

Both Mikan and Meyer will remember the game fondly, once the sting of the season's second loss has subsided. Meyer promises different results when he meets his old boss next time, but it will never happen. George Keogan will be gone, victim of another heart attack, within a couple of months, leaving Mikan and Meyer with unfinished business that they'll take out on his replacement.

The loss to Notre Dame signaled the beginning of a skid that saw the Blue Demons dropping three of four games, including two tough ones to Camp Grant, the top-ranked army-base team in the country, which had the distinction of handing Illinois University's "Whiz Kids" their only defeat of the season. Guard Stan Szukala, a DePaul alumnus and future Mikan teammate in the pros, led the team to a 31–2 record, including victories over Oklahoma and Michigan State.

The three DePaul losses were by less than 10 points, but they were significant, not only as temporary setbacks in the continuing development of Meyer's squad, but because they damaged DePaul's chances of postseason play. Prior to the losses, DePaul appeared to have a good chance to make the NCAA tournament, which chose its entries by region, or maybe even the prestigious National Invitation Tournament, which invited the very best of the collegiate crop. The losses dropped the Blue Demons out of NIT consideration, and, at best, they were longshots, ranked just behind Illinois, to represent the Midwest in the NCAA tournament. It didn't help, either, that DePaul had to face Kentucky the game after their second loss to Camp Grant.

Any school scheduled to play Kentucky regarded the contest as one of its premier games of the season. Coached by Adolph Rupp, the "Baron of Bluegrass," Kentucky owned the Southeast Conference, not to mention almost any other non-conference opponent standing in its way. Rupp had begun his coaching career at Kentucky in 1930, and he had recently notched his 200th career victory with the school. Kentucky had just beaten Notre Dame with very little trouble, and they entered the game against DePaul as solid favorites.

While scouting Kentucky, Ray Meyer consulted with Edward "Moose" Krause, a former teammate at Notre Dame and Keogan's replacement as head coach, and Krause had briefed him on Kentucky's hot-shooting starting guards. Rupp liked to run a fast-break offense; but with two guards capable of pulling up and hitting from anywhere inside twenty-five feet, the Kentucky offense boasted of a very potent inside–outside attack. Meyer decided to station Mikan closer than usual to the basket, where he could block layups and, if all went well, bat away some of the long-range shots.

Mikan played a very strong defensive game, knocking away more than a dozen Kentucky shots and leading the Blue Demons to a relatively easy 53–44 win. Most of the blocks were outright cases of defensive goaltending—still legal in college at the time—drawing angry outbursts from Rupp, who would use his considerable influence to see that the rule would be changed in the near future. In the meantime, he told Ray Meyer after the game, he would not schedule another game against DePaul until Mikan was out of the school.

One sportswriter saw the contest as a kind of coming-of-age for Mikan. Writing for the *Chicago Tribune*, Wilfrid Smith offered his highest praise yet for Mikan's defensive prowess: "The 6–8 center never played a better game, using his height to advantage and yet moving as nimbly as a forward."

DePaul closed out its season with three more wins, giving them a surprising 18–4 overall record. The season, however, wasn't quite over. As expected, the NCAA invited Illinois and its "Whiz Kids" to its tournament, but the school declined, arguing that the tournament would keep their student-athletes away from the classroom for too long. DePaul was the selection committee's second choice, and Meyer was pleased to accept the invitation, making DePaul the first school outside the Big Ten to represent the Midwest in the tournament.

Staged in New York's Madison Square Garden, the NCAA tournament featured an exceptionally competitive eight-team field, including New York University, Georgetown, and Dartmouth in DePaul's bracket. For their first game, the Blue Demons drew Dartmouth, one of the tournament's favorites and the darling of the New York press. Meyer again positioned Mikan close to the basket, and Mikan responded by rejecting or catching shots, often within the basket's cylinder. Ozzie Cowles, Dartmouth's coach and a member of the NCAA's Rules Committee, howled in protest, but there was little else he could do. As Mikan pointed out afterward, Meyer had instructed him to goaltend until a rule prohibiting it was passed.

DePaul shocked the college basketball experts by taking a relatively easy 46–35 win. Mikan scored 20 points to lead the scoring; but, even more important, he batted away 17 shots.

Sportswriters took notice, although they tripped over Mikan's name. The Associated Press, in a wire-service article published across the country, reported that "Dartmouth was rarely in the ballgame against the hard-driving Chicago quintet which was sparked by elongated *John* Mikan." In a United Press International article, Mikan was referred to as "Big Mike." *George* Mikan was amused.

Georgetown, DePaul's quarterfinal opponent, had a huge center of its own. John Mahnken, who would face Mikan on numerous occasions during his eight-year pro career, stood six-eight and could muscle inside, but he also had a soft outside shot that promised to give Mikan trouble. If Mahnken took Mikan outside on defense, he had guard Billy Hassett, a future teammate of Mikan's, to hit when he was cutting to the basket. If Mikan stayed inside, there was a good chance that Mahnken would beat him with medium-range shots.

Ray Meyer elected to go with the defense that had been so effective against Kentucky and Dartmouth, and for a while it looked as if it might work. DePaul led 9–2 in the opening minutes of the game, and 28–23 at halftime, with Mikan blocking shots at will. Mahnken fouled out with 10 minutes left in the game, but before he did, he hit four key outside shots and led a charge that put Georgetown in front for keeps. Georgetown won, 53–49, with Mahnken winding up with 17 points. Mikan, tiring noticeably and held in check by a swarming Georgetown defense, finished with only 11.

Henry Hyde, a future Republican congressman from Illinois and chair of the House Judiciary Committee, then a Georgetown freshman assigned to guard Mikan after Mahnken fouled out, held Mikan to a single point, although, by his own admission, his defensive methods were suspect. "I can only say about the way I guarded him that I will burn in purgatory," he admitted. "The rules were considerably bent."

Georgetown advanced to the finals against Wyoming, while DePaul returned to Chicago, victims of an upset but finishing the season with a .791 winning percentage.

Meyer, not surprisingly, felt DePaul should have won even more, including the disappointment against Georgetown, but, years later, as he reflected back on his first year coaching, he was pleased with the team, and even more so with Mikan's development, both on and off the court.

"I noticed a great change in Mikan's personality during that first season," he stated. "When he used to walk around the school halls with his shoulders slumped, as though he were ashamed of his height, he now seemed to be proud of his stature. He walked with shoulders back and head up. When he had been quiet, now he was more outgoing."

Three

BLUE DEMON

M IKAN GREW ANOTHER inch over the summer of 1943, putting him somewhere between six-nine and six-ten. His height might have given him a tremendous advantage over his opponents on the basketball court, but it presented problems almost everywhere else. A person that size wasn't buying clothes off the rack in many stores. Being a passenger in a car, even in the larger, roomier automobiles of the time, meant riding around in cramped conditions, with your knees, it seemed, up in your chin. Feeding someone the size of the Mikan brothers, any one of whom could easily consume two full chickens and still have plenty of room for the fixings, could be expensive. Everything in the house, from doorways to countertops, seemed to be built too low. When Mikan tried to enlist in the armed services, he was turned away, his height (and poor eyesight) keeping him from serving his country.

Height was becoming a big issue in basketbal as well. Three players— George Mikan of DePaul, Bob Kurland of Oklahoma A&M, and Don Otten of Bowling Green—had so completely dominated the pivot that other coaches were presently scrambling to find big centers of their own, while collegiate basketball officials pondered the effects that this latest development might be having on the game. Fans held conflicting views of the big man: they hated what they perceived to be his unfair advantage over shorter players—unless, of course, the big man was on their team—but they were nevertheless excited by that very domination. Big men could score more points, sweep more rebounds off the rim or backboard, make more spectacular blocks, and, in general, entertain in ways that hadn't been seen before.

Still, with influential coaches bending their ears about how goaltending was ruining the sport, NCAA officials felt they had to do something, and they decided to ban goaltending, on a trial basis, for the 1943–44 season. The ban would be in effect for conference games only. At the end of the season, the NCAA would revisit the issue and see how the ban had affected play.

Ray Meyer had warned Mikan that such a day would come. Other rules were bound to follow, and players like Mikan and Kurland would find themselves in the center of the debates. Ironically, considering the problems their heights presented, especially when they were young boys growing up, Mikan, Kurland, and others might have been happier if they'd been eight to ten inches shorter.

And they certainly wouldn't have been alone in that line of thinking.

Mikan never denied that his height was problematic, especially when he was just starting out. In his early days at DePaul, he actually tried to make himself seem shorter, just to avoid comments.

"I became round-shouldered, ungainly, and so filled with bitterness that my height nearly wrecked my life," he said. "Later, I found that a tall man didn't have to accept clumsiness."

Until Mikan, Kurland, Otten, and a few others came along, anyone taller than six-five or six-six was regarded as a big, slow-footed, uncoordinated oaf, maybe capable of jumping high enough off the floor to win a jump ball or scrape a rebound off the backboard, but hardly capable of competing with the fleet-footed guards and forwards. These giants had heard the taunts of their schoolmates, when they shot up in height during their adolescence and towered over everyone else in their classes. Even when they turned to basketball and excelled in the sport, they still endured rude remarks from other players and fans.

Ray Meyer recalled a time, early in Mikan's college career, when DePaul was playing in Philadelphia and the press had been cruel in its attacks.

"They were calling him gargantuan, a freak," Meyer remembered. "Then he played. The next day the newspapers came out with the words, 'Our apologies to George Mikan.'"

Mikan shrugged off most of it, but he had a boiling point too. He hated being called a goon, in reference to his height, and he had a standard reply on those rare occasions when he lost his patience when someone asked, "How's the weather up there?"

"It's raining," he'd say, spitting on the ground next to him.

Even compliments could have a backhanded quality to them. In a feature story on Mikan published in 1949, *Look* magazine praised Mikan by claiming he wasn't your garden-variety big man. "'Goon' best describes most players near seven feet," the article stated. "But Mikan, from Joliet, Ill., is an athlete."

Bob Kurland probably spoke for many of basketball's big men when he recalled the difficulties of always being the tallest kid in the group when he was growing up.

"It was an embarrassing, difficult time, and I didn't like it," he recalled matter-of-factly, with only the slightest trace of bitterness in his tone. "I was a big gangly kid, and height at that time was not looked upon in the same way as it is today. I had to carry my birth certificate when I went to the show, because the show was ten cents for a kid under twelve, and fifteen or twenty cents for a guy over twelve. I'd have to show them my birth certificate."

Basketball, Kurland pointed out, wasn't necessarily receptive to the taller kids, either. Hank Iba, Oklahoma A&M's coach and as astute a judge of talent as you could find, didn't know what to make of Kurland when he brought the seven-foot center to the school for a tryout.

"He said, 'You know, Bob, I like your attitude, I like your enthusiasm and your effort, but I've never coached a kid as big as you,'" Kurland remembered. "He said, 'I don't know whether you'll be a good basketball player or not, but I'll tell you what I'll do. If you come here, go to class, and stay eligible, I'll see that you get a college education.' I was interested in the School of Engineering and Oklahoma A&M had one, so I said, 'You got a deal.' I went down there with a tin suitcase and got off the bus and all the kids gawked and said, 'What the hell is this?'"

They would find out when Kurland, George Mikan, and Don Otten made headlines for their respective schools. Along the way, they changed the way the center position was played, first in college, and eventually in the pros.

"If you go back to the early days of basketball, the big man was there for only one reason: to get the jump ball," observed Arnie Risen, another big center who influenced the way the position was played. "Then Dutch

Dehnert came along with the old New York Celtics, and in their standard routine, he set up a high post and the others cut off of it. Fans thought that kind of thing was exciting, so pivot play began. Until that time, everybody faced the basket. As a matter of fact, back in the thirties, the American [Basketball] League played with a rule that said you couldn't play with your back to the basket for more than three seconds."

With the arrival of George Mikan and Bob Kurland, the rules were changed to give the shorter players a better chance to compete with these huge men who clogged up the middle of the court, blocked shots, misdirected play, and, in general, created holy havoc around the basket.

The most significant change addressed the previously acceptable practice of defensive goaltending. Ray Meyer and Hank Iba positioned Mikan and Kurland close to the basket, where they could catch or bat away any shots about to go through the hoop. Both players excelled at it, leading opposing coaches to scream about how the skill and athleticism in basketball was being ruined by a handful of players who used sheer height as their primary weapon.

There was more to it than that, of course, but as Bob Kurland himself admitted, goaltending—or the threat of it—was a powerful defensive tool.

"We did it in an organized fashion," he said. "In my freshman year, in our last game against Oklahoma, Mr. Iba decided that we were going to goaltend. The rule said you couldn't hit the ball on the downward arc once it was inside the cylinder. Well, the OU game started and Mr. Iba said, 'We're going to goaltend.' We set up a defense where I was under the basket. Bruce Drake, who was coach then and later head of the Rules Committee for the Coaches' Association, just about had a hissy-fit when I knocked down the first ball, the second ball, the third, fourth, and fifth. They had beaten us the week before, but we beat their butts. The next year, that was our defense: my knocking the ball down. The rule was changed in my junior year because of that."

Ray Meyer made goaltending a critical part of DePaul's defense. He had heard the complaints from opposing coaches, and he knew that goaltending would eventually be outlawed, but as long as it was permitted, he instructed Mikan to bat away anything around the basket, in or out of the cylinder.

Meyer and Iba knew something about their star centers that other coaches either didn't realize or accept: legislating against the game's big men would not reduce their effectiveness. In fact, time would prove it to be quite the opposite. These players had the skills and ability to adapt. They'd learn to play further away from the basket, improve their passing skills, and hone their shot-blocking techniques to new levels of effectiveness. Rather than restrict the effectiveness of centers who towered over other players on the court, the new rules forced the centers to become more complete players.

"The changes just gave me more opportunities to improve my game," Mikan asserted years later.

Wilt Chamberlain, the former University of Kansas great who began his career in 1959 with the Philadelphia Warriors and became the most dominating center of his era, acknowledged Mikan's contribution in changing the world's thinking about the big man in basketball.

"He showed the world a big man could be an athlete," he said. "He showed a big man was not just a freak, not just a [goon], not just some big guy who could hardly walk and chew gum at the same time. He was a splendid athlete. He was the first true superstar of the league, and lucky for us he was a big man."

DePaul opened its fall practice season with all kinds of questions about the strength of the team. George Mikan and Dick Triptow, named co-captains by Ray Meyer, were back, but the Blue Demons had lost key players. Tony Kelly, the previous season's team captain, and stand-out super-sub Bill Ryan, had graduated. Others had gone into the service. Meyer had spent the summer trying to round up enough players for a team, but it hadn't been easy, even for someone with Meyer's persuasive skills. Uncle Sam was busy doing some recruiting of his own, and, more often than not, great prospects were donning military uniforms rather than basketball jerseys. Meyer worried that he might wind up canceling the season due to a lack of players.

Anyone capable of playing a reasonably good level of basketball was a potential candidate. Gene Stump, one of Meyer's recruits, made the team before he'd even formally registered for classes.

"The first day I got there, we worked out and he offered me a scholarship," Stump said. "He needed bodies. The first day of school, I didn't go get books. I went over to the gym. We were shooting free throws and I said,

'I gotta register.' He said, 'Don't worry. We'll take care of that. Be back here at three o'clock for scrimmage.'"

Fortunately for Meyer, who had been found unfit (bad knee) for the military, there were enough recruits in the area, either too young or unable to go into the service because of physical problems, to put together a full roster. Triptow (double hernia) and Mikan (too tall, half blind) were joined by freshmen Ernie DeBenedetto (poor eyesight), Gene Stump (too young), Jack Dean (too young), and Ed "Whitey" Kachan (perforated ear drum) as the nucleus of the team. Ed Mikan, who had graduated from high school but was still too young for the service, earned a spot on the team as his brother's backup.

George Mikan, who only a year earlier was trying to find his own place on the team, suddenly found himself sharing a leadership role with Triptow.

"We were the logical ones, and the guys looked up to us," Triptow remembered. "The freshmen on the team were all good buddies of ours. They would razz me about my girlfriend and everything else, and we always had big talks about it. It was a great thing."

Stump, a guard who would become one of DePaul's all-time scoring leaders, was a superb practical joker, and George Mikan became his favorite target. Mikan's glasses might disappear while he was in the shower, or he might be summoned to an imaginary interview with a reporter. Anything was possible. On one occasion, Stump gathered the innards of dissected animals from the biology lab and stuffed them in Mikan's shoes and pockets; fortunately, he was much faster than the victim of his joke, who probably would have chased him across the country if he believed he could have caught him.

On the basketball floor, the new version of the Blue Demons stood up well in comparison to the previous year's model. Meyer had put together a schedule that found DePaul playing both cupcakes and powerhouses. With such teams as Illinois, Ohio State, Purdue, Marquette, Notre Dame, and Valparaiso on its docket, DePaul needed to get off to a good start against their less-skilled opponents—and they did. The Blue Demons shot off to a 13–0 start, winning most by huge margins. Mikan averaged more than 20 points per game, and some of the final scores (82–31, 88–23, 55–14, 84–23, 78–26), including lopsided victories against Nebraska, Indiana,

Arkansas, and Long Island University, had sportswriters wondering if there was any beating this team.

Valparaiso provided the answer when DePaul traveled to Indiana and took its first loss, 65–57. Valparaiso played a physical, hard-nosed defense against Mikan, guessing correctly that Mikan might get rattled if he found the going rougher than it had been in DePaul's earlier games. Mikan complained about fouls he felt the officials were ignoring and, on a couple of occasions, he was whistled for committing retaliatory fouls.

Milt Schoon, a six-eight center-forward, guarded Mikan for much of the game. The rough treatment, he admitted, was aimed at finding a way to distract Mikan from his usual style of play.

"Oh, man, we would battle," recalled Schoon, who would go on to play against Mikan in the pros. "I finally got wise enough to know that you had to get the first blow in on George. Give him a crack. Then you had to play away from him. He was determined that he was going to get you back. And if he tried to get you, he'd get caught. He was aggressive under there, and the best way to do it was get him off key, because if he could play his game, he was really tough. It helped if you could bother him. When De-Paul came out to Valpo and we beat them, George was held to about nine points. The town and everybody went crazy. I'll bet Ray didn't sleep for two weeks after that."

The loss upset Meyer, not just because it was DePaul's first defeat, but because he felt Valparaiso might have used a couple of questionable players in the game. One of the players, Bob Dille, had actually played pro ball prior to enrolling at Valparaiso, and another, John Janisch, had enrolled at Valparaiso for the next semester, but had yet to attend a class. Dille wound up with 28 points in the game, and Janisch contributed 15—a huge percentage of Valparaiso's final total. Meyer had scouted Valparaiso to prepare for the game, and he wasn't happy with the team he saw on their bench at the opening of the game.

"They had a different team," he groused to reporter Jim Enright. "Their uniforms didn't fit. They didn't know how to spell the names of the players for the program or how to pronounce them. Boy, they'd dug up some good ones! It was a sad experience because I felt they were trying to make a reputation on one game—and they picked on our game because we had George Mikan in our lineup."

It didn't get any better the next game against Marquette. The Milwaukee team traveled down to Chicago for a game at the Stadium, and won a hard-fought 51–49 contest. In a matter of days, DePaul had gone from invincible to very vulnerable.

Mikan was glad to be home, even if the first game of a nine-game home-stand was a disappointment. DePaul had played four of their past six games on the road, and everywhere they went, they had to listen to sportswriters, fans, and players complaining about Mikan's defensive goaltending. Since it was an independent school and not part of a conference, DePaul was unaffected by the NCAA's goaltending experiment, and Mikan continued to snatch the ball from the rim. The rules, opposing coaches contended, had to change—and permanently.

DePaul had revenge on their minds when they played Notre Dame, Illinois, and Valparaiso in succession. They took a beating at the hands of Illinois for the second straight year, but soundly defeated Notre Dame, 61–45, and Valparaiso, 69–38, in their rematch. DePaul's record now stood at 15–3, and an invitation to either the NIT or NCAA tournament seemed inevitable, as long as the Blue Demons closed out their remaining four games without difficulty.

Mikan scared DePaul when he sprained his right ankle in a game against Western Kentucky. Mikan thought the ankle was broken—he swore it hurt more than the broken leg he'd suffered in his high school days—but X-rays were negative. With a game against Ohio State, the best team in the Big Ten, only a few days away, Mikan had almost no time to recover—if, in fact, he'd be able to play at all.

Ohio State based its offense around six-eight center Arnie Risen, one of the top pivot men in the country. Risen moved better than Mikan and had a much better outside shot, but he was rail-thin and Ray Meyer hoped Mikan could use his bulk to neutralize Risen around the basket. Ohio State had plenty of motivation to win: Big Ten schools weren't allowed to play in the NIT, so Ohio needed to win the game to edge DePaul for an invitation to the NCAA tournament.

With Mikan uncertain for the game, Ray Meyer tried to come up with alternative centers. Eddie Mikan was a possibility, but he wasn't anywhere near the scorer his brother was, and not nearly as tall. Jack Phelan was much quicker than Eddie Mikan but, at six-five, he would be giving Arnie

Risen an even greater height advantage. Somehow, there had to be a way to get George in the game.

"The game was on a Saturday," Phelan remembered. "On Thursday, they had George in a whirlpool, and they put a shoe on his foot to see if he could walk with it. They had to slice the shoe down the side and tape it to his foot. He went out and walked on it a little bit, but it was really hurting. He ran a few steps on Friday, and I said, 'Well, he'll probably start the game, but they'll pull him right out.'"

Doctors cleared Mikan to play on the day of the game, but it didn't look as if his presence would be enough. The Mikan-Risen confrontation shaped up to be the battle that fans expected, but Ohio State held the lead throughout most of the game. With less than two minutes remaining and DePaul trailing by six, Ray Meyer called a time-out.

"Ray was a very, very religious man," Gene Stump recalled. "He had a hand in his pocket and he was saying his prayers. He took his hand out and started talking and—I'll never forget this—George said, 'Coach, you can do all the praying you want, but the only way we're going to get to New York is if you get the ball to me.' He looked at all of us. 'I want the ball,' he said. And Ray said, 'Let's go.'"

From that point on, Mikan, heavily taped sprained ankle and all, was unstoppable. He and Dick Triptow combined to tie the game, with Triptow hitting the tying shot with time running out, and Mikan completely took over in overtime. First, he saw that Risen fouled out of the game, and with no one to defend him as effectively as Risen, he scored at will, hitting his hook shots all around the basket.

"He made the first nine points of the overtime," Jack Phelan said. "Near the end of the overtime, he looked at Stump and said, 'You shoot the ball and I'll kill you, you little bastard. You throw the ball to me.'"

Mikan wound up with 12 points in the extra period and 37 for the game, and DePaul won easily, 61–49. Ray Meyer said afterward that Arnie Risen, after fouling out of the game, walked past the DePaul bench, mumbling, "Nobody ever did that to me before."

Meyer wasn't at all surprised by Mikan's gutty performance. Mikan, he liked to point out, seemed to tailor his game to the level of his team's opponents.

"If you look at his record," Meyer said later, "you'll see that if we won by two or three points, he got 25 or 30 points. If we won by 20, he got maybe 10. He knew how to keep everybody happy."

The victory guaranteed DePaul another trip to New York. DePaul could pick its tournament. Ohio State, in all likelihood, would be returning to Columbus.

When Meyer visited Ohio State's locker room to congratulate Coach Harold "Ole" Olsen on a game well played, he saw the dejected OSU players sitting, heads down, by their lockers. Cheer up, Meyer exhorted them. DePaul wanted to go to the NIT anyway. Ohio State was free to play in the NCAA.

Meyer's visit to the opponent's locker room was testament to the faith he had in his team. DePaul still had two games to go before the invitations were made, but no one believed the Blue Demons were going to lose. Mikan's performance against Ohio State was all anyone needed to see.

"Even the last of the doubters must believe now that DePaul's Blue Demons have definitely arrived in basketball's biggest time," wrote James S. Kearns in the *Chicago Sun*. "This is championship class!"

DePaul had not been to the NIT since 1940, when the tournament was still using a six-team format. In that tournament, the Blue Demons had lost to Colorado, the eventual champions, in the semifinals, and then they'd lost the third-place game to Oklahoma A&M. The basketball program, it could be argued, wasn't the same after that—until Ray Meyer and George Mikan arrived.

The National Invitation Tournament, the oldest of the college basketball tournaments in America, was started up in 1938, when the Metropolitan Basketball Writers Association decided to stage a tournament to decide, if possible, the best college basketball team in the country. The annual competition was always held at Madison Square Garden, and, not surprisingly, there always seemed to be a couple of New York schools on the list of participants. The NCAA tournament began a year after the first NIT, but in terms of prestige and prize money, there was no comparison. The NIT was by far the more desirable.

"We preferred the NIT," Mikan remarked later when asked about the two tournaments. "New York was the hub of basketball. You could make a reputation in New York that would last forever."

Ray Meyer might have been confident of DePaul's chances of being invited when he offered the NCAA berth to Ohio State after the two schools' game, but he was pleased nevertheless when the official call came in. The invitation meant a big boost to his basketball program, especially when it came to future recruiting.

Mikan was still nursing his sore ankle when DePaul arrived in New York. He'd played three full games on the ankle since he'd injured it in the game against Western Kentucky, and he was confident that he'd be able to function on it in the tournament, even if it did cut back on his mobility.

DePaul was heavily favored in its first game against Muhlenberg of Allentown, Pennsylvania. The Mules had brought in a couple of "ringers" for the contest—the navy had a program on campus, making a couple of recruits eligible for the NIT—and the game stayed close until the Blue Demons closed out the game with a 24–5 run. DePaul, bolstered by Mikan's 37 points, came out on top, 68–45.

The win set up a highly anticipated second-round match against Oklahoma A&M and Bob Kurland, college basketball's other nationally acclaimed center. Mikan had heard plenty about the Aggies' seven-foot center, usually in connection with debates over goaltending, and he was eager to see if Kurland lived up to his advance publicity. Mikan was in for a surprise, though: Kurland, superior to Mikan on defense, was content to let his teammates do the scoring while he teamed up with other Aggies players to hold down Mikan's point production.

DePaul stumbled at the beginning of the game, unable to find a solution to Oklahoma A&M's defense, which collapsed around Mikan and smothered his early attempts to score. Ten minutes into the game, DePaul had fallen behind, 15–2, and the 18,353 fans in Madison Square Garden were watching Mikan do little other than work himself into foul trouble. Seeing that he wasn't going to dominate Kurland the way he'd humbled other big centers, Mikan abandoned his usual game on offense, choosing instead to pass to players left open by Oklahoma A&M's sagging defense. With Gene Stump and Jack Dean hitting key shots, the Blue Demons worked their way back into the game, trailing only 24–18 at halftime.

The physical contest exacted its price on both teams. Mikan fouled out with only four minutes gone in the second half, and Kurland followed a few minutes later. By the time the game ended, Oklahoma A&M had only four eligible players, and DePaul survived, 41–38. Kurland outscored Mikan, 14–9, in a matchup that never really measured up to its hype.

"I couldn't make it much of a duel," Mikan conceded. "Kurland clung so close to me that I wasn't good for anything except keeping the Aggies worrying about me while Gene Stump and Jack Dean did our scoring."

Mikan's aggressive play haunted him in the NIT final as well. St. John's, the hometown favorite, had earned a trip to the championship game by beating Kentucky in the semis, and even though the oddsmakers established the much taller DePaul as the favorite to win the match, the much quicker Redmen took the game, 47–39. Mikan fouled out six minutes into the second half, with DePaul behind, 35–31, and the Blue Demons' season was over.

Mikan took a philosophical approach to the defeat. DePaul had enjoyed a very good season, he said, and they'd made it to the championship game of the NIT, only to lose a tough game to a very good team.

"We'd come up short," he allowed, "but we were headed in the right direction."

Four

THE M&M BOYS

IN MIKAN'S FIRST two years of varsity ball, DePaul posted a 41–9 record, including tournament games. The Blue Demons had reached the championship game of two major tournaments. Best of all, their starting five was intact as the team entered the 1944–45 season.

Over the summer, while Mikan took a break from basketball by rehabbing an old farmhouse with his brother, Eddie, the NCAA Rules Committee permanently banned goaltending from college basketball, setting up speculation that the domination of the big man had ended as abruptly as it began. The world would now see how one-dimensional these big men really were.

Mikan, named DePaul's captain, must not have read the papers. He continued to rule the pivot, increasing his points per game on offense while tightening his defense to the point where he was blocking shots as they were being launched, rather than swatting them away from the rim.

On paper, Ray Meyer had put together another challenging schedule that included games against Wyoming, Long Island University, Marquette, Notre Dame, Purdue, and Oklahoma A&M, as well as two games each against Western Kentucky, Hamline, and rival Illinois. In reality, DePaul had little trouble with anyone other than Illinois, who beat the Blue Demons, 43–40, in Chicago before losing to them, 63–56, in the rematch. DePaul ran up a 17–1 record before running into an outstanding Great Lakes Naval Training Station team (with future Hall of Famer Dick McGuire) and losing, 64–56. Great Lakes, now regarded one of the best teams in the history of the service leagues, put together a 32–5 overall record, including victories over DePaul, Illinois, Notre Dame, Minnesota, and Ohio State.

If anything, DePaul had to work at staying focused and avoiding complacency. In a game against Western Kentucky, Mikan scored 30 points in a 63–37 fiasco, but all reporters could think to ask was why Meyer had taken Mikan out of the game in the middle of the second half, when he only needed four more points to reach the 1,000-point mark for his college career.

"Let him earn them against a tough team," Meyer responded.

There were, of course, a few close games sprinkled in with the blowouts. The two Illinois games were hotly contested matches, as were the two meetings with Hamline; Notre Dame gave DePaul a battle, and the Blue Demons slid past Bob Kurland and Oklahoma A&M by two points.

DePaul posted a 21–3 regular season record. The M&M Boys, as Meyer and Mikan were called, had made DePaul one of the country's most highly regarded basketball programs, and, as expected, the Blue Demons were invited to the NIT for a second straight year. In addition, DePaul agreed to play the winner of the NCAA tournament in a benefit game for the Red Cross, which meant an extended stay in New York.

Mikan looked forward to the trip. He enjoyed New York, and he'd been hoping to avenge DePaul's NIT finals loss the previous year. There was a good chance he would be facing either or both of the country's two other premier centers, Bob Kurland of Oklahoma A&M and Bowling Green's Don Otten, and he prepared for the prospects with such enthusiasm that he almost cost his team a player.

"He knocked four of my teeth out with an elbow the day we were leaving," teammate Jack Phelan remembered. "I was so mad. I hit him so hard in the face that he had two stitches under one eye. I had to have my teeth dug out. We got on the train going to New York and Eddie Kolker, our trainer, came over and said, 'Here are two ounces of whiskey. It'll help with the pain.' So Stump and all those guys go, 'Look at how sick I am, Eddie.'"

Mikan took out any of his other frustrations on DePaul's NIT opponents. In the opening-round game against West Virginia, he set a single-game NIT scoring record by posting 33 points en route to an easy 76–52 win. The Mountaineers started five freshmen, and West Virginia Coach John Brickels, in his pregame pep talk, had instructed them that they'd have a chance if they could limit Mikan's points. It was a familiar rallying cry, with all-too-familiar results. Mikan had 23 points by halftime, and two of West Virginia's starters were in foul trouble for their efforts.

"We were both hanging on to his arms, trying to keep him away from the basket," Leland Byrd, a future West Virginia athletic director, recalled. "That was as far as we could get."

Ray Meyer expected to win the West Virginia game, but he worried about DePaul's next opponent, Rhode Island State, a run-and-gun team famous for putting up a lot of points. At a time when there was no shot clock, and when the game clock continued to run when the ball was out of bounds, Rhode Island State had racked up mind-boggling point totals, exceeding 100 points in several games. DePaul hadn't faced a team like it.

Knowing that DePaul needed a very big game from Mikan if the Blue Demons were to have any chance of winning, Meyer decided to play amateur psychologist to fire George up for the game. Meyer had been wandering around Madison Square Garden during Rhode Island State's pregame shootaround when he overheard Frank Keaney, Rhode Island State's coach, talking to a small gathering of the school's alumni. Keaney called Mikan a bum and boasted that his team would run him all the way back to Chicago.

"He's never met anybody who can run like we can run," he declared.

Meyer knew he had all the ammunition he needed. He hurried back to Mikan and gave him a wonderfully embellished account of the overheard conversation. Meyer correctly anticipated Mikan's reaction. Under the usual circumstances, Mikan would see red when other players talked trash about DePaul; he blew his top when it became personal, when someone called him a goon or a freak or a bum.

The other DePaul players knew this as well. Getting Mikan worked up was an ideal way to enter a game.

"What you did was get him mad before the game," Jack Phelan observed. "Don't ever call him a clown. He'd get his temper up."

Rhode Island State had no idea what waited in store for them when an ill-tempered George Mikan walked onto the court for the semifinal game. His mood didn't improve when Keaney sent Ernie Calverley, a six-two forward, to jump against him on the opening tip. ("Everybody roared," Gene Stump said of Rhode Island's attempt to show Mikan up.) Neither Mikan nor Ray Meyer found much humor in the ploy.

Mikan won the jump ball, and the rout was on. He wasn't content to merely beat Rhode Island State; he wanted to humiliate them in front of the country's biggest basketball fans, in the country's biggest tournament.

He had 32 points by halftime, but he was nowhere near finished. In a game that shattered personal, team, and tournament records, Mikan scored 53 points, equaling the entire Rhode Island State *team's* point production in the 97–53 thrashing.

"Our guys rose up to the challenge," Mikan recalled. "They fed me, and I had more points at halftime than they did."

At one point early in the second half, with DePaul in complete command of the game, Ray Meyer decided to sit Mikan down in favor of his brother, Eddie. George had just matched his record of 33 points in the preceding game, but Meyer wasn't aware of it.

"When he got in the mid-thirties, I wanted to take him out," Meyer stated. "I got a note from a newspaperman across the way, saying, 'Leave him in to set the NIT record.' He passed that, and when I went to take him out again, the newspaperman said, 'The Madison Square Garden record is forty-five points.' So I left him in and he passed that up. When I tried to put the second team in, they refused to go in. They said, 'Let him set a record that will never be broken.' "

The whipping continued. The packed house at Madison Square Garden realized that something special was occurring. Mikan's teammates fed him the ball every time down the floor, hoping to see him add to his point total. Mikan, exhausted from the effort, was dragging his feet by the time the second half wound down.

"He was unstoppable," Gene Stump said of Mikan's performance. "Ernie DeBenedetto dribbled down the floor on the fast break, and he'd turn around and say, 'C'mon, c'mon, George.' George would run up and he'd hand him the ball. George would dunk, to make sure he had the record."

DePaul scored its 97th point—another NIT record—with just over a minute left in the game. Frank Keaney screamed at his players to hold on to the ball or dribble out the clock. He'd seen his boys ring up 100 points against opponents; he didn't want it happening to them. His instructions didn't matter. Meyer had already taken Mikan out of the game and inserted his reserves. He'd told them to back off, although he would later admit to having one regret about pulling Mikan from the game.

"I should have left him in a little longer," he said, still fuming over the remarks he'd heard before the game. "He would have beaten them himself."

The papers went wild in their coverage of the game.

GEORGE MIKAN IN GREAT SCORING SHOW, they exclaimed. DEPAUL'S GI-
ANT SETS RECORDS IN NEW YORK TOURNEY. When all the numbers were tallied and checked against the record books, Mikan had set six NIT
individual records in DePaul's pasting of Rhode Island State: most points
in a game (53); most points in two games (86); most field goals in one game
(21); most field goals in two games (34); most free throws in one game (11);
and most points in one half (32).

Reporters, however, weren't prepared to concede the championship to
DePaul. The Blue Demons would be going up against Bowling Green and
Don Otten, the team's seven-foot center, in the title game. Bowling Green
had won 24 of its 26 games that season, and the press, dubbing the game
"the battle of the giants," wondered if Mikan could control the pivot
against Otten the way he had in DePaul's previous tournament games. Otten was not only taller than Mikan; he outweighed him by a good thirty
pounds.

"They kept saying that Otten could handle Mikan because he was bigger and stronger, so I agreed with them on that," Meyer remembered with
a laugh. "I knew George would play a little better when he got angry."

Once again, Meyer tried to stoke Mikan's competitive fires by telling
him everything he'd read about Otten in the papers or heard about him at
the press conferences.

"I slipped the paper under Mikan's hotel room door," Meyer said. "I
knew he would come out ready. He murdered him."

For a while, things looked bad for the Blue Demons. When the game
began, Bowling Green built an early 11–0 lead and DePaul seemed sluggish. Meyer called time and chewed out his players. Mikan, towering over
the huddle, listened as Meyer made a few adjustments to DePaul's offensive scheme and, as the huddle broke, he turned to Meyer.

"Coach," he said, "don't you worry a bit. I'll take care of everything."

From that point on, the game was no contest. On DePaul's first possession after the time-out, Mikan took the ball in the pivot, faked Otten off
his feet, and moved around him for an easy dunk. As they had so many
times in the past, Mikan's teammates found his determination inspiring,
and they were more than willing to let him carry them to the championship. With teammates feeding him the ball on almost every offensive
possession, Mikan scored 34 points—giving him an incredible 120 points

for the three-game tournament—and DePaul won, 71–54. Otten ended up with seven points in the battle that was purely one-sided. Mikan, to no one's surprise, was named the tournament's Most Valuable Player.

A couple of days later, Oklahoma A&M won the NCAA tournament, defeating Long Island University and setting up another confrontation between George Mikan and Bob Kurland. DePaul's budget wouldn't allow them to return to Chicago for a few days between the end of the NIT and the Red Cross game, so the players, virtually broke, hung around New York and waited, their victory celebration limited to a modest night on the town, financed by the two dollars' meal allotment given to each player.

"We were all broke. We were all hungry," Gene Stump said. "We stepped out into New York's Times Square and tried to buy the most food we could get for two dollars. We ended up eating hamburgers instead of steaks. But we felt like millionaires."

March 29, 1945

This is the game everybody's been waiting to see: George Mikan versus Bob Kurland. The DePaul Blue Demons against the Oklahoma A&M Aggies. The NIT champs against the NCAA champs, in a rematch of the previous season's NIT semifinal match. It's Ray Meyer, one of the best young coaches in the game, who's built a powerful basketball program by teaching an awkward young kid how to play, versus Hank Iba, who's taken a team decimated by the war and rebuilt it into a national powerhouse.

The press can't get enough of it. Here are college basketball's two Goliaths facing each other in what's being billed as the game to determine the true national champs, staged in the country's most prestigious venue in the country's biggest city, with proceeds from the matchup going to the Red Cross. This game has so much built-in hype that the newspapermen don't have to manufacture any more; they just have to direct what's already there.

Mikan and Kurland know each other well. Their teams have met three times over the past year, with DePaul winning all three, but every game has been a war. Although capable of scoring a lot of points in any given contest, Kurland has devoted most of his energy to playing defense against Mikan. Iba's a big believer in the old idea of the best way of killing a dragon being to cut off its head, and Kurland is his executioner.

"*The best defense against Mikan was to keep the ball out of his hands, from a direct pass, if you could,*" *Kurland would explain, many decades later.* "*We used a sinking defense, where the offside would fall back and you had me alongside or in back of George, with one or two guys in front of him. It was like a rubber band: when the ball went to the other side of the court, the defense would spread out on that side. Our offense was set up with screens and blocks, with me passing off rather than depending on me to score points. In my opinion, that's the kind of game that wins championships. If you're depending upon a particular individual and he's sick or having a bad night, you're in a mud hole, boy.*"

Iba has added a wrinkle to tonight's game plan. He's seen enough of Mikan to know that Big George has a tendency to get a little too ratcheted up for the big games. The elbows will fly a little more than usual, he's more aggressive on both offense and defense—he tries to take the load all by himself. If Kurland can get inside Mikan's head, there's a chance Mikan will take himself out of the game, either by fouling out or by letting his anger reduce his overall effectiveness.

It doesn't take much to get into Mikan's head when it comes down to the subject of Bob Kurland. Win or lose, Kurland has given him more trouble than any man alive, and Mikan considers him his ultimate rival. Gene Stump, De-Paul's designated practical joker, has a favorite gag that he likes to pull on Mikan whenever DePaul is in New York. Mikan will be out on the street, and some kid, spotting him towering over everyone around him, will ask Stump about him.

"That's Bob Kurland," Stump will tell the unsuspecting soul. "Go get his autograph."

As soon as the kid approaches him, Mikan knows who is responsible for the prank.

"He'd chase me all over the place," Stump would recall, laughing at the mental image of the big guy's trying to run him down on the streets of Manhattan.

The Red Cross game begins and Kurland is all over Mikan, physically and verbally. He needles him mercilessly, apologizing for jabbing him in the ribs, offering mock sympathy whenever Mikan misses a free throw. By the middle of the first half, Mikan is totally steamed. The Blue Demons jump off to a ten-point lead, but Mikan's attention is focused more on his red-headed tormenter than on the game itself. As Iba suspected, Mikan's emotions, so often a great motivator, are now working against him. The elbows are flying, the play's getting rough.

Ray Meyer sees it as well. Mikan has used up three of his four fouls and is in danger of being disqualified before halftime. Without Mikan, DePaul is in big trouble.

Meyer calls a time-out to try to calm Mikan down.

"Just hold your arms up on defense," he orders Mikan. "There's no way they can beat us if you just stay in the game."

What happens next will be discussed and debated long after the fans have left and the popcorn swept off the floors of Madison Square Garden.

Kurland has the ball and is backing his way in toward the basket. Mikan, as instructed, holds up his hands and avoids contact. Kurland, now ready to take his shot, wheels around and runs into Mikan. Referee Pat Kennedy blows his whistle. Foul on Mikan. He's been disqualified at the 13:50 mark of the first half. Mikan and Meyer complain vehemently, but Kennedy's call stands. The battle between college basketball's two most prominent players has come to a very sudden ending.

Mikan, Meyer, and Kurland will never agree on the call, although all three will agree that Mikan's fouling out was the result of his playing too aggressively.

"He killed himself in that particular game," Kurland would remember. "He was feeling his oats about being a great scorer—which he was—but I stood up against him and that's where he got his fouls. The shot he fouled out on was one I had practiced but never used before. He had his arms up, and I went under his arms and scooped the ball toward the basket. He came down across my arms and Pat Kennedy fouled him out. The game was over, for all practical purposes."

Mikan would never admit that he committed a foul on the play, but he would confess to losing his cool and costing his team the game.

"Coach Hank Iba and his Ags were a little too smart for me," he'd lament.

Meyer scolds Mikan after the game, but it's really not necessary. Meyer's bothered by the 52–44 outcome of the game—"the only good thing about that game is that a crowd of 18,158 contributed more than $50,000 to the Red Cross," he'd complain in his autobiography—but he's even more concerned about a telephone call he'd received the day before from a friend, who suggested that something might be amiss. There had been a surge of heavy betting on Oklahoma A&M, and that just didn't make sense, given DePaul's status as a five-point favorite. Meyer didn't want to believe it then, but in the wake of DePaul's losing and Mikan's being fouled out so early in the contest, Meyer starts rethinking everything he's heard. There have always been rumors about *games being thrown or points being shaved in college basketball. In New York, betting on the games and point spreads is considered an art form. So who's to say that DePaul hadn't been victimized?*

Meyer calls his friend Ole Olsen, the coach of Ohio State. He outlines his suspicions and tells Olsen that he's thinking of going to the New York papers with what he's heard. He'll expose college basketball for the fraud it is.

Olsen tells him to stay put and stay quiet. Within minutes, he's at Meyer's hotel room door, urging him to leave the room and come with him. They retreat to Olsen's room, where they spend hours talking about the game, Meyer's suspicions, and the damage Meyer could cause college basketball if he starts tossing around a lot of unsubstantiated allegations. At one point, Meyer gets up to leave, but Olsen won't let him go.

By morning, Meyer's cooled down and he decides against saying anything further about the matter. With the passage of time, he'll conclude that the better team won the game, and that he'd just been overheated from losing his star player and the game.

However, there is one ominous footnote to the episode. Meyer learns that a lieutenant from the New York City Police Department spent the night knocking on his hotel room door and trying to track him down. He wanted a statement from the coach.

Meyer wasn't alone in his suspicions. Word of his meeting with Olsen leaked out to the press, and in no time, rumors were flying around in college basketball circles and in the newspaper wire services. OKIE-DEPAUL UPSET STARTS RUMOR MONGERS' FIELD DAY, read one newspaper headline over a United Press International piece examining the flap.

According to the article, there were four basic rumors, all based on Meyer's meeting with Olsen. One had Meyer registering an official protest with Olsen about the game's officiating. The second had Olsen bringing the game's two officials to the hotel room for an explanation. The third— and perhaps most disturbing—had a big-time midwestern bookie calling a New York connection and advising him not to bet on DePaul because Mikan was going to be fouled out of the game. Finally, a fourth rumor had *Olsen* threatening to go to authorities to demand a full investigation into the affair.

The author of the report had caught up to both Meyer and Olsen after their meeting in Olsen's room, and he'd asked for their comments about the rumors. Both denied filing—or having any intention of filing—protests with the NCAA or any other authorities. Both denied requesting any sort of investigation.

"You boys seem to have been misinformed," Meyer told the reporter, keeping a straight face. "Mr. Olsen was merely consoling me for our defeat. Why should I protest? We were beaten—and that's all."

When pressed further, Meyer conceded that he thought Mikan had been fouled out awfully quick in the game, and that he was "burned up" about having no say in selecting the officials for the game, but he reiterated his position that he had filed no protests.

Neither Ray Meyer nor George Mikan would ever publicly suggest that the DePaul–Oklahoma A&M game had been anything but aboveboard; but given the serious betting scandals that would rack college and professional basketball in less than a decade, the police were probably justified in checking out any rumors they might have heard, especially those involving a high-profile event like the DePaul–Oklahoma A&M Red Cross benefit game. College coaches were aware of the heavy betting that accompanied any big game—the bigger the game, the higher the stakes. Every bookie and gambler in town was looking for an edge. Coaches tried to shield their players from outside distractions, including probing questions from the press, but there was no way they could be one hundred percent successful. New York was just too big.

College players were especially vulnerable. They might have traveled a bit and played in some big cities, but they were still young—not much more than kids—and they could be victimized by all kinds of con artists. Bookies and bettors employed all kinds of methods, some innocent enough, to glean information that might help them out. During the 1943–44 NIT, when Mikan had injured his ankle, gamblers inundated his hotel room with queries about his physical well-being.

"We didn't have any restrictions on phone calls coming into the room," Dick Triptow noted. "I roomed with Mikan because I was taping his ankle for the games, and I got calls. 'How's his ankle?' 'Is he able to play?' We knew there was a lot of betting going on."

Jack Phelan recalled seeing some shady characters at the hotel where DePaul was staying. Like Triptow, he knew their purpose. "The bookies used to be sitting in the lobbies," he said, "and they'd watch ballplayers come in, to see who was limping and who was hurting, who was playing or not, and this would change the odds."

Ray Meyer imposed a curfew on his DePaul players, but it was mostly based on the honor system. For Gene Stump, who was seeing New York for only the first or second time, the temptation to slip out of the hotel and see the city at night was too great to resist.

"I used to sneak out at 10:30, 11:00," he said. "I'd never had corned beef, so I'd go down to a deli one block away. I was sitting there one night and Milton Berle walked in, and to me that was like heaven. I was there every night. One night, I walked back [to the hotel] and Ray was sitting on the couch. He took one look at me, and if looks could kill . . . I told him what I did. He said, 'Don't ever do that again without me. The next time you go, call me and I'll go with you.'"

The gambling scandals had yet to break, but it was no secret that fixing games or shaving points could be easily accomplished in basketball. A missed shot here, an overthrown pass there—it would be almost impossible to detect. And officials, whose whistles governed the game, certainly weren't exempt. Players claimed they could look up in the stands and tell who had money riding on the game—"the New York guys told me that everybody in Madison Square Garden had a bet on the game, one way or another," one player said, only half in jest—and more than a half century after the DePaul–Oklahoma A&M game, there were still DePaul players who wondered if anything fishy had been involved in Mikan's quick exit from the game.

Nothing would ever come of any suspicions swirling around that game, but trouble lay ahead—trouble that would severely damage the NIT and college basketball, destroy the careers of talented players, tarnish the reputations of coaches, and cause coaches, players, and fans to look back at other games and wonder.

Five

A Disappointing Finale

UNDER THE USUAL circumstances, the George Mikan era at De-Paul should have ended after the loss to Oklahoma A&M. Mikan had been attending classes at the school for four years, and he'd been playing varsity basketball for three. Nevertheless, Mikan hoped that he would be allowed to play a fourth year of varsity ball, mainly because he was studying in a five-year degree program.

Mikan began fall practices with the belief that he would be permitted to compete in the forthcoming season, but in the first week of December, he learned that his eligibility was jeopardized when the Faculty Committee of the Western Conference passed new eligibility rules addressing, among other things, the timeframe in which college players serving in World War II might be permitted to compete in collegiate sports. Mikan, of course, had not served in the armed forces, nor was DePaul, an independent, required to follow Western Conference dictates, but the overall picture was confusing. De-Paul played a number of games against Big Ten schools, and there was some question as to whether Mikan would be allowed to play in those games.

Rev. Joseph Phoenix, chairman of DePaul's athletic committee, shrugged off suggestions that his school might not comply with the new rulings.

"DePaul maintains the same standard of eligibility as the Western Conference and will continue to do so," he stated.

Other schools lodged protests, arguing that it was unfair to suddenly disqualify the winter sport athletes who had already practiced (and, in some cases, competed) in their sports. Western Conference officials relented, deciding that the new rules would take effect after the current winter sports seasons. George Mikan was free to play for another season.

DePaul couldn't have been more delighted. Mikan, now the team's sole captain, drew large crowds wherever he went, and, in just a few years, De-Paul's basketball program had rocketed from mediocre to top-shelf. With World War II ended and the troops returning home, there seemed to be no limit to the supply of student athletes just out of high school or back from the war, eager to resume their college careers. DePaul, once a haven for players who couldn't catch on with bigger-name schools, now enjoyed pre-ferred status among young men looking for a good, competitive basketball program.

Most of the squad was back from the previous year, making DePaul the odds-on favorite to head back to New York for a Mikan curtain call in the NIT. Other schools would be gunning for a win over the NIT champs, and, as usual, Ray Meyer had put together a schedule of tough opponents. After warmup games against the Cicero Merchants and the Joliet All-Stars, the Blue Demons headed down to Stillwater, Oklahoma, to face Okla-homa A&M in their first road game of the season.

For a while, it looked like they might not make it.

"We landed in Ponca City and had to take a bus to Stillwater," Gene Stump remembered. "The bus broke down. We saw people walking—men on burros and women walking beside them. They finally got the bus fixed and we got there, I don't know how many hours later."

When the game finally did get under way, George Mikan and Bob Kur-land engaged in another of their classic battles. Kurland and his teammates tried to aggravate Mikan with the trash talking that had been so effective in the previous year's Red Cross game. This time around, Mikan ignored them and concentrated on his play. He needed every bit of it. He'd loafed all through the previous summer and had reported to fall practices terribly out of shape; by his own later admission, it took him nearly half the season to get in peak condition. Playing against the likes of Bob Kurland in less than optimum shape was never a very good idea, and the Blue Demons might have been in serious trouble if Mikan hadn't been so motivated by his failings in his previous postseason encounter against Oklahoma A&M. Mikan played his strongest game to date against Kurland, outscoring him 25–18, and DePaul outlasted the Aggies, 46–42.

As Gene Stump recalled, getting out of Stillwater was almost as difficult as getting in.

"They were a Baptist community and we were a Catholic university," he said, "and they were throwing everything at us but you name what. We locked ourselves in the dressing room. The police came and walked us out."

Bob Kurland remembered seeing DePaul's starting five, huddled in a circle before the game, all but Mikan (who stood over the group) on their knees.

"We were standing around," Kurland said, "and here were these guys, all down on their knees, praying. I knew we were going to have a hard night—and so did everybody else—and I thought to myself, 'If they've got George Mikan *and* God on their side, we're going to lose.' And we did."

The Blue Demons returned home to Chicago Stadium, to host the first of two tournaments slated for the Stadium that year. The Blue Demons were now playing most of their home games at the Stadium, and most of these games were parts of double-headers. New York colleges had been enjoying enormous success with double-headers, pulling huge crowds at Madison Square Garden, and Ray Meyer and DePaul boosters were able to convince Arthur Wirtz, owner of Chicago Stadium, that double-headers were the wave of the future. Wirtz went along with it and was rewarded handsomely: during the 1945–46 college basketball season, 162,000 fans paid to see DePaul play in twelve double-headers. For DePaul, it was a huge boost over the exposure they were getting at the Old Barn, which seated only 2,500 per game.

The first tournament of the season enjoyed great attendance. In the opening round, Mikan found himself up against another familiar foe— Don Otten and Bowling Green—and the Blue Demons emerged from a physical contest, 59–54 winners. DePaul waltzed through their semifinal game, overwhelming Washington 75–50 and setting up a final against Indiana State. Mikan earned the tournament's MVP honors by scoring 37 points and breaking his own Chicago Stadium scoring record in a 74–56 win. Both Indiana State centers fouled out while trying to contain him.

DePaul followed up its tournament championship with an incredibly easy 56-point win over Arkansas State and a 59–40 victory against Oregon State, giving them an 8–0 record for the year. Mikan took an early lead in the national scoring race and DePaul seemed invincible.

Reality arrived in the form of a disastrous five-game road trip, with games against Illinois, Minnesota, Notre Dame, Western Kentucky, and Murray State. DePaul had been enjoying home cooking for nearly a month, with Oklahoma A&M as the only quality opponent on the road.

The first two games were wretched. Mikan played poorly against Illinois, and the Blue Demons were thoroughly trounced, 56–37, marking the third time in four games under Ray Meyer that DePaul had been defeated by their downstate rivals. Then Minnesota handed DePaul consecutive losses for the first time since the middle of the 1943–44 season when they defeated the Blue Demons, 45–36.

It might have been easy to shrug off the losses as defeats at the hands of two good teams, had the games been good, solid efforts, but they weren't. Mikan was struggling, game after game, to put together two strong halves. An alarming pattern was developing: after playing a solid first half, scoring at his usual clip, Mikan would run out of energy in the second half and finish the game slowly. Ray Meyer kept him in the game, despite his obvious fatigue, hoping that he would find a second wind and pull off more of his late-game heroics. Unfortunately for DePaul, Illinois and Minnesota were too talented to let that happen.

Nursing a two-game losing streak, DePaul traveled to South Bend, Indiana, for the first of the season's two scheduled contests against Notre Dame. Games against the Fighting Irish always took on added meaning for Mikan and Ray Meyer, and Mikan came out for this one all fired up, only to see DePaul suffer one of its most heartbreaking losses during his time with the team. DePaul led throughout most of the game, but had been unable to put it away, and with time running out, the Blue Demons clung to a one-point lead. Notre Dame guard Billy Hassett tossed up a high-arching, teardrop shot that swished through the net at the final buzzer, giving Hassett his first basket of the evening and Notre Dame a 43–42 win.

Meyer considered all that had been going on during the losing streak and concluded that Mikan was wearing out and needed a rest. DePaul still had nine games, plus a round-robin tournament, left on its schedule, and the team needed to win almost every game if the Blue Demons expected another postseason tournament invitation. Meyer thought it over and declared that, for the time being, all practices and scrimmages were off.

Eddie Kolker, DePaul's team trainer, owned Eddie's Web, a little restaurant not far from the campus, which the players liked to use as a hangout. The guys would gather there before and after classes, or during lunchtime, to chew the fat, replay the latest DePaul game, talk about girls, or complain about classes. DePaul's success had brought them celebrity status among the other students frequenting the place, and Mikan quite naturally stood out in the group, not only because he was a star player, but also because, like other teammates, he held a part-time job there and cut quite a profile behind the counter.

One day in early 1946, while standing at the restaurant's cash register, Mikan noticed an attractive young co-ed coming in, and he was immediately interested in meeting her. For Mikan, such an attraction was out of character, since, from his earliest days at DePaul, he felt enough self-consciousness about his height that he usually shied away from girls.

"I tended to steer clear of college dances and other social contacts, especially dates," he wrote in his autobiography. "I remember one blind date midway through my second year of college. I called at the girl's house and sat down in a light wicker chair in her parlor to wait for her. Unfortunately, the chair buckled and cracked under my weight. The girl's mother looked at me askance. 'Do you always break the furniture?' she demanded."

Patricia Lu Daveny, the young woman walking into Kolker's, had never heard of George Mikan. A freshman at DePaul, Pat had attended high school at Our Lady of Angels Academy, an all-girls Catholic boarding school in Clinton, Iowa. After graduating from high school, she returned to Chicago, not really sure what she wanted to do next. Her parents insisted that she go to a Catholic college, and she chose DePaul mainly because she knew a couple of others enrolled at the school. She didn't know the first thing about basketball, George Mikan, or the Blue Demons, but after exchanging pleasantries with Mikan, she did know that she liked his engaging, almost innocent style.

There were no formal introductions that first day. Although he was definitely interested in dating her, Mikan took a slow, cautious approach. Whenever they saw each other at the restaurant, Mikan would tease her, make small talk, or playfully tug on her pigtails. DePaul was still in the middle of a demanding basketball schedule, which Mikan decided to use to his advantage.

"Somehow, he'd gotten my telephone number and address," Pat recalled many years later, "and he sent me postcards while he was away, from wherever they went. When he got back, he said, 'Do you want to go out with me?' And that's how it started."

Not surprisingly, Mikan wanted Pat to see him play, and she attended her first DePaul game at Chicago Stadium, where she saw the reception the tall young man received from total strangers. It didn't seem to affect him, though; he was totally down to earth. One of Pat's closest friends was dating Ernie DeBenedetto, and Pat arranged a double date as an occasion to introduce George to her parents. She'd told them that she was seeing a basketball player, and that he was tall, but neither was quite prepared for the sight of George Mikan ducking through their doorway.

"My dad was about six-two," Pat said, "but my mom was a little Irish gal, maybe five-four or something. When my mom saw George, he was wearing a porkpie hat. She said, 'Oh, my, you really are tall.'"

Mikan invited Pat's family to a game at the Stadium, and the more they saw of George, off and on the court, the more they liked him.

"My mom and dad loved George," Pat remembered. "My dad and my uncle would even go on trips with 'Mike' when he was in the NBA. They just loved it."

Pat enjoyed George's family. George talked about his grandmother all the time, and Pat was delighted when she finally met Blondie, whom George had built up into almost mythical proportions. Pat liked the others as well, especially George's sister, Marie—"a beautiful girl with big dimples and a wonderful personality"—with whom she became very close. One only had to go out to Joliet and walk into Mikan's Tavern to see where George got his level-headedness and strong work ethic.

Oddly enough, Mikan's teammates were slow to warm up to Pat— probably, she speculated, because she was invading a very close-knit fraternity.

"The friends George played with really didn't like me in the beginning," she mentioned. "For some reason, they weren't fond of George's going with me. The basketball players were like a little family. But we got along afterward."

Not that it mattered all that much: Mikan almost had to pencil Pat into his busy schedule of classes, basketball games, and working. But he did so—and gladly. As far as he was concerned, she was about the best thing that had ever happened to him.

Mikan's years at DePaul were reaching an end. Although he wouldn't be receiving his law degree after the spring semester, as he'd originally hoped, his basketball days could be counted by the game. The Blue Demons had recovered nicely from their midseason swoon, winning four straight after the Notre Dame debacle, including decisive wins over Western Kentucky and Marquette. Mikan stepped up his game noticeably. He now led the nation in scoring, averaging 24 points per game, and the Blue Demons were rolling over their opponents, averaging a 62.1–46.4 margin of victory.

DePaul slipped only twice during the second half of the season, dropping a tough-to-lose 69–67 decision to an excellent Great Lakes Naval Base team, despite Mikan's 30 points, and taking an embarrassing third place in their own round-robin invitational tournament. In the tournament, DePaul had drawn Oklahoma A&M for its opening game, in what would be the final showdown between George Mikan and Bob Kurland.

As always, the papers played up the Mikan-Kurland rivalry to the hilt. The winner of the battle between the two big centers would probably be picking up the tournament trophy. In their previous four encounters, the *Chicago Tribune* reminded its readers, Mikan had outscored Kurland, 58–54; this tournament game would probably be another close match.

For the Aggies, the tournament held greater meaning than just the Chicago Writers' trophy presented to the winner. Coach Hank Iba was looking for his 400th win, and he would love to see it happen against DePaul. The early-season loss to DePaul in Stillwater represented Oklahoma A&M's only loss of the season, and since that meeting, the Aggies had strung together fourteen straight wins. Notre Dame, the country's only other undefeated team, had just lost to Northwestern, giving Oklahoma A&M something to shoot for.

"If the Aggies win," *Tribune* sportswriter Wilfrid Smith noted, "they may continue to claim top rank [in the nation]."

Mikan would remember the game as one of his poorest performances of the year, when, in fact, it actually saw him reverting back to his strong first half/weak second half earlier form. Mikan outscored Kurland, 19–10, but he managed only one field goal in the second half, when Oklahoma A&M broke open a game that had been tied five times in the first half and at 34–34 in the second half. With Mikan ineffective and Gene Stump, DePaul's other big scorer, fouled out of the game, Oklahoma A&M pulled away, winning 46–38. The final tally for the DePaul–Oklahoma

A&M series during the Mikan–Kurland years came up 3–2 in DePaul's favor.

The consolation game against Hamline, taken by DePaul, 62–51, might have been an unremarkable, forgettable contest for most of its participants, but for the two teams' centers, the encounter wound up memorably, not for the competitive aspects of the game but because it became Mikan's introduction to a lifelong friend and future teammate.

Vern Mikkelsen, Hamline's freshman center, had already taken his lumps from Don Otten when Hamline met Bowling Green in its opening-round game. That much had been expected. Mikkelsen received no mention in the reportage of a tournament dominated by the nation's three most highly touted centers.

Joe Hutton, Hamline's coach, viewed the tournament as a great learning opportunity for his sixteen-year-old center. He'd be playing against the best.

"Did I learn a lesson," Mikkelsen declared, remembering his first brush-up against Mikan. "George was a senior and a superstar and everything, and I was just learning what the heck I was supposed to be doing. I got a basket off George in the first quarter, and I was so embarrassed, I apologized to him on the way down the court. I don't know why, but I knew I wasn't supposed to be able to score against the guy. I didn't know what to say, so I apologized on the way back. He said, 'That's okay, kid. You won't get any more.' And I didn't."

Mikan recovered from his mediocre game against Oklahoma A&M with a huge game against Notre Dame. He'd been lugging a chip on his shoulder since the Irish had defeated DePaul with the buzzer-beater earlier in the year; and if that wasn't motivation enough, the second scheduled meeting between the two teams was held on Mikan's last collegiate appearance in Chicago Stadium. The game was totally one-sided. Mikan scorched Notre Dame for 33 points, and DePaul took a laugher, 63–47.

DePaul's record stood at 16–5, with three games remaining, when DePaul left for New York for a game against Long Island University in Madison Square Garden. The Blue Demons' five losses equaled the greatest number of defeats in any season during the George Mikan era, but Ray Meyer felt confident that a win over a highly regarded basketball program such as LIU, in the highest-profile basketball venue in the country, would be sufficient for a nod from the NIT.

He was mistaken. DePaul smoked LIU, 75–51, before a full house at the Garden.

But the game would be Mikan's last collegiate appearance in New York.

George Mikan played his final collegiate game on March 9, 1946, leading DePaul to a 65–40 victory in a meaningless game against Beloit. The Blue Demons finished the season with a 19–5 record, giving Ray Meyer an astonishing 81–17 overall record during Mikan's years with the team. Meyer expected another invitation to the NIT—or the NCAA tournament, at the very least—but the phone remained silent. Mikan and Meyer would always speculate as to why DePaul wasn't invited to one of these tournaments, but neither received any kind of official explanation. Meyer wondered if he and his team were being punished for the noise he'd made at the previous year's NIT, when he'd questioned if there had been any shenanigans involved in Mikan's early exit in the game against Oklahoma A&M.

"Maybe my grumbling got back to the people who handled tournament selections," he speculated. "Or maybe we weren't invited so other coaches could take their pick between the NIT and the NCAA without worrying about us, as I'd heard. I never did get an explanation."

Whatever the reason, Mikan was now free to play basketball wherever he wanted—if, in fact, he chose to play at all. He'd been approached by several amateur and pro teams when DePaul's season was winding down, but he wasn't certain he wanted to play pro ball. He wanted to complete work on his law degree, stay close to his midwestern home and family, and, perhaps most important of all, stay close to Pat. The two had fallen deeply in love, and Mikan didn't want to jeopardize their future by moving away and playing a game that, by all indications, promised only a marginal future.

Maurice White and the Chicago American Gears changed his mind by making an offer too sweet to turn down.

Six

THE CHICAGO GEARS

MAURICE WHITE OWNED the American Gear and Manufacturing Company, a Chicago-based plant that built gears and other machine parts. World War II and its big government contracts had made him a wealthy man. White used some of his earnings from the factory and his Lindahl Foundry to sponsor several very successful amateur softball and basketball teams, and his decision to try his hand at a professional basketball franchise was just a natural progression for a former athlete who got a vicarious thrill from the successes of his sports teams. The National Basketball League was eager to establish a foothold in a major market like Chicago, and the league awarded White a franchise in 1944. With the Chicago American Gears, White had the potential to become a big name in a big town.

The National Basketball League, or at least the name, had roots going back to the beginnings of pro basketball. The NBL's most recent permutation dated back to 1937, when three companies—General Electric, Goodyear, and Firestone—agreed to create a league that would be a notch up from the Amateur Athletic Union and the industrial leagues that had been amazingly popular in the Midwest. Many of the NBL teams bore the names of their corporate sponsors (Akron Firestone Non-Skids, Akron Goodyear Wingfoots, Fort Wayne General Electrics, Richmond King Clothiers), and in most cases, the players, like those in the AAU, were employed by their teams' sponsors. When players weren't actually practicing or playing games, they worked in the factories.

The Chicago American Gears would operate in a similar manner.

Dick Triptow, Mikan's former DePaul teammate and co-captain, was one of the first players contacted by Maurice White.

"He called me in and told me he'd like to have me play for him," Triptow remembered. "I could work in the gear company as an executive in five years. I had a couple of offers from Sheboygan and Oshkosh, but I decided to stay home.

"I had a number of different jobs with the Gears. I was a clerk in the store, selling stock gears. I worked in the foundry. I worked in the factory, inspecting gears, where we stood ten hours a day and still had to play ball. But we were young, and at that stage it really didn't mean too much. You were able to do it."

Maurice White, Triptow noted, ran a first-rate operation which seemed to conflict with an eccentric side that eventually gained him the reputation as an oddball sports team owner.

"He was a very, very meticulous guy," Triptow said. "The aisles in the gear factory were all painted red—red, with white borders—and he had them painted every two weeks. It was an immaculate place—the gear machines and lathes and everything else."

Most of the NBL teams were located in the Midwest, especially around the Great Lakes states. Such unlikely towns as Sheboygan and Oshkosh in Wisconsin, Fort Wayne and Hammond and Anderson in Indiana, Columbus and Toledo and Akron in Ohio, and Flint in Michigan—had pro basketball franchises, where larger cities did not. Such future Naismith Memorial Basketball Hall of Famers as Buddy Jeannette, Bobby McDermott, Al Cervi, Red Holzman, Bob Davies, and Arnie Risen all spent time on NBL teams, serving as pioneers for the future NBA.

Not surprisingly, the wealthier team sponsors tended to field the better teams. Fred Zollner, owner of the Fort Wayne Zollner Pistons (which eventually evolved into the Detroit Pistons) operated one of the most successful NBL teams during the World War II years, mainly because his government contracts rewarded him with enough money to pay the highest salaries to the best players. When you played for Fred Zollner, you were an employee in every way, and you received benefits, such as life and health insurance, that other NBL owners did not give their players. Zollner's factory, like Maurice White's, had the reputation of being a good place to work.

Zollner's and White's personalities could not have been more unalike. Both attended their teams' games and took active interests in their on-court activities, and both were involved in their communities, especially in youth sports. But the similarities ended there. Zollner was a behind-the-scenes kind of guy, content to let someone else run the Pistons' day-to-day operations; he owned a private plane for his team's travels—unheard of, in those days—and it was first-class all the way for his team. White, conversely, was more of a hands-on owner, involved with his team to such a degree that he had himself listed as an owner-coach on the Gears' programs, even though he never coached. He was known throughout the NBL as an quirky character. He liked to drink, often heavily, which led to some erratic behavior.

"He had another fellow, a partner, and they were a bit rascally. They hit the bottle quite a bit," recalled Bob Rensberger, who played with the Gears during the 1945–46 season. "Once, when we were playing the Pistons down in Fort Wayne, they went out in the hallway and were standing there, urinating in the hall. Guys of that stature. We were embarrassed."

"He was a little offbeat," allowed Dick Triptow, "but he was a great guy. He had a dog, and he would have the dog at the games. And he would go on road trips with us. Fred Zollner would be there, too. Fred was a great fan and a good guy. These were gentlemen, and they treated their players right."

Price Brookfield, a Gears guard, shrugged off White's more eccentric qualities—"he was independent, but he was pretty nice to us"—but like other members of the Gears, he appreciated White's maverick system of incentive rewards, such as the bonuses he paid when the Gears played their biggest rivals, the Rochester Royals, in a meaningless three-game exhibition series after the 1947 playoffs. "He told us if we won two out of the three, he'd give each of us a thousand dollars," Brookfield recalled, "and that's what he did."

Within days of DePaul's final game, Maurice White contacted George Mikan and asked if he'd be interested in playing for the Gears. The team had just completed its season and was registered to play in the World Professional Basketball Tournament in a couple of weeks.

As a team, the Gears were nothing special. They'd finished their inaugural season with a 17–17 record, good enough for third place in a four-team division race. They were presently stacking their roster for the tournament. White believed that, with Mikan playing on the team, the Gears had an excellent chance of winning it. And that was just for the current year. There was no telling how far the Gears might go the following year if they had Mikan on board for an entire season.

White's offer to Mikan would have turned anyone's head. At first, he offered a generic contract with a $5,000 salary, an average to slightly better than average figure for NBL players, but Mikan turned it down. White then increased his salary offer to $60,000 over five years—a figure that would make Mikan the highest-paid player in the history of professional basketball. Mikan stood to earn a goodly sum in incentives as well. White offered unprecedented bonus cash to his players: six dollars for each field goal made, and three dollars for every free throw or assist in a Gears' victory.

Mikan could smell the cash coming his way. He'd never been on a losing team, and he knew he'd be scoring plenty of points with the Gears.

But money was not the only deciding factor for Mikan. He had received lucrative offers from other teams, but those offers meant he would have to move out of the Chicago area and, when he wasn't on the court, work for the team's sponsor. Maurice White expected Mikan to eventually work for his company as a corporate attorney, but he wouldn't be doing that until *after* he'd completed his law degree and was licensed to practice. Until then, Mikan was free to pursue his degree or just plain loaf during the Gears' offseason.

It didn't hurt, either, that Mikan would be joining a team with several of his old DePaul teammates already on the team. Dick Triptow was the Gears' playmaker and one of their leading scorers, and Stan Szukala and Bob Neu were also major contributors. Bob Calihan, a forward from Detroit University, earned second-team "All-NBL" honors for the 1945–46 season, and forward Stan Patrick, a former Illinois All-American, had been named to the first team the previous season. And, if these players weren't enough to sell Mikan on the Gears' potential, Maurice White had just signed Price Brookfield, a supremely gifted forward out of the military leagues, making him available for the World Tournament.

The final decision was easy.

On March 16, exactly one week to the day after closing the books on his career with DePaul, Mikan signed a contract to play for the Chicago Gears. He felt confident. The pro basketball experience, he thought, would be similar to what he'd seen in college, from the way the game was played to his team's walking away an easy winner in most of its games.

He would find out, soon enough, just how wrong he was.

Mikan was quickly reunited with Ray Meyer, who had been hired by the Gears to be an "advisory coach."

Maurice White wanted Meyer as the Gears' full-time coach, but Meyer wouldn't give up his coaching job at DePaul, so White offered Meyer a flat fee—it was either $50 or $75, Meyer could never remember—for every practice or game that he attended. Swede Roos, the Gears' player-coach during the 1944–45 season, and full-time coach during the 1945–46 season, would still be listed as the team's official coach.

The extent of Meyer's affiliation with the Gears was one of the worst-kept secrets in basketball. Meyer ran most of the Gears' practices and, since DePaul's season was now over, he sat on (or somewhere near) the bench during the games.* To observers, Meyer appeared to be working as Mikan's personal coach and advisor when, as even Mikan himself admitted, White's hiring of the DePaul coach "was actually a thinly veiled, and failed, attempt to hire him as a coach."

Just how "failed" the attempt really was, was best left to interpretation.

"He was more or less a coach with us when George came in," said Price Brookfield. "He was practicing most of the time and working with George."

Bob Rensberger, a Notre Dame alum signed with the Gears, saw Meyer's involvement as much more involved than his just advising Mikan and running practices.

"He wasn't an assistant, he was the *coach*. He was doing double-work," Rensberger insisted. "It wasn't against the law or anything, but I don't think they tended to publicize the fact that he was coaching too much. If you weren't doing too well [at DePaul], the alumni might have wondered how much time you were spending with the pros."

---

*In the 1946 World's Professional Basketball Tournament, Meyer was assessed a technical foul while seated in the second row of the stadium, just behind the Gears' bench. When Meyer protested the call, saying he wasn't on the bench and couldn't be given a technical foul for anything he said to an official, Referee Dutch Kriznecky responded, "Yeah, but you are coaching them and it's a technical."

Meyer maintained his allegiance to DePaul, and he made certain that he had fulfilled his obligations to the school before he went out to Cicero for the Gears' practices. The Gears practiced and played their games in Cicero Stadium, a small 2,000-seater in the western suburb. Often, when he arrived at the facility, Meyer found the Gears players standing around, patiently awaiting his arrival.

"I felt sorry for them and I would only go a half hour to an hour and let them go," he remembered.

The addition of George Mikan required major adjustments in the Gears' offensive approach. The Gears, like most teams of the day, preferred a freelance style of offense, using very few set plays. Prior to Mikan's arrival, the Gears played an up-tempo game that utilized Dick Triptow's speed and Stan Patrick's scoring. The team's two centers, Dick Klein and Bob Calihan, were both half a foot shorter than Mikan—and considerably lighter—but were much more mobile at the pivot.

Mikan would never be convicted for breaking speed limits on the court, and though he was much quicker with his hands and more agile on his feet than his size might have led you to believe, he preferred to camp out in the pivot and either fire off his hook shots or pass to players cutting to the basket. Before Mikan, scoring among the Gears was spread among the five players on the floor; now, with Mikan on the team, the offense would concentrate on the pivot.

With the Gears, as with DePaul, Mikan would become an unofficial coach on the floor, directing the action, making suggestions during time-outs, demanding the ball in clutch situations. He and Meyer worked on making the necessary adjustments between the college and pro games, much of them involving the physical play and positioning beneath the boards. Mikan was accustomed to being the biggest and most physical player on the court. He would still have a size advantage over most of his counterparts in the pros, but what the other centers lacked in size, they compensated for with bone-jarring play rarely allowed in college.

Mikan's first professional basketball game, like the first game for hundreds of other players, proved to be a huge learning experience. The Gears had thrown together two exhibition games, one against the Anderson (Indiana) Chiefs and one against the Detroit Mansfields, to prepare the team for the upcoming tournament, and while neither team presented the level of competition the Gears would be facing in the upcoming tournament, they did give Mikan a taste of what he'd be facing in the days ahead.

Mikan, understandably enough, was sky-high for his first pro game, eager to prove that he was worth every cent of his highly publicized salary and worthy of his lofty reputation as a player. The Anderson players, unimpressed with all the advance publicity, played the kind of rough, trash-talking basketball that reminded Mikan of his college encounters with Bob Kurland and Oklahoma A&M, and, as in the earlier games in college, he let his emotions get the better of him. The Gears won, 68–60, but Mikan, after scoring 17 points, fouled out with two minutes left in the third quarter.

By his own admission, he still had a lot to learn.

"Since I'd reached the pinnacle in college, I naïvely figured that I would have my way in the pros, also," he confessed. "I found out, however, that I may have graduated, but my education was not complete."

Dick Triptow agreed. Reflecting on Mikan's first game with the Gears, Triptow believed that Mikan fell victim to a combination of first-game jitters and his lack of understanding of the way officiating worked in professional basketball.

"He was so eager to do well, he got a little aggressive and fouled out," Triptow said. "He came into the league with a reputation, but he wasn't established, so the referees were going to call the fouls. And sometimes there was a difference in the way fouls were called, in terms of what would be allowed. The officials were usually local officials, and they refereed in a certain way. If you were playing in the Midwest, you had officials who maybe let a little more roughhousing go. If you went East, they would be calling [closer] fouls. You had to play the way the officials refereed the game."

Mikan, Triptow allowed, would always face a special challenge due to the physical nature of his position. "We used to say that basketball was a game where four guys went against four guys and the two centers had a wrestling match."

The Gears won their final tune-up game against Detroit, 59–48, with Mikan managing to stay in the game and contribute 20 points. Mikan, in typical fashion, felt he should have played better. He consulted with Ray Meyer, and they agreed that he would have to step up his game if he ever hoped to achieve the degree of success that he had enjoyed in college. The pro game, almost as foreign to Meyer as it was to Mikan, was definitely different from what they'd seen at DePaul.

Mikan's education continued when the Gears took the court as the featured club in the fourteen-team World Professional Basketball Tournament. In all, thirty-nine teams, including such powerhouses as the Fort Wayne Zollner Pistons, New York Rens, and Dow Chemicals, applied for entry into the prestigious tournament held annually at Chicago Stadium, but the Gears, hailing from the Windy City and featuring the country's top collegiate player just turned pro, were the hometown favorites.

The World Tournament, founded in 1939 by the *Chicago Herald-American,* featured the best of the National Basketball League, Amateur Athletic Union, and independents, and could make a legitimate claim to crowning the top team in the country. An NBL team traditionally won or took the runner-up position in the tournament, though the first two were taken by the New York Renaissance and the Harlem Globetrotters, respectively, marking an important development in professional basketball: throughout the ten-year history of the World Tournament, the NBL was an exclusively white league, and the inclusion of the Rens and Globetrotters, both African-American teams, represented at least a small effort to recognize the excellence of black basketball players. When they won the tournament in 1939, the Rens, with a 112–7 record, were easily the best team in the country.

The Gears had little trouble in their first-round game against the Pittsburgh Raiders. Mikan played his best all-around game as a pro so far, scoring 17 points while thoroughly controlling play on the offensive and defensive boards. The 69–58 final score made the game seem closer than it was.

The second game—against the Sheboygan Redskins—was much tighter. During the regular season, the Redskins had taken first place in the NBL's Western Division, finishing four games ahead of the Gears. Ed Dancker, Sheboygan's star center, played an extremely physical game, and he tested Mikan on both ends of the floor. The Gears took the game, 51–50, but not without struggles. Mikan fought for his 14 points against Dancker, causing some reporters to speculate about how he'd fare against Cowboy Edwards, the all-star center with the Oshkosh All-Stars, the Gears' opponent in the tournament semifinals.

Leroy "Cowboy" Edwards, perhaps more than any other player of his day, typified the brutal style of play at the center position in the NBL. At six-four, he wasn't especially tall, nor was he especially heavy—certainly not in comparison to Mikan's dimensions—but he was exceptionally strong and reasonably quick, and he had a nasty, aggressive disposition that spelled a long night for anyone tangling with him in close quarters. He'd bang bodies with you, toss his elbows in every direction, throw a punch if he deemed it necessary, or use any other method of intimidation he could dream up. On the offensive end of the floor, he could shoot a first-rate hook shot with either hand, which had helped him claim the NBL's scoring title three straight years (1937–40).

"He was built and he was solid," recalled Milt Schoon, a six-foot-nine center from Valparaiso, whose pro career included stints with Detroit, Flint, and Sheboygan, and who'd had plenty of encounters with Edwards. "He'd come around with that elbow on the pivot, and one day he caught me square alongside the head. I saw stars. The best way to play him was to stay away from him, because he felt you all the time. His arm was going and he knew where you were, and when he got you in position, boy, look out. It was coming."

Ray Meyer knew all about Cowboy Edwards, and before the Gears' tournament game against Oshkosh, he warned Mikan to stay away from him.

Mikan, predictably, heard none of it.

"Coach Ray Meyer advised me to try to stay clear of him on defense. I thought better as I proceeded to lean all over him," Mikan said of the encounter. "At one point he pinched me on my knee and it stabilized me. The second time, I again decided to keep leaning on him and again he pinched me and scored. I looked over at Ray and he turned his palms upward as much as to say, 'I told you so.' From then on I gave him three feet and 'Cowboy' did not do much after that.

"It was, however, a different story on offense. When I got the ball on the pivot on our first possession, I was able to take my patented hook shot with no problem and when 'Cowboy' saw that this spelled trouble for him, the next time I got the ball he really racked me up and proceeded to ask me if I wanted to fight. My only response was, 'Not just yet.'"

Edwards schooled Mikan from the opening tip, pinching his legs when he went up for a shot, knocking the wind out of him with elbows to the gut, and eventually knocking out four of Mikan's teeth with a hard elbow to the face. Fouls meant nothing to him—if, in fact, fouls were called at all. This was Mikan's true initiation into pro basketball, and it wouldn't end on that one night.

Price Brookfield, a veteran of the wars fought on-court in the military leagues, took Mikan aside and offered his best advice.

"When we played Sheboygan and Ed Dancker, or Oshkosh and Cowboy Edwards, that bunch beat on George that first year," he remembered. "They had him so upset at times that he came to me and I talked to him. I said, 'George, you either have to give it back to them or quit the game. They'll keep doing it. If you give it back to them, they'll stop.' That's what happened. He started giving it back to them and they quit."

Mikan tried fighting back in the tournament game, but he was shown the same respect from officials that any rookie received. Mikan tallied 25 points against the All-Stars, but he also fouled out early in the third quarter. Without Mikan, the Gears were no match for Oshkosh, and they lost, 72–66. The Gears took third place in the tournament, whipping Baltimore two games of a three-game consolation series, while the Fort Wayne Zollner Pistons took home the tournament trophy by beating Oshkosh, two games to one, in their championship series.

Although less than what he'd hoped for, the short season with the Gears and the World Tournament weren't a total loss for Mikan. He'd scored an even 100 points in his five games and had been named the tournament's Most Valuable Player. It might have been difficult to detect at the time, but a changing of the guard was taking place, perhaps symbolized by Mikan's MVP award: the Zollner Pistons, an NBL dynasty during the war years, were on the way down, and the Gears, a new team with a fresh new superstar, were climbing to the top.

Seven

CHAMPS?

THE 1946–47 SEASON ushered in another new league—the Basketball Association of America—which moved pro basketball into some of the biggest cities in the country.

Basketball had always gone over well in the East, particularly in New York City, where college basketball was exceedingly popular and an all-black barnstorming team, the New York Renaissance, featured some of the best basketball talent found on the planet. Edward "Ned" Irish, a former basketball reporter for the *New York World-Telegram*, had seen the potential for marketing college basketball in large arenas, and he'd built a very lucrative career out of staging double-headers in Madison Square Garden. The National Invitation Tournament, always held in New York, attracted the top college teams in the nation and drew huge crowds of spectators.

The BAA founders might have used Irish's success at Madison Square Garden as a model, but the league was really formed more out of practical need than any great love of basketball. Hockey was immensely popular in the eastern states, where the National Hockey League and American Hockey League had franchises in such cities as Boston, New York, Philadelphia, Pittsburgh, and Providence. These and other cities housed large arenas that hosted hockey games and ice shows. These events generated handsome profits, yet the arenas sat empty more than they were actually used. A number of arena operators, including Walter Brown, president of the Boston Garden, wondered what might happen if these arenas hosted basketball games on those nights when they would otherwise be dark. After all, the National Basketball League was doing well in smaller cities, with much smaller venues. Given the popularity of Irish's college experiment in

Madison Square Garden, it stood to reason that professional basketball would stand at least a decent chance.

The early discussions between Brown, Irish, arena operators, and other parties—most notably, Max Kase, sports editor of the *New York Journal-American*, who had helped promote a pro benefit game in New York during World War II—produced a consensus that the idea might work, although, predictably, no one seemed to agree on how to run the league. Most of the people involved knew very little about basketball, and all were too involved in their individual endeavors to put in the necessary time and effort to research and organize the new league.

That job fell on the shoulders of Maurice Podoloff, a Russian immigrant who, besides being a lawyer and banker, happened to be president of the American Hockey League. Podoloff's interests were in business far more than in sports, but, as it turned out, his ignorance of basketball and its history might have worked in his favor. Rather than organize the league with a purist's hope of promoting basketball as a sport, Podoloff worked to make basketball succeed as a business. Many of the arena operators were hotshots in their respective cities, forceful personalities with strong ideas on how things should be done, and Podoloff showed a remarkable skill in keeping these men tacitly satisfied, if not happy.

On June 6, 1946, Podoloff chaired an organizational meeting of the BAA at the Commodore Hotel in New York City, and the basic ground rules for the new league were laid down. A franchise would cost $1,000, with each franchise limited to a salary cap of $40,000, excluding the coach and trainer's salaries. The teams would be named for their respective cities, rather than for the businesses owning them, and the home teams would keep the gate receipts. College players could not be signed until their class had graduated.

Basic stuff, but significantly different from the NBL.

Over the ensuing months, the rules were fine-tuned and the franchises ultimately chosen. The BAA would consist of eleven teams: the Boston Celtics, Chicago Stags, Cleveland Rebels, Detroit Falcons, New York Knickerbockers, Philadelphia Warriors, Pittsburgh Ironmen, Providence Steamrollers, St. Louis Bombers, Toronto Huskies, and Washington Capitols. The teams would play a sixty-game schedule, after which there would be playoffs to determine a league champion.

No one knew how the new league would affect the NBL, whose season opened a month after the opening of the BAA season. Was there a fan base for all these additional teams? Would the talent be too watered down? Would the BAA's head start in the opening of its season jeopardize interest in the NBL?

In Chicago, the only city with more than one pro basketball team, the Gears faced stiff competition from the Stags, who were playing their home games at Chicago Stadium, a much nicer, roomier venue than the International Amphitheater, the Gears' home court. Although Maurice White confidently predicted smooth sailing for his team, which happened to employ basketball's premier young player and the NBL's biggest draw, the bottom line would still be determined, as it always was, by wins and losses. The Gears had to compete for the title. It was really that simple.

George Mikan spent the summer and early fall months working on his law degree and relaxing, enjoying the benefits of financial success he couldn't have imagined a year earlier. He'd given a good chunk of his salary to his parents for help with their bills, and if he needed any reminders about his recent past and the bright future ahead, he received them shortly before the opening of the Gears' season, when he was invited to participate in the College All-Star Classic.

This annual event pitted the best of the previous year's college players against the World Tournament winners. The Fort Wayne Zollner Pistons, the All-Stars' opponent, had won three consecutive NBL titles and the past two games against the College All-Stars, but this year's college team was loaded with talent and Mikan believed the young players stood a good chance of defeating their older counterparts.

In George Mikan and Don Otten, the collegians had a tandem of the two tallest centers ever to play in the game. The team also had three of Mikan's future teammates on its roster: Tony Jaros, a three-sport star at the University of Minnesota, headed for the Chicago Stags (and, eventually, the Minneapolis Lakers); Billy Hassett, the Notre Dame guard who had broken DePaul's heart with his last-second shot, soon to be playing for the Tri-Cities Blackhawks; and Fritz Nagy, a forward from Akron University, headed for the Indianapolis Kautskys.

The game, staged before a capacity crowd at Chicago Stadium, more than justified its heavy advance billing. The College All-Stars, behind the scoring of Mikan, Eastern Kentucky's Freddie Lewis, and Notre Dame's Leo Klier, played the champs even, leading 27–26 at halftime and tied 52–52 at the end of regulation. Mikan fouled out with less than a minute in regulation, but his 16 points topped all collegiate players, and only the Piston's star guard, Bobby McDermott, with 22 points, registered more points for the game. The All-Stars outscored the Zollner Pistons, 5–2, in the overtime period and came away 57–54 winners.

For Mikan, the game was a treat. "I've been in lots of all-star games since," he mentioned later, "but that was the big one for me."

Months would pass before he had as satisfying an experience. The Gears, unable to play in the International Amphitheatre because of an extended livestock show, opened their 1946–47 season on the road, playing a total of 17 regular-season and exhibition games away from Chicago and managing only a 9–8 record. Travel was grueling under the usual circumstances, but being on the road for the better part of a month tested anyone's endurance, especially when nearly half of the games were exhibitions. The Gears opened their schedule with three straight exhibition games against the Rochester Royals, whom they'd have to face four times during the regular season. They dropped two of the three, leaving them in a sour mood. The games drew good crowds, which irked players, who received no extra pay for exhibition games, and it bothered them all the more when they were losing on the road to a rival team.

One trip the Gears did enjoy was a jaunt to the West Coast for a pair of exhibition games against the Los Angeles Red Devils. Mikan, like many of his teammates, had never flown, nor had he ever been to the West Coast, so the trip meant a new adventure.

"It was our first chance to fly," remembered Dick Triptow, "and it was very interesting because we were on a prop plane, one of those two-motor jobs."

The Red Devils, one of the few integrated teams playing pro or semipro ball, had an outstanding team, with Art Stoefen, the former Stanford star, at center, and Irv Noren and George Crowe, two players who would make their names in Major League Baseball, as forwards. Their biggest star, however, was a UCLA graduate named Jackie Robinson, who, in a year, would break baseball's color barrier and, in the process, become the National League's Rookie of the Year.

Robinson, the only four-sport letter-winner (baseball, football, basketball, track and field) in UCLA's history, brought the same aggressive, competitive spirit to the basketball court that he displayed on the baseball field, and the Red Devils had a perfect 4–0 record when the Gears flew into town to play them in the Olympic Auditorium. The Devils, who made a habit of scheduling two-game series against all their opponents, had opened their season with two close wins over the Sheboygan Redskins before taking a pair from the New York Rens. Mikan and the Gears represented their toughest test to date.

Mikan was the third dominating center the Devils had faced. After battling with Sheboygan's Ed Dancker and the Rens' Nathaniel "Sweetwater" Clifton, the Devils were prepared to take some unusual steps in playing defense against Mikan.

"I had to pull on the bottom of his pants when he and I went up, so I could outjump him," Irv Noren said. "He didn't like it too much."

The teams split the series, the Gears winning the first game, 59–56, and the Red Devils taking the next day's meeting, 47–46, with Robinson's 13 points leading his team. Emotions ran high, and Robinson and Bob Calihan had to be separated after some very physical play under the basket.

The trip wasn't strictly business, though. Some of the Gears managed to work in a round of golf, and most of the team took a tour of the 20th Century Fox studios.

Most of the Gears' exhibition games, however, offered nothing in perks, and the playing conditions could be downright bizarre. A week before flying out to Los Angeles, the Gears played a series of what Dick Triptow described as "very unusual but memorable games" on the East Coast. The first, against the Jersey City Atoms of the American Basketball League, taught the Gears a lesson about the way basketball was played in the ABL, which, like hockey, divided its games into three periods. After the second period, the Gears figured they were through for the night, and they had to be rousted from the locker room to finish the game. Two days later, the Gears took on the Baltimore Mets on a court that had two mirrored pillars stationed in the middle of the floor. ("As a player would dribble or run from one end of the court to the other, he would see the reflection of his own number coming right at him," Triptow observed.) After the game, the Gears' business manager had to go into the bowels of the stadium to receive the Gears' $500 payment for the game—and even that was unusual.

"We got paid off in singles," Triptow remembered with a laugh.

But it wasn't over. The very next night, the Gears were in Philadelphia, playing their fourth game in four nights, this one against the Philadelphia Sphas. The playing conditions here were as strange as the ones the night before in Baltimore. A makeshift court had been set up in the Grand Ballroom of the Broadwood Hotel. A huge crystal chandelier hung over the court, and an orchestra assembled on the stage at one end of the ballroom. This was another three-period game, with teams retreating to their dressing rooms between periods, and after each period, while the players were away, the fans went out onto the ballroom floor and danced.

"We played in a lot of unusual places," Triptow allowed. "In some places, the courts were smaller. Then you had high school gyms. One place out East had a curve around the gym—like a track—and we would trip and fall. Your big arenas today are standard size and the floors are so fantastic it's unbelievable."

In his game against the Gears, Irv Noren had played well enough to catch the attention of Maurice White, who hired him away from the Red Devils. In recalling his first game with the Gears, Noren probably offered the best possible explanation for why players worked for so little money, endured miserable travel arrangements, played on quirky courts, dealt with crazy fans, and put up with the idiosyncrasies of a game still trying to find its level on the sports scene.

"The first point I made was a free throw," Noren remembered. "When I stood at the line, I was thinking, 'Jesus, here I am in Chicago.' I was in Pasadena the night before, but I flew in and played the next night. I was making a hundred bucks a game, but back in those days, I would've flown from here to Japan to make a hundred dollars a game. I was thinking, 'I can't believe I'm here, playing with these guys in a league. Here I am. I'm in Chicago.'"

Mikan was in a foul mood even before he stepped through the doorway to Maurice White's office on the afternoon of the Gears' first home game in Chicago. The Gears had been playing mediocre basketball, which in itself would have been enough to frost the hyper-competitive center, but Mikan had personal reasons to be angry with White. Several days earlier, when the Gears were on the road and getting ready to board a train, four players had been pulled aside and informed that their services were no longer needed. Just like that: no warnings, no private meetings in the coach's or owner's office, no real sense of professionalism. One of those dismissed had been Joe Mikan, George's older brother. By anyone's definition, Joe had been a marginal player, added to the Gears' roster as a favor to George. White had been paying him, along with the other three players, to ride the bench. It was an expense White no longer could afford.

Mikan's mood darkened when he was summoned to White's office and the Gears' owner explained his predicament. The Gears, White said, were in financial trouble, and like any business going through rough times, the team had to find ways to cut corners.

"The biggest corner I can see right now is you," he told Mikan.

Mikan, who had entered White's office with the thought that White might be aiming to explain why Joe had been cut from the team, suddenly wondered about his future with the Gears. White wanted him to take a huge pay cut—from $12,000 to $6,500 that year—with the understanding that Mikan would be eventually compensated to his real worth, after the Gears recovered from their present financial hardships.

No way, Mikan responded. He was not going to take a pay cut under any circumstances. They had a legally binding contract, and White was going to pay every penny of it.

The meeting ended without an agreement. Mikan stewed for the rest of the afternoon and into the evening. He dressed for the game, but his mind was elsewhere. He played his worst game as a pro, scoring only nine points and drawing a technical foul when he threw a ball at an official. The Gears lost to Oshkosh, 44–41, but it mattered very little to Mikan. He'd determined his course of action during the halftime intermission, and he announced it after the game in an interview with *Chicago Tribune* sportswriter Maurice Shevlin.

The *Tribune*'s headline the next morning spelled out Mikan's decision in no uncertain terms: MIKAN RETIRES AFTER GEARS LOSE, 44 TO 41.

"I do not like the way Mr. White does business," Mikan said, "and my heart isn't in the game under existing conditions." Mikan told Shevlin that he'd tried to reach White after the game to inform him of his decision, but White wasn't available.

The legal chess game began. Mikan consulted with his attorney, Stacy Osgood, and he was advised that he probably had grounds for a breach of contract suit. It wasn't going to be a simple matter, though. Mikan was playing for a base salary of $7,000 a year, in accordance with league regulations on maximum salary; the remainder of his salary was paid out in incentive bonuses and honoraria paid "for peeking into the [Gears'] legal department every once in a while."

Mikan's biggest source of dissatisfaction stemmed from what he perceived to be a lack of job security. He seethed over the way the Gears had handled his brother's dismissal from the team, and the way he saw it, his contract was essentially one-sided, slanted in favor of the Gears. White could release him any time he wanted, but Mikan was stuck with the team, regardless of circumstance. Three days before the home opener, before an exhibition game against the Dayton Mets, Mikan had confided in teammates Dick Triptow and Stan Szukala. He was ready to walk out, he told them. The only reason he even considered playing in the home opener was because a lot of money had already been poured into promoting the game and he didn't want to upset what was expected to be a full house of fans paying to see him play.

In his public statements, Mikan made sure that his fans and teammates understood that his actions were aimed solely at the Gears management.

"I can't possibly have stability under the present arrangement," he complained. "The boys on the Gears are fine to play with. None of the matters which created the insecurity traces to the players."

As of the moment, he announced, he had no plans to play pro basketball. He'd let the courts decide whether his contract was fair. In the meantime, he would work on his law degree.

Maurice White, similarly unhappy, filed a countersuit charging Mikan with breach of contract. Mikan's absence was going to cost his team a bundle, and White wasn't going to passively stand by and let that happen. After making sure that Mikan wouldn't be earning any money by playing for other professional organizations while sitting out, White applied further pressure by seeing that Mikan was fined $150 for each game missed and $25 for every practice he failed to attend.

Mikan had other things on his mind beside basketball and law school. On December 15, three days after Mikan announced his retirement, the *Chicago Tribune* announced that Mikan was marrying Patricia Lu Daveny. No wedding date was supplied.

Meanwhile, the Gears slogged along, posting a 9–10 record regular season record during Mikan's absence. The Mikan holdout might have been the biggest factor contributing to the Gears' losing record, but the team also struggled under a new coach and a different system. Swede Roos, the team's coach the previous season, had been replaced by Davey Banks at the end of November, shortly after the trip to the West Coast, and Banks had his own ideas about how the team should play. Banks had impeccable credentials as a player with the old New York Celtics, leading the team in scoring in 1927 and playing alongside such greats as Nat Holman, Dutch Dehnert, and Joe Lapchick, but he never clicked with the Gears players.

"He wanted us all to shoot that set shot, and I never shot that in my life," Price Brookfield remembered. "Nobody could go for what he wanted them to do. We would never have beaten anybody."

Banks was dismissed just before the Gears' December 11 home opener, and White assigned Bruce Hale the role of player-coach. Hale, a star at Santa Clara University and, later, several service league teams, was the same age, with essentially the same experience, as the men he was trying to coach, and the dual roles were more than he was equipped to handle. The coaching situation, coupled with the loss of George Mikan, threatened to push the Gears into also-ran status before half the season was completed.

The coaching problem was resolved in the most unpredictable way when, on January 3, 1947, Maurice White announced that the Gears had signed aging superstar Bobby McDermott as its new player-coach. Labeled "the greatest player of all time" after leading the Fort Wayne Zollner Pistons to their three consecutive NBL championships and two straight first-place finishes in the World Professional Basketball Tournament, McDermott boasted of basketball skills equaled only, perhaps, by his colorful personality. A hard drinker off the court and a scrapper on the floor, McDermott was known almost as much for his fisticuffs as he was for his unparalleled two-handed set shot, which he would launch from anywhere on the court.

"He could hit that long shot better than he could hit a layup," remembered Price Brookfield, who played both with McDermott and against him. "I sat out there and practiced behind him. I watched him shoot that thing from thirty feet and more. If he was on a fast break, he'd stop and shoot rather than go in for a layup."

"In my eyes, he was the greatest outside shooter that ever played the game," Dick Triptow marveled. "He shot those two-handed set shots from anywhere on the court. He was quick, knowledgeable—the epitome of a guard that played the game. A fierce competitor. He didn't always follow the rules, and he spurned conditioning. He drank, but he was there, ready to play, when the game started."

McDermott signed several players after taking over as coach, including Gene Stump, Mikan's old DePaul teammate. Stump never recorded a single minute's playing time while he was on the Gears' roster. His role, he quickly learned, was to see that McDermott and his friends were supplied with liquid refreshments when the Gears were on the road.

"I'd just gotten out of college, and Bobby McDermott needed about four or five guys to fill out the team," Stump recalled. "I'd get two cases of cold Schlitz, and McDermott would get on the train and they'd play cards and smoke cigars all night. There was no such thing as training. But he was a great athlete, a great player."

Billy Gabor, who earned his own reputation as a rough, quick-tempered player, remembered an encounter early in his career, when he was confronted by McDermott before the opening tip of a game.

"I was a rookie," he said, "and I'd heard all about Bobby McDermott and how great he was. I'm a hotshot rookie, and when we started lining up for the jump ball, he started pushing me and I started pushing him. Before you knew it, we were in a fight. We were both thrown out before the game started."

As it turned out, it was McDermott's wild side that landed him on the Chicago Gears. The Zollner Pistons had just played the Royals in Rochester, and on the train heading back to Fort Wayne, a fight broke out among a small group of Pistons shooting craps in the men's room.

"I was in my bunk, sleeping, when Curly Armstrong woke me up and said, 'Carl, we've got a little fight out here in the men's room,'" said Carl Bennett, the Pistons' general manager at the time. "We always stopped in Buffalo and picked up a case of beer so the guys could put water back in their systems. Beer was a big thing to the players in that day because they used it as an excuse for putting water back in the system."

McDermott and the other players went a bit further than just hydrating their systems, and by the time Bennett and others had broken up the fight, several Pistons had been bloodied. They were all sent packing as soon as the team arrived in Fort Wayne.

"It was a sad day," Bennett recalled. "In Fort Wayne's era in the National Basketball League, we considered Bobby McDermott a franchise player. If you go by ten-year eras, he was the top of the rock between 1940 and 1950. But that was Bob. He was a feisty boy, on and off the court. He wasn't easy to handle, but he did his job and was a great player."

Back in Joliet, George Mikan followed his team's travails and awaited his court date. The addition of McDermott kicked up the Gears' hopes of reaching the playoffs—if, in fact, Mikan returned to the team and the Gears went on any kind of winning streak—but there was no way of predicting how the contract issue would be resolved. Harry M. Fisher, the judge appointed to hear the case, had a son who worked as one of the Gears' attorneys, and Mikan feared how that might affect his case. Still, when the two sides assembled in court, Fisher appealed to their sense of reason. Why not put all differences aside until the end of the season? he suggested. The holdout had already cost both parties more than they could afford, so why not go about earning some money now and worry about the contract details when Chicago was turning its attention and entertainment dollars to the Cubs and White Sox?

The two sides agreed. Mikan and White dropped their lawsuits, and Mikan started working out, to get himself in shape for what promised to be an intense second half of the season.

One big question remained: could two big stars like Mikan and McDermott play together on the same court?

Mikan had been a focal point—his teams' and his opponents'—since his earliest days as a starter for DePaul. He carried his teams on the offensive end of the floor, and he was the intimidator and rebounder on the defensive end. The word was always the same: stop George Mikan and you'd probably win the game.

Now, with the addition of Bobby McDermott, the Gears had "Mr. Outside" playing with "Mr. Inside." Logic dictated a serious problem for Gears' opponents: if you stopped Mikan inside, McDermott would kill you from the outside. In this case, though, it wasn't that simple. McDermott was the *coach*, and the potential for problems was enormous, if either—or both—of the two players' egos stood in the way. Both were accustomed to being their teams' high scorers, and getting the ball when the game was on the line; both exerted great influence in the locker room. Only one was in the position of having the final say.

It was a common problem in the era of the player-coach. Team owners favored having a player-coach if a good one was available; they were filling two positions for the price of one, or close to it, and player-coaches were usually well-established veterans with long-standing credentials. Bruce Hale had been an exception with the Gears and, given the team's struggles during his brief tenure as player-coach, Hale was glad to turn the Gears over to someone else and return to his role as a player only.

Still, if you asked a player about sharing the court with his coach, he would admit that it could be difficult. If you didn't feed him the ball when he wanted it, you could wind up on the bench. McDermott had established his authority, as a player and coach, immediately upon joining the Gears, and the other Gears players had no problem with it. With Mikan back, it could be dramatically different.

"We didn't know what the story would be," admitted Dick Triptow. "Here you had Mr. Inside and Mr. Outside, and we didn't know whether McDermott would feel that he had to have all the praise and glory, and make all the baskets, or if he would condescend to Mikan. In order to win, we had to have both of them operating at full capacity."

"I think it would have been a lot smoother for all of us if we just had a coach, someone like Ray Meyer," noted reserve forward Charlie Butler. "A player-coach had a disadvantage with George."

The disadvantages weren't immediately apparent. The Gears went on a tear after Mikan returned, losing only one regular season home game the rest of the season and notching a 6–4 record on the road. At one point, the Gears won eight of ten games played in a grueling twelve-day period. McDermott took an egalitarian approach to the Gears' offense, and, to the players' delight, the scoring was spread around. Mikan still put up the most shots and scored the most points (413 points in 25 games), but McDermott, at 304 points in 27 games, was not far behind. Mikan and McDermott were named to the first team of the NBL All-League team, and Bob Calihan landed a spot on the second team. Four Gears players (Mikan, McDermott, Calihan, and Hale) averaged double-figure points per game—the first time that had happened in NBL history.

The Gears never recovered enough to win their division, but they finished with a 26–18 record, only one game behind second-place Indianapolis and two games behind first-place Oshkosh, laying the foundation for a promising playoff series. The Gears would be meeting the Indianapolis

Kautskys in the first round, and if they managed to get by them, they would, in all likelihood, go up against Oshkosh, a team they hadn't beaten all year, for the Western Division title and the right to play the Eastern Division winner for the NBL championship.

For Mikan, this meant a rough road ahead. In Arnie Risen, the Kautskys had the best young center in the league, besides Mikan; in Cowboy Edwards, the All-Stars had a cagey old veteran who might have been the only man in the league capable of manhandling Mikan in the pivot.

Mikan wasn't too concerned. He'd played against Risen in college and knew his strengths and weaknesses; the Gears had beaten the Kautskys in both of their regular-season meetings after his holdout. Edwards gave him all kinds of trouble, but their meetings tended to be highly contested rumbles, with the winner barely squeaking by. The Gears had the momentum going into the playoffs, and Mikan's legs, thanks to his long holdout, were still fresh.

He was ready to play.

Mikan needed to bring everything in his basketball arsenal for the games against Indianapolis. Even so, the Gears barely managed to survive.

The series offered everything a fan could hope for, complete with nail-biting games, unlikely heroes, non-stop action, violence under the boards, and plenty of flash. Arnie Risen displayed the scoring and team-leadership skills that would eventually place him in the Hall of Fame, playing Mikan dead-even in some games and outplaying him in others. Risen had been a terrific player at Ohio State, but in their collegiate encounters, Mikan used his height and weight advantages to beat Risen in a game played mostly under the basket. The pros were a different story. Risen used his quickness to beat Mikan at every turn.

The series was knotted at two games apiece when the two teams took the floor for the fifth and deciding game in Indianapolis. Oddly enough, the home court meant nothing in the series. The Gears had taken two straight at the Butler Field House, only to return home and lose two tough one-point games at the International Amphitheatre. Through the four games, Risen had outscored Mikan, 86–70, and battled him for every rebound coming off the rim.

Mikan carried the Gears in Game 5, outscoring Risen, 26–9, in a 76–62

Gears victory and covering for Bobby McDermott, who was ejected for throwing a couple of punches at referee Norris "Gadget" Ward. With Mc-Dermott gone, the Gears looked to Mikan for leadership, and he rewarded their faith by almost single-handedly taking control of the game. He'd beaten Risen when everything was on the line when the two had met in college; now, he'd repeated his amazing performance and the Gears were advancing to the next round.

NBL Commissioner Ward "Piggy" Lambert slapped Bobby McDermott with a two-game suspension and $100 fine for his mugging of Gadget Ward, though McDermott was permitted to sit on the bench and coach the Gears in their first two games against the Oshkosh All-Stars. The suspension was significant because, for some reason, the series was only a best-of-three affair. The Gears would have to pull off one victory without one of their leaders—not an easy task, given the fact that Oshkosh had defeated Chicago in their last seven meetings.

Despite the setback, George Mikan liked his team's chances. He'd played in only one of the Gears' regular-season encounters with the All-Stars, a 54–52 loss in Chicago, and he believed that the Gears would have won at least a couple of the games that he missed during his contract dispute. The two teams always seemed to play close games. The All-Stars had such standout players as Cowboy Edwards, Gene Englund, and Bob Carpenter on their roster, but the Gears had their own talent to match. "I just couldn't believe they were too tough for us," Mikan said later, recalling the series.

They weren't. The Gears won two straight, though Oshkosh kept both games very close. In the first meeting, in as physical a contest as Mikan had played in all year, the All-Stars employed the now-familiar "stop Mikan at any cost" strategy. They double- and triple-teamed him on defense, challenging the other Gears to pick up the scoring with McDermott out of action. The strategy was only partly successful. Mikan was held to four field goals during the game, but he contributed ten free throws and, with all the body-banging going on, he was largely responsible for Edwards, Carpenter, and Englund fouling out. The Gears won, 60–54.

The second game, played before a tense crowd in Oshkosh's Washington Park High School gym, was a seesaw contest. Mikan led all scorers with 22 points, but, for the second consecutive series, Stan Patrick provided the difference, breaking a 60–60 tie by sinking a free throw with fifteen seconds left in the game. The 61–60 victory moved the Gears to the finals against the Rochester Royals, who had posted a league-best 31–13 record during the regular season.

The Royals' assent to the top had been one of the National Basketball League's great success stories. Owner/coach Les Harrison, one of the more colorful team executives in the NBL, had been around basketball for most of his adult life, running amateur and semi-pro teams in the Rochester area and building an interest in a sport that enjoyed its greatest popularity in downstate New York City. Harrison and his brother, Jack, wanted something bigger for Rochester, and when they bought into the league before the 1945–46 season, they paid dearly for it.

"My brother and I mortgaged everything we had or could lay our hands on and we got a franchise in the National Basketball League, the only big league at the time," Harrison remembered. "I think it cost us $25,000."

Harrison knew something about assembling a successful team, but he knew a lot more about business, and he put his knowledge to great use in putting together the Rochester Royals. He'd had Al Cervi, a scrappy, street-smart New York City kid, on one of his semi-pro teams, and he felt Cervi's take-no-shit demeanor might be just the right attitude for a team about to enter the rough, broad-shouldered NBL. On the other hand, Rochester was an affluent community, and fans plopping down money for tickets were likely to be a diverse lot. Harrison reasoned that, in a business sense, it might be wise to appeal to Rochester's different ethnic and religious groups.

This belief led to hilarious (although ultimately rewarding) results when Harrison contacted Andrew "Fuzzy" Levane, a Brooklyn native who had played his college ball at St. John's.

"He thought I was Jewish," Levane laughed. "I'd played a couple of exhibition games with Rochester before the league started. I was in the service at the time, with the Ellis Island team, and I went up to Rochester on weekends. Harrison was looking for a point man, and he thought I was Jewish and would play well at Madison Square Garden."

Harrison, like others, had mistaken Levane for *Levine*, so rather than enlisting a New York Jew for his team, he'd actually signed an Italian Catholic. Harrison, however, didn't allow his mistake to cloud his vision: as a New Yorker, Levane surely knew *somebody* who was Jewish.

"He said, 'We're going to get a franchise in the National Basketball

League next year,'" Levane recalled. "'Do you know a couple of Jewish players?' Well, I had played with Red Holzman when he was with City College, and I'd played with Dutch Garfinkle, who was a year or two ahead of me at St. John's. I brought both of them up. We also got those guys who later became famous in other sports. We had Otto Graham, Chuck Connors, and Del Rice on that team. They only played a year with us, in '45–46."

Graham, of course, would go on to become one of the greatest quarterbacks in NFL history, and Rice would enjoy a lengthy career as a catcher in Major League Baseball. Connors, who tried out as first baseman with the Los Angeles Dodgers and drove his teammates crazy with his constant recitals of "Casey at the Bat" in the locker room, eventually made his name as the lead in television's *The Rifleman* series.

Levane and Seton Hall All-American Bob Davies joined the Royals after they were discharged from the service, and the Royals looked like the dynasty of the future when they won the NBL championship in the team's first year of existence.

They were even better the next year, in 1946–47. Holzman, who would coach the New York Knicks to their first NBA title in 1970, and Cervi, who would lead the Syracuse Nationals to a championship in 1955, served as unofficial coaches on the floor, stressing strong basketball fundamentals and suffocating defensive play. The Royals' teams, Levane pointed out, might not have been flashy (though Davies was the first pro player to dribble behind his back), but they weren't self-destructive either.

"We had sort of a conservative team," he said. "We didn't just run up and down the court. We seldom threw the ball away. We never tried the difficult pass. Everything was solid, but the tempo of the game was a lot slower then than it is today."

Prior to the opening of the 1946–47 season, John Mahnken, Rochester's center, had bolted the Royals for the Washington Capitols of the BAA, and Harrison had to scramble to find a replacement. The man that he found, William "Dolly" King, a two-sport star at Long Island and one of the best players on the New York Rens, not only stepped in and played strong basketball for Rochester; he also bore the brunt of being one of only two African-Americans playing in the NBL—months before Jackie Robinson became the first African-American to play Major League Baseball.

Harrison couldn't have been less interested in the issue of integration into pro basketball, or in making history. He needed good players, and he'd taken note of Dolly King and William "Pop" Gates when he'd seen them in action in the Royals' exhibition games against the Rens. At six foot four, King was four inches shorter than Mahnken, but he could handle the pivot and he was seasoned enough that he wouldn't be going through the same learning process that Harrison might have faced if he'd taken a player straight out of college. Gates was two inches shorter than King, but more aggressive.

Harrison, however, wasn't color-blind. He realized that King and Gates would face racism, in one form or another, wherever they played, and just because *he* had no problems employing African-Americans, that didn't mean that other people, including members of the Royals, would see it the same way.

"We got together with our whole team and said we need players and I've played with them before and I feel we should accept blacks and would you guys go along with it, and they said yes," Harrison told basketball journalist Ron Thomas, author of *They Cleared the Lane*, an outstanding history of integration in the NBA.

No one had to brief the Royals on George Mikan, or vice versa. By the time the two teams squared off in the finals, they'd played each other eight times during the year, the Gears holding a 3–2 advantage in regular-season games, Rochester holding a 2–1 edge in exhibition encounters. Mikan had played in six of the games. He could handle any of their big men down low, but he worried that the Royals' talented guards might have too much firepower from the outside. And God only knew what might happen if McDermott and Cervi started shoving each other around.

The series opened in Rochester. To win the championship, the Gears would have to steal a game on the road—provided they won Games 3 and 4 at home. Opposing players viewed the Edgerton Park Sports Arena as one of the toughest arenas in the NBL. The place, holding around 4,000 fans, was small and intimate, with exit doors ten feet from the end of the court. Players felt as if they were playing in a bandbox. They were constantly pelted with coins and programs tossed by angry fans, or tripped by Royals' supporters seated courtside; returning to their dressing rooms at halftime, or the end of the game, was like running the gauntlet.

Bobby Wanzer, who played his entire ten-year career in Rochester, thought the dimensions of the building itself made the court seem smaller than it was.

"It was a small building," he said, "and the seats were down close to the floor. I think it was a regulation court, but it just looked narrow because you had the people all the way down, right against the court. That made it look like a small court."

Arnie Risen, who would join the Royals after the 1946–47 season, liked the arena but could laugh about its tiny dimensions.

"On one end," he said, "there was just a row of chairs, and there was a double door with a panic bar on it. I remember one night in the dead of winter we were playing a game, and Bobby Davies went under the basket, shot a layup, hit the door, and ran right out into the snow."

The Gears opened their first game well, taking a modest lead and holding it. Mikan, aided by his height advantage over Dolly King, scored on a variety of hook shots, but the game, as predicted, was very physical and Mikan quickly found himself in foul trouble. On top of that, Bobby McDermott could find no way to defend Bobby Davies, who was hitting shots from all over the floor. Mikan and McDermott fouled out in the third quarter, along with starters Stan Patrick and Bruce Hale. With Dick Triptow the only starter on the floor at the end of the game, the Royals were able to overcome the Gears' early lead and rally to win, 71–65.

The second game looked to be more of the same, except this time the Royals came out hot. Mikan kept the game within reach by beating the Royals inside—he'd wind up with 27 points for the evening—but, as in Game 1, Bobby McDermott had no answer for Davies. By the end of the first quarter, Davies had lit up McDermott for 11 points and McDermott had four fouls as a result of his desperate attempts to guard the future Hall of Famer. Worse yet, McDermott, exhausting himself on the defensive end of the floor, couldn't hit a shot and was scoreless at the closing of the first quarter.

McDermott had to make a coaching decision. If he kept himself in the game, he would have to play off of Davies or risk fouling out by halftime. He might have switched defensive assignments with Dick Triptow, but that would have found McDermott guarding Red Holzman, with no guarantee of any better results. Or he could sit out the second quarter and hope that his replacement would contain Davies and hold him to a minimal number of points. With any luck, the Gears would be within striking distance at halftime and McDermott could contribute in the third quarter.

McDermott approached Stan Szukala, a defensive specialist and DePaul alum known more for his ball-handling than his scoring.

"Go in for me and guard Davies," he instructed Szukala.

Szukala held Davies scoreless in the second quarter and, as McDermott hoped, the Gears trailed Rochester by only three points at the intermission.

As Szukala remembered, Mikan asserted his own team leadership at halftime, when McDermott announced that he was going to start the second half.

"I walk out of the locker room and look back to see Big George talking to Mac and telling him to leave me in since I had done such a good job on Davies," Szukala said. "Mac relents and I start the second half, play the rest of the game, and Davies doesn't make another point. We win, 67–63."

McDermott eventually entered the game in the second half, but he fouled out without scoring a single point—possibly the only time in his life that such a thing had happened. Mikan and his 27 points earned the accolades in the newspaper accounts, but Mikan might have provided his biggest contribution when he talked McDermott into staying on the bench and allowing another unsung hero to help things along.

The second game had been the turning point of the series. The two teams headed to Chicago, and though the Royals would battle the Gears in Game 3, the next two games were almost anticlimactic. Mikan hit for 23 points in the third game, and Bob Calihan, who threw in 22 in Game 3, led all scorers with 22 points in the fourth and final game. The Gears won the two games, 78–70 and 79–68 respectively, and the National Basketball League had a new champion.

Or did it?

Playoffs had determined the NBL champs since 1937, but for some reason that was never explained, Piggy Lambert and league officials decided that, for the 1946–47 season, the team with the best regular-season record would be crowned the official champions. So Rochester, despite losing the regular-season head-to-head meetings with the Gears, and losing to them in the playoff finals, were declared the NBL champions.

No one believed it—not Mikan, not his teammates on the Gears, not even the Royals.

And while no one could have known it at the time, the Chicago Gears, dubbed "the dynasty that never was" by Dick Triptow, would never have another chance to play for a title.

Maurice White would see to that.

Eight

THE MINNEAPOLIS LAKERS

M AURICE WHITE SUMMONED Mikan to his office shortly after
the conclusion of the 1946–47 NBL playoffs, but rather than plead
poverty and talk pay cuts, as he'd done in their previous meeting, the
Gears owner was now patting his star center on the back and telling him
what a cash cow he was, not only for the Gears but to the entire National
Basketball League. White had been going over the league's attendance figures, which supported what anyone paying attention already knew: George
Mikan filled arenas. Attendance figures spiked wherever the Gears played,
and White, ever the businessman, wanted a bigger share of the earnings.

Mikan listened to White, but he didn't like what he was hearing.

What would happen, White wondered aloud, if the Gears defected
from the National Basketball League and became the focal point of an entirely new league with even more teams? The league, of course, would re-
volve around Mikan and the Gears.

Although flattered by White's praise, Mikan was skeptical of the idea,
and he told him as much. Pro basketball, while enjoying a slight upswing
in popularity, was still in its growing stages, establishing itself as a legitimate contender in the sports market. Mikan felt secure in the NBL, and
could see no reason to jeopardize a good basketball team by leaving the
safety of an established league for the perils of a new one.

In all likelihood, Mikan's position was bolstered by what he *didn't* discuss with White. He would be marrying Pat in a matter of weeks, and
White's plan didn't offer the kind of security usually sought by a young
married couple trying to establish a serious future together. The last thing
Mikan wanted was to go home and tell Pat that his team's volatile owner—

the one who tried to cut his salary because the Gears were going through a rough financial period—had plans to start up and own an entire league.

No one would have blamed Mikan for questioning White's thinking—or even his mental stability. The Chicago Gears' success had elevated White's sense of self-importance to such an extent that he actually campaigned to take over Piggy Lambert's job as NBL commissioner. Other team owners, most notably Les Harrison, strenuously objected to the idea. Rather than shrug off the defeat, White reacted like the sulking kid who takes the game's only ball and goes home when he doesn't get his way: he had the league's best team and its biggest single attraction, and if the NBL didn't want to play the game his way, he'd start his own league.

Nothing was decided during Mikan's meeting with White. Mikan detailed his reasons for believing a new league was a bad idea, shook hands with his boss, and left for the summer. White said he'd consider everything they discussed. They'd talk again when Mikan returned from his honeymoon.

While Mikan pondered his uncertain future in pro basketball, a group of Minnesota entrepreneurs worked overtime to assemble a team in Minneapolis. The idea had been the brainchild of a twenty-four-year-old sportswriter named Sid Hartman. In the years ahead, Hartman would become one of the most revered sports journalists in Minneapolis; but in 1947, when he was spearheading the drive to bring pro basketball to the Twin Cities, he was still supplementing his meager writing income by delivering papers.

In the late 1940s, Minnesota might have been one of the last places you'd expect to find a major franchise for any pro sport. The weather could be absolutely brutal for up to a third of the year. Minneapolis and St. Paul already had semi-pro baseball and hockey teams, and there was concern about whether a professional team could compete with the strong backing that fans gave to the University of Minnesota teams.

Hartman felt otherwise. He'd spent a lot of time hanging around the university, schmoozing with Minnesota's and visiting teams' coaches, befriending players, and building up a network of contacts that would serve him well for years to come. Hartman was an interesting study. He could be brash, irritating, overbearing, egocentric, petulant, and insensitive; he also had a work ethic that was second to none, and, when he wanted to be, he could be charming, funny, thoughtful, and gracious. And there was no debating whether he knew sports. In short, he possessed qualities useful in pitching a product—in this case, a basketball team—to investors who might be inclined to put their money elsewhere. Hartman loved sports, and, like any other die-hard sports fanatic, he wondered what it would be like to run a team.

He'd been watching interest in basketball grow since the end of the war, and if other small cities such as Sheboygan, Oshkosh, Fort Wayne, and Moline could sponsor pro basketball franchises, he could see no reason why Minneapolis couldn't get its hands on one. The Detroit Gems of the NBL had just gone under, leaving a possible opening for a new team in the season ahead.

The Gems had been a miserable excuse for a team, setting a new low-water mark in futility by finishing the 1946–47 season with a horrible 4–40 record. The team, without a permanent home arena, had roamed from court to court, playing wherever it could find an opening, never quite building a fan base at any one place. The media ignored them, and the fans paying to see them often numbered in the dozens. One game attracted a grand total of six spectators, who were all given refunds afterward. After a single season in the league, Maury Winston, the Detroit jeweler who owned the team, had seen enough. If someone was crazy enough to want his franchise, he'd be all too happy to sell it.

This was precisely the opening that Sid Hartman had been looking for. He'd been diligent in assembling his investment team and selling them on his idea. He initially approached a Minnesota businessman named Morris Chalfen, who promoted ice shows and other events around Minneapolis. Chalfen listened to Hartman's pitch, and while he was intrigued by the idea of a pro basketball franchise in the area, he wasn't entirely sold on the idea. Chalfen suggested that Hartman talk to one of his business partners, a Polish immigrant named Ben Berger. If Hartman could talk Berger into the idea, Chalfen would go along.

Berger barely knew a basketball from a hockey puck, but that didn't matter. He'd earned his wealth as an owner of movie theaters in Minnesota and North Dakota, as well as a restaurant in Minneapolis, and now, having achieved the American Dream, he was all in favor of returning some of his earnings back to the Minneapolis community.

"He was in favor of anything that would improve the city," Bob Berger, Ben's son, remembered. "He was a civic booster that invented civic boosting, if there was such a thing."

A pro team, Hartman assured Berger, would be good for the city.

Like Chalfen, Berger found the idea appealing, but before agreeing to sink a substantial amount of money into the project, Chalfen and Berger decided to test it, in the form of an exhibition game, staged in front of paying customers. If there was enough interest, Hartman could pursue a franchise.

They brought in two NBL teams from Wisconsin—the Oshkosh All-Stars and the Sheboygan Redskins—and on December 1, 1946, the two teams played a highly entertaining game at the Minneapolis Auditorium, the All-Stars winning, 56–42. More than 5,000 turned up for the contest, and that was all the convincing Chalfen and Berger needed. They gave Hartman the green light to look for a franchise.

The Gems disbanded shortly after the game in Minneapolis, and the Gems' players were assigned to other NBL teams. Hartman, in negotiating for the franchise, was essentially working out a deal for a piece of paper. There were no players or coaches to bring to Minneapolis; they couldn't even use the uniforms. Hartman offered Maury Winston $15,000 for the franchise, and Winston quickly accepted. He'd lost more than that sum during his team's disastrous season, but the fifteen grand represented ten times the amount he'd originally paid to enter the league a year earlier. There was no ceremony in closing the deal. Hartman and Winston met in the Detroit airport on July 6, 1947, they signed the paperwork, and Hartman turned over the check.

"I think that was absolutely the right thing at the right time," Ben Berger said, looking back on the deal, "though Sid went over and bought a Detroit team that had gone bankrupt in the National League, and paid fifteen thousand dollars for nothing. He could have gotten it for free. Well, you don't know things."

Minneapolis had a team, even if that team had no name, no general manager, no coach, no players, no uniforms, and very little equipment other than a bunch of old basketballs.

And the opening of the 1947–48 season was only a few months away.

*   *   *

Throughout his pro career, George Mikan preferred to keep his off-season calendar as simple as possible: very few thoughts about basketball; many, many rounds of golf. Mikan loved golf almost as much as he loved basketball, and his idea of a good day was eighteen holes at one country club in the morning, eighteen more at another club in the afternoon. He'd find a way to work in lunch.

In the summer of 1947, however, he was busy basking in his role of newlywed. He and Pat had married in May, shortly after the conclusion of the Gears' season, and they'd honeymooned for a month in Florida, Cuba, and Nassau. While they were gone, Maurice White formally announced his new pro basketball league. Mikan, still skeptical about the league's prospects, tried to put it out of his mind.

Although he had no way of knowing it, his future was being decided about five hundred miles north of Chicago, in a small office in Minnesota.

The Minneapolis brass wasted no time in putting their team together. Morris Chalfen and Ben Berger wanted Sid Hartman to quit his sportswriting job at the *Minneapolis Tribune* and work exclusively for the team. After all, even though it wasn't technically prohibited, there was something not quite kosher about a sportswriter's running a team he might be asked to cover for his paper.

Hartman disagreed. To the young reporter, his work with the basketball team would merely be a way of supplementing his income. There was nothing more to it than that.

"In those days, every newspaperman had an outside job," he pointed out later. "They were publicity men for the wrestling promoter, the boxing promoter, or the local hockey and baseball teams. I worked closely with the Lakers, and in those days no one batted an eye."

Hartman talked to his bosses and made arrangements to work for the basketball team while continuing on at the *Tribune*, but all parties agreed that once the team was put together, Hartman would work behind the scenes and a general manager would handle the team's day-to-day business operations.

It didn't take long to find a general manager. Chalfen and Berger knew a Minneapolis restaurateur and sports promoter named Max Winter, who ran a place on Hennepin Avenue called the 620 Club, "Where Turkey is King," according to its slogan. Winter, as it turned out, provided the perfect balance to the team's front office. His temperament was more even-keeled than that of the occasionally abrasive and hyperbolic Hartman. Where Hartman knew his basketball from a sports perspective, Winter knew how to push it as a business. Winter could be a hard-nosed negotiator, as players would learn, and he was a master of the small promotional touch. His team would have cheerleaders recruited from local high schools, as well as a small orchestra that entertained fans before games and during halftimes. In one of his more creative moves, Winter provided a service to jump-start cars that refused to start in Minneapolis's bone-chilling weather.

He was also smart enough to stand back and let Hartman piece together the team.

Hartman wanted to stay local when hiring a coach, but his first choice, Joe Hutton, wanted no part in the job. Hutton had built a national reputation as the coach of Hamline University, a small liberal arts college in St. Paul. Hamline had won a National Association of Intercollegiate Basketball title in 1942, and would go on to win two others within the next few years. Hutton preferred the security and status of his present job to the uncertainty of coaching a pro team. Besides, he had two sons whom he hoped to coach in the near future.

Hartman's second choice, John Kundla, was also well-known in the area. As a collegiate athlete, Kundla had been a two-sport star at the University of Minnesota, lettering in basketball and baseball. He'd been part of the Gopher basketball team that tied Illinois for the Big Ten title in 1937, and he was good enough at baseball to play a season of Class C ball. As a coach, he'd won grade-school championships and state high school championships before moving on to coach at St. Thomas College, a small Catholic university in St. Paul.

Kundla, like Hutton before him, turned down Hartman's coaching offer. At thirty-one, Kundla had his life going in the direction he wanted it to go. He was married, raising two young sons, living in a nice, if modest, apartment on the northeast side of Minneapolis, coaching at a good school, and still had time to play on one of the city's better softball teams. There were no guarantees that this new, still-unnamed franchise, with no players on the roster and inexperienced people running the show, would last for any considerable length of time, and with the kind of money that Hartman was offering, Kundla wasn't even tempted to take a risk.

Hartman's persistence eventually paid off. He visited John and Marie Kundla on several occasions, and haunted the softball diamond where

Kundla played ball, jabbering with Kundla from behind the backstop. When trying to recruit Joe Hutton, Chalfen and Berger had offered the Hamline coach a guaranteed contract: they would deposit his total three-year salary into a bank account, assuring Hutton a decent amount of money even if the new franchise went under. Hartman now offered a similar proposal to Kundla. After conferring with his wife, Kundla finally relented. He signed his contract on July 15, 1947.

A long future might not have been guaranteed, but at least he knew he would be paid well for the next three years of his life.

"I got six thousand dollars in the first three years," Kundla remembered, laughing at how small that figure would become in the not-so-distant future. "That was twice as much as I was making at St. Thomas."

Not surprisingly, given his knowledge of the game, Sid Hartman had all kinds of ideas about the kind of players he wanted for his team. Pro teams made a point of keeping several local players on their rosters, and Hartman compiled a short list of University of Minnesota alumni whom he hoped to recruit for the team. Better yet, he knew of an incredibly gifted player, a young forward named Jim Pollard, who played AAU ball on the West Coast and might be persuaded to join a pro league. Finally, Hartman had heard rumors that Maurice White had stretched his finances very thin when he founded his Professional Basketball League of America. If, as some predicted, the league folded and a draft was held to disperse the league's players, Minneapolis, by virtue of its connection to the lowly Detroit franchise, would have a shot at signing that big Mikan kid from the Chicago Gears. With Mikan, the Minneapolis team could become the hottest attraction in basketball.

Signing Pollard became Hartman's number one priority. Few, if any, players in the country possessed Pollard's overall basketball skills. He was explosively quick, with leaping abilities that had earned him the nickname "the Kangaroo Kid." He could dunk the ball (although it was considered hot-dogging in those days), hit soft jump shots near the basket, or bomb away from the outside. To top it off, he was an exceptional passer and ball-handler.

"He could make you look silly," said Ephraim "Red" Rocha, who squared off against Pollard on any number of occasions during Rocha's playing days with the St. Louis Bombers and Syracuse Nationals. "As far as I'm concerned, he was the best all-around basketball player, from a standpoint of pure technical basketball, that I saw during the period that I played. He was as quick as any guard in the league. At the end of the game, they'd give the ball to Pollard, and he would dribble the ball and nobody could faze him. And rebounding—he could do all of it."

"He was the first guy who played above the rim," recalled Fuzzy Levane, who, like many of the early NBA pioneers, played in the National Basketball League and the Basketball Association of America. "Whoever heard of dunking in our time? I'm following him in there, thinking he's going to miss a layup, and—BOOM!—there he goes. Believe me, he was the first guy who dunked."

John Kundla coached Pollard throughout Pollard's career, and he, too, praised his athleticism.

"Jim was the most graceful player I had," he said. "If there was a full-court press, I'd have them give the ball to Jim, because Jim could get by anybody. He had speed and he could jump. In his first game of pro ball, he came out with a bloody elbow and I said, 'What happened?' He said he'd hit it on the backboard. Jeez. When I was in college, I couldn't even touch the net."

If anything, Pollard was so far ahead of the game that he could grow bored with it. He was known to loaf in practice, and, during games, he might eschew an easy layup in favor of a more difficult jump shot, just to challenge himself. He was famous for playing like a demon at home but only marginally on the road. When television networks started broadcasting games, Pollard would save his flashiest moves for the cameras. His self-assurance was occasionally mistaken for arrogance.

"You never knew what Pollard's outlook would be from one night to the next," Sid Hartman recalled in his autobiography. "When he wanted to play there was nobody who could contain him. He could play terrific defense, although many nights he would not bother to do it."

Pollard had played center at Oakland Tech High School, but he switched to forward the summer after he graduated, when he played with a local AAU team. He enrolled at Stanford, and quickly established his reputation as one of the best when he led the team that won the 1942 NCAA championship in his freshman year. World War II ended Pollard's career at Stanford, but not his further development as a player. He played for the Coast Guard in California's service leagues. After completing his service, he returned to the AAU, playing for the Oakland Bittners.

Interest in Pollard reached a very high level among owners in both the NBL and BAA. This was the kind of player who could jack up fan interest in any basketball team, if not an entire league, and Pollard found himself fielding offers from teams in both pro leagues. He declined the overtures, saying that he preferred to stay put in California and play in the AAU.

Oddly enough, when he heard from Hartman, Pollard was more receptive to joining—and starring for—the new franchise in Minneapolis.

"I liked Sid," he told sportswriter Roland Lazenby. "I had another team [Rochester] that actually offered me more money."

Money wasn't the only issue for Pollard. He'd been following pro basketball, and he'd seen how some of the game's biggest stars had become synonymous with their teams. He enjoyed such stature with the Bittners, but moving on to the pros would be taking it to a higher level. He would be the big name in Minneapolis, the star of a rising new team.

Pollard pushed Hartman into bringing along three of his Bittners teammates—Paul Napolitano, Jack Rocker, and Bill Durkee—to Minneapolis, and Hartman, needing players anyway, agreed. On August 27, 1947, Jim Pollard officially signed with Minneapolis for a then-whopping $10,000 salary, along with a $3,000 signing bonus.

Hartman was elated. As far as he was concerned, Minneapolis had the cornerstone to its franchise.

While officials in Minneapolis pieced together their team, Maurice White, working out of Chicago, tried to launch an entire league. As George Mikan had feared, White was in way over his head.

The Professional Basketball League of America (PBLA) had to be one of the worst good ideas in sports history. In time, Maurice White's idea of expanding pro basketball's geography to include cities as far south as Atlanta, Houston, and New Orleans, and as far west as Omaha and Kansas City, would seem almost visionary, a bold step forward from the largely regional pockets that hosted teams from the NBL and BAA. Unfortunately, the logistics of running such a league were a nightmare. It would have been tough enough for a large, experienced, well-organized staff to handle the scheduling, travel arrangements, promotions, payroll, and other day-to-day operations. In the hands of White and his small crew in Chicago, the league was headed for disaster before the opening tip of its very first game.

That game, featuring the Atlanta Crackers against the Oklahoma Drillers on October 24, signaled some of the problems ahead. The game itself was a thriller, with Atlanta prevailing, 44–43, but the attendance was disappointing, as it would be throughout the PBLA's short life. Part of the problem could be attributed to lack of publicity. Pro basketball had to fight for every column inch it could get in the sports pages, and the PBLA was no exception. It didn't help that the league's promotional efforts were spotty, at best.

George Mikan and the Chicago American Gears opened their PBLA season on October 31 in St. Paul, beating the Saints, 55–49. After spending a summer relishing their NBL championship, the Gears looked forward to establishing their domination in the new league. Three of the team's strongest contributors from the previous season were gone to other PBLA franchises—Bruce Hale to the Saints, Price Brookfield to the Waterloo Pro Hawks, and Stan Szukala to the Grand Rapids Rangers—but with Mikan, Bobby McDermott, Stan Patrick, and Dick Triptow returning, the Gears were definitely the odds-on favorites to take another title.

The opening of the Gears' schedule was trying, with Chicago playing seven of its first eight games, including its first four, on the road, all within a span of twelve days. Mikan wasn't worried. With no one in the pivot to give him much of a game, he manhandled the opposition, averaging 24.1 points per game through the Gears' first eight games. McDermott, similarly, enjoyed a strong opening to the season, averaging 17.5. The Gears won each of their first eight games, all but two by double-digit margins. They were on their way.

Then, without warning, it all came to an end. The Gears had no sooner arrived at the train station in Chicago, ready to play their second home game of the season, when McDermott was handed a message saying that the league had folded and everybody was out of a job. Maurice White, who had absorbed great financial loss in the PBLA's two weeks of existence, suffered a nervous breakdown and was hospitalized.

Players and coaches, though not surprised by the failure of the league—attendance at many games could be measured in the hundreds—were caught in a mad scramble to determine what had happened and what might happen next. The news had hit them very suddenly and without warning. Players not only had no immediate future; they wondered if they were going to get paid for the games they'd played. Coaches holding train and plane tickets were told to return them to the league offices immediately; some returned the tickets, while others cashed them in and used the money to pay players. Many players would eventually wind up suing to recover their back pay.

Charlie Butler, a former teammate of Mikan's on the Chicago Gears, had almost signed on as player-coach of the Waterloo franchise, but his wife had talked him out of it. Still, he was kind in his assessment of White when remembering the PBLA.

"He had the right idea," he said of White, "and with enough owners with money, he could have done it. But it was too big and too soon, and instead of growing, he jumped. But he sure flattered me with that kind of offer."

Mikan knew he'd have no trouble catching on with another team. He'd heard from several teams immediately after word of the PBLA's demise was out. Still, in the days following the announcement, there was some question about who, if anyone, owned the players' contracts. Rumors circulated that a proposed new version of the Gears, under completely different ownership and management, might be admitted back into the NBL, but the other teams would have to vote on it. (Not surprisingly, Max Winter and Minneapolis strenuously objected to the arrangement.) There was also talk about disbanding the teams and assigning their players to other NBL franchises. Adding to the confusion was the announcement, made by the PBLA's legal advisor, that all players were now free agents.

Mikan balked at being any other team's property. He reasoned that he was under contract to Maurice White and the Chicago American Gears, and if that business, like any other business, failed, he should be free to pursue his next job. He would have a say about where he played or he'd remain in Chicago and finish off his law degree at DePaul.

Offers poured in. The Rochester Royals and Fort Wayne Zollner Pistons were immensely interested in securing Mikan's services, but Mikan wasn't so sure. Rochester had one of the best teams in the league, but Pat Mikan didn't want to move that far away from her midwestern roots. As an only child, she wanted to remain geographically close to her parents, in-laws, and friends, and she liked the Chicago area. George also preferred to stay near the Windy City.

The NBL eventually decided to break up the PBLA teams and assign the players to already-existing NBL teams via a special draft. The new Minnesota franchise would get first pick.

No one questioned which player they'd select.

Mikan didn't care much for the idea of relocating to Minneapolis. Max Winter had called him shortly after drafting him, and Mikan decided that if he was going to play for the team, he was going to earn at least as much as he'd been paid by the Gears. This was a brand-new team located out in the sticks, and Mikan had bad memories of playing in Minnesota back in his college days, when DePaul lost to the University of Minnesota on New Year's Eve 1945. The temperatures had been so cold that Mikan would never forget it. "It reminded me of Siberia," he said.

At least the new team now had a name: the Lakers. Max Winter had wanted to call the team the Minnesota Vikings*, and he had even gone so far as to order stationery with Vikings letterhead, but in the end, the fans had the final say. Jack Horner, host of a sports show on KSTP radio, set up a name-the-team contest with the Minnesota front office, with the winner to receive either season tickets to the team's inaugural season or a $100 savings bond. Suggestions poured in, including such unlikely names as the Aquacagers and Millcitians, but Ben Frank, owner of a consumer finance company, suggested the winner. "Lakers" was perfect shorthand for the people who lived in the state known as "The Land of 10,000 Lakes," and also for the long, sturdy ore boats, known as lakers, that transported iron ore, limestone, and other cargo from Minnesota to ports around the Great Lakes. The winning entry was announced in the *Minneapolis Times* on October 2, 1947, less than a month from the Lakers' first game. Frank took the money over the seats.

The Lakers' colors—light blue and gold—also originated from the community. These were the colors of Sweden's flag, and Max Winter reasoned that, with the large Swedish population living in the Twin Cities area, it might be wise to cater to them as potential customers.

George Mikan had just opened his season with the Chicago Gears when

---

*Ironically, Winter would later become instrumental in helping Minneapolis secure an NFL franchise, and would become president of the NFL's Minnesota Vikings.

the Lakers traveled to Oshkosh and met the All-Stars for their first official league game. John Kundla started Jim Pollard at center, and Cowboy Edwards, the All-Stars' powerful center, made a painful point of showing Pollard the ways of the NBL. West Coast flash wasn't tolerated in the pivot, especially when it came from a thin, undersized center. Pollard, by his own account, whizzed by Edwards for an easy early score; the next time down, when Pollard tried the same move, Edwards stuck out his arm and clotheslined Pollard, sending him sprawling. "That's when I knew I wasn't a center," Pollard admitted, years later.

The Lakers won their first game, 49–47. The team wasn't the powerhouse it would become in just a few weeks but, thanks to Sid Hartman's job of rounding out the roster, the Lakers had enough talent to compete in the league. The Lakers had spent $25,000—$10,000 more than Chalfen and Berger had paid for the franchise—for the rights to Don "Swede" Carlson and Tony Jaros, both University of Minnesota alumni who had played for the Chicago Stags the year before. At an even six feet, Carlson was undersized for the forward position, but he was a strong defensive player and had been the Stags' Most Valuable Player the previous season. Jaros, a six-three swingman capable of playing any position but center, was a three-sport athlete who played semi-pro baseball during basketball's off-season. In addition to Carlson and Jaros, the Lakers had mined the University of Minnesota for two other players: Don Smith and Kenny Exel. Neither scored much, and Exel would last only a handful of games before leaving the team, but having local talent on the roster translated into urgently needed ticket sales.

And the biggest draw in basketball was on the way.

John Kundla would never forget the call from Max Winter, telling him the Lakers had signed George Mikan. He didn't believe what he was hearing.

"My God," he gasped. "I've already got Pollard. Now I've got Mikan."

Getting George Mikan had taken some work—and a dash of trickery. A couple of days after being drafted by the Lakers, Mikan and his lawyer, Stacy Osgood, flew up to Minneapolis to meet with Max Winter and Sid Hartman. The group talked for several hours but the Lakers and Mikan were unable to reach an agreement. Mikan, still prepared to walk away from basketball and pursue a career in law, asked Hartman to drive him back to the airport.

If he gets on that plane, Winter thought, there's no way he'll sign with us. It'll be with another team or nothing.

Hartman, as it turned out, was having the same thought. There had to be a way to prevent Mikan from returning to Chicago before signing a contract.

The Lakers' general manager quickly concocted a plan, and he communicated it to Hartman in an unusual way.

"Winter suggested, in Hebrew so the others couldn't understand, that we get lost," Hartman recalled. "And we did. I drove Mikan around for more than an hour, until I knew the last flight had left Minneapolis."

Later in his life, Mikan could laugh at the memory.

"They were supposed to be taking me back to the airport," he said. "Well, lo and behold, we start driving around for two hours, like they didn't know where the airport was. They finally found it, and by then they wore me down."

"The route to the airport," Hartman quipped, "took us to Anoka, New Brighton, and other suburbs, and when we got to the airport, the plane had left. The next day Mikan signed."

In retrospect, it's difficult to precisely measure which side got the better of the other. Hartman might have thought he was pulling off a sleight of hand by driving Mikan and Osgood all over the Twin Cities area, pretending he'd lost his way. Mikan, on the other hand, was practicing a negotiating ploy that he'd use throughout his career. Aware of his value to his team and the league, Mikan would threaten to walk away from the game whenever contract negotiations got sticky.

Both sides ultimately won. Mikan stayed overnight and, the following morning, he signed his big, fat contract—at an average of $15,000 a year, including his signing bonus. The fledgling franchise from Minnesota now employed the highest-profile player in the game.

What no one anticipated was the friction that developed almost immediately between George Mikan and Jim Pollard. When Mikan walked into the locker room and introduced himself to his new teammates, he was wearing his trademark homburg hat and long winter coat. Pollard, the transplanted Californian, couldn't believe his eyes.

"I thought that was the biggest-looking dumb character that I'd ever seen for a guy that was barely twenty-three years old," Pollard recalled. "He had these great big thick glasses, and he had this homburg hat on. I said to myself, 'What the hell's a guy twenty-three years old doing wearing a homburg and a great big storm overcoat?' "

First impressions aside, Pollard had heard about Mikan's on-court abilities, and the two players greeted each other warmly.

When Mikan joined the Lakers for their fifth game of the season, the Lakers didn't even have a uniform prepared for his first game with the team. Rather than hand him a uniform with his familiar number "99" on the front and back of the jersey, the clubhouse attendant simply gave him the biggest jersey he could dig up. So Mikan wore "21" for his first game as a Laker. Even more interesting, the Lakers didn't have a pair of shorts that fit Mikan, forcing him to improvise by wearing his old Chicago Gears shorts. No one seemed to notice.*

Thinking that he had to justify his big salary by carrying the Lakers the way he had carried the Gears and, before that, the DePaul Blue Demons, Mikan called for the ball almost every time the Lakers brought it down the floor. His teammates were all too happy to send it in to him. Mikan led his team in scoring with 16 points, but he took a beating in the process. The Lakers, accustomed to be playing a fast-paced style with Pollard in the middle, couldn't immediately adapt to Mikan in the pivot, and the Lakers wound up being drubbed by Sheboygan, 56–41.

Over the next few games, Mikan and Pollard weren't compatible on the basketball floor. Mikan liked to stake out his space in the pivot, and he didn't want teammates passing through and getting in his way. It cramped his style. Pollard, on the other hand, zipped all over the front court, including the pivot. When he saw Pollard driving to the basket, Mikan moved toward the basket with him, looking to pick up a rebound if Pollard missed his shot or layup. Unfortunately, Mikan's defender would move with him, and Pollard wound up taking a pounding in the congestion under the basket.

It didn't help, either, that Mikan was so damn big. He moved well for

---

*Ironically, the most famous picture that would ever be taken of Mikan would come from that first game. In the photo, Mikan is seen dribbling the ball, his face a mask of intensity and determination, the Gears' shorts and number "21" clearly visible to all sports trivia buffs of the future.

someone his size, but Pollard could fly, and since Mikan was the center of the Lakers' offense, there were too many occasions when Pollard and the others had to wait for Mikan to make it down the court and into position before they could begin to work their offense. Mikan was a terrific offensive player, but playing alongside him could be maddening.

In their early games, Mikan and Pollard played awkwardly together, each getting in each other's way, each diminishing the other's game. The Lakers lost four of their first five games with Mikan. John Kundla, still new to pro coaching, was at a loss as to what to do.

Veteran guard Herm Schaefer, whom the Lakers had picked up from Indianapolis three games into the season, had seen enough, and he confronted Mikan in the locker room after a home loss to Fort Wayne on January 2, 1948.

"Mikan," he started, "you're a fool."

Mikan tried to wave him off, but Schaefer wouldn't let him past him.

"Look, George," he went on, "this is the greatest thing that's ever happened to you, and you're not taking advantage of it. This Jim Pollard is a great basketball player. He can do anything with the ball, including pass it to you. But you've got to pass it to him, too."

The problem, Schaefer insisted, was Mikan's belief that he could win the games all by himself. That wasn't the way it worked in this league. Players were faster and better than the opponents he'd gone up against when he was playing with the Gears. Mikan and Pollard had to learn to work together, if Minneapolis was to have any hope of competing.

Schaefer's words stung, but Mikan knew he was right. He and Pollard had been the stars of their respective teams prior to joining the Lakers; both felt the urge to lead. Instead of helping win games, they were battling each other.

Mikan pulled Pollard aside in the locker room the next night, and the two discussed the best way to work together. They devised a two-man game that would be beneficial to both. Pollard would pass the ball in to Mikan, and if he felt he had a clean path to the basket, he would give George a hand signal and Mikan would pass it back and move to the basket for a rebound. If Mikan had an opening for a layup or his hook shot, he'd take it.

John Kundla was working on his own series of plays for Mikan and Pollard. The most successful play, simply called the "J&G" (for "Jim and George"), was essentially an early version of what would eventually be called the pick and roll. "George would set the pick and Pollard would drive across," Kundla explained. "Then they'd switch and George would get the basket."

Kundla would forge his Hall of Fame career as a coach not so much from his ability at the chalkboard as from his instincts as a kind of amateur psychologist. His teams, he would always concede, were stacked with great players who really didn't need a lot of coaching; his job was to keep all that talent working together—not an easy job when you had George Mikan on your team.

"If George didn't get the ball, he couldn't score," Kundla pointed out, stating both the obvious and one of his biggest challenges as a coach. "All I could think was, we got George Mikan, Mr. Basketball. But we lost four out of the first five games with him because we were awed by his reputation. We threw him the ball every time we got the ball, and the other team sagged on him. So we got a system: Don't bring your man to George. Isolate him so he could work one on one. We had a lot of inside weaves and so forth because, with George, we had to keep the defense honest. It worked out well."

The Lakers streaked through January, finishing the month with a 10–4 record, with Mikan and Pollard leading the way. On January 18, in a road game against the Rochester Royals, Mikan played the entire game and set a new single-game NBL scoring record, torching the Royals for 41 points. The Lakers needed every point. Mikan's final basket, coming with three seconds on the clock, broke a 73–73 tie and gave the Lakers the win.

Mikan loved the fact that he'd set the record against Rochester. The Royals, the Eastern Division leaders, were becoming the Lakers' biggest rival, and Al Cervi, the team's star guard and leader, could drive Mikan to distraction. ("I'd still rather beat [Al Cervi] than eat," he'd say later, when talking about a playoff series against the Royals.) If that wasn't incentive enough, Les Harrison, the Royals' owner and coach, had been a mortal enemy of Maurice White, and rumor had it that Harrison was the driving force behind the NBL's refusal to allow the Gears back into the league after the failure of the PBLA.

Four nights after setting the single-game scoring mark, Mikan struck again, besting Cervi's single-season scoring record, set during the 1946–47 season. With nearly half a season ahead, Mikan's point total was bound to add up to an astonishing final tally. Who, after all, was going to stop him?

The Lakers concluded their first year by winning 27 of their final 33 games, good for a 43–17 overall record and first place in the NBL's Western Division. Mikan finished with a 21.3 points-per-game scoring average, topping the NBL's previous 20.2 high-water mark and earning him the league's Most Valuable Player award. His 1,195 points shattered the 632 points that Al Cervi had scored when he set the most points per season mark the previous season. Mikan and Pollard were included on the All-NBL first team.

Still, there were no guarantees for the playoffs ahead. The Rochester Royals wound up with a 44–16 regular season record, one game better than the Lakers. The Royals would have the home court advantage throughout the playoffs. Nobody relished the thought of playing in the rowdy Edgerton Park Sports Arena. But that would be the finals—if both teams survived the preliminary rounds.

The Lakers needn't have worried. Entering the playoffs, they were the hottest team in basketball, and they continued their roll in the first round of the playoffs, beating the Oshkosh All-Stars three out of four games in the first round and then sweeping the Tri-Cities Blackhawks in the semifinals. The Royals, likewise, won their two preliminary rounds, and the confrontation between the Lakers and Royals was set.

By now, Mikan had adapted to the breakneck pace of professional basketball. The pro season, as today, was really two separate seasons—the regular season and a postseason—and by the time a champion had been crowned, after adding up the preseason, regular season, exhibition, and postseason games, the winning team had probably notched over 100 games in one year.

The Lakers took a "break" from their NBL playoff run on April 8–11, when they traveled to Chicago for the World Professional Basketball Tournament. The tournament, in its tenth (and final) year, offered the usual assortment of first-rate teams, including such familiar NBL foes as the Fort Wayne Zollner Pistons, Anderson Duffy Packers, Tri-Cities Blackhawks, and Indianapolis Kautskys. For this year's tournament, the number of invited teams had been pared down from sixteen to eight.

Mikan showed no sign of fatigue. His previous experience in the tournament, when the Gears had walked away with only a third-place finish two years earlier, provided him with all the incentive he needed, and he put on a show for his old home town. The Lakers opened with a 98–48 blowout win in their opener against the Wilkes-Barre Barons, a Pennsylvania team that had won the Eastern League championship. The semifinal round matched the Lakers against the Packers, who had posted a 42–18 record while finishing in second place, two games behind the Rochester Royals, in the NBL's Eastern Division. The Lakers struggled in this one, but ultimately came out ahead, 59–56.

Appropriately enough, the Lakers' opponent in the finals was the New York Renaissance, winner of the very first World Tournament back in 1939. The great barnstorming team had missed the tournament only one year (1943) during its ten-year run, and they were definitely crowd favorites in Chicago. The Rens' superb starting lineup included forwards George Crowe and Duke Cumberland, guards Sonny Woods and Pop Gates, and center Sweetwater Clifton, who would eventually be one of the first African-American players in the NBA. Clifton was huge and mobile, and he promised a rough night ahead for George Mikan.

The game went right down to the wire. The Lakers, behind Mikan and Pollard, took a commanding lead early in the game, but the Rens, behind balanced scoring from Clifton, Gates, Cumberland, and Crowe, fought back until they had pulled even in the fourth quarter. The Rens had gone up by a point in the closing minute and a half of the game, and seemed to control its outcome, when a turnover decided the final outcome.

"The Lakers came down with the ball, and Sonny Woods stole it," George Crowe remembered. "He gave the ball to Sweetwater Clifton at mid-court. We had a three-on-one break. Sonny went down the left side, and Duke Cumberland went down the right side. Sweetwater passed the ball behind him with his left hand, and threw it straight out of bounds, right at the scorer's table."

The Lakers scored off the turnover and tacked on an additional two points to close out the scoring, walking away with a 75–71 win. The Mikan–Clifton matchup turned out to be a dogfight, Mikan scoring 40 points to Clifton's

24. Mikan won the tournament's Most Valuable Player award, becoming the only player to win the award more than once during World Tournament history, but he had little time to savor the accomplishment.

The Lakers had another tournament to finish.

A day later, the Lakers were back in Minnesota, preparing for the NBL finals against the Rochester Royals.

The Royals posed major matchup problems for the Lakers. The team boasted five future Naismith Memorial Basketball Hall of Famers (guard/forward Bob Davies, guards Al Cervi, Red Holzman, and Bobby Wanzer, and center Arnie Risen), and they played an "East Coast" style of offense focusing on fast-paced, guard-oriented play. The quick, athletic Rochester guards, easily the best group of guards on any team in the league, had a lethal outside game, and if they were hitting their outside shots, they were almost unbeatable.

The "West Coast" style of offense, such as the one employed by John Kundla and the Lakers, also depended upon scoring from outside shots, but they preferred an offense that ran through Mikan, with the guards cutting to the basket for easy layups, or short jump shots from Pollard and the other forwards.

"In essence, we were two-handed set shooters," Wanzer said of the Royals' style of play. "The West shot one-handed, and some of them had a jump shot. The outside shooting was the difference."

Arnie Risen also noted the difference in styles, although he also included the West Coast AAU teams when he listed the differences.

"You had a diversification across the country—three different regions with three different types of influence on the game. The Far West had one-handed shooters and jump shooters. The Midwest had the runners and the big guys. And then you had the East, with the set shots and ballhandlers."

The Royals' outside shooting would be all-important in the series against the Lakers because Risen, who had broken his jaw in an earlier playoff round, was unavailable for the finals. The loss of Risen was enormous: not only did he contribute significantly to the offense, averaging 13.2 points per game over the regular season; he was also one of the few big men capable of playing Mikan to a standstill. Les Harrison had picked up Risen from Indianapolis in the middle of the season for the express purpose of stopping the

Lakers' center. Without Risen, the Royals had no answer for Mikan in the pivot.

Risen wasn't the only key player with injury problems. Al Cervi, nursing a nasty leg infection, would only be available on a limited basis. "The Digger," as he was called, was by far the Royals' best defensive player, and his team seemed to feed off his mental and physical toughness. His points, like Risen's, would be tough to replace.

Mikan capitalized on the Royals' vulnerability, scoring at will against his overmatched defenders, including his old Gears teammate George Ratkovicz, forced into the role of starter by Risen's absence. In the first game, played in the Minneapolis Armory, the Royals grabbed an early five-point lead and used balanced scoring to keep the game close throughout the first half, but Mikan, who wound up with 26 points, took over after the intermission and the Lakers won, 80–72. The second game was no contest. Mikan put in 25 points and the Lakers won easily, 87–67.

As strong as the Lakers' inside play was—Jim Pollard scored 24 points and Tony Jaros contributed 14 in the first two games—the real story involved the Lakers' guards. Herm Schaefer picked up 38 points in the first two games, and the Minneapolis guards played their more talented Royals counterparts to a draw. Suddenly, what sportswriters projected to be a close, hard-fought series was now looking like a Laker sweep. All they had to do was win their next game in Rochester.

It didn't happen. With Arnie Risen, Al Cervi, and Fuzzy Levane in street clothes on the bench, the depleted Royals came out firing, building a 15-point lead in the first half and holding on, winning the third game of the series, 74–60, despite Mikan's 32 points. Pollard, guarded closely by reserve Bill Calhoun, played a miserable game, scoring only three points. According to one newspaper account, "Pollard sulked most of the night, not getting too excited about the battle at any time."

Fair or not, it was an interesting observation. Pollard might have simply had a bad night, as all players do, or Calhoun, known for his defense, might have deserved more credit for the way he guarded Pollard. However, other players, Lakers and their opponents alike, noticed that Pollard had a way of shutting his performances off and on, depending upon his mood or, some said, whether his wife was in attendance. Arilee Pollard, as knowledgeable a fan as you would meet anywhere, could be very critical of her husband, George Mikan, or the Lakers, and she could be very vocal during the Laker home games. Some of the players joked that Pollard played better at home just to keep his wife off his back, and one Laker quipped that he went so far as to humorously suggest that the Lakers employ Arilee Pollard in an effort to make Jim's game more consistent.

"He was as good a small forward as there was," said Vern Mikkelsen, who would become a teammate of Pollard's and Mikan's the following year, "but he always played better at home, here in Minnesota, than he did on the road. We finally figured out the reason: Arilee was here, hollering at him if he wasn't doing what he was supposed to do. I told Max Winter, 'It'd be worth it to fly Arilee on the road with us, so Jim would play well both on the road and at home.' Of course, they all thought that was pretty funny."

"We always looked to Pollard to make the difference," noted Howie Schultz, who, like Mikkelsen, joined the Lakers the following season and, during his two-year stay with the team, observed Pollard's tendency to play whenever he felt motivated. "We knew what Mikan could do, and when Pollard wanted to play, he was tough. When he didn't have the urge to play, he was just very ordinary. There was no halfway with Mikan."

Mikan, well aware of Pollard's prodigious talents, had no tolerance for any player's sloughing off, and over the years he and Pollard exchanged angry words about it. Fortunately for the Lakers, the two players usually worked out their differences privately and quietly. Each respected the other's abilities, even if they were never going to be close friends. Both realized that the Lakers depended upon them for any success the team would ever enjoy, and in a championship series, the Lakers couldn't afford many down days from either player.

Pollard made amends for his poor game by scoring 19 points in the series's fourth and deciding game. Whatever hopes the Royals might have harbored of evening up the series were completely demolished early in the contest. The Lakers, perhaps embarrassed by their sloppy showing in the previous contest, controlled the game from the beginning, building huge leads before eventually leveling off and winning, 75–65. Mikan, the MVP of the playoffs, took special pleasure in beating the Royals, and he would bristle whenever someone suggested that the series might have been another story if Arnie Risen had played in it. This year, there would be no controversy over who reigned as the league's champion.

Mikan liked to view the Lakers' championship as a matter of a team's going from worst to first in one year, although there was no connection whatsoever between the old Detroit Gems franchise and the new Minneapolis franchise that replaced it, other than a deed of sale. The Lakers had been built from scratch.

The reality, though, was just as impressive and, to the other teams in pro basketball, more than slightly foreboding: the Lakers, with two of the best basketball players in the universe and a great supporting cast, looked to be the team of the future. A year earlier, Mikan had proven that he was the difference between an average team and a championship team; he'd done it again in his first year with the Lakers.

Fuzzy Levane had seen the damage that Mikan could do, during the regular season and in the championship series, and he was blunt in assessing Mikan's impact on the meetings between the Lakers and Royals.

"If it wasn't for Mikan, we would have won two or three [titles] in a row," he said. "We won our division but lost to them in the finals. He was the guy who broke our backs."

Nine

LAKERS VS. GLOBETROTTERS

February 19, 1948

It wasn't supposed to have been this difficult, but here it is, the clock winding down, less than a minute to go, and the game tied, 59–59.

George Mikan leads all scorers with 24 points, but as the seconds tick off the game clock, and 17,823 paying customers scream their approval, it's becoming clear that his efforts might not be enough. The Lakers are in danger of losing one of the most heralded exhibition games in basketball history.

The Lakers' opponent: the Harlem Globetrotters.

The Trotters rightfully boast of being the most entertaining team in basketball, combining comic antics with skills that would make them stars on any pro team in the business—if, in fact, they were allowed in the pros.

But, to this point, pro ball is strictly whites-only. Sure, there have been a few weak attempts to integrate professional basketball in the recent past, and there are no written rules prohibiting African-Americans from playing in either the NBL or BAA; but an unspoken agreement among the team owners, a kind of collusion by silence and inactivity, has kept some of the best players in the game in an "outside, looking in" position.

This is all fine and dandy, as far as Abe Saperstein, founder of the Globetrotters, is concerned. The short, stocky Chicago businessman is a savvy operator— "He was the only guy I ever met who could count the house in 32 seconds," one player would note—and he's got a good thing going in not having to compete with pro teams for black talent. There are other all-black teams, most notably the New York Rens and Washington Bears, and they've produced some outstanding teams, but Saperstein's barnstorming group is by far the most popular.

A game against the Minneapolis Lakers makes perfect sense, in terms of competition and marketing. The Lakers are the world champs. The Globetrotters are boasting a 100-something-game winning streak (the number varies, depending upon whom you're talking to, though the most commonly listed figure is 103), even if a fair number of those games have been staged against lower-caliber teams or designated patsies. A game between the two teams will decide the ultimate champ.

It will also translate into incredible gate receipts. Saperstein had correctly anticipated overwhelming ticket demand for a contest pitting George Mikan, the most popular player in pro basketball, against Goose Tatum, the Clown Prince of the most popular act in the game. Fans had braved the bitter cold and lined up at the ticket windows, some as early as 3 A.M. the morning of the game, for seating to this game, and by the time Mikan and Tatum jumped off the floor for the game's opening tip, the SRO crowd at Chicago Stadium represented the largest assembly to ever witness a pro game at the venerable court.

"It was electric, as charged an atmosphere as I've ever been in," Mikan would say fifty-five years later, when the game was still being discussed, not only as a great basketball game between two talented teams, but as a breakthrough in the slow process of integration in the NBA.

The game is a no-win situation for the Lakers. Outscore the Trotters and everybody yawns, So what? Lose the game and the press will turn it into the biggest upset story since David and Goliath. Max Winter and Abe Saperstein are old buddies, and they've got a nice little side-bet riding on the outcome, but other than putting a little extra change in Winter's pocket and a whole lot more in the Lakers' bank account, there's not much to be gained by a Laker win.

Mikan and his teammates approach the game with mixed feelings. They're happy to compete in such a festive environment, but they're less than thrilled to be doing so for nothing. Promoting the game is part of the standard agreement between the players and their teams, and this is considered promotion, regardless of gate receipts. The Laker players will appear in dozens of exhibitions over the course of any given year, though none with this kind of fanfare.

It's an entirely different story for the Trotters. A victory would be sweeter than Georgia Brown, but it would mean much more than that. As a business, the Globetrotters have advanced well beyond the lean early years, when dinner often consisted of hamburgers or hot dogs eaten on the fly; a win here promises a financial bonanza in the future. But that's not the real issue. Good as they are, the Trotters have always been in the position of being able to cook for the whites but not eat in their dining rooms. There were even days, down in the South, when they'd play two separate games on the same day—one for white audiences, one for blacks. The whites will occupy the good seats in Chicago Stadium, but there will be plenty of African-Americans in the cheap seats, and it's high time to give them something to cheer about, believe in, and, God forbid, hope for. It's time to shut down the "you boys are good, all things considerin'" idea.

The game turns into a classic battle between two very good teams, though it didn't start out that way. The bookies had established the Lakers as eight-point favorites, and for a while it looked as if they were just being charitable in predicting a game so close. The Lakers jumped off to a 9–2 start, and with Mikan and Pollard leading the way, they held a 32–23 halftime lead. The anticipated showdown between Mikan and Tatum—"the toughest test of Mikan's brilliant career," according to a Chicago Sun-Times *sportswriter—had been totally one-sided, with Mikan outscoring Tatum 18–0 by the break. The Trotters had tried everything they could dream up to stop Mikan, but the sagging team defense and double-teams hadn't worked.*

They developed a new plan of attack during the intermission: foul Mikan whenever he got the ball, before *he had the chance to shoot. Mikan would receive only one free throw per foul. The Trotters have players to spare. Unlike the Lakers, they weren't bound to carry a designated number of players on their team, and before this contest, they'd picked up several additional players for the game, each worth five fouls.*

The strategy works beautifully. The Trotters whack away at Mikan every time he touches the ball, and when they hit him, they hit him hard.

"We said, 'If they're gonna call a foul, be sure to make him bleed.' And that's what we did," Vertes Ziegler, one of the players coming off the Globetrotters' bench, would remember. "We went to beating on him and slapping them glasses off."

The Trotters chip away at the Lakers' lead, outscoring Minneapolis, 10–2, at the start of the third quarter, to make it a two-point game. The game will be close the rest of the way. The hacking has taken Mikan out of his game. He's angry at the players whaling on him, at the officials for letting it happen, and at himself for his failures at the line. Normally a reliable foul shooter, Mikan misses free throw after free throw, making only four out of eleven attempts for the game, giving the Trotters the chance to slip back into contention. His frustration finally gets the better of him, and he throws an elbow at Tatum, leading to a technical foul. Now determined to take on the entire Globetrotters team if need be, he ratchets up the intensity of his play, hitting on some shots, missing on more, and, in general, playing outside his usual game.

It's the Bob Kurland–Oklahoma A&M situation all over again.

In time, Mikan will look back on the game and regret some of his actions.

"I tried to beat the Trotters all by myself, completely forgetting that I was but one cog in a great basketball machine," he'd admit. "I was ashamed of myself."

The game gets rougher. Players dive on the floor for loose balls; you can hear the grunts from combatants fighting for each rebound. This might be a mere exhibition game, but it might as well be the seventh game of the finals. The Trotters are playing for keeps. Outside of a little razzle-dazzle early in the pregame warmups, they've played it straight up. They want to win. Maybe, for the sake of the world's taking notice of the great skills of African-American players, they need to win.

How else could you explain Marques Haynes, the Globetrotters' dribbling wizard? Late in the third quarter, he and Mikan go up for a rebound, both grabbing the ball and wrestling for its possession. Haynes's hand slips away, and in the sudden release of tension, he falls backward, flat on his back. He's slow to get up, but he stays in the game. Then, unbelievably, it happens again. Both Mikan and Haynes hit the floor, both shaken from the fall. The full house in Chicago Stadium goes silent, watching the two men fight their way back to their feet. The two stay in the game, although the next day Haynes, still in terrible pain, will visit a Chicago hospital and learn that he has a fractured fourth lumbar vertebra. For the time being, however, there's a game to finish.

So it's all come down to this, the Trotters holding the ball with less than a minute to go. Everybody in the place knows they're going to take the last shot—either win outright or go into overtime—but the final play is anybody's guess. The Lakers scramble on defense, cautious not to foul but determined to contest any shot. Mikan, who scored his 24th and final point of the evening from the free-throw line, tying the game with just over a minute left, clogs the middle and waits. Tatum has already fouled out of the game, so the odds are about even that Haynes will take the final shot, bad back be damned.

Haynes has the ball, but it's going to take a miracle for him to drive the lane. Mikan and Pollard are both stationed there, blocking his path to the basket, *both ready to try to reject an outside shot, should Haynes decide to take it. Haynes scans the forecourt for an open man, but before he's able to make a move, Herm Schaefer rushes up from behind and pokes the ball out of bounds.*

Ten seconds left. No one in the stadium is seated. Haynes inbounds the ball and it's immediately passed back to him. He dribbles away from the basket, up toward the top of the key, each step increasing the degree of difficulty of the shot he might take. With three seconds left, he makes eye contact with Ermer Robinson, quite possibly the best outside shooter on the Trotters team, who's streaking across the court toward him. Haynes hits him with a pass and tries to set up a pick on Jim Pollard, who's frantically rushing over to try to block Robinson's shot.

With time expiring, Robinson releases a one-handed set shot that rainbows at such a high arc that it seems as if it'll go up forever. Everyone on the court freezes and watches the ball head up and, just as the final gun sounds, descend through the hoop, giving the Globetrotters a 61–59 win.

In the bedlam that follows, the fans go absolutely crazy. Robinson is hoisted onto the shoulders of his teammates while Kundla pleads with the officials, arguing that time had expired prior to the shot; the Lakers file dejectedly off the court.

Marques Haynes would always remember the game as one of the most important that he ever participated in, though he'd be characteristically modest in his assessment of the way it turned out. ("It just happened that we got the ball last," he'd say.) Still, it underscored the talents of his team. "The Globetrotters were known for comedy stunts and tricks," he'd admit, "but our team was, foremost, a team. We could play against anybody, from any league."

Later, Mikan visits the Trotters' locker room and offers his congratulations; but, good sportsmanship aside, he's emotionally drained from what's transpired. The Lakers weren't supposed to lose to these guys. They were the better team, even if the final score denied it, and now he'll have to listen to Abe Saperstein going on and on ad nauseam about the Globetrotters being the champs. The Lakers could win another league championship, but this game is going to hang over their heads until the Lakers and Trotters square off again. Max Winter is already hollering for a rematch and, given the money and publicity generated by this one, Saperstein will be happy to meet again.

Sometime next year.

But in the meantime . . .

*   *   *

It could easily be argued that, had it not been for the Harlem Globetrotters, there would be no NBA today. When the NBL and BAA were trying to find ways to bring fans to arenas, the Trotters would blow into town and play an exhibition game as part of a package deal with the pros. There was never a question about the main attraction.

"Abe Saperstein kept a lot of franchises alive," noted Fuzzy Levane, who witnessed the early struggles of the pro leagues. "The Globetrotters kept Milwaukee alive, they kept Philadelphia alive, and so on. We'd play home games on another court, as part of a double-header, and we were guaranteed more money than we'd get in Milwaukee, where you drew four hundred people."

Bobby Harrison, who played a handful of games against the Globetrotters when he was with the Lakers, agreed.

"They would come in and play the feature game," he said of the double-headers. "The preliminary game would be the NBA game. They shared the receipts with the NBA team, so they did a lot to help the NBA survive."

You couldn't help but wonder about the bitter irony of an all-black team saving the hide of an all-white league—a league that, more out of deference to Saperstein than bigotry, wouldn't let blacks play on its teams, and which, in the future, would deny Abe Saperstein a franchise.

Saperstein knew something about bigotry and segregation. The son of Polish immigrants, he had grown up in Chicago, and he'd taken an interest in sports because, as an athlete and member of a team, he was less likely to hear the anti-Semitic remarks that his other Jewish friends had to endure. In 1926, he put together the Savoy Big Five, a basketball team named after Chicago's Savoy Ballroom, a popular dance hall on the city's south side. Within a year, the ballroom appearances had fallen through and a new team, the New York Globetrotters, was formed—the "New York" included because Saperstein wanted basketball fans to believe that his team was a barnstorming unit in the tradition of the New York Renaissance. The Globetrotters, wearing red, white, and blue uniforms designed by Saperstein's tailor father, played their first game on January 7, 1927, in Hinckley, Illinois, earning a whopping $75 for their appearance. The team would change its name to "Saperstein's New York Globetrotters" before settling on the "Harlem Globetrotters," the "Harlem" an emphatic nod to the fact that the team comprised all-black players.

At first, the Globetrotters barely survived. The Depression robbed the entertainment and sports industries of a lot of potential customers, and, in the Globetrotters' case, those white basketball fans who did have the money for admission weren't necessarily enamored with the thought of watching a group of African-American players defeat all-white teams. And, when the Globetrotters played, there was little question about which team was going to win: in the first year of their existence, the Globetrotters, playing serious basketball, posted a 101–6 record.

The team's trademark showmanship—the fancy dribbling and passing routines, the seemingly impossible shots—actually sprang from its domination of most games. Hometown fans didn't turn out to see their teams whipped in boring, one-sided affairs, so, to give the fans a little more for their money, the Trotters learned to mix entertainment along with their basketball. The comedy came later, supposedly by accident. As the popular story goes, the Globetrotters were playing in Willamsburg, Iowa, on a cold winter night, in a hall heated by pot-bellied stoves located at either end of the court. At one point in the game, Willis "Kid" Oliver, one of the original Globetrotters, backed into one of the stoves, setting his basketball shorts on fire. Fans, thinking it was part of the routine, roared with laughter while Oliver ran around, screaming and desperately trying to put out the fire. Saperstein took notice. If fans wanted comedy as part of the show, he'd see that they got it.

Mostly, though, it was great basketball. The Globetrotters customarily tallied huge winning streaks, and the combination of great sport and entertainment turned the Trotters into a snowballing success. Saperstein would be severely criticized in some quarters for amassing a fortune with a team that, some said, was essentially a traveling minstrel show playing into racial stereotypes. Sadly, some of the criticism was well-aimed, in the respect that the players *were* subjected to the worst of American bigotry, and the on-court antics reinforced the existing racist notion that African-Americans were okay as long as they entertained whites, made them laugh, stayed away from their women, and kept their hands off their wallets. That Saperstein was Jewish only added to some of the backstabbing.

But it was hard to argue with success. Once the Globetrotters were established and enjoyed immense popularity, the players were viewed, even if begrudgingly, as some of the best in the sport. The players, particularly the stars, were given good salaries, although their seasons, unlike the pro seasons, ran year round and the travel was hard.

In 1939, as they neared their 2,000th game as a team, the Globetrotters played in the first World Professional Basketball Tournament in Chicago, which boasted of a $1,000 prize to the winner. The Trotters lost a heart-breaker, 27–23, to the New York Rens in the final, but the next year, after posting a 159–8 "regular season" record, the Globetrotters avenged their ear-lier defeat with a 37–36 win over the Rens in the semifinals. They won the tournament by besting George Halas's Chicago Bruins, 31–29, in the finals.

The championship proved, to anyone still foolish enough to doubt it, that the Harlem Globetrotters ranked among the elite in all of organized basketball. They would take on all comers, good or bad, but there was never a question about whether they played to win. (Saperstein, in fact, ordered his team to refrain from the clowning until a game was well in hand.) Saper-stein's eventual hook-up with professional basketball was just an extension of the Globetrotters' increasing popularity and Saperstein's keen eye for promoting the team. The double-headers benefited the Globetrotters and the struggling pro teams, although it didn't take long for those marketing the games to realize one important truth: the Trotters were more popular than the pro teams. In the early days, the Globetrotters' exhibition games were held prior to the scheduled pro game, but to the dismay of the pro team owners, fans had a habit of leaving after the first game.

The order of the games was swiftly reversed.

On February 28, 1949, the Lakers met the Globetrotters for their highly anticipated rematch. Mikan had been waiting for this game for more than a year, and he and his teammates believed that they were to going to exact more than a small measure of revenge over the team that had beaten them with a last-second shot the year before. The fact that a crew from Mov-ietone News was on hand to film the game made the prospects all the more delicious: the newsreel of the game's highlights, to be played in movie the-aters from coast to coast, would show, once and for all, which was the bet-ter team. It didn't matter to the Lakers that two of their starters, Jim Pollard and Swede Carlson, were nursing injuries and wouldn't be playing; the Lakers had more than ample firepower to beat the Trotters.

Or so they thought.

Abe Saperstein had spent a year basking in his team's previous victory over the Lakers, and the Trotters had gone on winning and winning. Determined to keep the streak alive, Saperstein had once again loaded his roster with extra players for the Laker game. Most significantly, he'd picked up Sweetwater Clifton from the New York Rens and was grooming him to be the eventual replacement for the aging Goose Tatum. Clifton, who earned his nickname from the soda pop he liked to drink, wanted another shot at Mikan after the beating he'd taken from him in the previous year's World Tournament.

Saperstein's practice of beefing up his regular roster irritated John Kundla and the Laker players. The ringers, they felt, gave the Trotters an unfair advantage.

"I don't know how many teams Abe had," Arnie Ferrin remembered, "but he brought all of his good players for the team in Chicago. When we got there, we looked out and he had about fifteen or sixteen players on the bench. The league required that we could only have ten."

As before, the press built up the game as a contest for the ages. These were two heavyweights, about to slug it out again after an earlier knock-down, drag-out title bout. The racial implications, though never explored in newsprint for all the obvious reasons, were clear: here was an all-black, street-ballin' team going up against an all-white, highly disciplined professional outfit. The Globetrotters' clowning around was all fine and good from an entertainment standpoint—if nothing else, it made the black players more acceptable to white audiences—but it wasn't highly competitive basketball. The Lakers would set that straight.

And, at the beginning of the game, it looked as if the Lakers were going to do just that. With 20,583 in attendance looking on—a larger crowd than the first game, and the second-largest ever gathered to witness a basketball game of any kind, college or pro, in Chicago Stadium history—the Lakers built an early 8–1 lead before settling in for the long haul. The Trotters had started Goose Tatum at center and Sweetwater Clifton at forward, but after Mikan beat Tatum for two early baskets, the two Globetrotters switched positions. Each team enjoyed brief offensive runs, but the Lakers led, 24–18, at the half.

The Trotters plotted strategy. They had tried the foul-Mikan strategy during the first half, but it hadn't succeeded, mainly because, unlike the first game, Mikan was hitting his free throws and the Trotters were missing a good percentage of their own shots from the field. The other Lakers weren't scoring much, but it ultimately wouldn't matter, as long as Mikan continued to carry the team.

Ironically, it was the Lakers, not any special strategy on the Globetrotters' part, who let the Trotters back in the game. The answer arrived almost accidentally. John Kundla's defense, a source of Laker pride, broke down in the third period. The Globetrotters put together 12–0 and 6–0 runs, many of the points coming from easy fast-break layups. Mikan tried to keep up with the frenzied Trotters' running game, but he was out of gas by the end of the third quarter, which found the Globetrotters comfortably ahead, 41–32. The first game had been decided by a last-gasp heave; this one was turning into a blowout.

Mikan and his teammates had no answer for the Globetrotters. They struggled to climb back into the game, but the Trotters played them even-up, matching them point for point. By midway in the fourth quarter, the Trotters led by a dozen.

In the first game, the Trotters had kept their clowning to a minimum. Now, with the game all but decided and the Movietone cameras capturing their antics for posterity, they turned on the theatrics, delighting the crowd with their familiar routines. Marques Haynes went into his dribbling routine, falling to the court and dribbling inches from the floor, dribbling while he crawled on all fours, jumping and teasing any unfortunate Laker coming out to guard him. Goose Tatum pulled his hidden-ball trick on Mikan, faking a shot and then sticking the ball underneath his jersey and walking away as if he no longer had possession of it. No longer interested in scoring, the Globetrotters toyed with the Lakers, playing keep-away with them and letting them score whenever they managed to wrestle the ball away. The final score—Globetrotters 49, Lakers 45—offered no indication of just how one-sided the second half had been. The Lakers scored the game's final nine points, but they'd been badly beaten long before the sound of the final gun.

John Kundla, for one, wasn't going to stand for it. The game had been played on Abe Saperstein's home turf in Chicago, using officials that Saperstein hired for the occasion. Another game had been scheduled to be played in Minnesota, but before that would happen, Saperstein would have to agree to play under BAA rules, using at least one BAA official.

Kundla took a purist's approach to the games, even if they were exhibition games. He admired the Globetrotters' skills—"Marques Haynes could have played in the pros," he allowed—but he argued that the Trotters' brand of basketball wasn't really basketball at all.

He was still fuming about it years later. A friend, he recalled, had taken a trip to the Soviet Union, and had asked him for some films of the Lakers to take along with him to show the Russians. "He took them over," Kundla said, "and when he came back, he said the Russians were shocked. The Globetrotters had been there, and the Russians thought that's the way the game should be played. They looked at our pictures and it was a different game."

Marques Haynes wasn't buying any of the complaints, especially those criticizing the Globetrotters' brand of basketball. Winning the second game, he suggested, was perhaps even more significant than winning the first.

"After the first game, most people thought it was just luck," he explained. "The second game made people believe we were not only good comedians but good ballplayers."

Mikan tried to put the game out of his mind. The Lakers and Globetrotters would be meeting again, and while he hated losing as much as anyone who ever played the game, he wasn't a poor loser.

"I'll give the Trotters credit," he wrote in his autobiography. "They knew what to do. They controlled the ball from start to finish and beat us."

Fortunately for Mikan, he wouldn't have long to stew about the humiliation. The next game, played only two weeks later, on March 14, found the Lakers in top form. Pollard was back, and Mikan met with him for a pregame pep talk. The Minneapolis Auditorium was packed with 10,122 fans, and they were going to see the Lakers win if Mikan had any say in it. Saperstein had agreed to play under pro rules, using one BAA official, so the Lakers would have no legitimate beef if they lost—and they didn't.

This time, a one-sided game favored the Lakers. Mikan, held to just four field goals while scoring 19 points in the contest two weeks earlier, exploded for 13 field goals and a total of 32 points, outscoring Goose Tatum and Marques Haynes combined. Jim Pollard and Swede Carlson, back from the ankle injuries that held them out of the previous game, added 17 points between them—more than enough to compensate for the point difference in the final score. The Lakers even added a comic routine of their own, an answer to the humiliation they'd suffered at the hands of Marques Haynes: with time running down, Donnie Forman entertained the Minneapolis crowd with a dribbling exhibition of his own.

The Lakers won running away, 68–53. They would meet the Globetrotters on four other occasions during Mikan's career, but they would never lose to them again.

Ten

BIRTH OF THE NBA

MAURICE PODOLOFF WALKED up the slightly curving sidewalk leading to a modest frame house at 2920 Alexander Street in Fort Wayne, Indiana, hoping that the forthcoming meeting would boost the fortunes of the embattled Basketball Association of America. The BAA teams had been hemorrhaging cash, losing roughly a half million dollars the preceding season, and the short, stout BAA commissioner knew that the league, even with its big cities and arenas, was on the road to failure unless he found some way to reverse the losses.

The BAA and NBL had been squabbling from the day the BAA announced its formation. The NBL had been operating smoothly enough until the BAA came along, mainly by serving small- to medium-sized cities with rabid fans thrilled to support the only major sport in town. The BAA could brag about having teams in New York City, Boston, Washington, D.C., Chicago, Philadelphia, and even as far north as Toronto; in Madison Square Garden and Boston Garden, the league also had the two most prestigious arenas in the business. Prior to the formation of the BAA, the National Basketball League had its pick of the best players available. The BAA had changed all that. Suddenly, there was a bidding war for players' services and, ultimately, the fans' dollars. The two leagues had tried to reach a compromise involving a joint draft, but so far nothing had come of it.

This was brought into sharp focus when Adolph (Dolph) Schayes, a gifted six-eight forward from New York University, graduated and entertained offers from the New York Knicks in the BAA and the Syracuse Nationals in the NBL. As basketball historian Leonard Koppett reported in his book *24 Seconds to Shoot*, the demand for Schayes was "barely noticed at the time, and certainly not fully grasped" in terms of its eventual impact on the two leagues. The Knicks wanted Schayes for his local appeal. Schayes, who would develop into one of the greatest players in pro basketball history, demanded more money than the Knicks, under BAA salary cap restrictions, could pay him. As a result, Schayes signed with the Nats (who had no such restrictions in the NBL) and became the cornerstone of the franchise.

Unfortunately for Maurice Podoloff and BAA team owners, the NBL still had the biggest turnstile attractions, most notably the big center in Minneapolis, who drew huge gates wherever he went. If there was no way to entice George Mikan and other notables to the BAA without a lot of legal wrangling along the way, maybe there was a way to get select teams to defect to the new league.

Which was the reason for Podoloff's flying out to Fort Wayne. The Fort Wayne Zollner Pistons, owned by automotive manufacturing magnate Fred Zollner, was possibly the smoothest running operation in all of pro basketball. The Pistons had been one of the NBL powerhouses during World War II, when Zollner's factory was churning out pistons for the war effort and, while doing so, employing some of the best basketball talent available. Zollner could be a little eccentric, but he was, above all, a huge sports fan and an astute businessman. He also wielded great influence on NBL operations.

Podoloff hoped the Pistons might defect to the BAA. He had called Carl Bennett, the Pistons' business manager, to see if he could arrange a face-to-face meeting with Zollner. The meeting, of course, would have to be absolutely confidential: there was no telling what kind of legal eruption might occur if word got out that the BAA was trying to drum up a way to raid the NBL for some of its teams.

Zollner was lukewarm to the idea. He was busy running his plant, and he wasn't predisposed to getting involved in a league as unstable as the BAA appeared to be—unless the conditions were right. He liked the idea of having his name associated with such owners and high-visibility franchises as Ned Irish (New York Knickerbockers), Walter Brown (Boston Celtics), and Eddie Gottlieb (Philadelphia Warriors). Zollner instructed Bennett to meet with Podoloff. "See what he wants," he told Bennett.

Bennett and Podoloff met at Bennett's Fort Wayne residence and, for several hours, Podoloff outlined his idea of arranging for several teams from the NBL to "merge" with the BAA. Podoloff doubted that a handful of teams (the Toronto Huskies, Pittsburgh Ironmen, Detroit Falcons, and Cleveland Rebels) were going to survive, and he proposed that three or four NBL teams join the BAA. He was especially interested in persuading Fort Wayne, Indianapolis, and Minneapolis to enter the league; Rochester, Oshkosh, and Toledo were also possibilities. Marquee players, obviously a major factor in selecting teams for the BAA, were not the *only* consideration. Podoloff wanted teams that were financially stable, franchises that could endure the costs and rigors of extensive travel, promotion, and day-to-day operations of a long season. In short, the teams had to have wealthy ownership, or at least the potential to earn big money.

"You can have the greatest ideas you want to have," Bennett explained, recalling his meeting with Podoloff, "but if you don't have the capital to back it up, your ideas aren't much good. Oshkosh and Sheboygan were solid teams, but they were small cities, and the difference between Fort Wayne and those two—or any of the others—was Fred Zollner. As a franchise, Fort Wayne was solid as a rock."

Bennett liked what he was hearing from Podoloff, and he knew that Zollner would relish the thought of seeing his team's name on the marquee of Madison Square Garden. Bennett called Zollner and suggested that he get together with Podoloff. Zollner agreed. The two men met and reached an agreement: the Fort Wayne Pistons were in. They'd become part of the BAA.

Podoloff took his case to two other midwestern teams. The Indianapolis Kautskys signed on, as well, but it took some convincing to bring the Minneapolis Lakers on board. Max Winter was content to stay in the NBL, where the Lakers were clearly the team of the future. The Lakers were still new to the business, and, by Winter's thinking, there was no need to invite trouble, especially legal skirmishes, if you were already thriving in your present league.

Ironically, the Rochester Royals, the Lakers' old rival, proved to be the wild card in the negotiations. Podoloff felt Rochester might be too small a market for the BAA, which already had a New York team in the Knicks. Les Harrison wanted in—badly. With Arnie Risen, Red Holzman, and Bob Davies on their roster, the Royals were loaded with the kind of talent that would bring people to Madison Square Garden, Boston Garden, or anywhere else. Harrison tried every method of persuasion he could think of, including the threat of a lawsuit, before Podoloff finally relented.

With other teams already defecting, the Lakers finally decided to switch leagues, and, on May 10, 1948, the BAA held a press conference at the Morrison Hotel in Chicago to announce its new realignment. The remaining NBL teams, finding their league suddenly gutted of its main drawing cards, screamed bloody murder, hired attorneys, and filed lawsuits.

Podoloff never tried to pass off all the maneuvering as anything other than a matter of survival. By his estimation, the BAA would not have survived more than another season or two without the new teams—and their star players—joining the league.

"I had started this move in desperation," he admitted. "That wasn't a merger, it was a raid."

The 1948–49 season was still nearly half a year away, but the real games had already begun.

The BAA, George Mikan discovered, was different from the NBL. The games, for one, had twelve-minute quarters, as opposed to the ten-minute quarters he'd been playing in the NBL. Since he rarely sat down for any extended period of time, at least in close games, Mikan now had to pace himself differently or risk running out of energy when the outcome of a game was still in doubt. The travel in the BAA was different as well. With the exception of Rochester, the NBL teams had been stationed around the Midwest, making travel relatively easy. In the BAA, Minneapolis and St. Louis were the westernmost teams in a league in which half of the teams were on or near the East Coast. Travel would be much more strenuous. For Mikan, this spelled more time away from an expanding family; on April 8, 1948, Pat had given birth to George Lawrence Mikan III, who would be called Larry.

Mikan found that he had serious competition for the scoring title— something he'd never dealt with at DePaul, or with the Gears or in his first year with the Lakers. Two players—Joe Fulks with the Philadelphia Warriors and Max Zaslofsky of the Chicago Stags—were averaging over 20 points per game, and they were doing so in a manner that was reshaping the game itself.

The Warriors had won the BAA championship in the league's 1946–47 inaugural season, largely due to the efforts of "Jumpin' " Joe Fulks, who led the league in scoring with a 23.2 points per game average—nearly seven points per game higher than the runner-up. He'd taken second place, behind Zaslofsky, the following season, but had still managed a 22.1 average.* The Kentucky native, who'd been stationed on Guam and Iwo Jima during World War II, had torn up the military leagues, and, after he'd returned to the States, he found his services in high demand. Some coaches felt that, at six-five and less than two hundred pounds, Fulks might be too frail for the rough, broad-shouldered pro basketball leagues, but he'd already proven his ability to put the ball through the hoop, despite any perceived downside.

"Fulks is slow and he's not a great defensive player," declared Honey Russell, coach of the Boston Celtics and a future Hall of Famer. "How can he be a great team player when he takes so many shots? But I wish I had him. I'd sure build my team around him."

Which is precisely what Philadelphia did. When Fulks came around, the Warriors, like the other teams in the BAA, were still trying to find a way to make pro basketball a profitable business. Chicago had Mikan, and he filled the seats with his high-scoring performances, and Eddie Gottlieb, owner of the Warriors, figured a high scorer like Fulks would do the same for his club. Fulks could score from nearly anywhere on the court, and his arsenal included an assortment of two-handed set shots and left- and right-handed hook shots. He could blow by his defenders for layups or he could stop suddenly and unload a bomb with startling accuracy.

But it was his jump shot that earned him his nickname and electrified crowds packing arenas to see him. Over the years, other players had used a jump shot, but it had never caught on in pro basketball. Fulks, who played his college ball at Murray State, changed that. The jump shot became his primary weapon, affording him the opportunity to elevate his six-five frame and shoot over taller defensive players. Not only was it effective; it was fun to watch.

As for the accusations that he was a ball-hog, Fulks had a simple answer: "To win, you've got to have points, so I fire away at every opportunity."

---

*Fulks actually averaged more points per game (22.1–21.0) than Zaslofsky during the regular season, but Zaslofsky played more games due to a Fulks injury, and scored more points (1007–949). Thus, the BAA awarded the scoring title to Zaslofsky.

Max Zaslofsky, more of a traditional two-handed set shooter, was another superb scorer. A Brooklyn native, Zaslofsky had learned his basketball on the playgrounds of New York, and after spending two years in the navy during the war, he enrolled at St. John's. The Redmen posted a 17–5 record the year Zaslofsky played on the varsity, but it would be the only year he played college ball. He joined the BAA in 1946 and, in his first year in the league, he led the Chicago Stags to the BAA finals, but the Stags lost to Joe Fulks's Philadelphia Warriors.

Like Fulks, Zaslofsky had the reputation of never seeing a shot that he didn't like, and teammates were accustomed to never seeing the ball again, once it had fallen into Zaslofsky's hands.

"Max would honestly tell you that if he had the ball on a fast break, don't expect a pass," said Carl Braun, who played with Zaslofsky on the Knicks. "At least he was honest. It didn't make it right or smart, but I respected the honesty."

Fulks and Zaslofsky were voted to the first team of the All-BAA team for the 1946–47 season, and they would be first-teamers for the next two years. If Mikan and his high scoring had carried the NBL during lean times, Zaslofsky and Fulks did the same for the BAA. Now, with the Lakers part of the BAA, the scoring race was on.

Mikan was at a slight disadvantage in the battle for the scoring title, though his coach and teammates in Minnesota would have disagreed that it was any kind of a hardship: Fulks and Zaslofsky didn't have a player of Jim Pollard's caliber on their team. On any given night, Pollard could carry the brunt of the Lakers' scoring. Philadelphia and Chicago had other fine players on their rosters, and both teams would be in the playoffs at season's end, but Pollard's contributions spelled the difference between championship and also-ran status. Pollard's presence on the court made Mikan a better, more well-rounded player.

And Mikan seemed to be getting better every week he was in the league.

Joe Lapchick, coach of the New York Knickerbockers, who had seen Mikan in action in the NIT finals when Lapchick was coaching St. John's against DePaul, marveled at Mikan's depth of talent, even though Mikan drove him to the borders of his sanity whenever the Lakers played the Knicks.

"Big George reminds me of Babe Ruth," he said. "Everyone forgets that Ruth was once an exceptional pitcher and that he was a fine outfielder.

Everyone also forgets that Mikan was the best feeder out of the pivot that the game ever had. Cover him normally and he'd murder you with his scoring. Cover him abnormally and he'd kill you with his passes. Why, if he'd been playing when I was with the Celtics, he'd have scored a million points. I take that back. Make it two million."

The Lakers opened their 1948–49 season with an 84–72 win over the Baltimore Bullets, who had posted the BAA's highest winning percentage the previous year, but they struggled to find their rhythm over the next six games, going 2–4 and looking like anything but champions. Two Eastern teams appeared to be the teams to beat. The Rochester Royals adapted well to their switch of leagues, and the Washington Capitols, coached by Red Auerbach and brimming with talent, set the pace by winning their first thirteen games.

There was also another Mikan in the league. Eddie had graduated from DePaul and signed with the Chicago Stags, meaning there would be inevitable confrontations between the Mikan boys. After George's graduation, Eddie had taken over as the Blue Demons' center, and the team had continued to prosper, coming within two points of capturing the NIT title in 1947–48. Eddie's problems, then and always, were the comparisons to George. He wasn't as tall as George, his hands weren't as good, and his hook shot wasn't as explosive. Eddie would enjoy a six-year career in pro basketball, but he was doomed to always having to measure up to someone who was not only a better player than he was, but who was better than *anyone* playing the position.

It didn't help that George was so competitive. George had pounded lumps into Eddie when the two were playing together on DePaul, and it would continue on the professional level. George was intensely loyal to his family—he had tried, with only marginal success, to get his brother, Joe, on the Gears' roster, and he would try to talk Minneapolis management into finding a spot on the Lakers' roster for Eddie—but whenever the action began, either in practice or a game, George blocked out all thoughts of blood relations. His brother was now his foe, an opponent trying to beat him, challenge his authority in the pivot, and, in the process, take food off his table. That wasn't going to happen.

"He looked after Ed and tried to get him on the team," Bud Grant, a future Mikan teammate, observed, "but then he'd get him on the floor and he'd beat him up in practice. Ed couldn't make the team because George would beat him up."

Slater Martin, another future Laker teammate, liked to tell a story about a conversation between George and his mother after a particularly brutal game, in which George had bloodied Eddie, and beaten him in scoring and rebounding.

"Georgie, how come you hit your brother Eddie?" Minnie Mikan wanted to know.

"Momma," George replied, "we were playing a game. If you had been in there, I'd have hit you, too."

The first Mikan-brothers battle in the pros occurred on November 19, 1948, when the Lakers met the Stags in Chicago Stadium. Sportswriters built up the game the way they'd hyped the Mikan–Kurland clashes in college.

These kinds of remarks, though interesting from a human-interest standpoint and effective in publicizing the game, rang hollow to anyone following the arc of the Mikans' careers. The Mikan brothers joked about taking it easy on each other, but, from the opening tip to the final second of any game they played against each other, George proved his superiority. In their initial meeting on a professional court, George not only outscored Eddie: he shut him out, 20–0, and the Lakers got by the previously un-beaten Stags, 85–81.

The Mikans faced each other again a couple of weeks later, when the Lakers played in the annual College All-Star Classic staged by the *Chicago Herald-American*. The All-Stars had defeated the pros the previous year, and John Kundla had the Lakers prepared for what amounted to very little contest. The Lakers led, 33–13, at halftime before coasting to a 60–42 final.

George outscored Eddie, 18–1, in the game, though the two Mikans were on the floor together for only a couple of minutes. Besides Eddie Mikan, the All-Stars had Dolph Schayes and Alex Hannum as centers, and the two future NBA stars played most of the game. George fouled out shortly after Eddie entered the game, which, given the way things were go-ing, might have been a blessing. The last thing Eddie needed was to have injury added to insult.

One of the few bright spots in the game had been the play of Arnie Fer-rin, the Lakers' first-round draft pick, who joined the team shortly after the game. Ferrin arrived with a sterling basketball pedigree and an uncertainty about whether he even wanted to play pro ball. He'd been an All-American at the University of Utah, but at 160 pounds, he was so thin that he questioned whether he would stand up to the punishment of the long pro season. He had turned down decent contract offers from teams in both the BAA and NBL, including the Knicks and Lakers, prior to his appearance in the College All-Star Classic, only to change his mind when he played a strong game and was named his team's MVP.

"I was the only player with the college team who wasn't playing professionally," he explained. "The only thing I really remember asking the Lakers was how they saw me fitting in with the team, because I wanted to know if there was a place for me. It was one of life's funny fortunes. I took less money to play for the Lakers than if I had played in the other league. A year later, the other league wasn't in existence."

The NBL was indeed in a lot of trouble when Ferrin was making his decision. Without Minneapolis, Rochester, and Fort Wayne, the league could no longer boast, as it had at one time, of having the biggest names in pro basketball. The NBL hung on, but barely.

Not that the BAA was prospering. Compared to the players' multi-million-dollar annual contracts, the lucrative television and marketing deals, and other extravagances taken for granted by NBA players fifty years later, the pioneering professional leagues were strictly rag-tag, run on shoe-string budgets that seem unbelievable, if not totally ludicrous, today. George Mikan and his lofty (for the day) salary was the exception, rather than the norm. There were no health-insurance benefits or pensions, and few ways to earn additional income with product promotion. The arenas and playing conditions were primitive, the travel long and boring.

The Lakers traveled mostly by train, occasionally by bus or, later, by plane. A typical trip to the East would find them catching a train from Minneapolis to Chicago, where they'd switch to a train headed for New York or Boston. The schedule-makers tried to accommodate them by lumping other cities into a trip, but it was all but impossible to work New York, Rochester, Boston, and Philadelphia into a single trip.

John "Red" Kerr, who spent most of his twelve-year career in Syracuse, where he set an NBA record by playing in 844 consecutive regular-season games, found no comparison between the travails of moving from city to city in the early NBA and what players face today.

"When A. C. Green broke my consecutive-games record," he recalled, "somebody told me, 'Well, it's a lot harder today than when you played.' I said, 'What do you mean?' He said, 'You know, if you go from Chicago to L.A., it's about four, four and a half hours on the plane.' I said, 'We used to play in Syracuse, and then the next day in New York City. We'd be six and a half hours on the train and we never left the *state.*'"

The big guys had the most to contend with. With no legroom to speak of, George Mikan and other taller players had to find ways to stretch out without tripping anyone coming down the aisle or trying to move around them. They had to be even more inventive when trying to catch some sleep.

"We could not sleep comfortably in a six-foot berth," Clyde Lovellette, a six-nine center, recalled. Like Mikan, Lovellette was tall and beefy, and whenever he wanted to sleep on the train, he would remove a piece of wood at the end of a compartment and stick his feet through. "You'd tell the porter to wake up both ends," he joked.

"Can you imagine George Mikan in one of those six-foot chambers?" asked George King, a six-foot guard with the Nats. "We little guys were fine. We didn't have any trouble."

Planes offered a different set of challenges. Most teams, when they chose to fly, took slow, antiquated DC-3's, which seemed barely capable of climbing above the clouds and, if the trip was lengthy, had to land and refuel at some point during the journey. A number of players were afraid of flying—with good reason.

John Kundla hated to fly. He'd slug down his bottle of milk and pray for the best. Bud Grant remembered a time when the Lakers were playing the Celtics in Boston on a Friday night and, with a Sunday afternoon scheduled in Minneapolis, decided to take a plane, rather than the customary train, back home.

"We got up over the harbor," he said, "and one of the engines flamed out. If you're a passenger, you don't know what's going on. You can't see anything. All you can see are flames shooting out of the engine. You can't see the airport, you can't see the runway, and you don't know if you're going in the ocean. Well, the pilot turned the plane around and came downwind, and we landed."

The fire was put out and the plane hauled to a hangar for repairs.

Kundla, badly shaken from the ordeal, was horrified to learn that the pilot intended to take the same plane back up as soon as the mechanics completed repairs. The problem, he was assured, was minor.

"Kundla just about passed out," Grant recalled with a laugh. "He got on the phone with Sid Hartman and said, 'Hey, we're in Boston. There's no way I'm getting on an airplane. No way we're going to come back.' Sid Hartman told him, 'You get back here. We have a game on Sunday afternoon. You gotta be here.'"

According to Grant, the final decision came down to George Mikan.

"If George had said we weren't going to go, we wouldn't have gone," Grant insisted. "He was the lead cow. When he got on, we all went with him, Kundla included."

Players dreaded going to certain arenas on the road, and while each had personal likes and dislikes, Syracuse held a special status as the ultimate snakepit for opposing players. Anything could happen there—and often did. The Nats may have had the most boisterous, active fans in the league.

"It got wild," Nats forward George King said of the Syracuse home crowd. "They chased the officials out of there a few times."

"We had very hostile, nasty fans," Red Rocha allowed. "One time, this guy jumped out of the stands and started choking the ref. They had to take him away. The refs never came out for the second half."

No other team could claim to having a regular ticket-holder with the dubious moniker of "The Strangler." The short, stocky Strangler thought nothing of menacing officials or opposing teams' players. According to Hall of Fame official Earl Strom, "That fan got his name when he picked up [official] Charley Eckman at halftime and had poor Charley hanging by the neck." Norm Drucker, another HOF official, recalled the way The Strangler would "run up and down the sidelines during the game and stand next to a player, screaming, 'You SOB, you stink.'"

Drucker liked to retell a story he'd heard about the day when The Strangler finally got his comeuppance from the players he tormented.

"Boston was playing in Syracuse," Drucker said, "and they were really hated by the Syracuse fans. 'The Strangler' was doing more and more crazy things and he was rather close to the Boston huddle, screaming at the Boston players. The story goes that Jim Loscutoff grabbed him and pulled him right in the huddle, and they took a couple of shots at him. He came out bleeding from the eye."

In George Mikan, the Minneapolis Lakers had a natural target. As the league's biggest attraction, he expected (and received) all kinds of attention, from fans of all ages, when the Lakers were on the road.

Bill Calhoun, who spent much of his career with the Rochester Royals, recalled a funny, harmless incident involving Mikan, which occurred outside Madison Square Garden before a scheduled double-header.

"I was walking in with a couple of our guys at the same time as Mikan," he remembered. "Some kid asked Mikan for an autograph and he gave it to him. The kid set it on fire and then jumped on it with both feet. Mikan laughed his ass off. He thought it was hilarious."

Mikan was used to his role as the villain. It was part of the game, and he enjoyed the fan reaction unless things got ugly. He took hefty doses of verbal and, occasionally, physical abuse from fans almost everywhere he went. Fans shouted every kind of insult imaginable. They tossed coins, batteries, newspapers, and programs at him. Every so often, a cup of mustard or soda would come flying out of the stands.

"It was a bit distracting, but you generally laughed it off—if you didn't get hurt," Mikan said of the less disruptive of fan behavior. "That kind of stuff from the fans wasn't so bad, though it just made me want to beat their team all the more."

Some of the fan aggression toward Mikan was downright dangerous. The most frightening incident occurred in Rochester, after one of the Royals' players literally tackled Jim Pollard as he was cutting to the hoop for a basket. Mikan charged after an official and had just launched into a tirade about the Royals' rough play when a knife came sailing out of the stands and stuck in the court only a few feet from where he was standing. Mikan stared down at the knife and its wobbling handle, then turned and walked away without uttering another word.

"Luckily, it hit the floor," recalled Bobby Harrison, who witnessed the event. Mikan, he pointed out, was often targeted for both friendly and nasty attention. "George bore the brunt of almost all of it because he was the star and everybody liked to pick on him."

Each new season brought a more creative kind of nastiness and, by the time he'd reached the end of his career, Mikan had seen just about everything there was to see. He'd been shot in the legs by a Fort Wayne fan armed with a BB gun. He'd almost been brained by a heavy coat hook pitched at him from somebody in the stands. ("We were warming up,"

Arnie Ferrin remembered, "and I looked at George and said, 'It's not safe warming up with you.'") One elderly woman, with seats right behind the bench in Fort Wayne, made a habit of beating Mikan with her saddle-bag purse. At times, Mikan would be assigned a guard to escort him on and off the court.

Mikan wasn't alone by any means. Every player from that era could speak of witnessing fan violence or being victimized by overzealous fans. Security at the arenas was spotty, and players risked their safety if they so much as thought about retaliating.

"If you went up in the stands, you'd get killed," noted Gene Stump, who saw all kinds of inappropriate fan behavior during his career. One incident stayed with him long after he retired. "I was taking the ball out of bounds in Anderson, Indiana, and this woman stuck her lit cigarette on my leg. From the out-of-bounds area to where the people were sitting was something like a foot."

Jack Phelan, who played for Waterloo and Sheboygan after playing with Mikan at DePaul, recalled a time when he stole the ball and was streaking down the side court on a fast break. "A little old lady tripped me with her umbrella," he remembered. "She was sitting on the edge of the court. I went sprawling straight out, my hands and legs and everything else."

Wally Osterkorn, a Syracuse Nationals forward with a reputation for rough play, had the tables turned on him during an on-court fight with another player.

"I got into an altercation with Zeke Zawoluk, when he was playing with the Philadelphia Warriors," Osterkorn said. "All of a sudden, somebody's hitting me with an umbrella. It was his *mother*. She came out of the stands and started beating me on the head."

The Lakers began their quest for another championship with a first-round playoff series against the Chicago Stags. The Stags had finished the season in third place in the Western Division with a 38–22 record, and smart money said the Lakers would make short work of them in the best-of-three series. The Stags had Max Zaslofsky, who had finished third in the scoring race and was always capable of taking over a game, and they had Eddie Mikan to go up against his brother, but the team didn't match up well against the Lakers.

George utterly dominated the middle during the series, scoring 37 points in the Lakers' 84–77 win at Minneapolis, and dropping in 38 more in his team's 101–85 victory in Chicago the next night. George made a point of praising Eddie's abilities and effort in his comments to the press, but the Stags were little more than a warmup for what promised to be a much tougher second round: a reprise of their previous season's NBL finals matchup against the Rochester Royals. This time around, the Royals had a healthy Arnie Risen on the court, and Mikan knew he was in for some work. Since this was another best-of-three series, there was very little margin for error, especially against the Royals, who, by virtue of notching the better regular-season record, held the home-court advantage.

Mikan needed no pep talk from John Kundla or anyone else to get up for the game. Mikan still groused about how the Rochester papers had insisted that the Royals would have beaten the Lakers in the previous year's playoffs if Risen had been in the lineup. It was time to put all the talk and speculation to rest.

Mikan led the Lakers to a 2–0 sweep, but both games were trials. In the first, the Lakers controlled the Royals, leading by as many as 17 points in the second half before the Royals tore off a run late in the game and actually led by two points with less than two minutes to go. Everyone expected Mikan to get the ball for a game-tying shot, but the Lakers found their hero elsewhere. With eighteen seconds left, Tony Jaros tied the game and, twelve seconds later, Arnie Ferrin won it, 80–79, with a free throw.

The Lakers took the next game—and the series—by playing some of the toughest defense in playoff history. The game, held in St. Paul due to previous commitments at both the Minneapolis Auditorium and the Minneapolis Armory, was almost like a road game for the Lakers, who always struggled at the St. Paul Auditorium. The Lakers and Royals exchanged leads throughout the game, but Rochester had built up a convincing lead by the end of the third quarter. Mikan and his teammates turned up the defense. In one of the finest defensive efforts of his career. Mikan neutralized Risen in the middle and the Royals turned to their guards—Bob Davies, Red Holzman, and Bobby Wanzer—for points from the outside. Their shots, closely challenged by their Laker counterparts, didn't fall, and the Lakers held the Royals without a single field goal for the entire fourth quarter, outscoring them 18–3. The Lakers escaped, 67–55.

By now, Mikan had grown accustomed to playing in a championship round. He had to go back to his days at DePaul, and the team's agonizing second-round loss to Georgetown in the NCAA, to find a time when one of his teams wasn't playing for a championship trophy. He'd walked away with the NIT trophy at DePaul and a championship with the Gears, and here he was again, trying for still another trophy in still another league. All the Lakers had to do was get by the Washington Capitols, a 38–22 regular-season team guided by a thirty-one-year-old coach named Arnold "Red" Auerbach.

Auerbach would eventually become one of the most recognized names in basketball history. He would enter the Naismith Basketball Hall of Fame after leading the Boston Celtics to nine NBA championships, and he would coach such legendary players as Bill Russell, Bob Cousy, Bill Sharman, Sam Jones, K. C. Jones, Tom Heinsohn, and others. The Professional Basketball Writers Association of America would name him the greatest coach in the history of the NBA. But, in 1949, he was just beginning to establish himself.

The Washington Caps had won a division title two years earlier, but had fallen short of a championship. Auerbach now had his team in the finals. Auerbach, a fiery coach who stalked the sidelines with a rolled-up program in his hands and contested every marginal call against his team, was John Kundla's polar opposite in coaching style, just as his team played an entirely different style of basketball. Two of the Caps' key players, Bob Feerick and Fred Scolari, were nursing injuries, and Feerick would miss the playoffs entirely with a bad knee. However, with Horace "Bones" McKinney and Clarence "Kleggy" Hermsen on the front line, the Caps felt they could play even with Mikan and Pollard.

Mikan burned the Caps for 42 points in the first game, but the contest was undecided until Swede Carlson hit a pair of free throws in the final minute to give the Lakers an 88–84 win. A seething Red Auerbach promised the press that Mikan wouldn't be scoring anywhere near that many points in the next game—and he didn't. Auerbach double- and triple-teamed Mikan throughout the game, packing the pivot and keeping the ball away from the Lakers' center, daring Minneapolis to beat them from the outside. The strategy succeeded, inasmuch as Mikan took only nine shots and scored only 10 points, a season low, but the other Lakers responded, with Carlson scoring 16 points and Herm Schaefer contributing 13. The Lakers grabbed a 2-0 series lead with a convincing 76–62 win.

The series moved to Washington, D.C. The Lakers overwhelmed the Caps in front of their hometown fans, taking the third game of the series, 94–74, with Mikan scoring 35 points in a game that Bones McKinney missed while attending to his ailing wife in North Carolina. In the series' first three games, Mikan was averaging an unheard-of 29 points per game, and he was looking to sweep the finals when the two teams met at Uline Arena for Game 4.

For a while, it seemed as if he'd get his wish. Led by Mikan's 12 points, the Lakers charged out to an early 16–7 lead. However, the momentum of the game—and possibly the series—shifted suddenly and dramatically when Mikan and Kleggy Hermsen collided while fighting for a rebound and Mikan fell awkwardly on his right wrist. Mikan stayed in the game, scoring another 15 points while shooting his hook left-handed, but his efforts fell short. The Caps stalled an ending to the series by winning, 83–71.

X-rays taken after the game revealed a broken wrist, and Mikan was fit with a cast, which was about the last thing the Caps needed: an angry George Mikan, who used his elbows like lethal weapons, now swinging a cast around like a club.

"That cast was hard as a brick," Bones McKinney recalled. "It fit right in with his elbows. It would kill you. And it didn't bother his shooting a bit."

Mikan proved as much in Game 5, scoring 22 points, but once again, it wasn't enough. The Lakers lost by nine, 74–65, turning what looked like a runaway series into a suddenly tight 3–2 duel.

The sixth game, played in the St. Paul Auditorium, was a rout. Hampered by the cast which, as Mikan described it, felt as if it stretched "from my fingers up to my armpits," Mikan concentrated on rebounding and shooting left-handed. Jim Pollard and Arnie Ferrin helped out on the boards, limiting the Caps to one shot on many of their trips down the floor. The Lakers, controlling the game from the beginning, posted a lopsided 77–56 win.

The championship underscored Mikan's supremacy in pro basketball. Despite playing two full games and part of a third with a broken wrist, and facing aggressive defenses that double-teamed him almost every time the Lakers had the ball on offense, Mikan poured in 303 points in the Lakers' ten playoff games—this coming at a time when a 20-point game was considered exceptional, and when only a couple of the league's elite players averaged

20 points a game over the course of an entire season. Mikan had set a record by averaging 28.3 points during the regular season, outscoring Joe Fulks and Max Zaslofsky and proving that, until further notice, he was still the best player pro basketball had to offer.

By all indications, George Mikan's life might have been a blueprint for the American Dream. Here was a young man, raised in a modest background in a midwestern town, who, through sheer determination and hard work, had achieved unimaginable success in a fledgling professional sport, and he'd managed to do so while maintaining a stable private life and projecting a wholesome public image that made him one of the nice guys in American sports. He was doing exactly what he wanted to be doing, and he was being highly paid for it. He was the biggest draw in pro basketball. His teams had won championships. And, in the event that the pro basketball dream came to an end, either naturally (by his eventual retirement) or otherwise (such as the BAA's folding, like the PBLA), he had a law career to fall back on. He received his degree from DePaul on June 8, 1949.

At home, life seemed equally promising. He and Pat added another family member—Edward Terrence, named after George's brother but called Terry—in the spring of 1949. Unlike the majority of professional basketball players, who held down jobs in the offseason to supplement the modest incomes they earned in the sport, Mikan could relax and spend his summer on the golf course.

Things, however, were about to change. The depleted NBL had barely hobbled through the 1948–49 season, and the BAA, with its big arenas, had done only slightly better. Hostilities between the two leagues had escalated, and the rumor mill was rife with talk about lawsuits, the NBL folding, or a merger between the two leagues.

The NBL was down to just a handful of teams. The Denver Nuggets and Waterloo Hawks had dropped out of the league before the 1948–49 season was completed, and other small-town teams, such as the Anderson Packers, Sheboygan Redskins, and Oshkosh All-Stars, were barely getting by. None of the teams, however, were going quietly. They aggressively competed with the BAA for the best players graduating from college, and the league threatened to tie up the courts (and perhaps jeopardize the opening of the BAA's upcoming season) with a series of lawsuits addressing, first, the BAA's raiding the NBL for teams, and, second, its refusal to allow the remaining NBL teams to merge with the BAA.

The BAA couldn't afford any of this. Two of its own teams—the Indianapolis Jets and the Providence Steamrollers—had gone under, and other teams were losing alarming amounts of money. Competing for players and staving off lawsuits only meant additional financial troubles.

Something had to be done—and soon.

Throughout the spring and summer of 1949, Maurice Podoloff, the BAA executive board members, and team owners racked their brains to come up with a solution. Podoloff's answer was wonderfully pragmatic and ultimately Darwinian: allow any NBL teams desiring to enter the BAA the chance to do so, and let time and finances sort things out. The lawsuits would go away, there would be no more competition for college players, and, in the end, the weaker teams would fall away, leaving only the strongest teams to make up the new league.

In August 1949, the BAA reached a merger agreement with the remaining NBL teams that would change the course of pro basketball history. The BAA would take in the NBL teams and a newly named league would be formed. Ironically, the new league edged closer to Maurice White's old dream than anyone might have predicted. The new league would have more teams and more players, and would operate on a greater national scale, than any league in the history of professional basketball.

The new league would be called the National Basketball Association.

Eleven

THREE-PEAT

NBA DYNASTIES CAN usually look back and boast of a spectacular draft, or series of trades or free-agency signings, that gave them the nucleus of a team bound for long-term greatness.

Few drafts, however, produced the kind of "instant team" that the 1949 draft gave the Minneapolis Lakers. The Lakers already had two superstars in George Mikan and Jim Pollard; the 1949 draft gave them three significant new team components—Vern Mikkelsen, Slater Martin, and Bobby Harrison—all destined to start and star for the Lakers, two (Mikkelsen, Martin) to eventually join Pollard and Mikan in the Naismith Basketball Hall of Fame. All had played for winners in college.

The Lakers chose six-two guard Bobby Harrison as their regular first-round draft pick. Nicknamed "Tiger" for his aggressive defensive play, Harrison could also put up points. He earned an eventual entry in *Ripley's Believe It or Not* when, as an eighth-grade center at Lagrange School in Toledo, Ohio, he scored 139 points (69 field goals and one free throw) in a single game. After twice earning All-State honors on Toledo's Woodward High School team, Harrison served for fifteen months in the Marine Corps at the end of World War II. He went on to play for the University of Michigan, where he'd led his team in scoring during its conference-winning 1947–48 season. He'd been Michigan's Most Valuable Player and, in 1949, he played in the East-West All-Star Game (with, ironically, Vern Mikkelsen and Slater Martin) and the Midwest All-Star Game.

He would never forget how he earned his starting spot with the Lakers.

"We were playing Philadelphia, and Joe Fulks was tearing our guys up," he said. "John kept looking up and down the bench, to see if he could bring somebody in. I raised my hand and said, 'Hey, John.' He said, 'Go on in, Bobby, and take Joe.' I did a hell of a job on him, and after that I moved into the starting lineup."

Vern Mikkelsen, the team's territorial draft pick, was a puzzling choice. He was a big, powerful center, but the Lakers already had one of those—the best in the business. Was the Laker front office trying to cover its bets, come contract time? Mikan was a notoriously tough contract negotiator—call it the lawyer in him—so, in Mikkelsen, the Lakers had a replacement in the unlikely event that they couldn't reach an agreement with their big man.

When the Lakers' front office approached Mikkelsen after the draft, they tried to convince him that they had selected him as Mikan's replacement.

"George is going to retire next year," Max Winter assured Mikkelsen.

Mikkelsen was skeptical. Mikan was all of twenty-five years old and playing at the highest level imaginable. Why would he walk away from the game at this point? Even if Mikan did retire in a year, how did he, Vern Mikkelsen, fit into the team's *current* plans?

"You can play when George gets a little tired," Winter told Mikkelsen.

That idea was almost as preposterous as the thought of Mikan's hanging up his high-tops.

"George," Mikkelsen remembered with a laugh, "never got tired."

Mikkelsen had played under Joe Hutton at Hamline, and, like so many of Hutton's students, he had been so well schooled on the basics that he could overcome his physical shortcomings by playing sound, fundamental basketball. At six-seven, Mikkelsen was about average height for centers in those days, but he wasn't known for his speed or leaping ability. His shot was average, perhaps a tad below average. A classic overachiever, Mikkelsen succeeded by hustling, making very few mistakes, banging bodies beneath the backboard, and feeding the skills of his teammates. What he could do, he did very well.

Arild Verner Mikkelsen, son of a Danish Lutheran pastor, was born in Fresno, California, but moved to Minnesota with his family when he was in seventh grade. His father had a parish in Askov, Minnesota, a tiny town of about 350 people of mainly Danish descent, about a hundred miles north of Minneapolis. Mikkelsen had never seen a basketball game prior to moving to Askov, but he learned the game quickly and excelled at it on the town's high school team. An exceptional student, Mikkelsen was ready for college at sixteen, but it took a strange turn of events for him to wind up playing at Hamline.

"Some guy, a professor at Hamline, was recruiting for Joe Hutton," Mikkelsen explained, "and he was running all around a five-state area, looking for ballplayers. He was on his way up to the Iron Range when he got a flat tire in my little home town. He was sitting there, getting his tire repaired in the only gas station in town, when he got to talking with the repairman, who started telling him about me."

The University of Minnesota had heard about Mikkelsen and wanted him on its team, but the Golden Gophers already had an outstanding center in Jim McIntyre. Mikkelsen liked his chances at the smaller school in St. Paul. He not only made the team; he excelled, leading Hamline to three consecutive MIAC championships and a national championship in 1949.

In contrast to Mikkelsen, Slater Martin possessed all the natural gifts a basketball player could dream of—except height. At five-ten, he would spend a career moving among giants, and he compensated for his lack of height with speed that astounded his opponents. Like John Stockton of the future Utah Jazz, Martin had uncanny court awareness and an anticipation of how and where the action would develop. A tough defensive player with quick hands and feet, Martin would usually be assigned to guard the opposing team's best player, regardless of that player's height.

Martin grew up in Houston and learned about basketball when he was eight, when his grandfather put up a makeshift backboard in a vacant lot and taught him how to shoot. His grandfather, a fan of the *Mutt and Jeff* comic strip, dubbed him "Dugar" after Dugar's Bar in the strip, and the nickname evolved into "Dugie," which Martin would carry with him throughout his life.

Jeff Davis High School coach Roy Needham stressed fundamentals, particularly defense, and Martin, who stood five-seven when he was on the high school team, learned how speed, quickness, and playing tight defense could not only keep you in the game; it could make you a star.

World War II interrupted what looked like a promising career at the University of Texas. Martin played in two games in the 1943–44 season, knowing full well that he was probably going to be drafted; but rather than wait for Uncle Sam to induct him into the army, Martin enlisted in the navy and served as a gunner's mate in the Pacific.

Following his discharge from the service, Martin played a year of amateur ball before rejoining Texas in 1947. The Texas team, nicknamed the "Orange Mice" because of its short, quick, active guards, could run, run, run, which was just what Martin preferred. They could also shoot, and in one game against Texas Christian University, Martin broke the Southeast Conference single-game scoring mark by knocking down 49 points.

"That was a crazy night," he recalled. "Our coach, Jack Gray, held the school record, thirty-two points. The conference record was forty-five. Near the end of the half, I stole the ball three times in the final minute and went to the locker room with eleven points. Coach Gray tells the team he wants me to set a record. So they kept feeding me and feeding me and I wind up with forty-nine. Coach told me afterward that I must have been shooting from memory."

Texas advanced as far as the semifinals of the NCAA tournament that year, but lost to Oklahoma, 55–54, on a half-court buzzer-beater. Texas would not go that far in the tournament again until 2003. Martin, however, had left his mark. He'd been named to the All-Southwest Conference team his final three years, and was eventually voted the All-Time Best Player in the Southwest Conference.

Still, he had little desire to play pro ball. Martin figured he'd go to Bartlesville, Oklahoma, take a job with Phillips Petroleum, and play alongside Bob Kurland on the Phillips 66 team in the AAU. It didn't work out. Martin wanted a job working outdoors; Phillips wanted him behind a desk.

Then the Lakers offered him a contract for $3,500. Martin and his wife packed all their earthly possessions into their '49 Ford and headed for Minneapolis.

Martin, a lifelong Texan, was quickly educated about the ways of the North.

"I'd been there about ten days, and I woke up and there's snow about knee-high," he recalled. "I went out to my car, and it had frozen. My radiator busted and the battery had blown up. My car was a mess. I think the repairs cost me about thirty-five dollars, which was about all the money I had. The first thing I bought was a big overcoat with a collar that came up over the top of your head."

As an offensive player, Martin had always been a gunner, but that would have to change on his first pro team, which already had enough scoring punch to go around. On offense, he'd be expected to bring the ball upcourt and pass it, as soon as possible, to either Pollard or Mikan. Where he'd once loved to run the fast break, streaking up the floor with a couple of Texas teammates, he'd now have to settle for the slower, more deliberate Laker style. His job, simply put, was to play defense and keep Mikan and Pollard happy.

"All they expected out of me was to hold Bob Davies or Bobby Wanzer or Bill Sharman or Bob Cousy to twelve points and then we'd win the game," he remarked. "If I got six or eight points extra, I was home free."

George Mikan didn't know what to make of his team's newest guard. When he walked out for the team's first practice in the gym at the Men's Athletic Club in Minneapolis, he spotted a small guy shooting baskets from the side of the court. He figured the kid was a ball boy.

"Hey, throw me that ball," he ordered. "I'm going to throw some free throws. Will you fetch them for me?"

The kid did as he was told. Mikan swished free throw after free throw, tossing the ball in his distinct underhanded style. When he eventually missed one, he called it quits.

"That's enough," he told the kid. "You can go now."

Mikan apologized later when he learned that the "ball boy" was really the sharpshooter the Lakers had drafted from Texas.

Martin shrugged it off. "I'm just trying to make the team," he told Mikan.

"I hope you do," Mikan said.

Martin made the team, though his early days on the Lakers might have made him wonder why he'd ever left Houston. He didn't play nearly as much as he'd hoped, and when he did get into a game, he'd have to deal with Mikan, who would growl at him for having the nerve to cut through his space, bringing his man with him.

The young guard might have grown more discouraged if not for some unsolicited remarks from Herm Schaefer, the man he eventually replaced. The veteran Minneapolis guard had suffered an injury and Martin was taking his place in the starting lineup. Just before a game in Fort Wayne, Schaefer pulled Martin aside in the locker room and offered some encouragement. He'd been watching Martin tiptoe around Mikan, and it was hurting his game at both ends of the floor.

"Don't be afraid to take your shots," he advised. "You're letting the big guy cramp your style."

Martin took the words to heart. "I had one of those lucky nights where everything I threw up went in," he recalled. "I hit eight straight shots from the floor. They came just in time to save my job."

He led all scorers with 42 points, and after the game, while he, Mikan, and other Lakers were standing around outside the gym, signing autographs for some Zollner Piston fans, Martin heard from one of the sharper analysts in the crowd.

"Hey, Slater," the fan called out. "You sure were lucky tonight."

"Yeah," Martin responded, "it seems the harder I work, the luckier I get."

Martin, as it turned out, was the least of Mikan's concerns. Not long after the opening of the season, John Kundla had come up with the idea of playing Mikan and Mikkelsen in tandem as a double pivot. Mikkelsen, Kundla decided, was far too valuable to be dividing his time with Mikan at center. As it stood, Mik was getting only a few minutes a game. Kundla decided to experiment with a two-center lineup, with Mikkelsen playing the high post and Mikan on the low post, close to the basket. On defense, the middle would be virtually impenetrable. Mikan and Mikkelsen's height and girth would make short shots and layups all but impossible, forcing the action to the outside, where players would be facing defensive specialists Slater Martin and Bobby Harrison and taking lower-percentage shots.

In theory, the idea made good sense; on the floor, it was a disaster. Two huge men couldn't move around in such cramped quarters, in such a narrow lane—especially on offense, with a couple of the opposing team's defenders nearby. The two were constantly in each other's way.

"I messed it up for George," Mikkelsen admitted. "The lane was only six feet wide back in those days. It just was not working. After about three or four weeks, George came to me and said, 'Hey, Mik, this thing isn't going to work,' and I agreed with him."

Prior to the 1949–50 season, Kundla had used Swede Carlson as his other forward. At six feet even, Carlson was no taller than most of the guards in the game, but Kundla, like many of his contemporaries, chose to have a small, quick forward playing on the front line. They were there for defense and an occasional outside shot. The big men took care of the rebounding and inside scoring.

With the double-pivot experiment failing miserably, Kundla decided to drop Carlson from the starting lineup and convert Mikkelsen to a kind of modified forward position. Mikkelsen's duties would include rebounding at both ends of the court, blocking shots, picking up an occasional garbage basket on a Mikan or Pollard miss, setting picks, and, in general, disrupting the other team's path to the basket. His brawn would be his most significant weapon.

In the years to come, this newly created position would be given a name—power forward—and Mikkelsen would be credited with being the first to play it. Learning the new position, though, wasn't easy for a rookie who'd played center throughout his high school and college years, and who'd been struggling to adapt in the pros.

"I spent two years learning that job," Mikkelsen said of Kundla's newly created position. "I had to learn a new way of playing the game. I'd been a center in college, and that's the only position I knew. They turned me around, made me face the basket, go to the right corner, and spend most of my time rebounding. I'm now known as the original power forward, which is certainly an honor, but the interesting thing, in my opinion, is when I first started, I was playing against guys Swede Carlson's size. When I quit ten years later, I was playing against guys like Bob Pettit and Tommy Heinsohn—people who were six-eight, six-nine, six-ten. That's how the game had grown in ten years."

The game had been evolving in any event, but the recent additions to the Lakers had dictated a change—perhaps even a drastic change. Mikan had already changed the center position, which had evolved from the tallest man on the court being used for jump balls and rebounds and little else, to his being the focal point of his team's offense. Pollard, the "small" forward, was the 'tweener, as athletically gifted as a guard yet tall enough to work on the front line. Mikkelsen, the "power" forward, was the team's muscle up front, pounding the boards for rebounds and doing what would be known as basketball's dirty work. Martin, the "point" guard, would bring the ball up the floor, direct the offense, and play defense. Harrison, the "shooting" guard, played defense and took the occasional shot. Each player had specific duties, drawn up largely from his individual skills, and those duties would move the game further away from the old freelance style of basketball to a more methodical way of playing.

Kundla had no way of knowing it, but he had created the prototype for the NBA team of the future.

"They said I invented the power forward, but I was just lucky to get a guy who could play front forward," Kundla said with typical modesty. "Mikkelsen was a good defensive man, a great rebounder. He developed an overhand shot that he fed Mikan with if they were sagging off. He learned how to shoot, and he could hit that overhand shot."

With the new players and the new style, the Lakers were a work-in-progress, and some ragged play marked the early going. Mikan hadn't helped the cause by reporting to training camp overweight and out of condition. The Lakers stumbled, losing five of their first fourteen games. Kundla ragged at Mikan for being "fat and lazy," and Mikan started working out at the YMCA, sweating himself into condition while his teammates were at the movies.

"As it turned out at the end of the season," he confessed, "my not being in shape almost cost us a lot of money."

The press covering the opposing teams ate it up. Mikan was out of shape, Mikan and Mikkelsen were fumbling around in Kundla's newfangled double pivot, and the Lakers looked vulnerable. Even the College All-Stars gave them a tough game before losing, 94–86. The Rochester Royals and Syracuse Nationals were establishing themselves as legitimate contenders. Reporters chirped on about Mikan's feuding with Pollard, or Mikan's feuding with Kundla, or dissension on the Laker team in general.

Members of the Lakers saw the reports but didn't take them too seriously, even if there was a kernel of truth to them. They knew the whole story. Pollard and Mikan exchanged testy remarks all the time, but, more than anything else, it was a matter of their saying what was on their minds and moving on. The same applied to Mikan and Kundla: Mikan needed to be effective if the Lakers had any hope of repeating as champions, and as the team's captain and floor leader, Mikan felt justified in offering suggestions, sometimes pointed, at how things should be run.

Kundla, who called his 1949–50 Lakers team "our strongest team"—no small statement, given the number of championship teams that he coached in Minneapolis—attributed much of the success to the kind of men he had suiting up for him every night. Regardless of what the papers said, the Lakers were a *team*, on and off the court.

"I was lucky. I had players with talent *and* character," Kundla explained. "I think a lot of players lack character these days. They're looking out for themselves, their own salaries, their scoring and everything. Mikan and Pollard were team players. They were all looking for a team victory. They weren't individuals. So character played a big part."

Good coaching didn't hurt, either. Modest by nature and quiet on the sideline, at least in comparison to screamers like Les Harrison, Al Cervi, and Red Auerbach, Kundla would never receive due credit for his contributions to the game. Future historians would stumble over superlatives in praise of coaches with fewer team victories, lower overall winning percentages, and fewer championships; Kundla, they'd say, had enjoyed the benefit of coaching five Hall of Famers during his coaching run with the Lakers.

Clyde Lovellette, one of those Hall of Famers, believed that Kundla's strongest asset was his ability to keep all those good players satisfied.

"A professional coach has to be a psychologist," Lovellette said, "because you've got ten, twelve players on the team, and they were all pretty decent college players. They had to be All-Americans or All-Conference, or good scorers or defensive players—*something* had to trigger the drafting of these people. Only five can play at one time."

Kundla kept his intensity to himself. He battled ulcers throughout his coaching career, and he kept a bottle of milk with him on the sidelines, for those occasions when the action on court threatened to turn his stomach into a boiling cauldron. He'd mix it up with officials from time to time, but he was more inclined to discuss than shout. He recognized the enormous talent he had on the Lakers; but rather than watch his team play a totally freelance or even undisciplined game, he became one of the first professional basketball coaches to use a number of set offensive plays catering specifically to the strengths of his individual players.

Handling someone like George Mikan, who was known to behave like a prima donna from time to time, required, as Lovellette noted, a psychologist's touch. You were not only dealing with a superstar's ego and emotions; you also knew you were being watched closely by the players, all interested in seeing whether Mikan received preferential treatment.

"When he was going to bawl someone out," Vern Mikkelsen said of Kundla, "he would always start by bawling out George. It made sense, and George understood it. John didn't want anybody to think that George didn't get bawled out too. Then it would be my turn or Jim's turn or somebody else's turn. But George had already set the stage."

No coach, with the possible exception of Al Cervi, emphasized the importance of defense like Kundla did. Sound defense, he maintained, set up the offense, and on those occasions when he chewed out Mikan, it was usually over defensive lapses in the middle.

"To win championships, you've got to play defense," Kundla insisted. "When I substituted, it was for defense. I harped on that. We had great scoring, but people don't realize that we also had a good defense."

Mikan's play on defense depended upon his opponent. If the opposing player wanted to play an inside game near the basket, Mikan would use his size and muscle to his advantage. He could block shots, misdirect the flow of the game, rebound, and control the opposing player. Guarding a player away from the basket was a different matter. If the opposing player played outside, Mikan would labor to keep up.

Kundla recalled a game against the Philadelphia Warriors, when Mikan was having an especially difficult time with the Warriors' Hall of Fame center, Neil Johnston. By halftime, Johnston had lit Mikan up for 14 points, and Mikan was at a loss as to how to stop him.

"He's a hard guy to watch," he complained to Kundla. "He works in sections."

Slater Martin, sitting nearby and overhearing the conversation, chipped in his advice. "Watch the section that's scoring," he quipped.

Dick Schnittker, a teammate late in Mikan's career, remembered another game that found Johnston scoring at will against Mikan.

"Neil's got about twenty-five in the first half," Schnittker said. "When we came in at halftime, Pollard took George's hat and threw it over at him. 'Put this on,' he said. 'You're going to catch a cold from his going by you so much.' God, did George get mad. He almost went after him."

The newly created NBA, bursting with its combination of old BAA and NBL teams, worked out exactly the way Maurice Podoloff had anticipated. The big-city franchises, with their huge fan bases and large arenas, prospered—or, at the very least, held their own. Some of the franchises from smaller cities struggled. One brand-new team, the Indianapolis Olympians, enjoyed great success, on the court and in attendance, challenging the established teams for domination of the new league.

The Olympians turned out to be one of the most unusual experiments in the history of professional sports. It all began at the University of Kentucky, where Coach Adolph Rupp, with such players as Alex Groza, Ralph Beard, Wallace "Wah Wah" Jones, Cliff Barker, and Joe Holland, assembled a collegiate juggernaut. Kentucky destroyed any team in its path, winning the NIT and NCAA tournaments along the way. The team comprised the nucleus of the gold medal–winning 1948 United States Olympic team, and a standing joke at the time was that this group of college players could probably beat most of the pro teams in the business. As it was, the Kentucky team, when its star players banded together to form the Olympians, had played as a unit for as long as many of the pro teams.

"We'd already played four years together," Ralph Beard remembered. "We were that far ahead of everybody. Once you were drafted [into the pros], you'd go to camp and you'd learn, and then it'd take you a year or two to get used to it. As soon as we got out together, we knew exactly what we were going to do. We were tough dogs to keep on the porch."

The newly formed Olympians gave them the chance to prove it. While still at the University of Kentucky, some of the Wildcat players had formed a barnstorming team, which had been so popular that it made them consider the idea of forming a professional team after they had graduated.

"Babe Kimbrough, a sports editor of the *Lexington Herald*, got our guys together, and we picked up three or four other guys and toured around the state of Kentucky," Beard explained. "We traveled around and we split the money. Kimbrough said, 'Hey, we can making a living doing this.' He's the one who had the idea, and that's what we did."

Podoloff was intrigued about the potential for a team made up of such high-profile athletes. It certainly didn't hurt the league's coffers and, with the team forming just before the merger of the BAA and NBL, there was a practical matter as well. As Wah Wah Jones recalled, keeping the players together also translated into financial savings in the highly competitive bidding war between the two leagues.

"The two leagues were battling for players and paying bigger prices," he said. "So they offered us the chance to come together instead of going to different teams at the price they had to pay for players They decided to take this whole team and give us a franchise."

It wasn't just any franchise. The Olympians, unlike any other team in NBA history, was owned and controlled by the players. Cliff Barker acted as player-coach. When it came time to choose a location for the new team, three cities were considered: Indianapolis, Louisville, and Cincinnati. According to Beard, Indianapolis won out because the state of Indiana had a history of supporting all levels of basketball, and because Indianapolis boasted a facility that everyone wanted to use.

"We chose Indianapolis," Beard said, "because we had played exhibitions at the Butler Field House, which was the greatest place to play in the whole world. We filled that at seventeen thousand a couple of times. Babe Kimbrough said, 'This is the place that we want for the team.'"

The addition of the Olympians created an instant interstate rivalry between the Olympians and Pistons. Beard and Groza, as expected, became all-star anchors of a very good team, and Groza immediately provided George Mikan with a big challenge in the pivot. As far as anyone could tell, this was a team with a very big future.

Throughout the George Mikan era, the Minneapolis Lakers had a tradition of posting strong winning percentages in January and February. They'd start the seasons slowly, and gain momentum as it went along.

Some of this could be written off to Mikan's habit of reporting to fall practices out of shape and spending the early portion of the season working himself into game condition. There was also a health issue that appeared to favor Minneapolis. By midseason, most teams were dealing with an assortment of injuries that took their toll on the teams' performances, but the Lakers—particularly their starting five—missed very little time to injury during their championship run. Mikan missed only two games in his entire career, both due to a viral infection—an amazing feat when you consider the beating he took during games. By the time his playing days were over, he'd taken, by his own estimation, 166 stitches; he'd broken bones in his arm, both elbows, both feet, his nose, and several fingers. He'd lost teeth to opposing players' elbows, and he'd eventually have to have a kneecap replaced. There was never a time when he wasn't covered with bruises. Somehow, he played through it all, and the Lakers' record showed it.

Even the weather played a significant role in the Lakers' gain of momentum as the season wore on. Players knew they had a tough game ahead any time they played in Minneapolis, where the court was actually a few feet narrower than the standard-sized court, and revved-up crowds backed their team with a fervor rivaling fans anywhere, but Laker players and their opponents alike agreed that the brutally cold Minnesota January and February gave the Lakers a psychological advantage over their opponents.

"I'm a Kentuckian, and when it was twenty degrees below zero, and the wind-chill factor was I don't know what, it was really cold," said John Oldham, who spent his career in Fort Wayne. The Lakers, he said, were tough enough without nature's providing any added advantage. "You had a sort of defeatist attitude when you went up there."

"I always felt sorry for Pollard in that Minneapolis weather," offered Bill Calhoun, speculating that Pollard, a native Californian, must have suffered in the unbearably cold weather. Visiting teams, Calhoun noted, usually walked from the train station to the hotel, and it could be a nasty hike when temperatures plummeted. "It was only three or four blocks from the train station to the hotel," Calhoun said, "but I remember having to duck into a Walgreen's just to get warm. We couldn't handle it."

George King, whose five years in Syracuse gave him plenty of experience with wintry weather, saw no comparison between the weather in upstate New York and what he faced whenever the Nats traveled to Minnesota. "We used to come out of there after taking a shower," he recalled, "and we'd have to walk a couple blocks to get a trolley because the cabs would all be gone. By the time I'd get to the trolley, my hair was frozen solid."

The intense cold led to one of the Lakers' most unusual—and amusing—travel stories. The team was taking a train to Fort Wayne, but a cold snap over the Upper Midwest created all kinds of problems for travelers, including those taking trains. Delays and breakdowns were inevitable. The Lakers' train made it as far as Milwaukee, but after several delays along the way, it became evident that there was no way the team could possibly make it to Fort Wayne in time for its game against the Pistons.

Fred Zollner, the Pistons' owner, came to the Lakers' rescue. The Pistons were the only team in professional basketball with a private plane, and Zollner telegraphed the Lakers and offered to send his plane for them. The message was delivered to the players stalled on the train in Milwaukee, and everyone received the notice about the change in plans except John Kundla, who wasn't with the team when the telegraph arrived. He'd gone to the dining car for a glass of milk to soothe his ulcer. He was seated at the dining car window when the train finally pulled out of the station, unaware that his players were out on the platform, desperately trying to flag him down.

The Lakers caught Zollner's plane, arrived in time for the opening of their scheduled game, and played the first half without their coach. Kundla, carrying his bags, walked into the North Side High School gym at the beginning of the third quarter, much to the amusement of the players and those in attendance. The Laker players never let him hear the end of it.

"At the time, we were winning, but we wound up losing the game," Vern Mikkelsen recalled. "We gave John plenty of trouble on that."

The Central Division race turned out to be much tighter than George Mikan and his teammates anticipated. The Lakers held a comfortable three-game lead over Rochester with only eight games remaining, but the Royals were red-hot, winning their last fifteen regular-season games and forcing a one-game tiebreaker to determine the division champ. The Lakers, in control of their fate going into their final game of the season, dropped a close road game to Fort Wayne. Mikan wound up regretting a couple of early-season losses, brought on, he felt, by his being out of condition.

An extra game would be trying under any circumstances, but for the Lakers it meant competing in four tense games in four straight nights: the season-ending game with Fort Wayne; an already-scheduled exhibition with the Harlem Globetrotters; the tiebreaker against Rochester; and the first game of the Central Division playoff series.

By now, the games against the Globetrotters were more of an annoyance to the Lakers than the testy, all-out competitions that marked their earlier meetings. This was especially the case now, with two very important games looming over the next forty-eight hours, and there were some discussions among several Lakers, including Mikan, about boycotting the Globetrotter game unless the Laker players received some sort of compensation for their efforts. It seemed unfair that Abe Saperstein, the Globetrotter players, and the Laker organization would make a bundle of money while the Laker players came away empty. Nothing ever came of their grumbling, however, and the game went on as scheduled.

The Lakers pounded the Trotters, 69–54, in St. Paul. Mikan led a balanced Lakers attack with 21 points before fouling out, while Vern Mikkelsen added 18 and Jim Pollard 16. The Lakers had now taken three straight from the Globetrotters—two in less than four weeks' time—and Saperstein was tired of losing. No one knew it at the time, but the series was reaching an end.

The next night's tiebreaker against the Rochester Royals looked daunting. The Lakers had lost a coin toss for the home-court advantage, and the Royals never lost at home. (In fact, three teams—the Lakers, Royals, and Syracuse Nats—could boast of losing only one game on their home court during the entire 1949–50 season.) The Royals, established as three-point favorites in the contest, were the hottest team in basketball and the Lakers were exhausted from the two games they'd played over the previous two nights.

The game wound up symbolizing the ultra-competitive history of the two teams. Royals coach Les Harrison decided to concede Mikan his points while trying to hold down the other Lakers' scoring. The strategy almost worked. The Lakers, behind 10 Mikan points, led early, but the Royals closed out the first quarter strongly and jumped ahead, 23–20, at the end of the period. Rochester held the lead from that point on, and, by midway through the fourth quarter, they were up 70–62. Bob Davies, Red Holzman, and Bobby Wanzer, the Royals' backcourt trio, tormented the Lakers all night, but with the game on the line, the Lakers turned to their own strength—their huge front line—for an answer. Mikan, Pollard, and Mikkelsen hit key baskets, and the Lakers worked their way back into the game.

With time running down and the score tied, 76–76, the Lakers brought the ball up the floor for what they figured would be the last shot. John Kundla had drawn up a play for Mikan, who had already dropped in 38 points, and all 5,000-plus packed into the Edgerton Park Sports Arena expected as much. Arnie Risen, with help from his teammates, blanketed Mikan, denying him the ball. With the final seconds of regulation ticking away, Tony Jaros found himself forty feet from the basket, still dribbling, still hoping Mikan would find a way to break free. Mikan screamed at him to shoot and, with four seconds left on the game clock, Jaros released a high-arching set shot that seemed to drift to the basket in slow motion. The ball fell through the net and the Lakers dragged themselves off the court, 78–76 victors.

More than a half century after the game, Royals players still shook their heads over the way they always seemed to come up just a little short against the Lakers. Mikan, they all agreed, was the difference, but there seemed to be no answer to how to defend against him.

"We tried everything," said Bobby Wanzer, "from double-teaming him to trying to shut down everybody else and letting George get what he got. It never seemed to work. They were a great team, and they were tough to contain. A couple of years in a row, we all dropped in on George at the end of the game. We thought they couldn't shoot that well from outside, but they did. Tony Jaros and Herm Schaefer and some of those fellas knocked the ball down."

"We could never stop Mikan," added Bill Calhoun, a Royals reserve. "We tried to double-team him, with Davies coming off his man to help Arnie Risen out, but that left Herm Schaefer free, and he killed us. The first time we tried that double-teaming, Schaefer absolutely killed us. The game wasn't even close."

The game highlighted one of the league's biggest mistakes in its team alignment. For a half decade, the Lakers and Royals had been two of the best teams in basketball, but by placing them in the same division, the BAA, first, and then the NBA kept them from ever squaring off in the playoff finals. From a marketing perspective, it would have made more sense to exploit the rivalry by placing them in different divisions.

"If you read about the rivalry between Boston and the L.A. Lakers," Arnie Risen noted, "they were in different divisions and they got to meet every year in the finals. Well, our finals were in the division rather than the playoff finals."

The win over Rochester seemed to rejuvenate the Lakers. Beginning with a first-round series against the Chicago Stags, Minneapolis ran off six straight playoff wins, sweeping three-game sets against the Stags, the Fort Wayne Pistons, and the Anderson Packers. Mikan, all business as usual, went on a rampage, burning his brother and the Stags for 30 and 34 points in their abbreviated series. The Stags pounded Mikan relentlessly, sacrificing players to fouls with the hope that they might neutralize him, but the tactics only fired him up. The Lakers then made short work of the Pistons before utterly destroying the Packers, 75–50 and 90–71. By the time the last semifinal game had ended, Mikan was averaging more than 30 points per game for the playoffs and the Lakers were headed to the championship round for the third consecutive year.

Next up were the Syracuse Nationals, a team with the best overall record in the NBA, the league's toughest coach, the nastiest front line in the business next to the Lakers, and a following that would frighten Genghis Khan.

And, to top it off, they had the home-court advantage.

Mikan would call the 1949–50 NBA finals "the roughest, toughest series I ever played with anybody," and for sheer physical brutality, the series was unparalleled in early NBA history. The players punished each other, fought with each other, ran each other up and down the floor to the point of complete exhaustion, and, in the process, touched off a rivalry that would continue to grow as long as George Mikan played in the NBA.

To understand the cause of all the commotion, you only had to look as far as Al Cervi, the Nats' player-coach. When Nats owner Danny Biasone put his team together, he had Al Cervi in mind for a coach, not only because Cervi had an excellent basketball mind, but also because having Cervi coaching the Nats would be the ultimate jab, aside from a championship itself, at Rochester Royals owner Les Harrison. Harrison and Biasone didn't like each other much, and not just because the two upstate New York teams had become bitter rivals. Harrison had made life miserable for Biasone when Biasone was trying to enter the league, and if Biasone could pay back some of that misery in stealing Cervi away from the Royals, all the better.

Cervi had clawed and scrapped his way to the top. He'd learned the game on New York playgrounds and had never played college ball. He stood five-eleven, had the temperament of an ornery terrier, and fully expected everyone else on his teams to follow suit.

"Al was a fiery guy, a competitor," said Red Rocha, who played under Cervi in Syracuse. "He was not good at putting things on the blackboard, but when he was in the game, he knew exactly what needed to be done. His real strength was his motivational strength. He motivated us."

Hall of Famer Dolph Schayes admitted to being put off by some of

Cervi's hollering and courtside theatrics, but he was impressed by Cervi's ability to connect with his players.

"He was able to put across his message to 'play like I do,' and we did," Schayes said. "Al was a very feisty guy, defensive-minded—a hard-nose. We played very aggressively, and that was his style."

The Nats' roster was packed with tough guys. Alex Hannum, George Ratkovicz, and Paul Seymour were huge, brawling front-liners. Billy Gabor, nicknamed "The Bullet" because of his speed, was a guard with a prizefighter's mentality. All had been involved in their fair share of fights.

None of this concerned the Lakers too much. They had their own tough guys, and they'd been to the wars with the Nationals. In one of his more memorable fights, Mikan had clocked Seymour with a punch that players were talking about years after the confrontation.

What worried the Lakers—or any other team playing the Nats, for that matter—was six-eight forward Dolph Schayes, who, like Jim Pollard, combined height and athleticism into a formidable package. Schayes didn't have Pollard's natural quickness, but he compensated for it by relentless movement out on the floor—and he could hit his shot from anywhere on the court.

"Dolph was the only six-eight guy who could hit from the outside," said Fuzzy Levane, who, like Al Cervi, had been beaten by the Lakers when he was playing for Rochester, and who was now facing them with Syracuse. "In our time, big men were inside players, but Dolph could play inside and outside. The big guys couldn't play him outside."

Vern Mikkelsen, for one, had a tough time keeping up with Schayes.

"If they'd had a three-point shot at that time, he would have set scoring records," he said. "He was always running, and it was hard work. I kind of like those deals where you beat up on a guy. Stand still, don't run around, quit bothering me."

Schayes was just twenty years old when he joined the Nats in 1948, and as reserve guard John "Whitey" Macknowsky, Schayes's roommate, remembered, the Nats conspired to toughen him up to the NBA's—and Cervi's—standards.

"He was a good ballplayer but he was a very passive guy," Macknowsky remembered. "They were knocking him around and he never dished it out. A bunch of us on the team got together and said, 'If the guy doesn't toughen up, we're not going anywhere.' So everybody started taking shots at him during practice, and that went on for two, three, or four days. He was getting angry about the whole thing, and he and Seymour almost got into fisticuffs. We finally told him it was all a setup and he accepted that. It's what we had to do. We had to toughen him up."

The series opened with two games in Syracuse, and if it went all seven games, four would be played at the State Fair Coliseum. The home court seemed especially important in this series. The Nats had posted a 34–1 record at home during the regular season, compared to the Lakers' 33–1 mark, so if the Lakers were going to win their third championship in a row, they'd have to steal at least one game on the road. John Kundla firmly believed that Game 1 was the key to the entire series. The Lakers had to win it, plain and simple.

Mikan came out firing. Cervi tried every defensive combination he could think of, but nothing stopped him. The Lakers rarely lost when Mikan scored more than 30 points, but in this game, which saw him setting a new State Fair Coliseum record by putting up 37, the big offensive production didn't seem to matter. Syracuse had firepower of its own. With just over a minute left and the Lakers trailing, 66–64, Kundla called a time-out and set up a play for Jim Pollard. Syracuse, expecting the play to go to either Pollard or Mikan, sagged their defense on the two. Bud Grant, who had been inserted into the game to guard Cervi, suddenly found himself in the middle of the action.

Grant, a three-sport star at the University of Minnesota who played two years as a Lakers reserve before correctly deciding that football was his game, couldn't believe he had the ball in his hands at such an important point in the game.

"We were going to run a double pick for Pollard," he remembered. "Pollard was going to come around behind the two of us and shoot. He came around and went up in the air, and dropped the ball off to me. I shot and tied the game."

Cervi immediately called time-out. The Nats, he decided, would freeze the ball until the last few seconds of the game. The final shot would be taken by Dolph Schayes or, if he was covered, Whitey Macknowsky, who was having a good game. The plan called for Cervi to handle the ball and, at the last possible instant, dish it to either Schayes or Macknowsky. The rest of the team was to clear out of the way, leaving the lane open.

The Nats inbounded and the play began, as planned.

The team members would replay and second-guess the last moments of the game in their minds for many years to come.

"All of a sudden, instead of giving the ball to Dolph, Cervi's taking the ball down the center toward the basket," Macknowsky said. "None of us expected this. We had all cleared out, and we expected Dolph to have the ball."

Fortunately for the Lakers, Bud Grant wasn't at all surprised.

"I don't know if everybody else knew, but *I* knew Cervi was going to take the shot," he said. "I mean, he's the coach. He's a very good player, but I knew he was going to take the shot and look for a foul. I put myself in the position to block the shot."

Cervi drove the lane and tried an awkward, underhanded flip toward the basket, but Mikan got a piece of the shot and Grant came up with the ball. Bobby Harrison streaked up the floor ahead of everybody else, and Grant rifled a pass to him. With only a couple seconds remaining, Harrison had no time to call for a time-out or even think of what he was doing.

"I took two dribbles to the half-court line and fired," he remembered, "and the ball went in."

"Harrison threw it from mid-court," Macknowsky said of the improbable winning basket. "It banged off the backboard and went in. The game ended. The people were stunned. Cervi ran out of the gym, grabbed his clothes out of the locker, and jumped in his car. He never went to take a shower."

Cervi, of course, had a different take on his final shot. "I was fouled on that play," he'd always insist.

The Lakers celebrated as if they'd won the deciding game of the championship series—and, in a way, they had. Winning the opener on the road not only set the tone for the playoff series; it put the home-court advantage in their favor.

"That locker room after the game," Bud Grant recalled, "was about as happy a group of guys as I've ever seen."

In the celebration following the game, John Kundla let slip a juicy piece of information that would haunt the Lakers in the second game of the series.

"I told a reporter that Mikan hated the smoke [in the Coliseum]," he remembered. Mikan had trouble breathing in the cloud of cigarette and cigar smoke that hung over the court like a cloud. The papers published his remarks, with predictable results. "We came out the next day and you couldn't see across the court for all the smoke," Kundla said. "Everybody was smoking a cigar."

The game itself differed significantly from the opener. Mikan, ignoring the smoke, again topped the 30-point mark, hitting for 32, but the Nats played an up-tempo game that left the Lakers in the dust. Bud Grant, playing more than usual, held Cervi to a pair of field goals (and seven points overall), and Jim Pollard, with 16 points, was steady as usual, but six different Nats scored in double figures. Syracuse prevailed, 91–85, and Cervi confidently predicted more running when the Nats met the Lakers for the next game in St. Paul.

"Except for that big man Mr. Mikan we have a better ball club," Cervi wrote in a guest column published in the *Syracuse Herald-Journal*. "Make no mistake about that. Even with him in the game we're just as good."

Mikkelsen and Pollard, Cervi continued, had not been able to keep up with the fast-paced Nationals offense. They had to be rested, giving the Nats an edge on the boards. "Given a fair share of the breaks the rest of the way, we will win the overall championship," Cervi concluded.

Mikan reacted to Cervi's bulletin-board material the same way he responded to Ray Meyer's reports at DePaul. The Lakers mauled the Nats in Game 3, 91–77, with Mikan scoring 28 points. Vern Mikkelsen enjoyed one of his finest games as a pro, hitting for 27 points in a game thoroughly dominated by the Lakers. Billy Gabor missed the contest with tonsillitis, and Paul Seymour sprained his ankle during the game, leaving the Nats seriously shorthanded. But the real story was in the rough play under the boards. The officials called 53 personal fouls—30 against the Lakers—but Dolph Schayes was the only disqualification for either team. Without Schayes, the Nats were no match for the Lakers down the stretch.

The Lakers played the fourth game in front of the largest home crowd—10,512—in the team's brief history. Mikan, Pollard, and Mikkelsen combined for 59 points, and the Lakers won their second game at home, 77–69. Even the usually optimistic Syracuse press conceded that the Lakers' 3–1 lead in the series might be more than the Nats could handle. To win the championship, the Nats would have to take three straight from the Lakers.

"The Nats do not seem capable of turning the amazing feat," wrote the *Herald-Journal*, "but there is no compromise or surrender in their ranks and they still talk of the big rally."

But it wasn't over yet. The Lakers came out flat in Game 5, and Syracuse easily took its second game, 83–76. Cervi assigned Paul Seymour the task of stopping Jim Pollard, and the Syracuse guard held him to six points. The Nats played another fast-paced game, nearly running the Lakers out of Syracuse, leading by as many as 21 points before Minneapolis staged a futile rally toward the end of the game. Mikan dropped in 28 points, but after five games, the physical play was taking its toll. Mikan played the entire game without a rest, as he usually did, but his temper was running short. George Ratkovicz, Alex Hannum, and Ed Peterson took turns beating on Mikan, pulling 16 fouls between them, and referee Pat Kennedy had to separate Mikan and Ratkovicz when the two former Gears teammates tangled under the boards. Mikan felt fortunate to get out of Syracuse, bruised but intact.

The Nats still needed to win two games for the championship, but the Game 5 loss put the onus back on the Lakers. If they didn't pull off the next game at home, they were in for a lot of trouble in a seventh and deciding game in Syracuse.

This was precisely the kind of game Mikan thrived on. He and his teammates were finally back on their familiar home floor in Minneapolis, where they had never lost a playoff game, and Mikan was spoiling for a fight. He was still black and blue from his muggings at the hands of the Nats' front line. Pollard was equally testy. Paul Seymour had taken him out of his game with a combination of solid defense and outright thuggery, and Pollard had taken enough. If the Nats wanted to mix it up, he was more than willing.

From the onset, this contest more resembled a one-sided hockey game between two bitter rivals than an NBA championship game. Long after the tempers had cooled and the wounds had healed, Arnie Ferrin remembered more about the violence of the game than the game itself. "I just remember it because there were at least three fist-throwing fights during that game," he said.

Not that there was that much else to remember: the game itself wasn't very competitive. The Lakers established a comfortable early lead and never relinquished it. Mikan wanted the ball, and he got it—often. The Lakers led 51–30 by halftime, due largely to the efforts of Mikan and Pollard, though both were in foul trouble for much of the game.

Pollard, in particular, was taking nothing from anyone. He and Seymour were at each other's throats from the beginning. With only five minutes gone, the two went sprawling after a loose ball and came up swinging. Players and fans spilled out onto the floor, but the officials were able to restore order with little difficulty. This was not the case a short time later, when Pollard was flagrantly fouled by Whitey Macknowsky while going in for a layup. Still enraged from his earlier fight, Pollard threw the basketball at Macknowsky's head and the two squared off. This time, the police had to be summoned to break up the fighting and usher the fans back into the stands.

The Minneapolis fans, normally partisan but sedate, contributed to the tension. Al Cervi was accustomed to inciting Syracuse fans in his favor; in Minneapolis, his theatrics only riled up the spectators against him. They'd already done everything but hire a hit man to take care of Seymour and, in very short order, Billy Gabor would be added to the list. Like Pollard, Gabor was involved in two fights; one with Slater Martin, another with Swede Carlson.

The game officials tried desperately to keep the players, fans, and game under control. They called a tight game, with lots of fouls, hoping to keep the physical contact to a minimum, but this only led to an intolerable parade to the free-throw line. Ironically, Syracuse, normally an excellent free-throw-shooting team, hit only 33 of their 53 charity shots during the game.

Cervi worked over the officials relentlessly until finally, during the third quarter, the antagonism came to a head after Mikan, Cervi, Carlson, and others converged and collided during a chase for a loose ball. Rather than call a foul, referee John Nucatola called for a jump ball. Cervi exploded. He directed all his frustration—over the game and the series, which were rapidly slipping away—at Nucatola, and, in what might have been more an act of mercy than punishment, Nucatola tossed him from the game.

The rest of the game was anticlimactic. Despite Dolph Schayes's 23 points and Macknowsky's 17, the Lakers beat the Nats at their own fast-paced game, underscored by Mikan's actually running down the court and finishing three fast breaks. The NBA's first season was officially over. The Lakers were the NBA's first champions.

Mikan's share of the championship money came to $1,500—hardly a princely sum, but enough to further sweeten the taste of victory. The NBA's inaugural season had been rewarding but not entirely convincing: there had been too many teams, many barely scraping by, leading to a strange playoff structure that, at some times, seemed more a case of attrition than a matter of the best team winning. But there was no doubting, in Mikan's mind, that the best team had won.

It was time to get away and relax, play a little golf, enjoy the family, and forget about basketball for a while. The new season would begin soon enough.

And, as Mikan would learn, the 1950–51 season would be one of the most tumultuous in the history of professional basketball. The new league would be seriously tested.

Twelve

SHOCKS AND CHANGES

BY THE SPRING of 1950, George Mikan had won every conceivable basketball award on the college or professional levels. He'd been a three-time All-American at DePaul, two-time College Player of the Year, and Most Valuable Player in the National Basketball Association; he held scoring records, and he'd been on teams that won the NIT title, two NBL titles, a BAA title, and now the NBA title. His parents had kept scrapbooks of his (and Eddie's) achievements, and Gramps stored some of George's trophies in Mikan's Tavern, just in case the regulars had forgotten who George Mikan was. Unfortunately, a 1949 fire at George's parents' house had wiped out most of the scrapbooks, press clippings, and photographs of the Mikan brothers' DePaul days. As sad as it was, a new collection of trophies, awards, and scrapbooks was beginning to build up, with perhaps the greatest recognition of Mikan's achievements coming after the 1949–50 NBA season.

Half of the twentieth century had passed, and to mark the occasion, the Associated Press decided to poll its sportswriters and broadcasters and name the top figures in the country's major sports for the first half century. Babe Ruth was voted "Mr. Baseball," Jim Thorpe "Mr. Football," and Bobby Jones "Mr. Golf"; similar recognition was accorded Jack Dempsey (boxing), Bill Tilden (tennis), and Man O' War (horse racing).

George Mikan was named "Mr. Basketball."

The award, he'd say, long after he'd retired, made him happier than any other issued to him during his career, and for the rest of his life, he would often add "Mr. Basketball" to his signature when he autographed programs, basketballs, jerseys, and other memorabilia for fans. Friends and teammates would tease him about it; opponents would occasionally use the title in derision to fire him up. Mikan could afford to laugh it off. Only one person would ever receive such recognition, and there had been a lot of good basketball players who might have received the title.

Mikan was especially pleased and humbled to find himself on a list with Babe Ruth, the childhood idol who had signed his baseball more than a half a lifetime ago.

"I felt determined to live up to the honor in the time I had left," he reflected in his autobiography. "I never had to look any further than that award for inspiration."

"Mr. Basketball" wasn't George Mikan's only informal title.

His other popular nickname, "Gentle Giant," amused teammates and opposing players alike. Off court, he smiled easily and often. An effective ambassador for the early NBA, Mikan could always be counted on for a good quote or two for the next day's papers, and the press liked him. He enjoyed mingling with the fans, at home or on the road. His congenial personality seemed to belie his massive size and the way he used it to his advantage.

On court, there was nothing gentle or easygoing about him. Players marveled at his intensity, and they avoided his flying elbows at all costs. At DePaul, Ray Meyer had encouraged him to swing his free arm and elbow when he was turning to take his hook shot, and Mikan had perfected the move. If you were standing too close when he turned and threw out his arm-bar, you could be knocked senseless. It was like being clubbed with a baseball bat. The same thing with rebounds: you didn't want to be within range of his flying elbows.

"They called him the Gentle Giant, but he was physically tough," said Bobby Harrison. "He had what we called 'educated elbows.' "

Swede Carlson, who set Mikan up with many passes in the early Laker days, remembered just how educated those elbows were. "He could raise that left elbow and move to the basket, and the bodies would just start to fly," he said. And, Carlson noted, it wasn't just the elbows that made Mikan so rough. "I used to like to pass him the ball, cut out around him and then listen to the sound the guy guarding me made when he ran into George."

"Without a doubt, he had the sharpest elbows that God ever made, and I mean that sincerely," said Jack Phelan, who played with Mikan in college and against him in the pros. "You know that statue out there in Minneapolis?" he asked, referring to the life-sized statue of Mikan at the Target Center, home of the present-day Minnesota Timberwolves. "Part of my teeth are on that statue."

Mikan only had to refer to his first game back with the Chicago Gears, when he'd been schooled by Cowboy Edwards, for justification for his rough play. If you were new, you would be tested. You couldn't be intimidated.

Clyde Lovellette, drafted by the Lakers in 1953 as Mikan's future replacement, remembered how George taught him the ropes, much the way Price Brookfield had taken Mikan aside after his first game.

"I got more tattoos from him in practice," Lovellette said. "He taught me the game, how to survive. George told me, 'You can survive in the league, but you've got to be able to give it and you've got to be able to take it.'"

You had to be bold if you were going to pass through Mikan's territory near the basket. It didn't matter if you were friend or foe: he didn't want you around.

"He had a temper," John Oldham remembered. "He'd say, 'Hey, man, this is my territory. Don't come around the basket.'"

One by one, Laker opponents learned that Mikan's terrain could be a dangerous place to visit.

"He not only hated losing—he hated losing his stature in the league as top man," Red Rocha explained. "He liked that position and he wasn't about to give it up easily."

Most teams set up offenses similar to the offenses played in college. Guards would fire the ball in to the pivot man and cut off the pass. If the guard was open for a clear shot at the basket, the center would pass it back.

Passing the ball in to Mikan, more often than not, meant watching a ball disappear into a black hole. Mikan was a fine passer—some said exceptional—but he was more inclined to turn to the basket.

And God help you if you were a Laker guard and you cut anywhere near the pivot.

"We had to stay out on the floor," Bobby Harrison recalled. "We couldn't get under the basket because that was George's territory."

Paul Walther, a sharpshooting left-hander from the University of Tennessee, learned just how little patience Mikan had for intruding guards shortly after joining the Lakers for the 1949–50 season. Walther had a habit of cutting a little too close to Mikan's turf for Mikan's liking, and the Laker pivot man let him hear about it after the first few infractions. When that failed to make an impression, he took matters into his own hands—literally.

"I threw the ball in to him and was driving in without the ball," Walther said, "and George held the ball with one hand and he grabbed me by the other as I was going by. He said, 'This is my area.'"

A few weeks later, Walther was gone.

All sports have unspoken forms of retribution. In baseball, if you were pitching and you hit the opposing team's best player, odds stood just about even or better that one of your team's star players would get drilled before the game was over—maybe even during his next at-bat. The same with basketball. Rough play begat retaliation, and Mikan applied it as well as anyone.

"I was a very aggressive and fiery-tempered player," noted Billy Gabor, who faced Mikan and the Lakers many times during his career with the Syracuse Nationals. "One time, late in the second half, I was going in for a layup and Mikan clobbered me. Paul Seymour went up to Mikan and gave him a shove: 'George, you didn't have to hit him that hard.' Mikan said, 'He had one coming.' I was down on the ground, but I looked up at Seymour and said, 'He's right, Paul. I got him in the first half.' He waited for the right time to retaliate."

Any team coached by Al Cervi was bound to play rough, aggressive basketball, and with such players as Paul Seymour, Billy Gabor, and Wally Osterkorn roaming the hardwood, the Nationals could hammer with the best of them. Laker guard Myer "Whitey" Skoog recalled another incident between Mikan and the Nats, though this one involved George King, a relatively mild-mannered guard.

"Mikan was a hard competitor," Skoog said, "and one time he was going to shoot a layup and he got tunneled by George King. George went down flat on his can and he lay there for quite a while before he was able to get up and play again. Well, about a month later, we were playing in Minneapolis and King went in for a layup. Mikan didn't do much about blocking the shot, but he blocked King—right up into the third row. And I heard him say, right out loud, 'I'll teach that son of a gun.'"

Mikan could be testy when reporters called him on his rough play. One night, after a very physical game, Mikan pulled up his jersey and showed reporters how bruised he'd become during the course of a single game.

"Take a look at my body," he challenged a sportswriter who had been giving him a hard time about his nasty elbows. "How do you think I got all those welts?"

Today's NBA, although still plenty rough, penalizes players for flagrant fouls, and will suspend players for fighting. Rough play and fighting were the norm in Mikan's time, even if the league didn't like it.

"In my first couple of years, there was a fight in almost every game," remembered George King, who added that, at six feet, he was too small to take on guys half a foot taller and much bulkier that he was. "I always found the water cooler," he quipped.

Each team had at least one enforcer. These players committed hard "message" fouls on other teams' best players, intimidated smaller players cutting through the lanes, "mediated" on-court confrontations, and jumped in when a fight broke out. They weren't always the biggest men on the court. Players like Billy Gabor, Al Cervi, Al McGuire, and Slater Martin, who established themselves as tough customers during their careers, were usually the shortest players on the court—but they were fearless. They'd go up against anyone, large or small.

Most players avoided fighting with Mikan because of his sheer size, and Mikan preferred to limit the rough stuff to the game itself, when he would receive some protection from an official's whistle. He rarely started a fight or took off after a player. When he did square off against someone, he did so with some reluctance.

"We'd always kid George after he got in a fight," remembered Dick Schnittker, a teammate later in Mikan's career. "George was the best defensive fighter. He'd swing and back away. They still do that, to some extent. You didn't want to hurt yourself."

On April 25, 1950, two days after the Lakers had won their championship series against Syracuse, Boston Celtics owner Walter Brown made NBA history at the annual NBA draft meetings.

"Boston takes Charles Cooper of Duquesne," he announced to the small group of team owners and officials seated in a hotel room in Chicago's Bismarck Hotel.

For a few moments, no one in the room said a word. The announcement, although not entirely surprising, carried a lot of weight. Pro basketball, still struggling for a foothold on the American sports scene, was taking a giant step. Not everyone in the room believed it was for the better.

"Walter, don't you know he's a colored boy?" one of the owners finally chimed in, breaking the awkward silence.

"I don't give a damn if he's striped or plaid or polka-dot," Brown responded, his voice rising. "Boston takes Charles Cooper of Duquesne."

African-Americans had been playing basketball from the very beginnings of the game. Two of the greatest and most popular teams the sport had ever seen—the New York Renaissance and the Harlem Globetrotters, both eventually enshrined as *teams* into the Naismith Hall of Fame—had been strictly African-American teams. A handful of African-Americans played briefly in the old National Basketball League. College teams fielded black players. In short, basketball fans were used to seeing black players on the court. This wasn't the same as a few years before, when Jackie Robinson broke the color barrier of the National Pastime. Baseball was a sacred institution, an American tradition, a sport totally ingrained in the national consciousness; pro basketball belonged to the die-hards, whose numbers couldn't even begin to compete with baseball's.

Nevertheless, the game was about to change—significantly. Within fifty years, more than eighty percent of the NBA's players would be African-Americans.

Walter Brown's announcement ended a year of contentious debate between owners, league officials, and other insiders who believed, depending upon whom you were talking to, that allowing African-Americans to compete in the NBA would be either inevitable and beneficial to the new league, or a fatal blow causing the loss of an already thin fan base. There had never been a written rule prohibiting African-Americans from playing in the NBA, but there had been a strong, unspoken understanding among the teams' owners: it was just too risky to bring black players into the league, at least for the time being.

Ironically, this belief stemmed not from players' racist attitudes toward African-Americans, or even from the belief that fans would stay away from the arenas if teams employed black players; the fear sprang from how drafting black players would affect the NBA's relationship with Abe Saperstein and the Harlem Globetrotters. After all he'd done to bring fans out to see pro games, Saperstein was bound to be unhappy about the prospects of NBA teams competing with him to sign the best available black talent.

The discussions about signing African-American players had begun at a meeting at the NBA offices in 1949. Ned Irish wanted to sign Sweetwater Clifton to the Knicks. Clifton was playing for the Globetrotters, but he was unhappy with his pay and the amount of travel required in the Globetrotters' busy touring schedule, and he wanted out. The Knicks needed a big center to compete against Mikan and other big centers. Clifton seemed like the perfect fit.

Some NBA owners—particularly Eddie Gottlieb of the Philadelphia Warriors—opposed the move. The Trotters had been saviors to the Philadelphia organization, which struggled to attract fans, even with a first-rate talent like Jumpin' Joe Fulks. With the Globetrotters' exhibition games filling the Philadelphia Arena, Gottlieb owed Saperstein more than a small debt of gratitude. Gottlieb wasn't alone in his thinking. Other franchises depended heavily upon revenues from Globetrotter games to boost sagging attendance.

Carl Bennett, business manager of the Fort Wayne Pistons and a member of the NBA's Executive Committee, told the assembled group in Chicago that he'd had a conversation about integration with Fred Zollner, the influential Pistons owner, and Zollner had no objection to it. Getting Gottlieb, another Executive Committee member, and some of the other owners to go along with it was problematic.

"It was delayed somewhat because of the Globetrotters," Bennett recalled, reflecting on the discussions about integration. "The league was convinced that the Globetrotters wouldn't play exhibitions for them and sell out their houses."

The owners voted on whether to permit the signing of African-American players, and the first tally came out negative. Since there was no rule actually prohibiting blacks from playing, the vote wasn't binding—just an indication of where the owners stood. An angry Ned Irish went home and stewed, and Sweetwater Clifton continued on with the Globetrotters.

Irish broached the topic at another meeting about six months later, although he was much more forceful this time around. Irish was well aware of his clout in the NBA. He'd been instrumental in the founding of the BAA and, later, the NBA, and his Madison Square Garden facility, when it was actually used for pro basketball, was the envy of the other owners.

"Either I get Sweetwater Clifton or we may not stay in the league," Irish declared, beating his fists on the table for emphasis.

Another vote was taken. This time, the owners voted, by a 6–5 margin, to allow teams to sign blacks.

Eddie Gottlieb was apoplectic. After the vote was taken, he followed Carl Bennett out the door and confronted him in the hallway. "Bennett, you just voted to ruin pro basketball," he said. "In five years, it'll be seventy-five percent black and nobody will be coming to the games."

Years later, Bennett laughed when he remembered the conversation. "Well, he was fifty percent right," he said. "When you're in those stands, you're cheering for great ballplayers, not whether they're black or green or pink-skinned."

Sid Hartman, representing the Lakers at the meeting, also remembered Gottlieb's reaction to the vote, and how he again voiced his concern about how it would affect the NBA's relationship with the Harlem Globetrotters. "Eddie Gottlieb was sitting next to me, and he said, 'Oh-oh, Abe's gonna go crazy,'" he recalled. "Everybody knew that Abe Saperstein would cut out all the double-headers, and in those days they couldn't get along without the double-headers."

Irish didn't get around to signing Sweetwater Clifton until after Walter Brown selected Chuck Cooper in the second round of the 1950 draft.* In that same draft, the Washington Capitols, hoping to add an African-American fan base to bolster their slumping attendance figures, selected West Virginia State's Earl Lloyd in the ninth round and North Carolina College's Harold Hunter in the tenth round.

And, as Gottlieb predicted, Abe Saperstein responded immediately to the Boston and Washington owners' decisions to draft African-American

---

*Historically speaking, there were three important "firsts" in NBA integration: Chuck Cooper was the first African-American to be drafted; Sweetwater Clifton was the first to be formally signed; and Earl Lloyd was the first to actually play in a game.

players. The Globetrotters, he announced, the day after the draft, would no longer be appearing at the Boston Garden or the Uline Arena.

Walter Brown was unimpressed by the threat. "As far as I'm concerned," he retorted, "Abe Saperstein is out of the Boston Garden right now."*

A little over a week later, on May 3, Saperstein sold Sweetwater Clifton's contract to the New York Knicks for $12,500. Clifton, in the final year of his contract with the Globetrotters, had made it clear that he had no intention of re-signing with the team. Saperstein reasoned he might as well cash in while he could.

The Lakers opened the 1950–51 season relatively intact. Herm Schaefer and Swede Carlson, two valuable members of the original team, had retired, but the starting five—Mikan, Pollard, Mikkelsen, Martin, and Harrison— were back, as were Tony Jaros, Bud Grant, and Arnie Ferrin. In the draft, the Lakers picked up Joe Hutton Jr., son of Hamline's head coach and an All-American, and Kevin O'Shea, a highly sought-after six-two guard from Notre Dame. On paper, the team was stronger than ever.

But so were the other NBA teams, most notably the Rochester Royals, Philadelphia Warriors, and, perhaps making the most significant strides, the New York Knicks and Boston Celtics. The Indianapolis Olympians, Western Division winners in their first year in the league, looked to repeat with Alex Groza (second to Mikan in scoring in 1949–50), Ralph Beard, and Wah Wah Jones, and one could never dismiss the Fort Wayne Pistons or Syracuse Nats, who, like the Lakers and Royals, did very little retooling during the offseason, but who were strong, well-coached franchises.

The league's balance could be attributed to two major factors: a tremendous influx of new talent, and the distribution of players from teams that had folded. The 1949 and 1950 drafts had been extremely generous to the league, in terms of future superstars and Hall of Famers. The Lakers, of course, had signed Mikkelsen and Martin. Philadelphia landed Paul Arizin, the College Player of the Year in 1950. The St. Louis Bombers took

---

*Cooler heads would prevail, and the Globetrotters would appear in the Boston Garden in the future.

hometown favorite "Easy" Ed Macauley, who wound up with Boston when the Bombers folded. The Tri-Cities Blackhawks drafted Bob Cousy, the collegiate superstar from Holy Cross and easily the most popular college player on the East Coast. The Washington Capitols snagged Earl Lloyd; Dick Schnittker, Ohio State's six-five All-American; and Bill Sharman, who, in a few months, would become one of the cornerstones of the Celtics' franchise. The Knicks rebuilt their team by drafting Northeast Missouri's Harry "the Horse" Gallatin, Colgate's Ernie Vandeweghe, and St. John's "Tricky" Dick McGuire; all would enjoy successful careers in the NBA.

The balance of talent (and power) shifted again when six teams dropped out of the NBA prior to the 1950–51 season. Players were distributed, without a great deal of fanfare, to the remaining eleven teams, and very little was said until the Chicago Stags folded and their players were being dispersed. Three Stags players—Max Zaslofsky, Andy Phillip, and Bob Cousy—became the subject of a power struggle between New York, Boston, and Philadelphia. The three teams' powerful owners insisted on drafting the high-scoring Zaslofsky. Phillip, one of Illinois's former "Whiz Kids" and an outstanding playmaking guard, was the owners' second preference. Cousy, as good as he was, generated very little enthusiasm.

Maurice Podoloff, tired of hearing the owners bickering over Zaslofsky, placed the three players' names in a hat and had the owners draw. Ned Irish, choosing first, picked Zaslofsky, adding another piece to his suddenly rich-in-talent franchise. Eddie Gottlieb picked second and drew Phillip, leaving Cousy for a very disappointed Walter Brown.

Cousy may be the greatest unwanted player in the history of professional sports. His superlative passing and ballhandling were second to none, and the two-time All-American had led Holy Cross to national prominence. The Celtics could have selected him as their territorial draft choice, but Red Auerbach, the Celtics' new coach, wasn't going to buckle to popular pressure.

"I don't give a damn for sentiment, and that goes for Cousy," he said in his inimitably straightforward, often blustery fashion. "The only thing that counts for me is ability, and Cousy hasn't proven to me he's got that ability. I'm not interested in bringing someone in just because he's a local yokel. That won't bring more than a dozen people into the building on a regular basis. What will bring fans in is a winning team, and that's what I want to have."

Auerbach believed that Cousy possessed some major skills; what concerned him were what he perceived to be Cousy's weaknesses. Cousy was extremely quick, but he was short, and Boston needed a big man. As talented as he was on offense, Cousy couldn't play a lick of defense. And Auerbach wasn't impressed with Cousy's style.

"I had seen Cousy play," he remembered. "He was very flashy. He wasn't the first guy to dribble behind his back, a guy named Bob Davies was, but he was the guy who made it popular. The local press was all over me to take Cousy. I wasn't interested in making the press happy—I had a ball club to build. You don't build a club with guards, you build it with big men. So, when it was my turn to pick, I took Charlie Share out of Bowling Green. He was six-eight, [a] big, strong guy."

Cousy, drafted by Tri-Cities, was almost immediately traded to Chicago for former LSU guard Frank "Flash" Brian, who had a very strong local following.

Cousy, the booby prize of the three Stags players, only went on to lead the NBA in assists eight straight years; be selected first team All-NBA ten consecutive years; lead the Celtics in scoring four straight years, and in assists for thirteen years in a row. Then there was that little matter of all those NBA championships—nine, to be exact—over the course of Cousy's career. Next to George Mikan, he became the most popular player in pro basketball, and until Bill Russell and Wilt Chamberlain came around in 1956 and 1959, respectively, Mikan and Cousy *were* the NBA.

Cousy was on hand, along with Arizin, Schnittker, and a host of others when the College All-Stars tried to break the Lakers' stranglehold on the annual College All-Star Classic in Chicago. The Lakers had taken two straight, including the previous year's shootout, in which Mikan set the game's all-time scoring record with 31 points.

Mikan, who had led the All-Stars to a victory when he was on the team in 1946, and who'd led the pros to victories in 1948 and 1949, looked forward to the game. It was an informal opening to another new season, and after a summer of haunting the Twin Cities' golf courses, Mikan was ready to get back to work.

Mikan expected a tough game, and he got it. The All-Stars double-teamed him throughout the game, playing the kind of defense Mikan was used to seeing in the pros. With the opposition holding him to a mere five field goals (and 14 points overall), Mikan spent much of the game passing instead of shooting. Jim Pollard led the Lakers' scoring with 17 points, and Vern Mikkelsen contributed 12. Only Cousy, with 13 points, scored in double figures for the All-Stars. John Kundla was pleased with the Lakers' defensive effort which held the All-Stars' high-powered attack to a mere 54 points. The Lakers led by only two points at halftime, but poured it on in the second half, winning 61–54.

The Lakers' play in the game illustrated the kind of team they'd become. They expected to win—and usually did—but they could be sloppy at times, confident that their huge front line, in general, and Mikan, in specific, would bail them out in the close games. Kundla's offensive system quite rightly relied first on Mikan and then on Pollard, but this could be dangerous if one or both had a bad night. Victories, particularly on the road, could be difficult. The Lakers had all they could handle when they were playing away games against teams like Rochester, New York, and Syracuse. This was especially noticeable when Pollard fractured a cheekbone and missed fourteen games in the middle of the season. The Lakers remained almost impossible to beat at home, but they fought to break even on the road.

The first ominous sign came in the first game of the season, when the Lakers lost in Baltimore, 81–71, signaling the first time in team history that the Lakers ever lost an opening game, at home or on the road. Mikan started the season stronger than usual, but it didn't seem to matter. Teams were gunning for the champs, and until the midway point of the season, when the Lakers caught fire and took fifteen out of seventeen games, the Lakers looked very ordinary. Sportswriters predicted an end to the Lakers' stranglehold on the NBA and of Mikan's domination in the middle. The pared-down league, they crowed, meant more parity between the teams.

Mikan ignored such analysis. His point production was up, and he could see nothing wrong with his team—nothing that a decent winning streak wouldn't cure. The league *was* as competitive as it had been in any year he could remember, but that wasn't a problem. Mikan loved to compete. By the time the regular-season games had been played and the playoffs came around, the Lakers would be ready to defend their title. Of that, Mikan was certain.

After taking his first (and only) head coaching job at DePaul in 1946, Ray Meyer found himself working with a talented but clumsy George Mikan. Meyer's agility drills became legendary and led to Mikan's quick development as a player. (AP IMAGES/ED MALONEY)

Bob Kurland, Oklahoma A&M's star center, future Hall of Famer, and Mikan nemesis in college. (ASSOCIATED PRESS)

Mikan's dominating presence helped DePaul achieve an 81–17 record—and national prominence—during his four years with the team. Mikan was named to All-American teams for three straight years. (COLLEGIATE IMAGES/GETTY IMAGES)

Mikan's first game with Minneapolis, played against the Sheboygan Redskins. The Lakers didn't have a uniform that fit him, so Mikan wore his old Chicago Gears shorts and a "21" (rather than his trademark "99") on his jersey. (ASSOCIATED PRESS)

The 1950 World Champion Minneapolis Lakers: Slater Martin, Billy Hassett, Don "Swede" Carlson, Herm Schaefer, Bobby Harrison, Tony Jaros, Coach John Kundla, Bud Grant, Arnie Ferrin, Jim Pollard, Vern Mikkelsen, and George Mikan.

In the early years of the NBA, Mikan was the league's main attraction and biggest promoter. He played some of his most memorable games in the old Madison Square Garden. New York loved him—and vice versa.

The superstar and his coach: Mikan carries John Kundla on his shoulders following the Lakers' championship win over the New York Knicks on April 12, 1953. Mikan called the 1952–53 championship his "favorite title." (ASSOCIATED PRESS)

Ed Mikan. His pro career would include stints with six NBA teams. (PHOTO COURTESY OF RICH MIKAN)

Brother act: Ed Mikan took over the center position at DePaul after George graduated and moved on to play for the Chicago Gears. As professionals, the two would square off against each other on numerous occasions.
(PHOTO COURTESY OF RICH MIKAN)

George Mikan, as the first commissioner of the Amercan Basketball Association, presenting Larry Brown with the MVP award for the ABA's first all-star game on January 9, 1968. Hall of Famer Rick Barry stands on the right. (NBA PHOTOS/GETTY IMAGES)

A career in trophies, awards, and photos.
(ASSOCIATED PRESS)

Anchors to three Laker dynasties—Kareem Abdul-Jabbar, Shaquille
O'Neal, and George Mikan—in a 1996 photo for *Sports Illustrated*.
(NBA PHOTOS/GETTY IMAGES)

On April 11, 2002, during a ceremony at the Staples Center, the Los Angeles
Lakers honored the Minneapolis Laker teams by hoisting championship banners
and a plaque bearing the names of the Minneapolis team's Hall of Famers.
(AP IMAGES/MARK J. TERRILL)

November 22, 1950

Murray Mendenhall sits in a Northwestern Railroad car and tries to come up with a plan for the game ahead. Like every other coach in the NBA, he's had a bellyful of losing to the Lakers, and, in just a few hours, his Fort Wayne Pistons will be taking the floor in the Minneapolis Auditorium. The Lakers have won twenty-nine straight on their home court—nearly a season's worth of home games—and Mendenhall will be damned if he'll watch his team become victim number thirty. The Pistons usually play competitive ball against the Lakers, but that hasn't prevented George Mikan, Jim Pollard, and the rest from beating them the last seven times they've traveled to Minnesota. In fact, the Pistons have never beaten the Lakers on the road.

The solution, when it comes to Mendenhall, is unbelievably simple.

"We're on the train to Minnesota, and Mendenhall and I are sitting there, talking about the game," Carl Bennett would remember. "And he said, 'Why don't we just sit on the ball? There's no rule against it. Let's keep the ball away from them and see what happens. Maybe we'll get lucky.'"

The Pistons arrive in Minneapolis, and Mendenhall calls a team meeting at the hotel. He details his plan, and his players, as tired of losing to the Lakers as their coach, respond favorably to trying the unusual strategy.

"I don't think any of us felt comfortable that we could win," Pistons guard John Oldham would recall, years later, "so we sort of liked the idea of doing something to aggravate them."

The game plays out exactly as planned. The Pistons win the opening tip. Rather than move the ball up the floor, Larry Foust stands stock-still at center court, holding the ball on his hip. The Lakers, already in their defensive positions, look at each other, trying to figure out what's going on. The 7,021 fans in the stands can't believe what they're seeing. They've come to watch a fast-moving basketball game, and here are ten players standing around as if they're nailed to the floor. Boos and catcalls rain down on the court.

No one knows what to do. There's nothing illegal about what the Pistons are doing, and since this has never been attempted before—at least not to this extent—Stan Stutz and Jocko Collins, the game's officials, are at a loss as to how to proceed. They instruct the Pistons to play ball, but they stay put. The Lakers, Mendenhall shouts at the officials, are playing a zone defense, and his players aren't about to move until Mikan and company leave their posts and come out to play man-to-man defense. Johnny Kundla has no problem with this brand of "stall ball": the Pistons aren't scoring if they're not shooting, and Kundla has no intention of changing the Lakers' defense. If it's going to be a low-scoring game, so be it. The Lakers will win, regardless of how the game plays out.

"It was something we hadn't seen," Arnie Ferrin would remember, "but it really didn't bother me. We felt we were better than them, and that we'd win anyway."

The action is almost nonexistent. The Pistons spread the floor, and every so often Slater Martin attacks the man with the ball, usually with little result other than the Piston passing to an open man, who freezes the ball until someone comes after him. An occasional shot is taken, and every so often one of the teams turns over the ball. The game crawls along. The first quarter ends with the Pistons up 8–7. At halftime, it's 13–11, Lakers' favor.

As boring as it is for players and fans alike, the game demands more caution than usual on the part of the players. Every pass is a potential turnover, every shot a valuable commodity. Mistakes are magnified. Nothing can be taken for granted.

"Obviously, the early part of the game was a little dull for the spectators," George Mikan would recall, "although the drama of it produced terrific tension later in the game."

"If you got a basket," Laker guard Joe Hutton observed, "it was like a piece of gold. You didn't think much about the pressure in the first part of the game, but as the game wore on, you had to be really careful not to make a mistake."

The second half picks up where the first half left off. The Pistons, within striking distance of the Lakers, move even slower and shoot even less. The Lakers, content to protect their meager lead, stand around and watch.

"It was a terrible game," Vern Mikkelsen conceded, "but I didn't blame Johnny Kundla. He said, 'If we get a lead, let them hold the ball. They can't score.'"

The game's pace infuriates Mikan. "This isn't basketball," he screams repeatedly at the Pistons and the officials, to no avail.

The two teams score only nine points between them, and the third quarter ends with the Lakers still ahead, 17–16—a low score at the end of the first quarter of the average game. Murray Mendenhall, however, isn't remotely concerned. His team is one shot away from winning the game.

By this point, the fans have written off the game as a total disaster. For a *while, at the beginning of the game, they booed and threw coins, newspapers, and programs onto the court; some are still raising hell as the fourth quarter opens, but many have left, and others sit in the stands and read the papers.*

Not that they're missing much by not watching the men on the court. The futility has reached a new depth, and the score is still 17–16 with only 6:10 left in the game. Larry Foust breaks the scoreless spell with a free throw and, less than a minute later, Jim Pollard tosses in a free throw to give the Lakers the lead again. The free throw will be Pollard's sole contribution to the final score.

The game winds down, and the Lakers find themselves with the ball in the last minute. It's now their turn to stall, but the Pistons swarm the ball on defense, and the Lakers turn it over. With nine seconds on the clock, Mendenhall calls for a time-out, and the Pistons set up a play. The ball is to go to guard Johnny Oldham, who seldom shoots but who, with a total of five points, has the Pistons' "hot hand." ("He was our leading scorer that night. We called him 'The Gunner,'" Fred Schaus would joke later.) The Pistons inbound the ball, but the Lakers cover Oldham and, with the seconds ticking away, Curly Armstrong hits Larry Foust with a pass. Mikan rushes out as the Pistons center launches his shot near the free throw line. Mikan gets a piece of the ball, but not enough. The ball grazes the top of the backboard and drops through the hoop. The Pistons win, 19–18.

The Minneapolis fans go crazy. For the Pistons, the ordeal now switches to battling through the crowd to reach their dressing room.

According to Johnny Oldham, "Everybody was really upset. We had fisticuffs on the way to the dressing room. A pregnant woman hit me on the top of the head with her umbrella. I got hit on the back of the head with a wet towel. All we were trying to do was get to the dressing room, but we had a distance to go."

When reflecting on the game years later, Bobby Harrison, like many others, including basketball historians, would see the game as a turning point in NBA history: "Our fans got all upset, saying they weren't going to see another game and all that. The future of the league was really in trouble at that point. This had set the game back."

The passing of time would give the game's participants a different perspective. Nearly everyone would agree that it had been a disaster, but the game offered a number of memorable aspects. Between them, the two teams had taken only 31 shots, and they'd hit on only 8 of them. The bulk of the scoring—21 points—had come from the free-throw line. George Mikan scored 15 of his team's 18 points— and he'd had a horrible night, hitting on only 4 of his 11 shots from the field.

Johnny Oldham's 5 points would always stand as a record for the fewest number
of points recorded by a team's high scorer.

Oldham would be laughing about the game more than a half century later.

"My grandson was selling magazines," he'd say, "and I ordered Basketball
Digest. *The first issue I received was about the ball game. He thought his grand-*
daddy was the greatest. That's my only claim to fame: scoring five points and get-
ting four rebounds."

On January 12, 1951, Junius Kellogg, a six-eight center from Manhattan
College, walked into Coach Kenny Norton's office and told him that he had
been offered one thousand dollars to shave points in an upcoming game
against DePaul. Kellogg took his information to the Bronx district attorney, setting off a full-scale, city-wide investigation that sent shock waves
throughout college basketball, college basketball tournaments, Madison
Square Garden, and, later, the professional ranks.

Shaving points took very little effort, and it didn't involve betraying
your school or your teammates by actually throwing a game. All you had
to do was miss an occasional shot or rebound, overthrow a pass, or turn
the ball over. You just couldn't be obvious about it. If your team was favored by, say, eight points, you just had to see that you won by seven or
less. You weren't losing the game—just helping out a lot of people who
bet on it.

That was the pitch the bookies and gamblers used on the college kids.

And a lot of kids bought it.

The big money, naturally, was in New York, in the games played at
Madison Square Garden, which regularly sold out its high-profile college
games. The city had several top-notch teams—St. John's, Long Island
University, Manhattan College, New York University, City College of
New York—that were featured regularly at the Garden. These games, especially those featuring other strong teams, attracted enthusiastic fans and
hard-core gamblers, many of whom were one and the same.

Prior to 1951, professional basketball had run a very distant second to
college basketball in the public's—and gamblers'—eyes. The pros were already earning money in the sport and would be tougher to persuade than
college kids, who were perennially broke. Interest in the pro game wasn't
anywhere near what it was in college, and since the gambling business was

controlled by actual numbers—the gamblers and their dollars—it made sense that the focus would be on college.

Junius Kellogg's story was just the beginning, a snowball that grew and grew as more tales of misconduct hit the news. As bad as it was, the Manhattan College scandal paled in comparison to what investigators turned up on players from LIU and CCNY, the latter the winner of both the NIT and NCAA tournaments in 1950. When investigators trained their sights on Adolph Rupp's great Kentucky teams of the late 1940s, Rupp counterpunched in his typically brash, aggressive style. "Gamblers couldn't get at my boys with a ten-foot pole," he growled.

He'd wind up eating those words within a year's time.

The point-shaving scandals would reach beyond New York City, to such schools as the University of Toledo and Bradley University. All told, six colleges and thirty-three players would be implicated, and Madison Square Garden, the Mecca of college basketball, free-fell from grace. No one was beyond suspicion or scrutiny, including some of the biggest names in recent college hoops. Members of the National Collegiate Athletic Association's Council convened and proposed a Madison Square Garden boycott. No future NCAA championship games would be held there, the Council declared, and schools belonging to the NCAA should consider avoiding the Garden for *any* future games.

For Ned Irish, the scandals and their aftermath constituted the ultimate nightmare. He'd earned his reputation and fortune from the good work he'd done in staging college games and double-headers at the Garden, beginning with an NYU–Notre Dame contest back in 1934. He'd scheduled twenty-eight college double-headers during the 1950–51 regular season. He'd now have to scramble to get much of anything for the following season. His Knicks, accustomed to playing second fiddle to the colleges, held a good percentage of their games at the tiny 69th Regiment Armory instead of the Garden. They now felt the percussive effects of the scandals, not only in terms of where they'd be playing their games, but also in the players the team would be drafting in the future. The Knicks feasted on local talent. Dick McGuire and Max Zaslofsky had played their college ball with St. John's, Ray Lumpp had been a star at NYU. Connie Simmons and Ernie Vandeweghe had roots in the city. For the Knicks, the territorial draft pick meant first dibs on the city's finest graduating players.

The scandals had an immediate effect on their plans for the 1951 draft.

The Knicks had their hearts set on selecting Sherman White, LIU's six-eight center, but White's involvement in the point-shaving scandal brought his—and the Knicks'—future plans to a very abrupt halt.

"I don't think anybody got hurt more than we did," Vince Boryla said of the scandals. "Sherman White was probably the most outstanding big man in the country at that time, but he got involved in the scandals and we never got him. Had we drafted him, I think we would have had a chance of having an outstanding ball club."

The rest of the NBA teams held their collective breath. There were locker-room murmurings about which, if any, of their members might have been involved in past indiscretions, but the players, teams, and the league itself avoided issuing public statements, choosing instead to wait for the storm to blow itself out. Things might have been going very poorly on the college level, but the NBA was actually benefiting from the scandals, as disgruntled basketball fans shifted their attention from the colleges to the pros. There was a delicious irony to the whole thing: in the past, fans had gravitated to the college game, where kids played for the love of the sport and the glory of their schools, uncorrupted by the money that professionals accepted in plying their trade. It was different now.

The college point-shaving scandals were at their height of publicity when George Mikan headed out to Boston to participate in the NBA's first All-Star Game on March 2. Vern Mikkelsen and Jim Pollard had also been selected for the team, and with John Kundla coaching the West, the Minneapolis Lakers had plenty of representation in the first convening of what, over time, would become one of the biggest spectacles in pro sports.

Nothing was certain, however, in that first game. Fan interest was not a given, especially with basketball trying to repair image problems. Maurice Podoloff was convinced that the game would be a disaster. As late as a week before the game, he thought it might be better to cancel it rather than face embarrassment of no one's turning up to see it. As it was, the game wouldn't be broadcast on either television or radio.

"It was at the time of the college scandals, and basketball had a black eye," Celtics' owner Walter Brown, the game's sponsor, remembered. "Things were going so badly that even my wife wanted me to get out of the business."

The idea for an all-star game came from Haskell Cohen, the NBA's publicity director, who had been tracking the enormous popularity of baseball's midsummer classic and felt basketball could do the same. He'd been able to sell the idea to Brown, who offered the use of the Boston Garden for the event. A minimum attendance of ten thousand was required for the league to break even. When skeptics predicted that this wasn't possible, Brown volunteered to cover any losses that the NBA accrued.

He certainly wasn't breaking the bank with player remuneration. Each team had a ten-man roster, and Mikan and the others were each given a $100 savings bond for their efforts.

Nevertheless, Mikan liked the idea of playing with and against the best his sport had to offer. "It was a pleasure to play with fellows that you always played against," he said. "It was good for the morale of the players in the league."

The two teams almost perfectly reflected the differences in eastern and western styles of play. The West, with Mikan, Mikkelsen, Indianapolis's Alex Groza, and Fort Wayne's Larry Foust in the front court, had a big, aggressive team that could do a lot of damage around the basket; Ralph Beard and Bob Davies, two of the slickest guards in the business, could run the fast break if the occasion arose. The East, with Bob Cousy, Andy Phillip, and Dick McGuire in its backcourt, was flashy and quick, as was the starting front line of Jumpin' Joe Fulks, Dolph Schayes, and Easy Ed Macauley. The game would pit brawn against speed.

John Kundla admitted that he was at a loss as to how to handle so many stars on the same team.

"I was scared," he said. "I didn't know what to do or how to handle them. We just ran some simple patterns. We had several of our players on the team, so it worked out all right."

Joe Lapchick, the East's coach, felt that containing Mikan was the key to the game, and in Easy Ed Macauley he had someone who matched up well against him, at least in terms of offensive production. The two usually fought each other to a draw, each scoring liberally off the other.

Macauley had a few ideas of his own, including a way of slowing down Mikan's offense.

"I know a lot of guys play as individuals in the All-Star Game," Macauley remembered, "but I said, 'I'm going to play in front of him. Give me help.'"

The strategy worked beautifully. Mikan normally had a difficult night when playing against Macauley or Schayes, but he would usually get the better of them by simply outscoring them. In this game, with Schayes and Fulks playing behind him and Macauley playing in front of him, Mikan had to fight to get open, and, more often than not, his teammates shot or worked the ball elsewhere rather than risk a turnover by passing it inside. The East jumped out to a nine-point lead by the end of the first quarter, and the West never recovered, losing 111–94. Mikan was held to 12 points on 4-of-17 shooting. He managed to pull down 11 rebounds, but he was badly outplayed by Macauley, who scored 20 points and won the game's Most Valuable Player award.

More important than the game's final score or the players' individual statistics was the fact that the game was a big success. The 10,094 in attendance, although far from a sellout, represented a better showing than average for a pro game, especially at a time when basketball was fending off a glut of negative publicity, and it proved the naysayers wrong. The game didn't lose money. With the playoffs just around the corner, there was a good chance the NBA would hold its fans' attention long enough to make it through the storm.

Mikan's 1950–51 season was his finest as a professional. At twenty-seven, he was hitting his prime, and his 28.4 points per game scoring average was a personal best—nearly seven points a game better than Alex Groza's second-place finish. The NBA had started keeping track of a new statistic—rebounds—at the beginning of the season, and Mikan's 14.1 rebounds per game average was second only to Dolph Schayes's 16.4.

At 44–24, the Lakers notched the best record in the NBA, nosing out the Rochester Royals by three games. But it had been a struggle. The influx of talented young players had provided greater parity among the league's teams, and with only eleven teams, the fewest since the BAA's opening season, the NBA had rosters loaded with talent. The Washington Capitols, playing before an ever-diminishing number of fans while posting a miserable 10–25 record, had tossed in the towel at midseason, resulting in several teams benefiting greatly from the dispersal of the team's players. Earl Lloyd signed with the Nationals, who urgently needed another big man to shore up their defense up front. In the most significant move of all, Bill Sharman signed with the Celtics, giving Boston a formidable trio of players in Sharman, Macauley, and Cousy. The Celtics, the perennial door-mats of the BAA and NBA, were no longer to be taken lightly.

The playoffs were going to be as competitive as ever, and if the Lakers hoped to add another championship to their string, they were going to have to do so with George Mikan playing at considerably less than full strength. During the Lakers' next-to-last game, a meaningless road game against Tri-Cities, Mikan had suffered a hairline ankle fracture. He wouldn't consider sitting out a game, though. The Lakers were facing the Indianapolis Olympians—and Mikan's rival, Alex Groza—in the first round of the playoffs. They would need every one of Mikan's points.

John Kundla agreed. He could have moved Vern Mikkelsen into the center slot, but Mikkelsen hadn't played in the middle since the failed double-pivot experiment during his rookie season. The more mobile Alex Groza would give him a lot of trouble. Mikan had played in the Lakers' final regular-season game, a victory over the Knicks. If he could play with his ankle heavily taped, as he had in that game, the Lakers might get by.

Mikan not only played on the bad ankle in the opener; he had one of his best games of the year, scoring 41 points in a 95–81 Laker win. The next day, however, the pain in his ankle was so severe that he could barely walk when the Lakers took the court for their pregame warmups. Kundla pondered using Mikkelsen at center, but Mikan persuaded him that he could start, that he'd let his coach know if the pain was too much. Twelve minutes into the game, Mikan had had enough. He left after scoring only two points, the lowest point production of his career, and the Olympians went on to bury the Lakers, 109–88.

It would have been easy to second-guess Kundla for using Mikan in the '50–51 playoffs. Kundla could be stubborn in some of his coaching decisions, and even if he did allow Mikan to talk him into playing on a bad ankle, as was the case in Game 2 against the Olympians, Kundla was gambling with the prospects of an even more serious injury to his star center.

Vern Mikkelsen, for one, understood Kundla's reluctance to bench Mikan, though he had a hard time endorsing the decision.

"I didn't make a big stink about it, but I knew I was a good center," he said. "George had a broken ankle, and I knew he wasn't going to be able to play like he should—and he didn't."

Mikkelsen, a staunch Kundla supporter and a lifelong friend, was absolutely correct in his assessment, but Mikan, more than any player in his time, had a way of playing with pain that would have sidelined anyone else in his position. In the third and final game of the first round, Mikan dropped in 30 points in a close contest that the Lakers won, 85–80, finishing off the Olympians.

The next round of the playoffs, for the Western Division title, had the Lakers meeting the Rochester Royals in a best-of-five series. The two teams matched up almost evenly with a healthy George Mikan in the Lakers' lineup, but with an injured Mikan, the decisive edge went to the Royals. The Lakers appealed to the league offices for a one-day postponement of the series's opening game in Minneapolis. Incredibly, the league went along with it. The Royals' owner/coach, Les Harrison, excitable in the best of times, had a total meltdown, to no avail.

If the four-day rest between games helped Mikan's ankle, it was only marginally so. Mikan would never be compared to Jim Pollard when it came to leaping ability, but now he could barely get off the floor. Kundla inserted Mikkelsen at center in the starting lineup of the opening game, but Mikan saw thirty minutes of action. He scored 22 points and the Lakers won, 76–73.

The Lakers were hopeful. They had another game at home, where they almost never lost, before they flew out to Rochester for two games on the road. If they took the second game at home, they'd only have to pull out one of the next three to win the Western Division title.

Unfortunately, Mikan's ankle showed no improvement in the two days between games, and he was hobbling badly throughout Game 2. Les Harrison changed his starting lineup for the game, starting Red Holzman at guard, with great results: Holzman led the Royals in scoring, hitting on 10 of 13 shots for a game-leading 23 points.

"I got off hot," he remembered. "I hit my first couple of long two-hand set shots and I knew I couldn't miss. I played the whole game, which was tough since I hadn't had all that much playing time during the year."

As effective as Holzman was, the big difference in the game was in rebounding. Mikan, by his own assessment, was "useless on the boards," while Arnie Johnson, the big forward who had grown up in northern Minnesota, controlled the boards and set up Holzman, Davies, and Wanzer on the fast break. Mikan managed 18 points, but the Lakers dropped a close one, 70–66.

The teams shared a plane on the trip to Rochester, and, during the flight, Mikan discussed his ankle problems with Jack Coleman, a Royals forward. Coleman was sympathetic.

"We were friends when we weren't on the court," Royals reserve Bill Calhoun remembered. "Jack told George about a way to shoot your ankle with Novocain or something. So he shot up his ankle and I think he was okay after that."

Arnie Risen probably wished that Coleman had remained silent. He and Mikan had rough encounters whenever they squared off against each other, and the one area where Risen enjoyed a significant advantage over Mikan was in getting up and down the court. Now that Mikan was greatly hampered by injury, he had an enormous edge.

"We tried to take advantage of it," Risen recalled. "George would lumber up and down the court, and they played that slow-down offense, waiting for him to come down. But once he got into position, George was pretty quick. He had quick hands and quick moves, which belied the way he ran up and down the court."

When he arrived in Rochester, Mikan consulted a physician about receiving a shot of Novocain before the game, but the doctor suggested ethyl chloride, another local anesthetic. He sprayed a small amount on one of Mikan's hands to show him how it worked, and Mikan was impressed. He had the ankle numbed before the next two games.

The anesthetic worked, but not enough to save the Lakers. The Royals had little trouble with Minneapolis in the first game, beating them, 83–70, in a sold-out arena. Down two games to one, the Lakers now faced the improbable task of having to defeat the Royals two straight games in order to advance to the finals. The New York Knicks and the Syracuse Nats were engaged in a fiercely competitive series for the right to represent the Eastern Division in the finals, and Mikan knew, even if his ankle held up for two more victories against the Royals, he was in for a long, difficult championship series.

For a while, it looked as if the Lakers were going to force a fifth and deciding game in Minneapolis. The Lakers hit from all over the court, scoring on ten of their first eleven offensive possessions before the Royals fought their way back into the game. Mikan scored 32 points but fouled out with less than two minutes left and the Lakers hanging on to a one-point lead. Mikkelsen and Harrison fouled out in quick succession, and the Royals scored the last six points of the game, winning 80–75.

Just a few years earlier, the Royals had used an injury to Arnie Risen as an excuse for losing a tough series to the Lakers. Now, the roles were reversed. Mikan had put on a gritty performance during the four-game series, but it hadn't been enough.

"He still did a lot of damage," Bobby Wanzer remembered, "but I don't think you could hold it to one man. We played extremely well. We shot very good fouls, and we caught them on a night when they weren't hitting. We split the games up there and capitalized at home."

It had taken some time, but the Royals had finally advanced beyond the Lakers in a playoff series. Mikan was none too pleased—"I've always felt they stole one of our titles," he complained—but it would be the only time in the history of the Lakers–Royals rivalry that Rochester won a playoff series against Minneapolis. The Royals went on to capture the '50–51 championship, beating the Knicks, four games to three, in an intrastate showdown that turned out to be one of the most entertaining finals fans ever could have expected.

Mikan went home and dreamed about starting a new string of titles. He'd never forget the one that got away.

Thirteen

MIKAN RULES

DURING THE SUMMER of 1951, the NBA's Rules Committee enacted a new rule aimed at cutting back the dominance of George Mikan. The new rule widened the lane, from the free throw line to the end line beneath the basket, from six feet to ten feet. (This would almost immediately be amended to twelve feet.)

The "Mikan Rule," as it was called, came after years of lobbying and complaining by coaches and owners. Mikan, they argued, enjoyed an unfair advantage because of his height and girth. On offense, players were only allowed in the lane for three seconds, but Mikan could anchor himself just outside the lane and, with the narrow lane, move in and out of it and still be so close to the basket that there was no stopping his hook shot. He was also well positioned for tip-ins and rebounds. The players were getting taller each year, but Mikan still towered, literally and figuratively, over his opposition.

Joe Lapchick of the Knicks and Les Harrison of the Royals were especially vocal in pushing for the widening of the lane. Harrison was sick to death of Mikan. He'd tried everything humanly possible to offset Mikan's game in the middle, but even the addition of Arnie Risen, one of the best centers in the business, hadn't worked. As far as Harrison was concerned, the Royals' fast-paced, guard-oriented East Coast style of basketball was wasted on a team like the Minneapolis Lakers. They were slow, plodding, and dull, thanks mainly to the big guy who ambled up the court and then proceeded to beat the living daylights out of his competition. "He's just a monster," Harrison bellowed about Mikan after one Lakers victory, "just a basketball monstrosity."

Lapchick, who had carefully constructed a deep, talented team that could compete with anyone, but which still lacked a big man capable of playing even against Mikan, was similarly distressed. "See these gray hairs?" he challenged a reporter. "Mikan put most of them there."

Lapchick had heart trouble, and he swore, only half-jokingly, that Mikan would kill him one day. He especially hated playing the Lakers in the Minneapolis Amphitheatre, which had a floor two feet narrower than anywhere else, leading Al Cervi to remark that Mikan, Pollard, and Mikkelsen could stretch out, arm to arm, fingertips touching, and span the width of the court.

The rule change didn't come easily. Mikan, after all, still drew the league's biggest gate, and fans queued up to see the Lakers the way fans of all sports would always be inclined to see games featuring the better teams. Besides, with Mikan on the team, the Laker organization had clout. When he got wind of the proposed rule change, Sid Hartman called college coaches and asked them to write letters of protest to the league offices. Widening the lane, the coaches argued, would ruin the game. Max Winter took it one step further. The Lakers, he said, would not widen the lanes on their home court, regardless of the new rule. He then threatened to withhold Mikan from the Lakers' road games.

"If the lanes are widened in other arenas," he warned, "I shall advertise in advance of our games in those towns that George Mikan will not appear on the floor."

One of the more creative arguments against expanding the lane contended that there would be more three-second violations with the wider lanes. Fort Wayne's Carl Bennett, a member of the NBA's Executive Committee and a proponent of the new rule, conducted an experiment during three Pistons' exhibition games to see if there was any merit to the argument.

"I got this tape that you use to tape players' ankles, and I measured three feet on each side of the six-foot lane and put it down so it was a twelve-foot lane," Bennett remembered. "We played the three exhibition games, and I think the ball was lost out of bounds seven times to three-seconds [violations] in the three games."

After much discussion, the Mikan Rule was passed, effective for the 1951–52 season.

Mikan wasn't happy about having the league legislate against him, but he'd been down this road before. Back in his college days, he and Bob Kurland had been directly responsible for the change in goaltending rules, and they'd both survived that change. If anything, the change had made him a more complete player. The same might be true now. His point production might dip as a result of his being moved further away from the basket, but a wider lane to the basket also meant more room for the Laker guards cutting through. Mikan had always been a better-than-average passer; now he'd have an opportunity to demonstrate it.

In any event, Mikan tried to remain philosophical about the change.

"They tell me the new twelve-foot free-throw lane was written into pro basketball rules just to make it tougher for a guy named Mikan," he wrote in a guest column, published in the *Minneapolis Star* shortly after the opening of the season. "If that's true, the rules-makers did themselves a double favor. They not only made things tougher for me, but they also made the game better than it has been since Doc Naismith hung up his first peach basket."

On October 19, just before the opening of the '51–52 season, the NBA took another major hit when Alex Groza and Ralph Beard, two of the league's premier players, were arrested at the annual College All-Star Classic in Chicago. The Indianapolis Olympians had a preseason game scheduled against Tri-Cities in Moline, and Groza, Beard, and other teammates had dropped by Chicago Stadium to watch the game between the College All-Stars and the Rochester Royals, and to visit with their old coach, Adolph Rupp, who was coaching the college team. As the game ended and they were leaving the stadium, Groza, Beard, and two other members of Kentucky's Fabulous Five team (Cliff Barker and Joe Holland) were approached by detectives, who detained them and drove them to the Cook County Jail for questioning about their possible involvement in the point-shaving scandals.

"They told Barker and me that they knew we were not involved," Holland remembered. "They knew who was involved and who was not. They took Beard and Groza in back and put them under the bright lights, and they kept them under the bright lights all night and finally broke Beard down. They brought us out about 6:30 in the morning and told us that Beard and Groza had confessed to taking money, and that just shocked us.

I asked Groza, 'What can we do for you?' Of course, we had to get them out of jail, but he wanted me to call his brothers and tell them about it. I called them, but they already knew. It was all over the radio stations."

Word of the arrests spread like a brushfire. Players and league officials sifted through hastily written news accounts, television and radio reports, and a white-hot rumor mill, all in an attempt to determine what had actually occurred and how widespread the gambling scandals might be among players active in the NBA. Groza and Beard confessed to shaving points (but not throwing games) while they were playing at Kentucky. Dale Barnstable, another Kentucky teammate, was arrested in Louisville in the wee hours of the morning of October 20, and he, too, admitted to being part of the point-shaving scheme.

The media trained their sights on Adolph Rupp. What did he know? Was he involved? Rupp, as revered in Kentucky as the state's top politicians and civic leaders, seemed untouchable. Rupp could counterpunch with the best, and he defended his players as being pawns in a much bigger game. "The Chicago Black Sox threw ball games," he declared, "but these kids only shaved points. My boys were the inexperienced victims of an unscrupulous syndicate."

The NBA acted swiftly. The league couldn't afford the kind of scandal that had so heavily damaged college basketball—not on the eve of a new season, not when the sport was finally gaining a foothold on the pro sports scene. Since Groza and Beard had admitted their guilt, they were out, banned for life from the NBA, and they had thirty days to sell their interests in the Olympians. League officials hoped for the best. With any luck, those stern, decisive actions would mollify the fans. They would see that the NBA was capable not only of policing its own players; it was willing, if necessary, to kick out two of its top stars for their actions *before* they even joined the league.

The fans might have bought it, but players remained skeptical. Many insisted—and would continue to insist for the rest of their lives—that Groza and Beard were far from alone in shaving points while they were playing college ball. Other names were bandied about in private, and at least one other superstar was implicated in New York District Attorney Frank Hogan's investigation. There was talk of threats and backroom deals consummated to spare other players of Groza's and Beard's fates. According to Charley Rosen, whose account, *Scandals of '51*, details the scandals at the different schools, Maurice Podoloff had been briefed on at least one superstar's involvement in collegiate point-shaving, but Podoloff buckled to pressure. "The owner of the star threatened to fold his franchise and go home if Podoloff touched his player," Rosen reported. "The star remained in orbit."

Players, although not sympathetic to Groza or Beard's actions, strongly felt that the league, while publicly condemning the actions of the point-shavers, had been less than forthright in its investigation of the scandal and the punishment of the guilty. The league, they contended, made scapegoats of the two players, forcing Beard and Groza to pay the ultimate price if, in exchange, it meant saving face and having the problem go away.

Then, in the midst of all the talk and hand-wringing, Sol Levy, a veteran NBA official, was arrested for agreeing to help fix six NBA games, including one involving the Minneapolis Lakers, during the 1950–51 season.

It didn't take a great imagination to see how easily an official could influence a game. All he had to do was whistle fouls on key players. In the Minneapolis game, Mikan had fouled out, as arranged, but not before he led the Laker offense to a big enough lead to win the game.

No one will ever know exactly how widespread the practice was among NBA officials, but at least one player, speaking anonymously to Charley Rosen for his book, contended that there were other officials involved in fixing NBA games.

"Levy wasn't the only ref doing business," the player told Rosen, "but all the other guys are safely dead by now. Even after the scandals broke, there were plenty of games dumped in the NBA."

The interest in the scandals, as the NBA hoped, faded and the new season commenced without any more serious damage to the league's reputation. Levy was eventually convicted of a misdemeanor bribery charge—and that conviction was overturned in appeals court—and, on March 30, 1953, Alex Groza, Ralph Beard, and Dale Barnstable were given suspended sentences for their roles in point-shaving while they played at the University of Kentucky.

Beard, a likely Hall of Famer if he'd been allowed to play out his career in the NBA, accepted his fate with some reluctance. He admitted his guilt and went on with his life, going back and earning his degree from the University of Kentucky and, in time, becoming vice president of sales of a wholesale drug company in Louisville. But he would always struggle to come to terms with the way he, Groza, and Barnstable had been singled out for punishment while others walked away.

"It all didn't come out, okay?" he said in 2006, when questioned about the scandals. "I know the ones that were involved in the scandal, the ones who were banned and the guys who weren't banned. *They* know how it is. Maybe we will meet in heaven sometime and I'll say, 'How were you so lucky and I wasn't?'"

There would be other headline-making scandals in the future—most notably Bill Spivey, of a later Kentucky team, and Ralph Molinas of the Fort Wayne Pistons—but the NBA managed to overcome the negative publicity, largely because the scandals were limited in number and the NBA, at least as far as the public could tell, seemed capable of internally handling such problems.

The Mikan Rule affected the Lakers more than by just diminishing George Mikan's scoring figures and making him a more multi-dimensional player; it helped create a stronger, more balanced team. For the new season, the Laker management, recognizing the need to relieve some of the pressure on Mikan, picked up a pair of guards with excellent outside shots. Whitey Skoog, a five-eleven star out of the University of Minnesota, arrived via the draft, while Frank "Pep" Saul, a hot-shooting reserve with the Rochester Royals, found his way to Minneapolis through sheer trickery.

Skoog, chosen All-Big Ten during his three years of varsity ball, had played on the front line of the excellent Minnesota team with Jim McIntyre and Bud Grant, and he'd been the first player in the Midwest to use a jump shot as his featured offensive weapon. He'd developed the shot in college, where he'd played the forward position, as a means of shooting over much taller forwards and centers; with the Lakers, who converted him to guard, he used it to launch his outside shot.

Saul, on the other hand, was a traditional two-handed set shooter with exceptional range. The Lakers had seen plenty of him in their games against the Royals, and they knew that the former Seton Hall star was unhappy with the very limited playing time he was getting behind Bob Davies, Bobby Wanzer, and Red Holzman. They also knew that Les Harrison would have slugged Drano straight from a can before trading him to the Royals' biggest rival.

Sid Hartman had an idea. He was friendly with Clair Bee, the legendary coach at Long Island University and currently head coach of the Baltimore Bullets. The Bullets were barely staying afloat financially, and Hartman proposed giving the Bullets $5,000 for the rights to Pep Saul. The Royals weren't really interested in keeping Saul around, Hartman told Bee, and Les Harrison would probably let him go for about $1,500. Baltimore could keep whatever they had left over from the $5,000 if they agreed to transfer Saul's rights to the Lakers.

Bee went along with the idea, the Bullets wound up making $3,500 on the deal, the Lakers acquired Saul, and Harrison, as expected, raised hell with the league offices. Ironically, Saul found himself in much the same position as he'd been in with the Royals: the Lakers already had Slater Martin, Bobby Harrison, and Whitey Skoog competing for backcourt minutes, and he could only add to the competition.

Saul remembered: "I got into Minneapolis, thinking, 'Here's a championship team. I'm pretty much the last guy on the totem pole, so I'll have to work my way up.' I wound up with the Lakers to take the pressure off George because of the widening of the lane."

The Lakers made adjustments to accommodate the Mikan Rule and get the guards more involved in the offense, although the guards still remained a secondary option. Slater Martin was a fine offensive player, but he earned his spot in the Hall of Fame more for his passing and outstanding defensive work than for his scoring prowess. Mikan and Pollard remained the Lakers' primary weapons on offense.

In the first year after the widening of the lanes, Mikan's scoring dropped off dramatically—from 28.4 points per game in 1950–51 to 23.8 in '51–52. Pollard and Mikkelsen benefited most from the change. Both set personal scoring bests by averaging more than 15 points per game for the first time in their respective careers.

And the Lakers were a much better team for it.

Mikan celebrated the opening of the new year in Chicago, in what proved to be his final game against the Harlem Globetrotters.

For a while, there had been some question as to whether the game—or any future games between the Lakers and the Globetrotters—would be played. The last meeting, which found Mikan scoring 47 points in a narrow,

72–68 Laker win, had just about pushed Abe Saperstein over the edge. Saper-stein was tired of the losing. His team had just come off an enormously suc-cessful tour of Europe, and a feature film about the Globetrotters was in the works. The loss to the Lakers had been too much. After the game, he had called Max Winter and, without offering an explanation, canceled the sec-ond game of the '50–51 season.

He had cooled down since that time, and he brought in his usual assort-ment of regulars, crowd-pleasers, and ringers with the hope of finally put-ting an end to the Lakers' string of victories over his team. Instead, the Globetrotters were utterly humiliated in a game that, for all the 20,004 spectators in Chicago Stadium could see, was over by the end of the first quarter. The Lakers scored more points in that single period than the Glo-betrotters accumulated during the entire first half. The 45–26 halftime score infuriated Saperstein to such an extent that Max Winter felt com-pelled to visit the Laker dressing room during the intermission.

Winter's rare appearance left a lasting impression on Whitey Skoog.

"The only time I remember Max coming down in the locker room was when we played the Globetrotters in Chicago," he said. "We were beating them by twenty points at halftime, and Max came down and said, 'Boys, you've got to let up.'"

"We were destroying them," Laker backup center, Lew Hitch, remem-bered. "We were told we had to ease up, so we did. They made it at least respectable."

The Lakers eased up in the second half, but the outcome of the game was already well in hand. Vern Mikkelsen enjoyed a huge game, and he and Mikan shared the high scoring honors with 25 points each. Slater Mar-tin, besides limiting Marques Haynes to 6 points, added 17. The 84–60 final score represented the largest margin of victory in the two teams' seven-game history.

After the game, a very frustrated Abe Saperstein stormed out of Chicago Stadium and was missing in action for hours. His Globetrotters had now lost five straight to the Lakers, three of the last four by double-digit mar-gins. He was more than a little hurt by the NBA's drafting of African-American players—Chuck Cooper, Earl Lloyd, and Sweetwater Clifton, the very first black players signed by NBA teams, had all played at least briefly for the Trotters—and he worried about finding talented replace-ments for some of his aging players. Goose Tatum, Marques Haynes, and

Babe Pressley had been on the circuit for a long time. Fans loved to see the Globetrotters clowning around, but the Lakers, with their intense play and superior skills, offered them little chance to do so.

As Saperstein saw it, there was no point in continuing the Lakers–Globetrotters series, and he told Max Winter as much. The Lakers would have to find somebody else to beat up on.

This was just fine with George Mikan, who had grown tired, long ago, of risking his neck in games that didn't count in the standings, and for which there was no additional pay. The demise of the Lakers–Globetrotters series, he'd say later, was probably symbolic of the end of the barnstorming era.

"As the NBA was growing in popularity," he reflected, "basketball fans were turning to the established league. The days of playing fifty to sixty exhibition games a season would soon be a thing of the past."

Mikan's prediction came true. There would come a time when the idea of playing an exhibition game or making a promotional appearance for no additional pay would be laughable; but in the early years of pro basketball, players signed contracts requiring them to participate in these activities. Players visited schools, dropped by church socials, conducted clinics, appeared at local businesses, made promotional appearances at radio stations, and traveled in caravans and played exhibition games all over the United States—all in an effort to drum up publicity for their teams. Publicity from the traditional sources was hard to come by. Box scores of pro basketball games in newspapers were unheard of outside a team's home city, and teams had to all but beg local media outlets to give them a mention in their sports coverage.

Carl Bennett, general manager of the Fort Wayne Pistons, noted that newspaper editors rarely assigned reporters to cover a game. If the Pistons wanted anything in the papers, they had to contact the sports desks themselves.

"We'd play, and somebody would call the *Fort Wayne Gazette* with a box score and about four or five lines," he said. "That's all you got."

Arnie Risen had similar memories of his early days with Indianapolis and Rochester.

"The first couple of years that I played," he said, "newspapers didn't carry box scores or anything. They hardly ever sent anyone around to cover the game or mentioned the game. You called in the results and pleaded with them to put the results in the papers, just so you'd get your team's name in front of the public.

Ed Kalafat, a successful businessman after he retired from basketball, recalled a time in the mid-1950s when he and Slater Martin were dispatched to Fargo, South Dakota, two days ahead of the Lakers, to participate in grand opening festivities for a grocery chain.

"We were going to play a game up there two days later," he said. "We set up a portable basket out in the parking lot and conducted clinics for two days. We didn't get extra pay for it. They gave us a room and provided our meals. Today's players won't go out unless they're paid thousands and thousands of dollars."

The Lakers usually followed their playoff runs with a tour of the Upper Midwest or plains states. The newly crowned champs would bounce from city to city, bringing basketball to people who never saw it outside of local high school or college games. Arnie Ferrin and Bob Berger (son of the Lakers' owner, Ben Berger) eventually put together a postseason tour that paid the players, but most of the exhibition games were simply part of the job.

The players would complain about it but, as Fuzzy Levane pointed out, they enjoyed it to some extent.

"We were making more money than we ever made," he said. "My father was making twenty-five dollars a week back then. He'd say, 'They're paying you that money just to bounce a ball?' He'd ask me what else I had to do. I'd say, 'Well, I kind of clean up the gym afterwards.'"

January 20, 1952

It's one of those nights where every shot seems to be dropping through the net, and Mikan lets them fly like well-aimed daggers. The Lakers are up against the Rochester Royals, and Mikan's memories of the way the Royals booted his team from the previous year's playoffs are as fresh and urgent as the sound of Les Harrison's hollering from the Rochester bench.

The game plays out like the seventh game of a championship series. The Royals, as always, are in a dead heat with the Lakers for first place in the Western Division, and even though the Lakers are still a slightly better team (and will win the season series with the Royals), Mikan is keenly aware that every single game matters from this point on. Barring the intervention of some very bad luck to one of the two teams, the Lakers and Royals will be duking it out for the division title come the last week of the season. The two teams meeting in the playoffs is about as predictable as the icy winds and snowdrifts that torment Minneapolis and Rochester every year at this time.

Arnie Risen hangs nearby, playing Mikan one-on-one, trying to keep the ball out of Mikan's hands, trying to cut his angle to the basket. The league could have widened the lane to twenty feet, for all the good the twelve-foot lane is doing tonight. Mikan's teammates feed him the ball almost every time down court, and, in a motion all too familiar to the Lakers and their opponents alike, Mikan takes his drop step, turns toward the basket with his left elbow swinging out like a lethal arm-bar, and pops in a hook shot with about the same degree of difficulty as he might experience when trying to drop a wad of paper into a waste basket two feet away.

At first, Les Harrison isn't concerned. Mikan's not going to score every one of his team's points, so all the Royals have to do is see that Pollard and Mikkelsen or any of the others don't go off on their own little rampages.

The Royals hang tight. Mikan continues to score. By halftime, he has bludgeoned the Royals for 36 points.

Mikan would never admit it out loud, but he wants another scoring title. It doesn't matter that he already has a handful of them in his trophy case; Mikan enjoys the past, but he dwells in the present. Paul Arizin, the jump-shooting phenom for Philadelphia, has been at the top of the scoring list all season. The former Villanova star has been averaging 20-plus points per game, and reporters have been hitting their typewriters with stories about the scoring race, predicting a usurper to Mikan's throne. Mikan's heard the talk and pretends it doesn't bother him. But it does. A big game tonight could add as much as another point to his average.

Harrison's no fool, and he makes his adjustments at halftime. His new defense will focus on Mikan. He stations his three big men—Alex Hannum, Arnie Johnson, and Odie Spears—in a collapsing, triple-team defense designed to cut off any pass to Mikan, or, if Mikan does manage to get the ball, block any move he might make toward the basket. In the meantime, Harrison works the officials. He complains that they're playing favorites, allowing Mikan to charge every time he turns toward the basket. He's absolutely right, but it doesn't matter. The officials aren't listening.

Harrison's defensive strategy slows Mikan down—but only a little. Regula-
tion ends in a tie, as does the first overtime. Harrison had hoped that Mikan
would foul out at some point, as he often does, but not only doesn't he foul out,
he's played every second of the contest.

The Lakers take over in the second overtime period and win, 91–81. Mikan
winds up with 61 points—an incredible 66 percent of his team's total. Mikan's
total is two points below Joe Fulks's NBA record of 63, set in 1949, and eight
points better than his own personal best, the 53-point barrage against Rhode Is-
land State in the 1945 NIT.

Les Harrison goes bananas after the game, calling Mikan a monstrosity in a
postgame interview. Mikan couldn't care less. He has been called worse. He's
just posted what will stand as his all-time high in a winning effort against his
team's biggest rival, and he's done it when the league has been doing its level
best to keep him from doing just such a thing.

It simply doesn't get any better than that.

The NBA's second annual All-Star Game took place at the Boston Garden
about three weeks later, on February 11. The Lakers sent the same three
players (Mikan, Pollard, and Mikkelsen) as they'd sent the previous year.
John Kundla coached the West All-Stars again, but this time around, the
East had Al Cervi as their coach.

Unlike the previous year, there were no objections to the game, no
doubts about its appeal. Mikan and Paul Arizin (the game's MVP) showed
why they were the league's top scorers, putting on a dazzling exhibition of
scoring and leading their respective teams with 26 points each. Unfortunately for Mikan and the West, the game had an element of déjà vu to it,
with the East taking charge from the beginning and holding the lead for
most of the game. The West came back in the fourth quarter, but the Eastern stars countered with a 16–3 run, ending any hope Mikan and company
might have had of evening the score. The East took the game, 108–91, the
17-point differential identical to the spread in the first game.

Entering the playoffs, the Eastern Division looked to be more competitive and well-balanced than the Western Division. Only three games separated the top three teams—Syracuse, Boston, and New York—in the final
standings. Syracuse had posted the same regular-season record (40–26) as
the Lakers, winning the division for the second time in three years, mainly

on hustle and defense. Boston, with Bob Cousy, Easy Ed Macauley, and Bill Sharman, ran a full-throttle offense, leading all NBA teams in team points-per-game average, but they stumbled on defense. The Knicks boasted the deepest team in the playoffs, though they lacked an overpowering big man in the middle. Philadelphia, the fourth-place finisher, with a strong nucleus of players in Paul Arizin, Joe Fulks, and Andy Phillip, promised to be competitive in a playoff series.

In the West, it was basically the same two-team race. The Lakers and Royals had sprinted to the finish of the regular season, both concluding on hot streaks, but the Lakers' slow start cost them the division. The Royals, with a 41–25 regular-season record, were one game better than the Lakers, winning the title and the critical home-court advantage throughout the playoffs.

The Lakers drew the Indianapolis Olympians in the first round. Alex Groza had been banned from the game, meaning Mikan wouldn't be matching up against one of the toughest players he'd faced during his career, but there was still reason for concern.

That the Olympians were still in existence, let alone in the playoffs, was testament to the players' determination to overcome almost overwhelming obstacles. The devastating loss of Groza and Ralph Beard, the twin engines driving the team, had meant more than just the loss of vital personnel; the team's remaining nucleus of University of Kentucky stars, although never indicted or implicated in the betting scandal, had to contend with the suspicions of the public, not to mention the stress of watching two friends and former teammates denigrated in public and dragged through the legal system. Rather than let the distractions dump them into standings oblivion, the Olympians regrouped and rallied, actually posting a better winning percentage than the previous season.

The Lakers swept the two-game series, but had a surprisingly difficult time in doing so—not the kind of start they were looking for. After taking the opener, 78–70, in Minneapolis, the Lakers headed for Game 2 in the Butler Field House. A small crowd of 7,016 partisans watched the Olympians grab a lead and hang on to it for three quarters. Mikan couldn't handle his counterpart, Joe Graboski, on defense, and Graboski enjoyed a 29-point night. Mikan countered with a big night of his own, especially in the third quarter, when he demanded the ball nearly every time the Lakers brought it up the floor. An eight-point Olympians' lead evaporated to a single point going into the final quarter. Mikan, who finished the game with 36 points, hit seven straight shots during the Lakers' third-quarter spree. He then surprised the Olympians by going into passing mode in the decisive fourth quarter. Jim Pollard and Bobby Harrison picked up the slack in a quarter that found the Lakers hitting on 10 of 19 shots, and the Lakers sneaked out of Indianapolis with a 94–87 win. For the Olympians, the two close games against the three-time champs became a final gasp for a franchise that, only three seasons earlier, looked like the team of the future.

Mikan was sky-high for the division championship series against the Rochester Royals. Still annoyed by the Royals' nosing them out for the regular-season division title, and by Les Harrison's remarks following his huge performance against the Royals two months earlier, Mikan looked forward to schooling Harrison and his team on the Lakers' version of the natural order in the basketball universe. Both the Royals and Lakers were in good health, so there would be no excuses from the loser this time around.

Time would show the Lakers–Royals rivalry to be one of the most evenly matched in history. Between the NBA's inaugural year in 1949 and Mikan's retirement after the 1953–54 season, the teams would win 533 regular season games between them. The Lakers would win 267 contests, the Royals 266. The Lakers would win four division titles, the Royals two. The main difference was in head-to-head competition: including the playoffs, the Lakers held a 38–28 advantage.

The two teams relied on their contrasting styles throughout the first game in Rochester. The Lakers tried to establish a slow pace by bringing the ball up the floor very deliberately and then leaning on Mikan to shoulder the scoring load. Mikan responded with a 47-point night, but it wasn't nearly enough. The Royals sped up the pace every time the Lakers tried to slow it down, and their backcourt duo of Bob Davies (26 points) and Bobby Wanzer (24) proved to be more than the Lakers could overcome. Despite Mikan's efforts, Minneapolis dropped the opener, 88–78.

The next night, the Lakers took a dramatically different approach. Rather than depending so heavily on Mikan, the Lakers distributed the ball almost equally among their three front-line players, resulting in balanced scoring between Mikan (17), Pollard (17), and Mikkelsen (19). Pep Saul burned his former team for 17 points while playing a suffocating defense on Wanzer, holding him to only seven points. The Lakers evened the series with an 83–78 overtime win. They had come to Rochester with a goal of splitting the two games, and they returned home confident that they could finish the series on their home floor.

The third game was a defensive battle, with both teams' big scorers never getting untracked. Mikan had a horrible night, hitting only two field goals, while, in the worst game of his career, Bob Davies was held completely scoreless. Pollard came through with 22, and Minneapolis posted a 77–67 win.

The Royals might have expected Mikan, Pollard, or Mikkelsen to provide the difference in a series with the Lakers, but the real catalyst in this series was Pep Saul, the guard the Lakers had stolen from the Royals only a few months earlier. Les Harrison, in particular, must have been especially frosted when he watched Saul break the Royals' backs with the last-minute, overtime basket that salted away Game 2. Then, in the very next game, he had started and contributed 11 points.

Saul sent his former teammates packing in Game 4, scoring a Laker-high 18 points in one of those fan-pleasing confrontations that went down to the final seconds. Arnie Risen and George Mikan waged another war in the pivot, and Mikan had another miserable night, hitting on only three of his shots from the field. The teams traded leads and went on brief runs that looked as if they might make the final difference, but the Lakers and Royals had been too evenly matched, for too many years, for anything to come easily. Davies bounced back from his poor performance in Game 3 with 21 points, and Wanzer scored 16.

The game was dead-even, 65–65, going into the final quarter, and the lead seesawed throughout the period. The game was deadlocked with only seconds left in regulation, and everyone in the house knew what that meant: Mikan might have been struggling from the field, but he would be getting the ball for the game-deciding shot.

Unfortunately for the Lakers, Mikan couldn't deliver. With two seconds left on the game clock, he spun in the pivot and attempted a left-handed hook shot that clanged off the rim. Jim Pollard, however, leaped above the Royals' defenders and tipped in Mikan's miss, giving the Lakers an 82–80 win in one of the tensest games the Lakers and Royals had ever played against each other.

The Lakers would be playing the winners of the Nats–Knicks series for the title.

If the betting scandals had dampened New York's enthusiasm for basketball, you wouldn't have known it from the two divisional playoff series. Three teams from New York state—the Rochester Royals, the Syracuse Nationals, and the New York Knicks—ended up in their respective division finals, and the two series were exhibitions of pro basketball at its best. By defeating the Nats in their Eastern Division championship series, the Knicks moved to the finals for the second straight year.

The Knicks were no longer anyone's surprise team. They'd defeated the two teams finishing above them in the Eastern Division standings, beating the second-place Celtics, two games to one, in a tight series culminating with a heart-stopping, 88–87 double-overtime final-game win in the Boston Garden. It had been a little easier when the Knicks met first-place Syracuse, though the games had been very competitive. If anything, the Knicks were exhausted by the time they met the Lakers in the first game of the finals.

The matchups were intriguing. Big George Mikan vs. Sweetwater Clifton, in a renewal of a matchup that began back when Mikan was with the Chicago Gears and Clifton was playing for the New York Rens. Vern Mikkelsen vs. Harry "the Horse" Gallatin—two strong, hard-working forwards muscling for rebounds. Jim Pollard vs. Ernie Vandeweghe, in a battle of athletic forwards. Slater Martin vs. Dick McGuire—two floor leaders more inclined to pass than shoot. Pep Saul vs. Max Zaslofsky, a third-year long-range-shot specialist pitted against a former scoring champ, now part of a balanced attack less dependent on his putting up the big numbers he'd had in Philadelphia.

The Knicks rounded out their roster with Al McGuire, Dick's younger brother, known for his fiery defensive play; Ray Lumpp, who had played on the 1948 Olympic team; and George Kaftan, a former Holy Cross star and teammate of Bob Cousy. Few, if any, rosters in the NBA went as deep.

Which suited coach Joe Lapchick fine. He wasn't looking to build a team around a single go-to superstar like George Mikan, or even a starting five that played all but a few minutes of the game.

"I always considered our club to be kind of like minestrone soup: a little bit of this and a little bit of that," said Vince Boryla, the Knicks' regular-season scoring leader, out for the playoffs with an injury. "Maybe we weren't that good individually, but collectively we played better than average."

Whitey Skoog agreed. "They really had good talent," he remembered, "and it was spread out among the whole ball club. The offense wasn't geared around one or two or three ballplayers. Different players scored on different nights. They had that kind of talent. So how do you work on defense? You don't say, 'We've just got to shut this guy down.' You had to shut them all down."

Skoog, unfortunately, had banged up his knee and hadn't been available for the final few weeks of the regular season or the playoffs, which left the Lakers thin at the guard position. Kundla could bring in Bobby Harrison or Joe Hutton off the bench, but neither posed Skoog's scoring threat. Not that guard play mattered in this series as much as it had in the games against Rochester: the McGuire brothers shot only as a last resort, and the Knicks played the kind of front-line game that the Lakers favored.

The Lakers held the home-court advantage, which couldn't be underappreciated, since the Knicks had won twenty-three consecutive games at home. The advantage, however, wasn't as big as it could have been. As in other playoffs, the Lakers were forced to play in St. Paul, which had never offered the kind of advantage they enjoyed in the Minneapolis Auditorium.

Officiating played a huge role in the first game. Sixteen fouls—twelve on the Lakers—were called in the first period alone. Mikan would be saddled with foul trouble all night, limiting him on both ends of the floor. But it's what the officials *didn't* whistle that had the Knicks' players talking for years after the game.

Ironically, the dispute rose out of a shot taken by Al McGuire, the least likely person on either bench to be shooting early in the game. The Knicks were up, 13–9, when McGuire drove the lane and was hammered while taking a shot. The officials whistled the foul, but, to the astonishment of the Knicks (and probably everyone else in the building), the officials missed one crucial detail: McGuire's shot had dropped through the hoop for a score.

"Al drove the lane and he threw the ball up," Ernie Vandeweghe recalled. "He was stumbling and falling, and it wasn't a very good-looking shot. No one looked at the basket, but the ball went in! It didn't go in clean. It hit the backboard, it hit the front of the rim, and it went around and around and fell through. Al was making so much noise *he* didn't even know it went through. He got up, feisty as he was, and says, 'Foul, foul, foul.' And the referees, because it was Al acting up, turned to make sure that he wouldn't be going after anybody or anything. No one looked up at the basket. We were sort of laughing, because Al did create a scene. I was standing next to Jim Pollard, and he turned to one referee and said, 'Aw, it went in. Give it to him.' A lot of people saw it go in."

Neither official—Sid Borgia, one of the league's best, or his colleague, Stan Stutz—saw the shot go in. Joe Lapchick pleaded with them to verify it with others in the building, but the refs stood firm. The basket would not count. Al McGuire was awarded two free throws for being fouled during the process of shooting.

"Everybody in the arena saw that it went in," Ray Lumpp remembered, "but the two officials never saw it. So they gave him two shots."

The memory would haunt Lumpp and his Knicks teammates for decades. The Knicks knew that they were in for a tough, competitive series—one that could, and did, go the full seven games—and this seemingly small incident could have been a turning point. McGuire converted only one of the two free throws, and, three quarters later, the game was tied at the end of regulation. One or two points became very important.

"If we'd won that game," Lumpp asserted, "that could have been the difference in the championship."

But they didn't win the game. Mikan, bottled up by the Knick defense for much of the game, fought for 15 points, well below his average, before fouling out in overtime. He might not have been scoring, but he was passing, and his favorite target was Jim Pollard, who was having his finest night as a pro. The two hooked up on the first two Laker baskets of the overtime, forcing the Kicks to play catch-up. Pollard put the game out of reach with four free throws in the final minute, giving him a career high 34 points in the Lakers' 83–79 win.

It was going to be that kind of a series.

Game 2 was a disaster for the Lakers. Mikan, partly because he couldn't find his shot and partly because he was being pushed around near the basket, connected on only four of his shots from the field, and Pollard was held to 13 points, 21 below his previous game. Pep Saul kept the Lakers in contention with 16 points, but a huge 30–14 second quarter spelled the difference. The

Knicks, behind Gallatin's 18 points and Lumpp's 15, left Minnesota with a tied series.

The teams alternated victories throughout the series, the Lakers winning the odd-numbered games, the Knicks taking the even-numbered ones. Home-court made no difference—until the seventh and deciding game; each team, usually unbeatable at home, lost in front of its fans.

Mikan improved his scoring in Game 3, putting up 24 points in the Lakers' narrow 82–77 win in New York's 69th Regiment Armory. The Knicks, like the Lakers, hated the fact that their usual home court was unavailable during the most important games of the year. The Armory, they claimed, was like playing in a neutral court, even if they played more regular season games there than at Madison Square Garden.

The Lakers lost more than just a game in their next contest, a 90–89 overtime defeat. Jim Pollard, who had been picking up Mikan while he struggled in the playoffs (Mikan managed only 11 points in Game 4), hurt his back and was declared out indefinitely. If the Lakers were going to win what was turning into as competitive a playoff series as they'd ever played, George Mikan would have to figure out a way to beat a Knick defense that, to that point, had neutralized him.

As he had done so many times before, Mikan took the team on his back, and the Lakers buried the Knicks in Game 5, 102–89, pulling the Lakers to within one victory of the championship. John Kundla inserted Bobby Harrison into Pollard's starting lineup spot, and Harrison responded with 13 points. Mikkelsen, in another strong playoff performance, hit for 32 points, more than compensating for the loss of Pollard's points.

The game, however, belonged to George Mikan. His 32 points tied him with Mikkelsen for high-scoring honors (and put him over the 10,000-point mark for his career), but it was his dominance on the boards that defeated the Knicks. The Mikan Rule, he pointed out afterward, had made no difference when the series was on the line.

He scored 28 points in Game 6, another rumble in the Armory, but the Knicks, behind Max Zaslofsky's 23 points, prevailed, 78–68. The Knicks had gone the distance against the Royals the year before, only to lose in the seventh and deciding game; they could only hope for better luck this time around.

The intangibles were clearly stacked in the Lakers' favor. Jim Pollard, after sitting out two games, was back in the lineup for Game 7. Better yet, the Lakers were playing the deciding game in the Minneapolis Auditorium, where they had never lost a playoff game in any round.

Ray Lumpp, who enjoyed a strong series for the Knicks, remembered the games as being hard-fought and evenly matched, but he had no trouble analyzing the Lakers' ultimate advantage.

"It came down to a seventh game," he said, "and the difference was George Mikan."

Kundla had always insisted that defense won championships. Mikan scored a game-high 22 points in the final game, but his shot-blocking, defensive rebounding, and overall intimidation in the middle wiped out any chance the Knicks might have had for winning their first NBA championship. Sweetwater Clifton and Connie Simmons, alternating at center, managed only five field goals between them. The game was never a contest. The Lakers stomped the Knicks, 82–65, and Minneapolis had its fourth title in five years.

For Mikan, it was the perfect ending to an up-and-down season. He'd lost his scoring title and watched his team finish in second place in the division race. Neither sat well with him. On the positive side, he'd posted single-game personal bests in scoring (61) and rebounding (36); he'd been named to the All-NBA first team for the third consecutive year, and to the All-Star team for the second straight year. And now, in what mattered most, the Lakers had reclaimed the title they'd lost the year before.

New rules or no new rules, he was back on top.

Fourteen

ROLLING ON

MIKAN NEVER STRAYED far from his midwestern upbringing. He had accumulated enough in fame and wealth to live an extravagant lifestyle, and while he certainly never lacked the benefits of both, his blue-collar Catholic background kept him grounded in the values of his youth.

This came through clearly in his book, *Mr. Basketball*, the first of two autobiographies that he would publish. Co-written with *Minneapolis Star* sports columnist Bill Carlson, *Mr. Basketball* covered Mikan's life from birth through the Lakers' loss to the Rochester Royals in the 1951 championship series, with heavy emphasis on his upbringing in Joliet. The book's easy-going, conversational style had an "aw, shucks" quality to it—a contrast to Mikan's hard-hitting reputation on the court, but definitely the George Mikan that friends and family knew. This was the Gentle Giant telling his tale, his ego showing through only on occasion, his values stamped on every page. Mikan guarded his family's privacy, mentioning Pat and their children only in passing, but a reader couldn't help but come away from the book with the thought that, as much as he loved the game, Mikan viewed basketball as a means to some end. But he was still too young to know exactly what that end might be.*

His domestic life was more typical of suburban American life in the

---

*In 1997, Mikan would team up with Minnesota writer Joseph Oberle on a second, longer and more detailed autobiography. *Unstoppable*, which featured interviews with Mikan's family members, teammates, opponents, and friends, would cover his entire career, as well and two decades following it.

1950s than the privileged life one might have expected of a highly paid superstar. He and Pat had their third child, Patrick, two weeks after the conclusion of the 1952 playoffs, giving George occasion to reflect further on
his life away from basketball. He was the father of three boys and, in all
likelihood, there would be more children in the future. He liked the Twin
Cities area, which was growing steadily, but without a lot of the problems
usually associated with big cities. If he continued to play with the Lakers,
he could see his career lasting another five years, or maybe even longer,
meaning he'd have to move into bigger digs to accommodate his expanding family.

With this in mind, Mikan spent the summer of '52 planning and de-
signing a seventeen-room house, complete with seven-foot doorways and
large, custom-built furniture. Mikan hoped to take his Minnesota bar
exam before the opening of the new season, and with a new house and career ahead of him, he felt very optimistic about his future.

To the casual fan, the 1952–53 NBA season opened with the league looking
almost identical to the previous season. The same ten teams were
returning—the first time in the NBA's brief but rocky history that that
had happened—and the Minneapolis Lakers and New York Knicks still
looked like the teams to beat. The Lakers had added Jim Holstein, a six-
three guard from Cincinnati, and Jim Fritsche, a six-eight forward from
Hamline, but very little else had changed. Fritsche was quickly moved to
Baltimore, and Holstein, as expected, found a spot on the bench. The Lakers' starting five remained the same. There was no reason for change, or for
John Kundla to tweak his substitutions. The team was coming off another
championship season, and the Laker starters were the best in basketball.

Mikan faced another rule change aimed at least indirectly at him. In the
past, in the final three minutes of a game, a jump ball occurred after a
team took its free throws, the jump taking place between the person who
was fouled and the player fouling him. This led to a lot of strategic fouling
at the end of a game, with a big man often fouling a smaller player, creating mismatches in the ensuing jump ball. Mikan often found himself in
this situation. The new rule called for a jump ball between the fouled individual and the player he'd been playing on defense. This, too, was doomed
to fail.

The '52–53 season would always be remembered as a season of excessive fouling. Players fouled opponents for three reasons—to send a message, for strategy, or by accident—and the trend of strategic fouling had turned the end of games into lengthy, boring free-throw contests. During the '52–53 season, the fouling spiraled out of control. The average game featured 58 fouls per 48-minute contest.

Mikan was no saint when it came to fouling. He often hammered his opposing center early in the game, just to intimidate him and establish his territory near the basket, and he was also famous for the hard retaliatory foul. Opposing players complained—and rightfully so—that officials let a lot of Mikan's fouling go uncalled because he was the game's biggest attraction, but he was not immune to fouling out, either. Over the course of his career, Mikan placed second only to Vern Mikkelsen in Laker disqualifications.

The excessive fouling brought a lot of attention to the officials, and fans got to know them almost as well as the players. The home team usually received the benefit of the doubt on calls, mainly because the officials feared for their physical safety if they made calls against the team. The early NBA did very little to protect the officials from players or fans, leaving them to fend for themselves.

Norm Drucker, who began his career as an NBA official during the foul-happy 1952–53 season, remembered times when the police had to be summoned to escort officials to their locker rooms or from the arenas. The officials would try to defend themselves, but the fans usually outnumbered them.

"We used to complain to the league office," Drucker recalled, "but very little security was put in place."

Maurice Podoloff tried to address the issue during the 1952–53 season, after he and official Chuck Solodare required a police escort to leave the Boston Garden after a game in which New York Knicks defeated the Boston Celtics. Podoloff was particularly concerned by what he saw as a pattern of fans being incited to violence by the words and actions of the home team's players, coaches, and owners. He'd witnessed this firsthand in the Knicks–Celtics game, and in a memo to team owners, he cautioned that such behavior could lead to the league's not having a staff of officials willing to risk such abuse.

"After a recent game, one of our Governors, in a voice that could be

heard all over the building, told all and sundry what he thought of the officiating," Podoloff wrote. "How he can expect to inspire confidence in the
officials on the part of the spectators is beyond me."

The '52–53 season, with all the foul-calling, especially late in the game,
would bring the problem to a boiling point. The NBA would have to correct the problem or face losing a fan base that had been slowly increasing
in recent years, but which had little tolerance for games that, toward the
end, were starting to look more like a visit to the library than an action-
packed sporting event.

Although his point production was down from previous years, Mikan was
an easy selection to the NBA's third All-Star Game. The Lakers, as usual,
were well represented. John Kundla was coaching the West for the third
straight year, and Vern Mikkelsen was also chosen for the third time. Slater
Martin was also selected for the team, marking his first of seven consecutive appearances in the classic.

Mikan wanted to win the game—badly. The East had taken the first
two games fairly easily, and Mikan was tired of it. Maybe the change of
venue would help. The first two had been held at the Boston Garden, before a partisan crowd favoring the East. This one was being staged in Fort
Wayne, home of a Western Division team, and two Piston players (Andy
Phillip and Larry Foust) had been selected for the game, ensuring strong
hometown interest.

Mikan found himself up against Easy Ed Macauley, one of four Celtics
selected to the team, and he quickly tried to establish his territory in the
pivot. Macauley refused to back down. The officials, perhaps fed up with
calling tight games during the regular season, let them play.

The first quarter ended in a 20–20 tie, and the West held a slim 35–34
lead at halftime. Mikan, playing nearly all of the first half (he would be on
the floor for forty of the game's forty-eight minutes), treated the game as if
another world championship was on the line. He led the team in scoring,
as expected, but he made his biggest contribution on the boards, making
sure that sharpshooters like Bill Sharman, Carl Braun, and Dolph Schayes
wouldn't get a second chance off a miss.

Offensive rebounding made a huge difference in the outcome of the
game. The West ended up taking a whopping 31 more shots than the East,

hitting on second shots that proved to be the difference. The East stayed close by outscoring the West, 25–11, from the free throw line, with Cousy, Macauley, and Schayes hitting a perfect 19 for 19 between them.

The West carried a 57–55 lead into the fourth quarter. Unlike the previous year, when he found himself in foul trouble in the final period, Mikan avoided the cheap hacks that normally meant trouble. He would lead both teams in scoring with 22 points, but it was Bob Davies who kept the West ahead. The Rochester guard scored eight of his nine points late in the fourth quarter, when the East, behind Macauley, Cousy, and Philadelphia's Neil Johnston, was trying to overtake the lead.

In the end, Mikan had his victory. The West topped the East, 79–75, in the closest, lowest-scoring All-Star Game to date. Mikan took home the MVP award—one of the few awards he hadn't already won.

Mikan looked forward to the playoffs each year, when the NBA's *real* season began. The opening round of the 1952–53 playoffs against Indianapolis offered him a little more than usual to look forward to. By now, meeting the Olympians in the playoffs had become old hat: this was the third straight year the Lakers had met them in the postseason, and they'd only lost one game to them in the previous two series combined. The Olympians, as a team and a franchise, had struggled after the loss of Alex Groza and Ralph Beard; the team had finished the regular season with a 28–43 record. Nevertheless, the Olympians had a group of scrappy overachievers and a strong backcourt that had to be taken seriously. For Mikan, this would have ordinarily been enough to get up for the series, but he found added incentive: his brother Eddie played at the power forward spot.

The series, though, wasn't much. The Lakers had finished atop their division with a 48–22 record, four games better than second-place Rochester, and they were vastly superior to the Olympians—and proved it in their brief two-game set, blowing out Indianapolis, 85–69, in Minneapolis before hanging on to win, 81–79, on the road. The Lakers' biggest concern was George Mikan's left ankle, which he'd turned midway through the fourth quarter of Game 1; while Lew Hitch had filled in admirably for him during the remainder of that game and as a substitute during the second one, the Lakers needed Mikan at his best if they were going to beat the Fort Wayne Pistons, surprise winners in their first-round series against the

Rochester Royals. Fortunately for the Lakers, Mikan's ankle improved considerably while they waited for the next round of the playoffs to begin.

The series ran the full five games, with the home team winning each of its games. Mikan led Minneapolis in scoring in all five games, and the Lakers' supporting cast proved to be too much for the Pistons. The games, typical of the rough games played in the NBA throughout the season, became foul-a-thons, ultimately resulting in both teams hitting a greater number of free throws than field goals, leading critics to mutter that something had to be done to bring a quicker pace to the NBA. In Game 4 alone, each team lost four players to fouls. John Kundla would always claim that the tough physical nature of the series, along with its extending to the full five games, put the Lakers at a notable disadvantage when they met the Knicks in the first game of the finals.

The Knicks came prepared to avenge their previous year's loss to the Lakers in the finals. The team was stronger and, hard as it was to believe, even better balanced than the previous year's group. Max Zaslofsky was gone, via a midseason trade, but his replacement, Carl Braun, was a better shooter and playmaker. Braun's career with the Knicks had been interrupted by two years in the military service, but his game hadn't fallen off at all. During the regular season, he'd led the Knicks in scoring with a 14.0 average—an amazing statistic that pointed to the team's remarkable balance. Five other players—Harry Gallatin (12.4), Ernie Vandeweghe (12.0), Connie Simmons (11.2), Sweetwater Clifton (10.6), and Vince Boryla (10.2)—averaged in double figures. The home-court advantage promised to play a significant role in the series, though, under the NBA's new 2-3-2 format, the Lakers needed to win their first two games at home to provide them with a cushion before they played the following three games in New York.

The Knicks realized this as well. Coach Joe Lapchick emphasized the importance of the Knicks' taking at least one game in Minneapolis, and his team responded, winning Game 1, 96–88, in a contest played at the Minneapolis Armory rather than the Lakers' usual Auditorium. Mikan staked his team a game-high 25 points before becoming one of four Lakers to foul out. The team, however, seemed sluggish as a whole. The Lakers led by one point entering the fourth quarter before the deeper Knicks outscored them, 30–21, in the final period to take the game.

Minneapolis rallied the following night, winning Game 2, 73–71, in a contest that could have gone either way. The Knicks played for a game-tying shot at the end of regulation, working the ball to Carl Braun, whose 21 points were second only to Harry Gallatin's 22 for the Knicks' scoring honors. With Bobby Harrison guarding him closely, Braun took what he thought was a successful shot.

"With ten seconds to go, I had a shot that tied the game, to send it into overtime," Braun recalled. "It was a fifteen or twenty-foot jumper, a tough shot. Sid Borgia, the ref, called traveling and negated the basket. So we lost the game. We might have lost it in overtime—we'll never know—but we might have gone back to New York 2–0."

The Knicks, although unhappy about the loss, considered the game a moral victory. New York had never been a strong road team, and they'd always had an especially difficult time in Minneapolis. They had played the Lakers to a draw, nearly winning both games of the all-important opening of the championship series. Mikan, held to 18 points in the second game, looked tired and vulnerable, as if the long season and postseason had finally taken their toll on his six-ten frame and bad knees and feet.

Even after losing the second game of the series, the Knicks were a cocky group, and they weren't afraid to show some swagger around the reigning world champs.

This, as it turned out, was a huge mistake.

"We were probably the cockiest we had ever been," Vince Boryla admitted. "We should have won two games there. We beat them that first game, and then we played them a hell of a game that second game. We were very, very cocky, and that got the best of us. We went to New York and they just wiped the floor with us."

According to Vern Mikkelsen, the Lakers got all the motivation they'd ever need after the second game, when the two teams were leaving the Armory.

"As we were walking out of the arena," he remembered, "Sweetwater Clifton hollered at me, 'We're not coming back. See you in New York.'"

Boryla admitted that these words were spoken, but he disputed Mikkelsen's memory of Clifton's saying them.

"It wasn't Sweetwater," he insisted. "Sweets wasn't that kind of player. That was Al McGuire, with his big mouth, who said that."

The New York papers did their part to fire up the Lakers as well. The oddsmakers had established the Knicks as five-point favorites for Game 3, and when the Knicks arrived back in New York, several of the Knicks players confidently predicted that they'd make quick work of the Lakers at home.

"They were telling the newspapers, 'We're not going back, we're going to end it here,'" Lakers reserve forward Jim Holstein said, recalling the boasts the Laker players had heard back in Minnesota. "*We* ended it up there. We won three in a row."

"I can still see the clippings," Mikkelsen said. "The New York newspapers were all saying that the series wouldn't go back to Minneapolis. They were right. It didn't."

Mikan heard the boasts, and he dealt with them the way he always responded to opposing players' boasts: he made the players eat their words. In Game 3, he played some of his most intense defense ever, blocking 20 shots en route to the Lakers' 90–75 stomping of the Knicks. Mikan even experimented with a jump shot during the first half, though it kept clanging off the rim and never seemed to fall. At halftime, Ray Meyer, brought out to New York as an assistant coach in the playoffs, scolded Mikan as only he could.

"Take that jump shot and stick it up your ass," he snarled at Mikan.

Mikan stayed away from the jump shot from that point on.

He turned up his offensive game the next night, scoring 27 points before fouling out with two minutes left in the game. Reserve guard Whitey Skoog supplied the last-minute heroics, putting in two key baskets at the end, making the difference in the Lakers' 71–69 win. The Knicks, full of confidence just forty-eight hours earlier, were all but beaten, even if their coach refused to recognize it.

"We're not dead yet," Lapchick told the skeptical New York sportswriters. "We're just breathing hard."

But they were dead. In Game 5, the Lakers mounted a twenty-point lead, 55–35, early in the second half, and were still ahead 62–48 early in the fourth quarter. The Knicks staged a furious rally, closing the gap to 85–84 with only forty seconds left in the contest, but they exhausted themselves in doing so. The Lakers had the last word. Mikan converted a three-point play and Minneapolis posted the final six points of the game, winning 91–84.

The Lakers flooded the court and Mikan hoisted John Kundla up in the air. Mikan would always call the '52–53 championship his favorite one, and

Kundla would say that his finest moment as a coach came "when we won in New York and George put me on his shoulder and carried me."

The Lakers celebrated well into the wee hours of the morning. After beating a very good Knicks team three straight on the road, New York City seemed to be the ideal place to let off steam from another banner season.

"After we won the championship," Whitey Skoog remembered, "we all went to the Copacabana and had steaks. We had quite a night."

"That was an evening to remember," Mikkelsen agreed. "It was high-test stuff, even in those days."

Mikan couldn't resist a little gloating after all he'd read and heard from the Knicks and the New York sportswriters. The Lakers were not only the world champs; they were going to hold that status for as long as he and his teammates had anything to say about it.

"We're going to win again next year," he predicted. "We'll keep the title as long as this bunch keeps playing. And nobody here is ready to quit."

Fifteen

GOING OUT ON TOP

GEORGE MIKAN HATED being pulled from a game. It was bad
enough when he got a little too physical and had to be removed because he was in foul trouble; he'd stew on the bench, cheering on his teammates while counting off the seconds until it was safe for Kundla to
re-insert him into the game. But to be taken out because Kundla thought
he needed a rest? Or because the Lakers had a whopping lead and Kundla
wanted to give the bench players a little court time? That was unthinkable.
Mikan was the heart and soul of the Lakers' offense, the team's leader and
highest-paid player, and he didn't care how tired he was, or whether his
team was up by two points or twenty. He expected to be on the floor, and
Kundla risked an earful of complaints if and when he removed Mikan
from a game.

Still, at the opening of the 1953–54 season, Mikan, although still a powerful presence on the court, had lost a step. The Lakers were accustomed to
his reporting out of condition to training camp, only to work himself into
game shape during the season's first ten games or so. But this was different.
By halftime, Mikan would be laboring up the court; by the end of the
game, he'd be totally gassed. It made sense. No one knew how long a man
his size could play such a physically demanding game, especially at the intensity level that Mikan brought to the court.

Besides, the Lakers knew—even if the front office hated to discuss it
and fans refused to consider it—that Mikan's career would end one day
and the Lakers' run of championships would probably end with it—
unless, of course, the team tracked down a replacement good enough to
cover for Mikan or pick up for some of the others, particularly Jim Pollard,

who wasn't getting any younger, either. The Lakers believed they had found such a player in Clyde Lovellette, the former University of Kansas star, who, like Mikan, had always elevated his teams to championship level.

Lovellette had grown up in Terre Haute, Indiana, and he'd led his high school team to the state tournament finals. Unlike Mikan, he'd done most of his growing by the time he had graduated from high school, and at six-nine and 235 pounds (if the scales were being charitable), he had college scouts drooling. Although he was recruited by an estimated fifty schools, including Notre Dame and Purdue, sportswriters assumed that he would be attending the University of Indiana. After all, he'd be staying close to home and his high school coach was a close friend of Branch McCracken, Indiana's coach.

What McCracken and others hadn't counted on was the persistence and persuasive power of Forrest "Phog" Allen, the University of Kansas's legendary coach. Allen had learned his basketball under the tutelage of none other than James Naismith himself, and Allen had invented and refined the idea of a team's having a full-time coach. His Kansas teams had fared well over the years, despite the challenge of trying to recruit players coveted by bigger and better-known schools. Still, by mid-century, with Allen getting older and retirement becoming more of a realistic future than a young man's dream, he had yet to achieve either an NIT or NCAA title. Lovellette, he thought, was just the player needed to put his team over the top, and he brought his "A" game when pitching Kansas to Lovellette.

"Clyde," he told the kid from Indiana, "I've got a nucleus of guys that is going to make us a real good ball club, but I need a big man in the middle. If you come, we'll win the national championship, and after your senior year we'll go to the Olympics and win a gold medal."

"Sometimes," Lovellette recalled, many years later, "coaches kind of blow you up a little bit, to see if they can convince you that you're the greatest thing since sliced bread, but I felt he was being sincere. And his predictions came true."

Lovellette listened to Allen's sales pitch and came away impressed. What kid wouldn't want to hear that he had a chance to be the star on national championship and Olympic gold medal teams? In addition, Lovellette worried that Indiana was too big a school for him, that he'd be lost on the campus and in the bigger classrooms. Kansas, he decided, was the perfect fit.

To say that he came as advertised would be an understatement. In his three years as a varsity starter, Lovellette averaged 24.5 points per game and was named to the All-American and All-Big Seven teams each year. He led his team in scoring all three years, and the nation in scoring his senior year; he was voted NCAA Player of the Year in 1952. As Phog Allen predicted, Kansas won the NCAA tournament, beating favorite St. John's, 80–63, in the finals. Later that same year, the U.S. Olympic team beat the Soviet Union in Helsinki for the gold medal. Rather than go immediately into pro ball, Lovellette spent his first year out of college playing AAU ball with the Phillips Petroleum 66ers; that team won the AAU national title.

Lovellette's bringing such a resume to the Minneapolis Lakers left other teams grumbling about the rich getting richer, but there was never a doubt about Lovellette's immediate role on the team. He wouldn't be dislodging Mikan from the lineup. For the first time in his life, he'd have to fight for playing time. That, Lovellette admitted, long after his 1988 induction into the Hall of Fame, could be frustrating.

"Sometimes," he said, "when I was sitting on the bench, I'd think, I'm young. Maybe I don't have George's experience, but I'm young and maybe I can help. But you couldn't go to Kundla and say, 'It's time to change.' You had more respect for your coach."

Lovellette understood Kundla's position. The Lakers' front line had no equal in pro basketball. The Lakers hadn't won all those championships because their coach was soft or sentimental.

Lovellette would be compared to Mikan for as long as the former Kansas star played with Minneapolis. Some of the remarks cut deeply. As good as he was, he was Mr. Basketball's replacement; he was the constant reminder that there was an end to the ride. It didn't help, either, that Lovellette was only a so-so defensive player. Mikan was only adequate when it came down to guarding a man on the move or on the outside, but Lovellette struggled to such an extent that Kundla often called for a switch in the middle. Mikkelsen would guard the center and Lovellette would handle the opponent's power forward. On occasion, Kundla would have Mikan and Lovellette on the floor at the same time, but he didn't repeat his failed attempt at a double pivot.

Mikan had no problem with Kundla's decisions, as long as they didn't interfere with his game. He still hated coming out of games, but, with someone of Lovellette's caliber replacing him, it made the move more palatable. If anything, it covered up what Mikan already knew but couldn't bring himself to say out loud: his days of playing an entire game were long gone.

The NBA was down to only nine teams for the 1953–54 season. Indianapolis, after two seasons of trying to carry on after the losses of Alex Groza and Ralph Beard, finally called it quits, making the NBA's great experiment with a player-owned franchise a part of history. The Western Division now had only four teams—Minneapolis, Rochester, Fort Wayne, and Milwaukee—and the Milwaukee franchise, competing for attention with baseball's Milwaukee Braves, who had left Boston and moved to the Midwest, wasn't faring much better. In the Eastern Division, Baltimore was having its own troubles.

The league needed more exposure. Televised games had been only marginally successful, but Maurice Podoloff believed that regularly televised games might be an answer. He was finally able to come to terms with NBC—a move that elicited mixed reactions from team owners. The more successful teams, fearing a loss of attendance, weren't happy; the less successful teams, looking to generate any kind of publicity, welcomed it. As a result, in contrast to the direction televised games would take in the future, fans were more likely to see Baltimore or Milwaukee than they were to see New York, Boston, or Minneapolis.

Antiquated stadiums had also become a problem. The Fort Wayne Pistons had moved into a new facility in 1952, after years of playing in a highschool gym, and the Syracuse Nationals had dumped the old State Fair Coliseum in favor of the Onondaga County War Memorial. However, Rochester was still playing in the old 5,000-seat Edgerton Park Sports Arena, and the Knicks were playing a majority of their games in the 69th Regiment Armory.

Even such venerable arenas as Madison Square Garden and the Boston Garden, with their hockey rinks built right under the basketball floors, were a problem. Players liked the big-time exposure of these facilities, but they hated having the ice under the basketball floorboards. It could get downright dangerous.

Arnie Ferrin remembered a game, early in the NBA days, when the Lakers played a game in Washington, D.C., where they had a similar setup. "It was the finals of my first year," he said, "and they put a floor down over the ice. Washington had a heat wave and the floor was absolutely slippery from the ice melting underneath the floor."

Not that things were much better in the Twin Cities. The Lakers divided their games between the Minneapolis Auditorium, the Minneapolis Armory, and the St. Paul Auditorium. All held between 9,000 and 10,000 spectators, but they were anything but modern.

The Lakers especially disliked the Armory, which had been built during the Depression and, to the players, felt every bit of it.

"We didn't like to play in the Armory," John Kundla remembered. "They had a sportsman's show every March in the Auditorium, and we'd go to the Armory. It had a hard floor, and the players got shin splints."

Mikan blamed the Armory for his creaky knees. "Playing on that floor in the Armory," he maintained, "ruined my knees."

The All-Star Game was supposed to be fun, a treat for the fans, but you wouldn't have been able to sell George Mikan on the idea. It was more than just a game—it was the best the NBA had to offer competing against each other, and winning the All-Star Game, while not as significant as winning the final game of a championship series, was important. Mikan proved as much in the NBA's fourth All-Star Game.

With only seconds left in the game, he stepped up to the free throw line and waited for the official to hand him the ball.

Mikan, like almost every other player who ever walked onto the court, had his own ritual that he went through before shooting free throws. If necessary, he would remove his glasses and wipe the moisture from the thick lenses. Then he would step up to the line, gaze at the target in front of him, and make the Roman Catholic Sign of the Cross before taking his shot. He always threw his free throws underhanded, as was customary for many players at that time.

The Sign of the Cross became his trademark. His teammates would occasionally tease him about it, opposing players were known to make their own Signs to offset any influence Mikan might have had with his creator, and it ultimately gave John Kundla an anecdote that he liked to repeat.

"Marques Haynes told me a story about an audience he had with the Pope," Kundla said, referring to a meeting in Rome between the Harlem

Globetrotter and Pope Pius XII. "The Pope came out and blessed himself, and the guy next to Haynes asked, 'What's he doing?' Haynes said, 'I don't know, but I think he's going to shoot a free throw.'"

For Mikan, this wasn't just a show; this was serious stuff. He still practiced his Catholic faith, and he didn't care what others thought about it. He and Kundla regularly attended Mass together, sometimes with other Lakers, and at a time when Catholics were still forbidden to eat meat on Fridays, Mikan would make a point of visiting a rectory to seek a special dispensation if the Lakers happened to be playing a Friday night game. ("I remember we were playing in Oshkosh on a Friday, and George said you could eat certain duck or chicken on Friday," Kundla recalled. "We laughed about that.")

Mikan, a better than average free-throw shooter, probably would have sunk 75–80 percent of his charity shots without divine intervention, especially if the game was on the line, as it was at this point. The 16,487 fans at Madison Square Garden had been treated to a great game. The Western Conference, represented by Mikan, Jim Pollard, Slater Martin, Arnie Risen, Bob Davies, Bobby Wanzer, Andy Phillip, and others, had fought back from a first-half deficit to take a two-point lead going into the fourth quarter. Pollard, who would lead all scorers with 23 points, had almost single-handedly kept the West in the game. The East, with Boston Celtic greats Bill Sharman, Easy Ed Macauley, and Bob Cousy, and Knick hometown favorites Harry "the Horse" Gallatin, Carl Braun, and Dick McGuire, had opportunities to put the game away, but could never build beyond modest leads.

Mikan found himself at the line after he was hammered while taking what could have been a buzzer-beating, game-tying shot. Sid Borgia, the official responsible for making the call, hadn't blown his whistle, but Mendy Rudolph, his partner, did. Rather than simply go to the free-throw line and quietly take his two shots, Mikan harassed Borgia for missing the call.

Not to be upstaged by basketball's premier player, Borgia grabbed the ball and handed it to Mikan.

"Well, Mr. Basketball," he chided Mikan, "your team's down and you've got two free throws. We'll see who chokes now."

Mikan crossed himself, bounced the ball several times, and sank his first free throw. The East's lead had been trimmed to 84–83.

This January 21, 1954, game would be one of the closest in NBA history. As Ed Macauley remembered it, Mikan was at the free-throw line because a play was botched.

"He never should have shot those two free throws," he said. "Joe Lapchick called a time-out with twenty seconds to go or whatever it was, and the first thing everybody said was they were going to get the ball to Mikan. We had a two-point lead, and since they didn't have the bonus free throw in those days, everybody said, 'Foul Mikan before he can shoot.' I forget who was playing him, but he didn't foul him before he shot. George turned, and in the process of shooting, he got fouled. He had two free throws with five seconds to go. That didn't bother George."

"The crowd was yelling and trying to distract him," Carl Braun remembered of the final moments in regulation. "I was standing at the side, and I saw Mikan wink before he shot. I don't know who he winked at, but he was very cool at that moment."

Mikan launched his second foul shot and it swooshed through the net. Game tied, 84–84. Mikan, not about to let things go without a final word on the subject of whether he'd choke in the clutch, turned to Borgia.

"I can't tell you what he said to the official," joked Arnie Ferrin.

In Ferrin's opinion, the league employed outstanding officials, but that didn't prevent Mikan from giving them an earful if he disagreed with their calls.

"George was hard on officials," Ferrin said. "He had that indomitable will to win, and if the officials weren't doing a very good job, he would very nicely—or sometimes not so nicely—explain it to them. He'd complain if he didn't get the calls. I thought we were going to get fined or get technical fouls, to try to control George."

Mikan collected his share of technical fouls throughout his career, but not just because of his fiery, competitive spirit. He felt obligated, as a team captain and leader, to see that the games were called fairly and correctly. He was the first to admit that he received star treatment from officials, especially when the Lakers were playing at home; he'd heard other teams protest that he was given way too much leeway with his elbows. He disagreed. He received as much as he dished out, and he demanded at least equity in the way games were officiated.

Mikan's late-game heroics only prolonged the '54 All-Star Game. In overtime, Bob Cousy conducted his own clinic on basketball, scoring 10 of the East's 14 points and leading his team to a 98–93 win. Cousy took home the MVP award, and Mikan found himself on the losing end of the All-Star Game for the third time in four years. He'd never play in another.

Over the course of his career, Mikan had seen just about every kind of rule change one could imagine, usually designed to level off his domination of the game. Goaltending rules had been enacted while he was still in college. The lane had been widened to move him farther away from the basket. Every time the league changed the rules, he adjusted his game, proving to his naysayers that there was much more to him than just height.

The NBA unveiled its most outlandish experiment on March 7, 1954, when league officials decided to raise the basket from ten feet to twelve feet for an exhibition game between the Lakers and the Milwaukee Hawks. The Lakers, just back from a road trip, had not been informed of the league's latest brainstorm, and the players got quite a surprise when they walked into the Minneapolis Auditorium and saw the elevated baskets.

No one liked it.

"It was a huge mistake—a *huge* mistake," Vern Mikkelsen declared. "I said, 'This isn't going to work, but I'm going to have the best night I ever had.' I was a brute force guy, and now that we were at twelve feet instead of ten feet, I would be getting more second shots than I ever had in my life."

As Pep Saul recalled, there was a good reason for Mikkelsen's getting so many shots off the rebound.

"The ball just came off at an entirely different angle," he said. "When the ball came off the backboard, it came down almost flat. It didn't come out at all. That was an amazing thing to me."

Mikkelsen's prediction came true. He led Minneapolis in scoring with 17 points, and the Lakers squeaked out a 65–63 victory. Mikan had a nightmarish night, hitting on only 2 of his 14 shots. His hook shots needed a higher trajectory to the basket, and he couldn't make the adjustment in just one game.

"George couldn't hit his ass from second base," said Dick Schnittker. "He could not adjust that quickly. We hadn't practiced on the baskets. We just went out and played."

The league had found a way to neutralize Mikan's domination of the game, but no one enjoyed it.

"It took away a lot of the excitement of the game," Bobby Harrison said of the twelve-foot basket. "There were no hook shots or tip-ins. You'd get an occasional layup, but you had to shoot it fifteen feet high to make it."

"The first time I jumped during the layup drill, I wasn't even at the bottom of the net," Jim Holstein said. "I thought, 'Oh my God, what am I going to do with this?' We all laughed a little bit. Then we started shooting and we had a real laugh."

Bill Calhoun, never known for his point production, wound up leading Milwaukee with 20 points in what he'd see as one of the more memorable games of his career, even if the game itself was, in his words, "a bust."

"It took the driving layup out of the game, and it pretty much took the jump shots out of there, too," he said. "The only thing you could make were set shots. We couldn't make layups, and all the players were laughing when we tried to shoot free throws. Mikan got only four points in that game, I think."

Calhoun laughed at the idea of his and Vern Mikkelsen's being their respective teams' high scorers. "A friend of mine had seen that game, and he said, 'The two slop-asses got all the points.' "

The fans hated the game as much as the players, and any ideas for moving the basket up on a permanent basis were scrapped. For their efforts to make the game a bigger challenge for the taller players, league officials had made it almost impossible for the shorter ones.

The advantage, Clyde Lovellette pointed out, noting what the league should have foreseen, was still with the big man.

"He was still closer to that basket than the six-foot guy," he said.

All that stood between the Minneapolis Lakers and the NBA's first "three-peat" were the Syracuse Nationals. Al Cervi had put his playing days behind him the season before, but he still coached the team with the same hard-nosed, chip-on-the-shoulder style that had marked his tenure with the Rochester Royals and, for the last five years of his career, as player-coach of the Nats. Cervi was nothing less than a perennial test: of the players he belittled and outraged in the name of guidance; the officials who had to listen to his every complaint about every single call that went against his team; and opposing players and coaches, who came to see a game against the Nats as a contest that was part war, part sideshow. The fans packing

Syracuse's new arena loved him, and the local press nicknamed his team the "Cervi-men."

Most important, of course, was the fact that the future Hall of Famer produced a winner, year after year after year. The Nats had posted a sub-.500 season only once in Cervi's five years as coach, and had won the division title twice. Somehow, despite all the success, Cervi was able to sell his players on the idea that they were underdogs doomed to go unnoticed and unappreciated by everyone outside the Syracuse city limits. The press, he was able to convince them, was dedicated to kissing the backsides of the guys playing downstate in Madison Square Garden or, worse even yet, those occupying seats in the Boston Garden. Other teams had marquee names like George Mikan and Bob Cousy and Neil Johnston and Bill Sharman; the Nats had each other.

The us-against-the-world spirit, which would evolve into a tiresome cliché decades later, when any team not named the Los Angeles Lakers or Boston Celtics or Chicago Bulls would employ it as a rallying cry, was remarkably effective: the players bought it, even a half century later, when the Nationals players characterized their team as a group of no-names that had battled the odds on the way to the top.

"We were a small market and we got very little publicity," Dolph Schayes would assert, comparing the Nats with football's Green Bay Packers. "Syracuse was the David against Goliath. Nobody ever heard of us and nobody ever will."

"The press supplied us with ammunition," Earl Lloyd would say. "They couldn't figure out why we were winning. We didn't have a lot of big names, but we had some people who were good at what they did, and the way we played embodied the word 'team.' We got some ridicule from the press: 'How are they winning with that rag-tag bunch they got?' We just took it as a challenge."

The Nats, as their opponents knew all too well, were anything but a rag-tag group. Dolph Schayes, who had finished the 1953–54 season sixth in the league in scoring, fifth in rebounding, and first in free throws made, was easily among the league's elite players. Paul Seymour, another member of the '49–50 Nationals team that had given the Lakers all they could handle, had just enjoyed one of his finest seasons as a pro, finishing among the league leaders in scoring, assists, and free-throw percentage. Seymour and Billy Gabor, along with relative newcomers George King and Bill Kenville, played a relentlessly aggressive (and occasionally nasty) defense molded strongly in the image of their coach. They would never be compared to the backcourts in Rochester or Boston, but they were quick and talented, and certainly a good match for the Lakers' backcourt. The men up front—Earl Lloyd, Wally Osterkorn, and Bob Lavoy—set picks and crashed the boards, freeing Schayes to pursue his hyperkinetic style of play.

The '53–54 season had been a good one. The Nats finished in a tie with the Celtics for second place, two games behind the Knicks in the extremely competitive Eastern Division. The three teams had pounded the daylights out of each other during the regular season, setting the tone for a round-robin playoff series that exacted its price in terms of player attrition. Syracuse won every game in the round-robin series, beating the Celtics twice and the Knicks twice. They went on to sweep the Celtics, two games to none, in the Eastern Division finals, but by the time the final second had ticked off the clock in Syracuse's 83–76 victory over Boston on March 27, the Nats were such a conglomeration of broken bones, sprains and strains, cuts and bruises, and battle fatigue that the press labeled them the "Bandage Brigade."

The Syracuse–Boston rivalry had heated to a boil over the past couple of seasons, leading to brutal confrontations in the playoffs. The Celtics, with future Hall of Famers Bob Cousy, Bill Sharman, and Easy Ed Macauley, scored at will against most of their opponents, but Cervi's dedication to strong team defense had led the Nats to a tense 96–95 overtime win in the two teams' initial round-robin game. The Nats went on to defeat the Celtics in the final game of their preliminary round, and the first game of the best-of-three conference finals.

By this point, the Nats were hampered by a number of physical ailments. Earl Lloyd had broken the middle finger on his right hand and had been fit with a cast that hindered his play. Wally Osterkorn was slowed down by calcium deposits that would require surgery during the offseason. George King's heel was so badly bruised that he had foam cushions installed in his shoe. Billy Gabor was limping on a sprained ankle. Cervi, however, wasn't worried, at least when he addressed the problem with the press.

"We were in bad shape before Monday's win over the Celtics, and my fellows didn't act as though they were crippled," he boasted. "I guess all they see are dollar signs on the hoop when they get out there. Let's hope their eyesight doesn't dim."

The second game against the Celtics, known thereafter as the "Boston Massacre," proved to be one of the most violent encounters in NBA playoff history. Fifty-seven fouls were whistled by officials, and the Nats suffered two more key casualties that would play an important role when they met the Lakers in the finals. Tempers flared throughout the game, accompanied by the usual pushing and shoving, but a near-riot broke out with three minutes left in the third quarter, when Dolph Schayes was undercut while going up for a layup. Schayes fell hard to the floor, cutting his face and breaking his right wrist. Wally Osterkorn, nicknamed "Ox" for his size and strength, exchanged heated words with Easy Ed Macauley, and within seconds a full-blown donnybrook was taking place on the floor of the Boston Garden.

"Somebody tunneled Dolph and Wally Osterkorn got pretty upset about it," remembered Bill Kenville, who found himself near the white-hot center of the action. "Wally threw a punch and that's when it started."

"I punched out Macauley, and after I hit him, he fell backward and Seymour hit him," Osterkorn recalled. "And then the crowd poured onto the floor."

Both benches emptied. Players squared off. Police and Garden security struggled to keep fans from attacking the Syracuse players. Nats forward Bob Lavoy remained near the Syracuse bench because, by his own admission, he could find no one he could beat in a fight. He calmly collected the watches flying off fans' wrists during the fighting.

Osterkorn wound up matched up against Bob Brannum, one of the Celtics' enforcers and one of the toughest players in the league. However, if those watching the fisticuffs expected a battle royal between the two, they were disappointed. The two players had been teammates earlier in their careers, and Brannum feared for Osterkorn's safety.

"I had played with Brannum in Sheboygan," Osterkorn explained. "Bob grabbed me from behind and squeezed tight. 'Goddamn it, Wally, don't struggle,' he said. 'They'll kill you, for Chrissake. Let me hold you.' So he held onto me and nobody bothered me."

It took an estimated fifteen to twenty minutes for police to restore order and the game to resume. Cervi called five consecutive time-outs with the hope that Schayes would recover enough to toss up his two free throws. The Nats, playing from behind for most of the game, went on a tear and took the game, 83–76, earning the right to face the Lakers for the championship title.

Schayes was not the only Syracuse player lost in the melee. Paul Seymour had sprained his right thumb when he punched Macauley. He, like Schayes, would have to play with a cast—if, indeed, the two were cleared to play at all.

And the first game of the finals was only three days away.

March 31, 1954

Mikan and the Lakers aren't too concerned about meeting the Nats. They've never lost a playoff game in the Minneapolis Auditorium—not one, in the history of the franchise—and the opening game of the series is in Minneapolis. Granted, Mikan's feeling the effects of another long season, as are Pollard and Mikkelsen, but there's absolutely no reason for anyone to think that the team can't marshal enough energy to take out a team with 60 percent of its starting lineup sporting casts. Besides, if Big George wears down, Kundla can always bring in Clyde Lovellette, who's young and relatively rested and shouldering a big chip for the lack of playing time he received during the regular season.

No, lack of confidence isn't a problem. Looking back on the scene decades later, Lovellette, for one, would wonder if the Laker swagger might have worked against them.

"I think we came in with the wrong attitude," he'd remember. "Once you've won championships and you come up to a team that isn't one hundred percent, it's like a step down. They came to play, and I think we left a little bit in the locker room."

Dolph Schayes isn't even on the floor for the first game's opening tip. He'll play in this and other games, but only for a limited amount of time, with mixed effectiveness. Seeing Schayes on the bench comes as a big relief to Mikkelsen, who's sick to death of chasing the big Syracuse forward all over the floor in an effort to limit his points and rebounds. Schayes wears Mikkelsen out, and, on more occasions that he'll ever want to remember or admit, Mikkelsen's had to resort to fouling Schayes just to keep him from blowing past him and scoring easy baskets.

Earl Lloyd, similarly limited by the cast on his hand, is back after missing the Celtic series, but he plays only sixteen minutes of the game. Mikan finds himself working against Jim Neal, who's big and burly but nowhere near as effective as the smaller but much quicker Lloyd. On offense, the Nats move guards Paul Seymour and George King into the pivot, where they can use their superior speed to frustrate Mikan. Cervi's philosophy is simple: wear the big guy out on both ends of the floor. With any luck, he'll pick up a few quick, cheap fouls, and Kundla will be forced to sit him for a while. Cut Mikan's points and you might not miss the production you might have been getting from Schayes and Lloyd.

The strategy is effective. Mikan hacks his way into early foul trouble, and Kundla replaces him with Lovellette. Whitey Skoog, who's enjoying a good game, also lands on the bench with foul problems. The Lakers stagger under the constant pressure applied by Cervi's tough brand of defense. Pollard can't find the basket, making only one the entire game. Mikkelsen, rarely a big scorer, manages only three field goals. With only minutes left in the game, the Nats are running even with the Lakers and looking to end the Minneapolis streak. Three games in Syracuse loom in the near future, so an opening-day loss would be as devastating to the Lakers as when they stole a game in Syracuse four years earlier.

But this game belongs to Clyde Lovellette, who winds up leading all scorers with 16 points, including two huge three-point plays in the closing minutes, when the Lakers are pulling away for good. By the end of the game, Jim Neal, bothered by a chest cold, is so winded he's walking up the floor, and Lovellette takes full advantage of it. He's not only the tallest man on the court; he also packs enough beef to clean off the boards and move around anyone in his way. Lovellette and Mikan put together 31 points between them, leading a frustrated Al Cervi to comment after the game that "those giants just wore us down."

In the end, the Lakers prevail, 79–68. Schayes plays only six minutes and Lloyd sixteen. Between them, they score all of three points. Schayes, in a postgame interview, tells the press that the pain in his wrist didn't limit his effectiveness, but that the heavy cast definitely made a difference. Lloyd, too, complains about his cast, saying that he had a hard time handling the ball with his hand encased in plaster. Cervi, determined to find some way to overcome his team's injuries, promises to put his team through a series of rigorous drills designed to help them learn to dribble better with their casts.

The series's low-scoring first game only hinted at what lay ahead for the Lakers.

Cervi had devised a brilliant game plan that took George Mikan and

Jim Pollard out of their games. Pollard's quickness was always a problem for the forwards trying to guard him; Cervi countered by having his guards switch to Pollard on defense. The ploy worked from two standpoints. First and foremost, Pollard wasn't able to use his speed to blast around his defenders for cheap baskets; he would have to earn his points the hard way. Cervi's strategy also affected Pollard's passes to Mikan. The Nats' guards had quicker hands than the players on the front line, and they were capable of intercepting, misdirecting, or knocking away passes going into the pivot—a lesson that Pollard and Mikan learned in the first game. Fans had to wonder if Cervi's unconventional strategy had finally succeeded in neutralizing the Laker stars.

A larger question must have been hanging in the air as the two teams readied themselves for Game 2: Was the Lakers' heralded front line losing its domination after years of intense competition, injuries, and time itself? Mikan would be turning thirty on June 18; Pollard was nearly two years older.

Mikan conceded that he was feeling the effects of all the pounding he had taken during the regular season, the postseason, and the many exhibition games the Lakers played.

"My eight-plus years as a pro had started to take their toll on my body," he admitted.

Some things, though, didn't change. Mikan might have been slowing down with age, but he still fought every minute he was on the court, and when the game was on the line, he still expected the ball.

Syracuse forward Bill Kenville recalled a conversation he overheard coming from the Lakers' locker room, a fiery speech that attested to Mikan's continuing competitiveness.

"We were coming out at halftime," Kenville said, "and we were doing pretty well. I think we were up on them. As we were walking out, I heard George's voice coming out of the locker room. 'You guys have fooled around for a half now. If you want to win, just get the ball in to Big George.' That was the message."

Mikan, however, didn't fare much better in the nationally televised second game of the series. He duplicated his disappointing 15-point production of the first game, though he managed to avoid the foul troubles that bothered him in the earlier contest. Pollard dropped in 13 points and Lovellette 11, but the Lakers struggled. Once again, Al Cervi had made important adjustments to thwart the Lakers' attack. If the Nats were going to score fewer points with Schayes and Lloyd competing well below their usual standards, a snail's-paced, lower-scoring game might give the Nats a chance. It worked: at halftime, Syracuse led 28–27.

Syracuse poured it on in the third quarter, outscoring the Lakers 16–1 at one stretch. The Lakers chipped away at the lead throughout the fourth quarter, and with eighteen seconds left in the game, Mikan grabbed a pass from Dick Schnittker and tied the game at 60. The Nats had plenty of time to work for a last-second shot to win the game, but rather than work the clock and look for a high-percentage shot, Paul Seymour took a two-handed set shot from forty-three feet away. To the amazement of everyone in the building—except, perhaps, Seymour himself—the ball dropped through the hoop. The Lakers' playoff winning streak at the Auditorium had ended.

After the game, Jim Pollard approached Seymour and asked him why he'd taken a shot from so far away, when there was still time left on the clock. "I was open," Seymour replied coolly.

Seymour would never regret launching his game-deciding bomb, but he would wonder later if it might have changed the course of the finals. "We made 'em mad then," he commented. "Mikan showed us how to play after that."

The victory came with another price. With a minute and twenty-nine seconds left in the game, George King, who had led the Nats' third-quarter charge, tried to drive to the basket for a layup. Mikan and Schnittker charged over to defend, and King found himself sandwiched between the two much bigger men. King wound up on the floor with a broken wrist. Like several other of his teammates, King was fitted with a specially designed cast that allowed him to join the Bandage Brigade for the remainder of the playoffs.

"The doctor put a basketball in my hand and put a cast on my wrist, with my hand open, so it would fit a basketball," King explained.

But the carnage wasn't over for the Nats. The Lakers and Nationals split the next two games, the Lakers taking Game 3, 81–67, behind Mikan's 30 points and 15 rebounds, the Nats grabbing Game 4, 80–69, behind Paul Seymour's 25 points. Unfortunately for Al Cervi's team, Billy Gabor tore up his right knee in the fifth game and was lost for the playoffs. Desperately short-handed, the Nats seemed all but finished.

The Nats would win the NBA championship a year later, but to Earl

Lloyd, who played injured and watched his teammates do the same, the Nats' survival in the '53–54 finals was nothing short of astonishing.

"To me, this was much more amazing than winning the championship," he said. "We had six people who were healthy."

"Amazing" would be the proper term to describe the Nats in Game 6. In another foul-plagued, low-scoring match, the two teams traded leads until the final minute. Mikan finished with 30 points, but the Nats refused to let him completely take over the game. With a minute to go and the game tied, 63–63, Al Cervi called time-out to set up a final play.

Four years earlier, in a similar situation, Cervi had taken the shot himself and the Nats had lost. He was no longer playing, so he'd have to trust one of the five exhausted players on the floor—or, perhaps, four of them. Jim Neal, the Nats' six-eleven backup center, playing mainly by default, was to clear out of the lane and, if necessary, set a high pick for one of his teammates. The ball would go to one of the other four. The Lakers, however, played very tight defense and the play broke down. Neal, standing near the top of the key, suddenly found himself with the ball after an errant Paul Seymour pass. With only four seconds left in regulation, he unleashed a two-handed prayer from twenty-seven feet away. The ball dropped through the hoop, and the Nats had tied the series by stealing another game in Minneapolis.

Mikan couldn't believe it. The Lakers were the superior team, even when the Nats were healthy, yet here they were, facing a seventh and deciding game. If Syracuse found any more tricks in their gym bags, the Lakers stood to lose to a team they should have put away in Game 6.

The Lakers were ultimately too good and too healthy. The Nats put the defensive clamps on Mikan in Game 7, but Jim Pollard took on the scoring load with 21 points. Dolph Schayes countered with 18, but the injury-depleted Nats were never in the game. The Lakers built a huge 61–45 lead in the third period and coasted to an 87–80 win. Minneapolis had another championship, their third in a row, in the books.

The Laker fans didn't know it, but they'd never see another. They had just witnessed the last championship game of the George Mikan era.

The series had taken a lot out of Mikan. Although he probably had several more good years of basketball in him, he was beginning to question whether it was worth the wear and tear on his body, or the time it took from his family. Clyde Lovellette was a very capable center, and the Lakers' front office had made it clear that he would be succeeding Mikan, sooner or later, depending upon how long Mikan chose to stay in the game.

There was also an issue of money: Mikan wanted a new high-buck contract, and the Lakers' weren't willing to pay it.

Mikan spent the summer mulling over his future, weighing the pros and cons of continuing his career in basketball. On September 24, 1954, he announced his decision: he was retiring, effective immediately. He needed to spend more time with his family, he told the press; he was ready to pursue a new career as a lawyer.

The Lakers, perhaps sensing another contract-negotiation ploy in the announcement, or maybe knowing how futile it would be to argue against Mikan's strong will, made very little effort to change his mind.

The greatest player the NBA had ever seen was hanging up his sneakers.

Sixteen

FAILED COMEBACK

GEORGE MIKAN DIDN'T want to retire any more than any other athlete wants to call it quits after a long, successful career. He knew he'd miss the competition, the camaraderie with his teammates, the attention from reporters, and the adulation from Minnesota sports fans. Younger players were quicker and, in some instances, stronger, but Mikan never doubted that he could still compete at a high level. He would not accept the contention that he wasn't worth the top salary that he'd been receiving since he graduated from DePaul and took his first pro job with the Chicago Gears.

What he didn't discuss with reporters—to do so, in those days, would have been tacky beyond belief—was just how much the issue of money had affected his decision to retire. He meant what he said about wanting to spend more time with his family and establish a law practice, but if the money had been right, he probably would have played at least another season or two.

Mikan had approached Max Winter at the conclusion of the 1953–54 season. He'd earned $35,000 for the season, and he hoped to duplicate it the next year. Winter, who had gritted his teeth and given Mikan his hefty salaries throughout his stay in Minneapolis, turned down Mikan's salary demands, and the two had never been able to come to terms. If retiring was another one of Mikan's negotiating ploys, it didn't work.

Fortunately for Mikan, the failure to come to terms on another contract spared him from another rule change that probably would have had a much more profound effect on his play than the earlier goaltending and lane-widening changes. Over the summer of 1954, the NBA adopted a rule requiring the offensive team to take a shot within a 24-second timeframe. The rule was designed to speed up a game that had become so hopelessly bogged down—by stoppage of play and stalling tactics—that fan interest was beginning to wane.

Mikan, not surprisingly, was at least partially responsible for the change. The idea of a shot clock had been discussed among players, coaches, and team officials since the Laker–Piston debacle on November 22, 1950, when the Pistons had frozen the ball in an effort to keep Mikan and the Lakers from playing offense. Teams throughout the league had informally agreed that such a game, if repeated, could spell the death of fan interest in the sport, and they had agreed, although not in writing, to avoid that kind of game in the future.

There had been no repeats of the Laker–Piston game, but teams still froze the ball if they had a lead in the last few minutes of a game.

"In my first year [1950–51], we won the championship of the Eastern Division," recalled Paul Arizin, who spent his entire ten-year Hall-of-Fame career in Philadelphia. "We played Syracuse at home in the playoffs, and the first game went into overtime. We got the tap in the overtime and Joe Fulks, I think, took a shot and missed it. Syracuse got the ball and held it for, like, four minutes and fifty seconds. With ten seconds left, Freddie Scolari took a one-hander. It went in and we were done." Syracuse beat the Warriors, 91–89, in the first game of a best-of-three series. The Nats took the second game in Syracuse and Philadelphia was eliminated.

Teams also used excessive fouling as a strategy, and this, too slowed the game to a crawl.

"The game was going down the tubes at that time," Rochester guard Billy Gabor remembered. "If my team was ahead by ten points going into the last quarter, I'd say, 'Okay, let's foul the other team.' So we'd foul the guy, hoping he'd get one free throw. Then we'd get the basket. We called it trading two for one. Well, they'd say, 'Hell, if you're going to foul me for one shot, I'm going to foul you for one shot.' The last quarter was just people going back and forth to the foul line. The game was getting pretty bad."

The fouling had escalated with each new season. During the '52–53 season, officials called an average of 58 fouls per 48-minute game. The fiasco bottomed out on March 21, 1953, in a playoff game between the Boston Celtics and the Syracuse Nationals. The game had gone into four overtimes, with Boston prevailing, 111–105. Bob Cousy scored 50 points, with 30 coming from the free-throw line. All told, 107 fouls had been called on the two teams, with each team attempting 65 free throws. The game had been so horrible that the television network broadcasting it had cut away before the game concluded.

Big changes were necessary.

The fouling part was easy. Beginning with the 1954–55 season, teams would be allowed six fouls per quarter. If this number was exceeded, the other team would be given a bonus free throw, allowing it the opportunity to score the two points it might have recorded if it had shot successfully from the field. There could still be strategic fouling—to stop the clock, for instance—but the worst of the excessive fouling was eliminated.

Owners weren't so sure about what to do about the stalling tactics.

Enter Danny Biasone, owner of the Syracuse Nationals. Biasone, an Italian immigrant, had never played basketball. He was not a big-time arena operator like Boston's Walter Brown or New York's Ned Irish, nor was his city one of the league's bigger markets. Biasone came from a more modest background. He owned a restaurant with a ten-lane bowling alley on the second floor, and he'd sponsored a semi-pro football team before the war. He started up the Nats in 1946, and the team had done very well, first in the NBL and, eventually, the NBA. Biasone became a student of the game. Whenever the Nats played a game at home, you could usually find Biasone sitting on the Syracuse bench next to Coach Al Cervi, impeccably dressed, chain-smoking cigarettes and giving the officials the business whenever a call went against his team.

As Biasone told basketball historian Terry Pluto, he'd been concerned about the excessive fouling and the ball-freezing tactics since the Laker–Piston game, and he favored the idea of putting a time limit on offensive possessions.

"Baseball has three outs an inning, football has four downs, every game has a limit on possessions except basketball," he explained. "Finally, I sold the idea to Maurice Podoloff."

The 24-second limit, not exactly the first number that would jump into anyone's mind, was arrived upon after Biasone did some simple math. He studied a sampling of box scores of moderately high-scoring games, and concluded that each team shot about 60 times in these contests, for a total of 120 shots per game. Each 48-minute game came down to 2,880 seconds, which translated into a shot every 24 seconds.

The idea of a time limit on offensive possessions was almost universally accepted among players, coaches, and team owners (although Max Winter screamed that it was another case of the league's legislating against big men like George Mikan), but not everyone embraced the actual 24-second limit. Some felt that 24 seconds was inadequate time to set up a good shot, and some argued that it might result in more turnovers and sloppy play.

"I'm an old-timer," admitted Carl Bennett, who had seen some high-scoring games in Fort Wayne, but who had also witnessed the 19–18 Laker–Piston game. "Basketball takes time to set up a play. It's finesse, instead of just running up and down the court. I think thirty seconds [would have been better]. As we well know, six seconds is a long time."

Bill Calhoun, who had earned his reputation for his play on defense, had another reason for having initial doubts about the 24-second clock. "I thought it was going to be bad, because I thought it would be running up and down and shooting, with no defense of any kind," he said. "It actually turned out good for me. Defense played its part. You had to play defense for fifteen of the twenty-four seconds, and that seemed plenty long enough."

Dick Schnittker, a Mikan teammate on the Lakers, also confessed to being skeptical of the rule, but, like Calhoun, he found that it eventually helped his game.

"It was good for me because I was a mover without the ball," he said. "I got a lot of garbage baskets because I would slice in and out, and pick up rebounds and loose balls. When you know the clock is running down, you know there's going to be a rebound. So it really helped me a lot."

Once he had come up with his 24-second time limit, Biasone decided to test it in a game situation. He assembled a group of Syracuse-area pro and college players and, on August 10, 1954, they played an exhibition game at Vocational High School in Syracuse. Since an official 24-second clock had yet to be designed and built, a timekeeper watched the second-hand of his watch and shouted "TIME!" whenever 24 seconds had elapsed. The players, aware of the time restrictions, moved the ball around at a decent clip and very few time violations occurred.

The NBA adopted the rule. As for Biasone's contribution to the game,

Maurice Podoloff didn't mince words when asked about the historical importance of the 24-second clock.

"The adoption of the clock was the most important event in the NBA," he told an interviewer, "and Danny Biasone is the most important man in the NBA."

George Mikan's retirement announcement, as the sports world learned soon enough, did not mean that he was finished with pro basketball. Max Winter had grown more and more interested in pursuing an NFL franchise for the Twin Cities area, and on October 5, 1954, the Lakers announced that Mikan would be replacing Winter as the team's general manager and vice president. Mikan's retirement had lasted all of eleven days.

The Lakers were still a formidable team. Clyde Lovellette now assumed Mikan's place in the middle, and Minneapolis, behind very balanced scoring, finished the 1954–55 season with a 40–32 record, the NBA's third-best record behind Western Division winner Fort Wayne and Eastern Division winner and NBA champion Syracuse. The Laker guards, in particular, benefited from Mikan's retirement: Slater Martin and Whitey Skoog, rarely called upon to score when Mikan was in the lineup, each enjoyed career highs in their point production.

Mikan attended Laker home games, taking a seat near the bench, and it was clear to anyone watching him that he was itching to be back out on the floor.

"You'd take one look at George, sitting right behind the Laker bench, and he would be almost sick," said forward Ed Kalafat, who began his career with the Lakers the year Mikan sat out. "You could tell he was chomping at the bit to come back."

Mikan was the first to admit as much. The game was faster and more youthful, but he still felt he could compete. He was never a big suit-and-tie, sit-at-the-desk kind of guy, although he was adept at using his name and easy, outgoing personality to help convince people that Minnesota was a great state in which to play college or pro basketball.

Kalafat was a case in point.

"I'm Croatian by nationality," he said. "My dad was born in the Old Country, and George was a Croatian from the north side of Illinois. I'm originally from Montana, and I visited Minnesota a couple of times and hated the school. I had twenty-six offers to go to college and I wanted to go to the West Coast. George wrote a letter in Croatian to my dad, and my dad said, 'You're going to Minnesota.' I said, 'Dad, I don't like Minnesota.' He said, 'I don't give a damn. That's where you're going because Mikan's there.'

"When I came to the University of Minnesota, George took me under his wing like a brother. Compared to Montana, it was colder than heck in Minnesota, but George took me down to his tailor and got me the best storm coat. I was sixteen when I got there—I turned seventeen about two weeks later—and he gave me four tickets right behind the Laker bench for every Laker home game. When he'd see me, he'd talk to me in Croatian. Then they made me their territorial draft choice. George talked to me about it because I had some offers to go somewhere else. I was thinking about a long-term career with the Phillips Oilers, because they were after me, and I thought I should maybe go someplace where I could play basketball and have a career."

Kalafat not only signed on with the Lakers; he wound up having Mikan as a teammate.

In the most ill-advised move of his professional career, Mikan returned to the court on January 14, 1956. The 1955–56 version of the Lakers was off to a horrible start. Jim Pollard had retired after the '54–55 season, and the Lakers floundered without him. Attendance was way down, and Mikan could barely stand to watch the once-dominant franchise sinking into mediocrity.

Mikan played twelve minutes in his first game back, scoring 11 points in a Laker victory over the Pistons. The Lakers' record gradually improved with Mikan in the lineup, but Mikan's bigger value to the team was in his name. Prior to his return, the Lakers would have been lucky to attract two thousand fans to their home games; with Mikan back, attendance shot up, not only in the Twin Cities but all around the league.

His play bore no comparison to the George Mikan of a few years earlier. It took him several weeks to work himself into game shape. His knees, shot from all the punishment they'd taken over his career, took an even greater pounding. With a 24-second clock ticking away, he had to run as hard as he could to get in position for the offensive plays. Suddenly, after a career of being the best ever to play his position, Mikan was looking very average.

"He played well his first couple of games, but then, the next thing you knew, he wasn't doing so well," Whitey Skoog remembered. "He was fresh to begin with, but he started getting beat up a little bit and he didn't return to that. He didn't get in that groove. I don't think he could have gotten into that groove again."

"You just don't do that, at that age," noted Dick Schnittker, who, with Ed Kalafat, had inherited Jim Pollard's spot at forward. "It's been proven over the years. He's not there physically; the reflexes are gone. Then you start pressing and you look worse."

Jim Holstein actually had the nerve to address the issue with his former Laker teammate. Holstein had been traded to Fort Wayne twenty-seven games into the season, and it was almost painful for him to watch Mikan struggling to keep up

"I was at the free-throw line with George," Holstein recalled. "I looked at him and said, 'George, get out. You can't do it any more. You're making a fool of yourself.' Well, he didn't like to hear that, so I shut up real quick."

Mikan's return, Schnittker suggested, had a negative effect on the team's on-court chemistry and development. The Lakers hadn't fared well prior to Mikan's coming out of retirement, but they had been learning to play together, adapting to Clyde Lovellette's talents, rather than Mikan's, in the middle. The team had young, quick players, but with Mikan back on the team, the offensive game changed. John Kundla quite naturally wanted Mikan in the lineup, so the future was put on hold.

"It changed the whole dynamic," Schnittker explained.

Chuck Mencel, the University of Minnesota star brought to the Lakers as part of the rebuilding process, agreed.

"When he came back, the rest of us didn't really know how to deal with it," he said. "He wasn't the player he once was, but you had to give him the ball, and that took away from the ongoing efforts to find the combinations that could have been effective in rebuilding. It takes time to find the right combinations and for players to contribute in their roles; it takes time to build a chemistry. We felt obliged to involve George—beyond, perhaps, his best capability—and that impacted on our effectiveness."

No one was more affected by Mikan's return than Clyde Lovellette. He'd suffered through the inevitable and often cruel comparisons to Mikan during the '54–55 season, when he was holding down the center position after Mikan's retirement. He would have been the first to acknowledge that he didn't compare to Mikan, in style of play or impact on the game, but nevertheless Lovellette had led the Lakers with an 18.7 scoring average—slightly better than Mikan's 18.1 the year before—and he was developing into a very strong offensive player.

With Mikan back, he was again relegated to second string, watching the fading Laker superstar trying to regain his form, knowing full well that he could do better.

He didn't dare broach the subject with John Kundla.

"It bothered me," he said about the time he spent on the bench, "but I knew it was going to happen. George shouldn't have come back, but it wouldn't have been right for him to go behind me. When George left, it seemed like we were going to have two guards, two forwards, and Clyde. We were all going to get in the action. The game became more wide-open."

The problem, Lovellette and some of the others agreed, was a problem of transition. Pollard was gone, and Martin and Mikkelsen were hitting their peaks. Pep Saul and Bobby Harrison, mainstays on three straight Laker championship teams, had moved to other teams. Minneapolis wanted another championship, especially after being knocked out of the '54–55 playoffs, but the team would have to go through a rebuilding process first. Mikan, Lovellette suggested, was not part of that process.

"You can't start from where he was and keep going to the top of that mountain," he insisted. "He's already been there. There was only one way to go, and that was to flatten out or start down a little bit."

That much was evident as the Lakers lurched through a mediocre season, finishing the '55–56 campaign with a sub-par 33–39 record, tying them with St. Louis for the second-worst record in the NBA and saddling them with the first losing season in franchise history. Mikan averaged a meager 10.5 points per game in the thirty-seven games he played after his comeback—his worst average as either an amateur or professional. Then, to cap off the miserable season, the Lakers lost to the St. Louis Hawks in the first round of the playoffs. Mikan had seen enough. On March 21, 1956, immediately following the Lakers' elimination from the playoffs, he retired again—this time for good.

He'd always insist that his decision to return had been a good one. It had been impossible to simply walk away from the game, and he needed an unsuccessful comeback to convince him that he really did need to retire.

Ironically, his comeback might have affected the Lakers' future in adverse ways that wouldn't become apparent until years later. The best young center in college, a kid from San Francisco who would change the game in dramatic ways, was about to graduate, and Sid Hartman wanted him for the Lakers in the worst way. The center would be available to the team with the worst record, since Rochester, the team with the first overall pick, already had a center and didn't want him. Hartman concocted a trade that would have sent Vern Mikkelsen to the Celtics for three players who were in the service and unavailable for the season—a trade that would have all but assured the Lakers the first pick in the draft.

"Without Mikkelsen, we were almost a cinch to wind up with the worst record in the league," Hartman remembered. "That's what I wanted. That would have given us the number one draft choice."

John Kundla wanted nothing to do with the proposed trade. "I objected and Mikkelsen objected," he recalled. "I still think it was the right thing to do. As a coach, you never think of losing games on purpose."

The Boston Celtics also wanted the young collegiate star, and they were willing to part with outstanding talent to get him. The Celtics traded Easy Ed Macauley and Cliff Hagen, both future Hall of Famers, to last-place St. Louis for the rights to their pick. Boston used the pick to draft the center from San Francisco.

The player's name was Bill Russell, and beginning with the next season, the Celtics would win the Eastern Division title nine consecutive years, and the NBA championship eight of those years.

The Lakers wouldn't enjoy another winning season during the remainder of the team's stay in Minneapolis.

Mikan accepted the reality that his days as a player were over, but, at thirty-two, he had a lot of life after basketball ahead of him. He had his law degree and was a full partner in the Minneapolis firm of Ryan, Kain, and Mikan. He'd dabbled in law while he was still playing with the Lakers but, by all accounts, he was only marginally good at it. This was not a career where you could trade on your name for success, at least not in court. Besides, in the immediate aftermath of his retirement as an active player, Mikan returned to the Lakers' front office and his duties as general manager.

Mikan was used to others' trading on his name. Sometimes he profited from it, as he did when he endorsed such commercial products as

Wheaties, Gillette, Pabst beer, and Keds tennis shoes. But there would be occasions when others would try to capitalize on his name recognition, good-natured disposition, wealth, or naïveté for their own gain, with very little concern for how their actions affected Mikan and his family.

Such was the case in the spring of 1956, when the state's Republican party talked Mikan into running for the Third U.S. congressional seat in Minnesota. Mikan viewed the campaign as another opportunity, even though he was politically inexperienced and, by all indications, the Republican party was using him as a sacrificial lamb or, if enough luck was with them, someone to ride on Eisenhower's coattails and squeak out a win in the fall election.

The sum total of Mikan's political assets was his name, organizational skills, and abilities to move and speak well in public. He was not politically astute, experienced at any level of public service, or especially well connected. He'd met a lot of people, including powerful political and business figures, while he was playing basketball, but there was a world of difference between a handshake or casual conversation and the backroom deal. The Republican party promised to assist him along the way, in everything from providing him with political briefings to recommending his law practice to potential clients. Mikan, who probably learned more about politics in his family's tavern than in any hallowed halls in Hennepin County, took them at their word. Pat Mikan, a Democrat, wasn't thrilled with her husband's decision, but she backed him anyway.

Mikan knew from the onset that he had a tough road ahead of him. The Democratic incumbent, Roy Weir, was enormously popular among voters. He'd been a congressman for more than twenty years, and he was heavily favored to win the upcoming election. The Republican party wanted to exploit what it judged to be weaknesses in Weir's character, but Mikan would have no part in mudslinging. He would beat him fair and square, or not at all.

When it came to campaigning, Mikan had one serious problem: he didn't enjoy campaigning. He resented all the time he had to spend on the road, away from his family, and there were times when he felt as if he was doing everything alone. As he soon discovered, there was a huge difference between political campaigning and playing pro basketball. In basketball, all you really had to do was show up for practices or games; everything else was taken care of for you. Even the tough stuff, like travel, was arranged for you by someone who made the schedules, bought the train or plane tickets, and, at least in more recent years, took care of your uniform and equipment. You'd be traveling with friends, playing the game you loved with them, going out to dinner with them. In politics, you'd be driving alone from one stop to another; meeting with strangers who had set up your appearances; talking to groups, large and small, who held your fate in their hands, and who, in exchange for their support, wanted some measure of say in what you thought and how you behaved. Campaigning left Mikan exhausted. One night, after a stop in Braham, he dozed off at the wheel and put his car in a ditch, narrowly escaping serious injury.

Vern Mikkelsen, who lived in nearby Minnetonka, couldn't figure out why Mikan put himself through the grind. Political campaigning, he felt, was not part of Mikan's makeup.

"Politicians would start at the crack of dawn and go through the Minneapolis Moline Tractor Plant, shaking hands," he said. "George would never do that. He would even be late when he was coming to a place where he was supposed to be."

Despite his political deficiencies, Mikan defeated six other Republican contenders in the September primary. In the vigorous two-month stretch running to the general election, he tried to project himself as a populist candidate battling against an incumbent beholden to special-interest groups. His campaign was bolstered by visits to the state by President Eisenhower and Vice President Nixon. Roy Weir, who had avoided Mikan's earlier challenges to a debate, finally squared off against him and, unfortunately for Mikan, exposed him as a nice guy but a weak political candidate.

Election day rolled around on November 6, 1956, right about the time Mikan's old teammates were readying themselves for another season, and Mikan lost an extremely close election, coming within one half of one percent of winning the seat. For Mikan, it was a bitter setback.

"Except for one NBA title," he said later, "it was the first time I had been defeated for anything significant, and it was especially hard to have put all the work into it and still have come up short."

The defeat itself hadn't left him nearly as bitter as the political education he received along the way. Although he shouldn't have been, he was surprised when his party forgot all about him as soon as the votes had been counted. There were no more calls, no new clients for the law firm of

Ryan, Kain, and Mikan. Not only was there no new money coming into the coffers; Mikan had spent his savings on the campaign and, in its aftermath, he had to cash in his life insurance policies to replenish his funds.

The election loss was Mikan's first experience with people willing to use and abandon him, leaving him with the check. Sadly, it wouldn't be his last.

After his retirement as a player, Mikan's relationship with the Lakers was complex. Mikan needed the Lakers—and vice-versa—and while he did report to work and fulfill his duties as general manager, the position was nowhere near what it is in today's NBA. Under the old regime, prior to Mikan's moving into the front office, Max Winter had handled the business end of day-to-day operations, while Sid Hartman oversaw the personnel decisions. This changed dramatically when Mikan assumed the position. Financed by a loan from Ben Berger, Mikan bought out Max Winter's interest in the team, and then he'd sold these interests to Berger when he left his desk and returned to playing. Hartman left the team shortly after the failed trade that would have brought Bill Russell to the Lakers, leaving a void in personnel decisions, since Mikan wasn't as familiar with pro and college players as Hartman.

The team, in a word, was a mess. Mikan could only stand by and watch forlornly as the Lakers slumped through another losing season. Slater Martin was gone, traded to New York for seven-footer Walter Dukes. Whitey Skoog was sidelined by injuries for much of the season. The Lakers had Dick Garmaker, a forward from the University of Minnesota, and Bob "Slick" Leonard, a newcomer from Indiana, and both showed great promise. The team played well enough to finish with one more victory than the previous season, but they played poorly enough, and drew poorly enough, to make Ben Berger and Morris Chalfen look into selling the franchise to a couple of investors from St. Louis.

Mikan approached Berger and offered to mortgage his home and buy the Lakers, if doing so would keep the team in Minneapolis. Berger turned him down. The franchise, he said, would only be sold to a civic or investment group. The issue was resolved when a local group of more than one hundred investors, organized by *Minneapolis Star* sports editor Charlie Johnson and led by investors Bob Short and Frank Ryan, ponied up Berger and Chalfen's asking price. The Lakers would remain in Minneapolis.

The deal might have kept the Lakers in the Twin Cities, but with more than a hundred "co-owners" demanding at least some say in the team's operations, no one was quite sure what was going on.

The 1957–58 season saw major changes. In the most significant move, Mikan and Kundla switched positions. Mikan was now head coach, and Kundla took his spot as general manager. Neither was suited for his new job.

It didn't take long for Mikan to see that he was in way over his head. Much of his problems could be traced to his coaching style, which differed greatly from Kundla's. Off-court, Kundla had been easy-going, one of the guys; on-court, he was the boss, and everybody knew it. Mikan had a different relationship with his players. He had played alongside some of them, which made discipline a sticky issue, while some of the newer players on the team had problems with discipline of any sort.

"It was hard for George, I think," Clyde Lovellette observed. "As great a player as he was, to sit there on the bench and coach the team—it didn't work out very well. George should have stayed in the front office and looked for players and do whatever general managers do."

Vern Mikkelsen agreed. "Some people can be coaches and some can't," he said. "I was the first one to recognize that I was not going to be a good coach, so I didn't do it. But George did, and he got fired."

Under Mikan, the Lakers were absolutely abysmal, winning only 9 of 39 games before the front office pulled the plug on him on January 15, 1958. For Mikan, the firing was more like a mercy killing. He'd never really wanted the job in the first place. He'd only agreed to take it because the new Laker ownership wanted to fire Kundla. In taking over as coach, Mikan was leaving a vacant position for Kundla in the front office. The move had a negative effect on Mikan. Early in the season, in an effort to trim the payroll, Kundla had traded Lovellette, Kalafat, and Dukes for three journeyman players. Angry about losing three of his better players, Mikan threatened to quit but was talked out of it.

Mikan soldiered on, though he never found the right rotation of players to guide the Lakers back to their old winning ways. He knew how to call plays; handling the needs and egos of a new breed of young players was something he simply couldn't do. The Lakers were a hodgepodge of older and new players, and many of the newer team members, like Rodney "Hod Rod" Hundley and Slick Leonard, were more interested in drinking and carousing than in playing basketball. Both were exceptional basketball players, but they were virtually uncoachable.

"George's coaching skills were good," Kalafat said of the short time he played under Mikan before the trade. "But when George took over as coach, we didn't have a big superstar or anything, and there were a bunch of newer players who were not so much team players as individuals."

Dick Schnittker felt the same way.

"George was a good coach," he agreed, "but some of the guys on our ball club weren't disciplined and wouldn't react to his coaching. George knew what he was doing, but some of the other players did not respond, putting him in a bad position. Management put pressure on him. They wanted him to resign, but they actually fired him."

Kundla was reinstated as the Lakers' coach. Mikan, no longer interested in a front-office position of any kind, decided to leave basketball and practice law. His involvement with the Lakers, at least in any official capacity, was over.

Seventeen

ABA COMMISSIONER

W HEN, IN 1966, Mikan first heard Bill Goff's sales pitch about a new professional league, he reacted with skepticism.

Mikan knew Goff through an insurance company he had invested in, and Goff was calling on behalf of a friend, a California businessman named Dennis Murphy, who was the brains behind the plans for starting up another professional basketball league.

Murphy, the mayor of Buena Park, California, had originally wanted to invest in an American Football League franchise, but that ended when the AFL merged with the NFL. Murphy quickly changed direction. Maybe, he thought, there was room for another pro basketball league. Getting Mikan on board as the league's first commissioner would do wonders for establishing the league's credibility.

Mikan wasn't interested, and he told Goff as much. The idea of a new league was hardly original. He'd heard from an East Coast promoter, Connie Seredin, who was also interested in starting a new league and naming Mikan its commissioner, but Mikan doubted that the world was ready for a competing league. Abe Saperstein, who knew a lot more about promoting and marketing basketball than almost anyone in the business, had fallen on his face when, a few years earlier, in 1961, he'd founded a new version of the American Basketball League. That had lasted all of one and a half seasons. True, the NBA only had twelve teams, leaving plenty of room for expansion, but pro basketball was hardly striking fear into pro baseball or football for popular attention.

Mikan had a number of reasons for not wanting to get involved in a new league. He'd learned to live without basketball. His travel agency,

George Mikan's Viking Travel, was doing well enough to support his family, which, with the addition of Michael (1956), Tricia (1959), and Maureen (1963), was now a family of eight. A new league would almost certainly be financially risky. Pat was glad to have him out of basketball, and there was something to be said about keeping Pat happy. Then there was the memory of his political campaign, still strong enough to raise suspicions of anyone wanting to use his name or reputation to further a cause. Finally, he wasn't about to move away from Minneapolis, and a new league would probably require his relocating to a larger big-media city.

No, he told Bill Goff, and then Dennis Murphy, he wasn't interested.

Murphy wasn't giving up easily. He and Connie Seredin hooked up and the new league began to take shape. Bill Sharman, the former NBA great and a friend of Murphy's, suggested that they call the league the American Basketball Association. The name stuck. Murphy continued to campaign for Mikan's joining the ABA as its first commissioner, but Mikan remained adamant in his decision. He wouldn't be joining the league, he informed Murphy, unless he was convinced that the league had its financial affairs in order.

This included, of course, a substantial contract for its commissioner. Mikan wanted a three-year deal worth $50,000 a year—no small piece of change in the mid-1960s. In addition, Mikan demanded almost total autonomy in decisions regarding the way the league should be run; as commissioner, he would decide what was best for the game. Finally, he insisted on running the league offices out of Minneapolis—or, more specifically, out of an office down the hall from his travel-agency offices.

Mikan's demands were not without merit. The investors in the ABA franchises were more businessmen than sports fans, and Mikan, ever the basketball player, was as concerned about keeping the game strong as he was about turning huge profits.

The key, he felt, was making the game more entertaining. Purists had been attending pro games for years, but that hadn't been enough. To take the game to the next level, the ABA had to find ways to attract new fans, especially women and children, and the best way to do that was to entertain them. The game itself had to be more exciting; plus pro basketball needed to steal a page from pro football by making each night an event. Mikan had a list of ideas on how to accomplish that, but, as commissioner, he needed to have the final say in order to prevent these ideas from being debated to death by businessmen who knew nothing about basketball.

Some of his ideas, considered quirky or even radical at the time, would eventually be taken for granted.

Mikan waged his biggest battle over what became the ABA trademark: its red, white, and blue basketball. The idea, he explained, had sprung from his own poor eyesight. When seated in the stands or watching a game on television, he had a difficult time following the movement of the standard brown basketball when it was being passed or shot. A colorful ball would be easier to see. Choosing red, white, and blue for the colors had been the easy part. The league, after all, was the American Basketball Association.

Mikan also believed that his proposed ABA basketball offered marketing opportunities that some of his opponents might have overlooked. The ABA was reaching out to a younger audience, and kids preferred the colorful ball to the standard one.

"The young kids really liked it," Mikan pointed out. "In fact, we ran product comparison tests and the youngsters invariably chose our ball over the others."

The naysayers, from coaches to players to the media, continued to ridicule the idea—"I believe I was the first one to say that the ABA ball belonged on the nose of a seal," Alex Hannum said, only to later confess that he wound up changing his mind—and the more he heard, the more defensive Mikan became.

"People will stand and cheer when they see our balls," he insisted to a group of amused reporters.

Mikan won the argument and, as he predicted, the ABA basketball became immensely popular—so much so that league marketing officials would regret not formally licensing the design. Sporting-goods stores had trouble keeping them in stock.

Another ABA staple—the three-point shot—distinguished the new league from the NBA. Abe Saperstein had used it in his ill-fated American Basketball League, and Mikan really liked the idea. There was an irony to it that he appreciated: as a big man and the game's most dominant player, he'd watched helplessly as new rules were passed to reduce his effectiveness; his proposed three-point field goal, awarded for long-range shots, promised to do more to shift the action away from the big man than anything the NBA had done.

"Guards get killed when they come inside," Mikan noted. "But if they could become proficient from a long way out, they should be rewarded."

The three-point shot, which Mikan likened to a home run in baseball, turned out to be one of the most important and innovative changes in pro basketball history. Teams that might otherwise be hopelessly out of contention could work their way back into games via the three-pointer. Late-game strategy changed. Long-distance shots became as popular with fans as the dunk. The NBA eventually adopted the three-pointer, and it became so popular that the NBA featured a three-point shooting contest as part of its All-Star Game festivities.

Mikan knew from the beginning that the ABA would face its greatest competition with the NBA in its recruitment of players. Very few players were going to defect from the NBA to the ABA,* and the competition for the country's best college players would be fierce. Unless something unforeseen occurred, the NBA would still have the best players. Mikan then came up with an idea that would also have long-term effects on the pro game: if you couldn't sign the best players, feature the most colorful ones.

From his own experience, Mikan knew that fans would pack arenas to watch great individual players, even if their own home teams were mediocre or poor. To compete with the established league, the new one would have to offer a change in style, which started with the players themselves. This was part of Mikan's overall entertainment package, a way to make the ABA a feast for the eyes as well as a quality sport. The new league, he felt, should have memorable players, lots of lights and sound, halftime entertainment, cheerleaders—anything to keep the fans' eyes on the court.

The ABA would eventually be remembered as much for its flamboyant characters, outrageous promotions, and innovative All-Star-Game events as for its great players, high-octane action, three-point scoring, and memorable games. The league that introduced the public to Julius Erving,

---

*The most notable defection was future Hall of Famer Rick Barry, who left the San Francisco Warriors to play across the Bay for his father-in-law and former college coach, and former Mikan Gears teammate, Bruce Hale, who was coaching the Oakland Oaks.

Moses Malone, George Gervin, and Dan Issel also offered bikini-clad cheerleaders; the first woman to play professional basketball (Penny Ann Early, who played long enough to inbound the ball); a team owned by a dog (the Kentucky Colonels); and big hair and platform shoes. Larry Brown, Doug Moe, and George Karl played in the league; Pat Boone and Morton Downey Jr. owned teams. Bob Costas got his start as the radio and television voice of the Spirits of St. Louis. Then there was Marvin "Bad News" Barnes, whose supreme court skills were matched by his propensity for finding trouble.

The league could be crazy, but, as Bob Costas told *Basketball News* writer Brett Ballantini, the focus was still on the game.

"I thought the most significant contribution—and Dr. J epitomized this more than anybody—was to legitimize flamboyance, that flamboyance and selfishness were not synonymous," noted Costas. "You could entertain and still play the game in a way that deserved respect."

For all his planning and meetings with league officials and team owners, Mikan wasn't a lock for the position of commissioner until ten minutes or so before the February 2, 1967, press conference announcing the league. He still hadn't signed his contract, and he refused to meet the press until he had done so. It was all very simple: no contract, no commissioner. Mikan watched the hotel conference room filling with reporters and invited guests while his business representative, Bill Erickson, worked out the final contractual details with the team owners. Mikan, as tough a negotiator as ever, realized that he could still walk away from the deal and make his living through his travel agency. The league needed him.

He was right. With just minutes to go before the scheduled press conference, he signed his contract and prepared to introduce the new league.

The press conference was as garish as the ABA promised to be. Red, white, and blue ABA basketballs were passed around to people in attendance. Drinks and press releases were distributed by cheerleader-types wearing hot pants. Celebrities mingled with reporters. According to one report, the whole thing wound up costing $35,000.

Mikan was appalled. The press conference had plenty of flash, but little substance. No one seemed to know what was going on, and no one seemed to be taking charge.

"This is all a bunch of crap," he complained to Dennis Murphy. "I'm gonna get up there and run the show."

Mikan took the lectern and addressed the media, briefing reporters on the new league, its red-white-and-blue basketball, and why the ABA was going to be able to compete with the NBA. Only a few minutes earlier, the press conference seemed headed for disaster; now it looked like a well-planned media event.

"I'm convinced that we would have died at that first press conference without him," Dennis Murphy recalled. "Let's face it, when a guy who was the greatest basketball player of his era, a guy who is a successful business-man and a guy who was six foot ten with the charisma of Mikan stood up, people listened."

The team owners, however, were not as easily impressed. They were busi-nessmen, and they couldn't have cared less about Mikan's visions for the game. When the ABA was still in its planning stages, many prospective owners hoped that their investment would eventually pay off handsomely when the NBA and ABA merged, which seemed as inevitable to them as the NFL and AFL's merger in football. When that didn't happen, and when it became clear that the ABA was in it either for the long haul or for failure, the owners grew restless. Not only was their investment not paying the big dividends they'd envisioned; they were losing money while they waited for the payoff.

The ABA turned out to be good, entertaining basketball, as Mikan had hoped, but the commissioner's job was much more demanding that he had anticipated. As a decision-maker, Mikan scored early when he followed his instincts and allowed Connie Hawkins, the incredibly gifted and entertain-ing six-eight forward from Iowa, to play in the ABA. Hawkins had been banned from the NBA* for his rumored (but never proven) involvement in a 1961 point-shaving scandal, but Mikan believed in offering Hawkins a sec-ond chance—a faith that was rewarded many times over, when Hawkins became the league's leading attraction.

But victories such as this didn't offset the downside of running the league. Mikan eventually grew tired of dealing with disgruntled owners, disciplining players and coaches, and handling the finer but boring points

---

*Hawkins would eventually play in the NBA and earn a place in the Hall of Fame.

of day-to-day operations. He worked out of Minneapolis, as he'd insisted, but he always seemed to be on a plane, flying to important meetings.

"We called him the 'En Route Commissioner,'" Vern Mikkelsen quipped. Mikkelsen had taken a position in the front office of the Minnesota Pipers, and whenever he called Mikan's office, he never seemed to find him in. "I'd call Lee Meade, who was doing the PR for the league, and I'd say, 'Is George around?' 'No,' he'd say, 'he'll be back tomorrow or the week after.' I'd say, 'Is he en route?' And he'd say, 'Yeah, that's a good phrase.' So he became the En Route Commissioner."

The ABA team owners, however, weren't interested in an En Route Commissioner. They didn't want the league's offices located out in the sticks when it should be closer to the nerve center of the real world—i.e., New York City. The NBA had its offices in the Empire State Building; the ABA's offices, the owners felt, should be located in a similar high-profile location. Mikan disagreed. Going head to head with the NBA for attention in the media capital of the United States, he countered, would be suicide. Mikan proposed that the offices, if they had to be moved, be shifted to California, as far away from New York as possible.

He was fighting a losing battle, and he knew it. His relationship with the owners had eroded beyond repair.

This dispute, along with his failure to persuade Lew Alcindor (later Kareem Abdul-Jabbar) to join the ABA, led to the end.

Alcindor, the most sought-after college player since Wilt Chamberlain, might have changed the ABA's fortunes. The New York Nets had the rights to draft him, and Mikan reasoned that the ABA had a legitimate chance of landing him, since Alcindor was from New York and would probably want to play close to home. The league cut a certified check for one million dollars, and Mikan and trucking magnate Arthur Brown, owner of the Nets, set up a meeting with Alcindor and his parents in a New York hotel. The plan was for Mikan to present Alcindor with the check, so no one would doubt the ABA's intentions or seriousness. The million dollars would be an advance on the final contract figure.

There are conflicting accounts of what happened at that meeting.

According to former ABA executive Mike Storen, who talked extensively with basketball writer and historian Terry Pluto for *Loose Balls*, Pluto's oral history of the ABA, Mikan never showed Alcindor the check. Instead, he talked to Alcindor and his parents, figuring he'd show them the check on another occasion, when serious negotiations began. Dick Tinkham, the chief attorney for the Indianapolis Pacers, told Pluto that Mikan and Brown offered Alcindor a million dollars, but said it was the league's best offer. In his autobiography, Mikan disputed these accounts. He showed Alcindor the check, he said, although he admitted that he hoped to lead another round of negotiations before the final deal was made.

Whichever version is true ultimately doesn't matter. Alcindor signed with the Milwaukee Bucks, and the ABA lost a player who might have done for the ABA what Mikan had once done for the NBA. Mikan always believed that Alcindor had already agreed to a deal with Milwaukee prior to the meeting, but that didn't matter either. The owners had had enough of Mikan, and vice-versa.

Some of the owners favored firing Mikan on the spot, but it would have been a PR nightmare. Instead, they informed him that the ABA offices were being relocated to New York City. This, they correctly assumed, would spell the end of Mikan's involvement with the ABA, since Mikan wouldn't leave the Midwest. The two sides reached a settlement on Mikan's contract, the ABA agreeing to buy out the last year of his three-year deal. Mikan turned his attention back to Minneapolis and his travel agency.

ABA teams would come and go, and the ABA and NBA would be involved in all kinds of legal skirmishes during the ABA's volatile up-and-down existence. A merger between the NBA and ABA seemed possible in 1971, but the agreement fell through. Finally the two leagues merged in 1975, with the NBA taking in the San Antonio Spurs, Denver Nuggets, Indiana Pacers, and New York Nets.

Mikan never regretted his involvement in the ABA. Things might not have worked out exactly as he'd hoped, but many of his ideas withstood the test of time and, as he wrote in his autobiography, they helped make the game better.

"I see the spirit of the ABA in every game I watch," he stated.

Eighteen

In Honor of the Pioneers

April 9, 2001

George Mikan watches a game between the Los Angeles Lakers and the Minnesota Timberwolves at the Target Center in Minneapolis.

His legacy is apparent down on the floor. Shaquille O'Neal, the game's premier center and the most dominating player at that position since the glory days of Kareem Abdul-Jabbar, places himself just outside the paint and waits for Kobe Bryant to zip the ball in to him. Nobody's moving Shaq anywhere. This man's thick, seven-one frame makes everyone around him look small.

The Timberwolves counter with Kevin Garnett. Although six-eleven, Garnett is nowhere near O'Neal's weight. Nevertheless, he's a force to contend with. Garnett's a forward with a center's mentality, and, like Shaq, he wants the ball at crunch time.

Mikan loves watching these guys play.

Both men, in turn, know their history and are quick to show their respect for the man who helped pave the way for them.

"He's definitely a milestone," Garnett told a reporter covering the game. "Without George Mikan, there wouldn't really be any big men or be any hook."

O'Neal found a similarity between Mikan in his time and Shaq in his. "George Mikan was the first dominant big man," he said. "Because of him, they changed the game. And because of my dominant play, they're thinking of changing the game and rules again."

The game, between Minnesota's original pro team and its current one, is almost beside the point. This day belongs to George Mikan, who will be honored at half-

time for his contributions to the state's pro basketball teams. Pat Mikan is at her husband's side, as are the Mikans' children, grandchildren, and great-grandchildren. Ray Meyer is on hand, as is John Kundla. Some of the old Minneapolis Lakers sit nearby.

Mikan could use a day like this. His health has been steadily declining. Diabetes, which ran in his family, has been creating serious problems for him. In March 2000, his right leg was amputated just below the knee, and he's been trying to make the transition from wheelchair to walker to prosthetic leg. He's remained positive throughout the ordeal, as well as in handling kidney problems requiring dialysis three times a week, four hours per session.

"I'm feeling fine and learning to walk better with a walker," he'd told a USA Today reporter a few days earlier. "I hope to one day get out of that and get to a cane. The next step would be getting ahold of the golf clubs again."

He's more hopeful about the future for others battling diabetes. One of the day's important events is a silent auction to benefit the Max McGee Research Center for Diabetes. McGee, the former Green Bay Packers star receiver, founded the Milwaukee-based center after he learned that his son had diabetes. Mikan is pleased to be attached to such a worthy cause.

"Max tells me that within the next five years, so many wonderful things may happen that children's diabetes may be pretty well cured," he said optimistically.

The first half ends, and the attention shifts to Mikan. He's always been graceful in the spotlight, and today is no exception. In his speech, he makes a point of thanking his coaches and former teammates—the people who made him the player he was. He's humbled, of course, that the Minnesota Timberwolves, a team he never played for, have chosen to honor him.

And that honor is no piece of paper, no banner, no plaque. It's much bigger, literally and figuratively. A life-sized bronze statue of Mikan, wearing his Lakers jersey and shooting his trademark hook shot, has been placed just inside the Target Center, where it will be seen by fans for many years to come. The statue, people will agree, makes him look a little like Clark Kent in a basketball uniform.

Which suits Mikan just fine. Shaq has a Superman logo tattooed on his arm. It's only right that the original Superman of pro basketball be set in bronze, standing out like a symbol of a time long past, when players took the court for the love of a game now being played in bigger arenas, by higher-paid athletes, in front of international audiences.

"I'm very happy that the NBA has taken it upon itself to bring the history of

*the NBA up to speed so a lot of young people know what we had done," he says.
"The young people are finally starting to see some of those old films that were
taken and they're starting to realize that they wouldn't be here today if it were
not for us. I felt like we were in the covered wagons that went across the United
States."*

The departure of the Minneapolis Lakers in 1960 left a void in professional
sports in Minnesota, but not for long. After leaving the Lakers, Max Winter had gone to work on helping to bring a National Football League franchise to the Twin Cities. The Minnesota Vikings experienced the usual
expansion-team growing pains during their first decade of existence, but
under the leadership of Bud Grant, Mikan's old teammate with the Lakers, who had left basketball to play and coach football, the Vikings became
one of the most successful NFL teams of the seventies. In 1961, Min-
neapolis/St. Paul inherited the old Washington Senators, now called the
Minnesota Twins. In professional hockey, the NHL's Minnesota North
Stars started up, meaning that the area had three of the four major sports.

Professional basketball had returned to Minneapolis in 1967, with the
ABA's Minnesota Muskies, replaced in 1968 by the Minnesota Pipers, but
each team lasted only a year in the new league before relocating to a different city. For the next two decades, the NBA continued to expand, but
Minnesota never seemed to be on the list. Nearly three decades had passed
since the Lakers left town.

When the NBA announced that it was expanding by two teams in 1988,
and by two more in 1989, Minnesota civic and business leaders decided to
make a major effort to bring pro basketball back to the area. Minnesota
Governor Rudy Perpich called Mikan and asked him to chair a committee
devoted to organizing a franchise proposal to present to NBA Commissioner David Stern.

Mikan didn't have to be asked twice. His post-NBA business adventures
had been hit-or-miss. His law firm had fizzled, and some of his investments
were disastrous. The travel agency had been steady, his work in real estate
a mixed bag. All told, he would never achieve anywhere near the success in
the business world that he'd seen on the basketball court.

He missed basketball. His experience as commissioner of the ABA had
led him to believe that he still had something to contribute to the game

and, with the possibility of an NBA franchise coming to his home town, he hoped to be seriously involved in pro basketball again.

Mikan was a natural as a spokesman to drum up support for a new franchise. He'd lived in the area for almost all of his adult life. He knew a lot of the politicians and businessmen. He'd worked in professional basketball on every level, from player to coach to front office to commissioner, and while he wouldn't be working on founding an entire league, as he had with the ABA, his experiences gave him ideas about what worked and didn't work. He'd watched the NBA grow into an exceptionally successful business, moving from pure sport to high entertainment. Minneapolis had two strong ownership candidates in Marv Wolfenson and Harvey Ratner. Mikan threw himself into the task, and when he and his committee presented their Minnesota proposal to David Stern on April 3, 1987, they had a winner on their hands.

Mikan saw a bright future ahead. He'd been promised a position with the new franchise, and he was ready to move back into basketball full-time. In his own words, he felt "energized."

His high hopes faded quickly. Wolfenson and Ratner named Bob Stein, Wolfenson's son-in-law, president of the Minnesota Timberwolves. Stein made it almost immediately clear that there was no position available to George Mikan on the team. Everyone appreciated all he'd done to bring pro basketball back to Minnesota, but . . .

For Mikan, it was another bitter pill, similar to the one he'd swallowed after putting so much work into running for office, only to be dumped by his party after the election results were in. He'd come out a winner this time, but he still was being pushed aside. He puzzled over it unhappily, wondering if he'd been used, or been on the losing end of a power play, or, perhaps worst of all, been unrealistic about his importance to basketball. Maybe, he thought, the game had passed him by.

His conclusion was characteristically optimistic.

And forgiving.

"The truth is," he wrote in his autobiography, "my time hadn't passed; it was just someone else's arriving."

The face of the NBA changed dramatically after Mikan's retirement. The game would never overtake baseball or football in popularity, but it exploded as a business, moving from its very modest beginnings to becoming an international phenomenon, with players and fans from every continent in the world. The league had teams in every region of the United States; it had expanded into Canada. Product merchandising, along with huge network and cable-television contracts, brought in revenues that Maurice Podoloff had never imagined back in the days when he was scheming to come up with ways to keep the league above water for one more season. Individual players earned more money per year than the entire *league* realized in profits during a season in its early days. Michael Jordan's 1996 contract earned him more for a single season than George Mikan, Wilt Chamberlain, Bill Russell, and Oscar Robertson earned in their *combined* NBA careers.

Mikan watched it happen with mixed feelings. Like other players of his era, he was amazed by the players' athleticism and the pace of the game, and he was pleased to have been instrumental in the development of the pro game. He chose his words judiciously whenever he issued public statements or talked to reporters eager to record his thoughts on the current state of basketball affairs.

"It's hard to imagine what the league is going to be like in fifty years," he told a reporter, in an interview filled with optimism and superlatives. "The progress the league has made since Day One is amazing and fantastic."

In private, however, he was less effervescent. He harbored darker feelings that he only let surface in conversations with family and friends. He wondered if the NBA's pioneers were being forgotten, their names lost on a generation of players and fans with no interest in history. He still felt used and discarded after his involvement in bringing the Timberwolves to the Twin Cities. His pension was pathetically small, both in comparison to what the current players would be earning when they were eligible to collect pensions, and as compensation for what he'd meant to professional basketball when it desperately needed stars to promote the new league. Some of his bitterness would come out in conversations with friends. To someone like Vern Mikkelsen, who spoke to him regularly, Mikan seemed conflicted about the game he loved.

Not that he was alone—not by any means. Players from the Mikan era (and beyond) shared the same mixed feelings as the years passed and the pro game surged to new heights. They envied the beautiful new arenas, complete with luxurious locker rooms and training facilities. They couldn't help but be amused by the sight of the modern player entering the arena, isolated from the media and fans by the headphones he wore or the cell phone he was using, accompanied by an entourage ready to carry out his every wish. They marveled at the basketball-shoe contracts and other endorsement deals—some negotiated before a young player so much as bounced a ball off the hardwood in his first regular-season game.

"I think today's kids are so catered to, from the time they're in high school through college, that they just expect more," said Bobby Wanzer, who followed his playing days with a coaching career. "I don't know. They love the game as much as we did, but . . . if I got a pair of sneakers when I was playing on the team, that was a lot."

Ed Kalafat laughed at the sneakers idea. "We had one pair of shoes that they gave us, that we'd wear all year," he said. "These guys go through their shoes every game."

Players didn't even pretend to understand the financial rewards. Even allowing for inflation, the difference was incredible.

"I played in the NBA All-Star Game in '53," Billy Gabor remembered, "and I got a hundred-dollar war bond that you had to hold for ten years to get your hundred dollars. When we won the championship in 1955, we got fourteen hundred dollars a man. We did not get a championship ring. I'd tell somebody I was on an NBA championship team, and they'd say, 'Yeah? Let me see your ring.' When I'd say I didn't have one, they'd say, 'Yeah, you played in the NBA. Yeah.'"

Wilt Chamberlain, always at the top of the pay scale during his playing days, and never one to shy away from supplying a direct answer to a reporter's question, no matter how pointed, admitted that the escalating salaries worried him.

"For years, people have been saying as an athlete you should get whatever you can get," he said in a 1996 interview, "but it gets to the point where there's a law of diminishing returns. Guys making $100 million, well, someone has to pay it."

But were they worth it? Or were they overpaid?

Bill Russell, who earned a fair nickel during his lengthy Hall of Fame career playing for the great Boston Celtics teams, and who, after retiring as an active player, discovered that coaching younger players could be difficult, couldn't help but wonder.

"The league is bigger today, players make a lot more money, and the league is successfully selling the sport all around the world," he told a reporter from the *Chicago Sun-Times*. "But we had better teams when I was playing, and I believe the average player was better than the average player today."

It was the kind of argument that would never be resolved. Pro basketball had evolved enormously and quickly, making definitive comparisons impossible. Mikan and his contemporaries were quick to agree that the basketball player, as an athlete, was getting better by the year, and that players like Michael Jordan, Shaquille O'Neal, Magic Johnson, Larry Bird, Hakeem Olajuwon (a Mikan favorite), or any number of others possessed natural and developed skills that eclipsed those of their predecessors.

They only hoped that the young players would learn and remember NBA history.

Mikan needn't have worried. The names of the stars of his era might not have jumped immediately to the minds of younger NBA fans, but older fans, basketball historians, sportswriters, and the NBA itself saw that they would never be entirely forgotten. George Mikan's name would always be near the top of any list of historically significant players.

The first assurance of that had arrived in 1959, with the establishment of the Naismith Memorial Basketball Hall of Fame. The Hall, named after basketball's inventor, was unique, in that it wasn't created for NBA players only. Instead, it would honor players, coaches, contributors, and officials from both the professional and college ranks. At the time of its formation, the Hall of Fame didn't even have a home, a building where, as in baseball and football, fans could see exhibits on the sport's history and important figures. This wouldn't happen until 1968, when a Hall of Fame museum was built on the Springfield College campus, in Springfield, Massachusetts.

Mikan became a charter member and the first NBA player selected for the Hall of Fame. The honor, he'd say, was the biggest thrill of his life, outside of being named "Mr. Basketball" in 1950.

This was only the beginning of the recognition given Mikan after his retirement from the game. In 1996, XPRO, an association of retired NBA players, announced what it called the "All-Time Super Team" of thirteen of the NBA's greatest players ever. Mikan made the list, along with such luminaries as Wilt Chamberlain, Oscar Robertson, Bob Cousy, Elgin Baylor, and Jerry West. XPRO named Red Auerbach, who had led the Boston Celtics to nine NBA titles, coach of the super team, and Auerbach proved that he hadn't softened since his retirement by using the occasion to offer an assortment of opinions comparing the players of yesteryear with the players of today.

"These are the players who invented the game we see played today," he said of the players on the super team, adding that the players on the XPRO team could have beaten any team in the game's history. The current game, Auerbach maintained, was much easier with its "jets, food, and assistant coaches," but as a coach who liked to teach, he doubted if the modern players would have bothered to listen to him.

"If you're making $400,000 as a coach, how are you going to tell a player making $14 million what to do?" he wondered.

Later that same year, Mikan received a similar honor when a panel of former NBA players and coaches, along with current team executives and media members, compiled a list of the "50 Greatest Players in NBA History." The NBA, celebrating its fiftieth anniversary, wanted to pay tribute to select players from each position—players who had advanced the game to its present popularity. Mikan found himself on an impressive roll of centers that included Kareem Abdul-Jabbar, Wilt Chamberlain, Dave Cowens, Patrick Ewing, Moses Malone, Hakeem Olajuwon, Shaquille O'Neal, Robert Parrish, Willis Reed, David Robinson, Bill Russell, Nate Thurmond, Wes Unseld, and Bill Walton. There was the predictable controversy over inclusions and exclusions, including some discussion about why Jim Pollard, arguably the best forward of his time, had been left off the list. But such was the nature of these kinds of lists. If nothing else, it gave ESPN, sports talk radio, sportswriters, and fans in bars and restaurants across the country something to debate.

The players were honored in a halftime ceremony during the February 9, 1997, All-Star Game. Mikan, the oldest of the players on the list, was introduced last, to a huge ovation from the 20,562 in attendance.

Mikan couldn't help but consider how far the NBA had come. He'd been on the league's first championship team, and he'd participated in its first All-Star Game. In his day, he'd have been lucky if he'd walked out on the court and found ten thousand turning out to see him play. Now here he was, honored in a ceremony that had more glitz and glamour than he'd ever seen during his playing time.

"When we first started out, we didn't even have a halftime," he noted. "But this one was the tops."

Recognition came from the college ranks as well. Mikan had been named to DePaul's Hall of Fame, and his number "99" had been retired by the school's basketball program, but that much had been expected. No one in DePaul's history, with the exception of Ray Meyer, had done more for giving the school a name in college basketball. A more unexpected award came Mikan's way in 1997, when a media panel selected an "All-Time NIT Team." Hundreds of players had participated in the National Invitational Tournament over its sixty-year history, and Mikan felt honored to have been a unanimous selection to a team that also included Tom Gola (La Salle), Ralph Beard (Kentucky), Maurice Stokes (St. Francis), and Walt Frazier (Southern Illinois).

Mikan treasured the awards given him for individual achievement. During his playing days, he'd collected them after every season. Now, all these years later, he was being honored for his entire career. If there was anything missing, it was recognition for his old team, which somehow seemed to have been forgotten in all the hoopla raised around the championship Lakers on the West Coast.

But that, too, was about to change.

When Lakers owner Bob Short moved his team to Los Angeles in 1960, he left the team's Minneapolis history behind. As far as he was concerned, the Los Angeles Lakers were a brand-new team. They would develop their own history and identity on the West Coast. The Minneapolis Lakers' championship trophies were tossed out—literally—the broken pieces retrieved and eventually restored and saved for fans with longer memories. Short did retain the "Lakers" name for his Los Angeles franchise, a curious decision, given the fact that Los Angeles had its own large body of water nearby, and it was anything but a lake.

In time, the names of George Mikan, Vern Mikkelsen, Jim Pollard, Slater Martin, John Kundla, Clyde Lovellette, and those of other Minneapolis Lakers slipped from memory. Only old-timers or diehard fans remembered their achievements. Basketball, it seemed, was not only one of the fastest-paced pro sports; its fans had the shortest memories.

In time, the Los Angeles Lakers did indeed develop their own history and identity. The names of the West Coast version of the Lakers read like a Who's Who of NBA greats: Elgin Baylor, Jerry West, Wilt Chamberlain, Bill Sharman, Kareem Abdul-Jabbar, James Worthy, Bill Walton, Magic Johnson, Shaquille O'Neal, Kobe Bryant, and Phil Jackson—and this was only a start. In a run of excellence spanning several decades, only the Boston Celtics had won more championships.

The Los Angeles Lakers raised one championship banner after another to the rafters of, first, the Los Angeles Forum, and, later, the Staples Center. The team retired the numbers of its star players and ceremoniously raised replicas of their jerseys to the rafters. The Minneapolis Lakers' numbers—Mikan's "99," Pollard's "17," Mikkelsen's "19," Martin's "22," and Lovellette's "34"—were never officially retired. From time to time, a fan or sportswriter would ask about why the Los Angeles Lakers had done nothing to honor their predecessors in Minneapolis, but nothing came of the inquiries.

"Jerry Buss, the team's [current] owner, would send a polite response through an intermediary," wrote *Chicago Tribune* columnist Mike Downey, one of those who campaigned for years on Mikan's behalf. Mikan's jersey, Downey argued, belonged on the arena wall with all the other Laker greats. Buss only agreed to a point: "Mikan was one of the true greats of the game," he'd say, "but the Lakers wall of honor was meant for the L.A. Lakers."

Mikan shrugged off the snub, even though it irritated him. He had never played or lived in Los Angeles, he reasoned. Minneapolis, his home town for most of his adult life, had put up the big statue in the Target Center, and Mikan had won enough awards for his individual achievements to keep him satisfied. *He* knew what Minneapolis meant to the Lakers'—and NBA's—history, and that would have to do.

He was surprised and deeply moved, then, when the Los Angeles Lakers announced that the team intended to honor the Minneapolis Lakers during the halftime of an April 11, 2002, game between the Lakers and Minnesota Timberwolves. The Lakers planned to raise two banners honoring the pioneering team, the first listing the championship years of the BAA and NBA Lakers (but, curiously, not the NBL Lakers), the second listing the names of the Minneapolis Lakers inducted into the Hall of Fame.

Jerry Buss was pleased to be doing what the team's two previous owners—Bob Short and Jack Kent Cooke—had deemed unnecessary.

"This puts it all together," Buss told the press. "I like the completeness of it all. It should have been done before, but I didn't recognize the necessity. Now I really feel the continuity of the organization."

Mikan, too, was happy to see the Minneapolis Lakers linked to the current team. The NBA's pioneers, he'd always felt, deserved recognition for their contributions. The early Lakers were a case in point.

"It's a history we're proud of," he said.

The tribute to the Minneapolis Lakers was more than four decades coming, but when the big day arrived, the Los Angeles organization staged their tribute in style.

"It was the first time I flew first class," John Kundla remembered with a laugh. "It was a great tribute. They gave us rings with fourteen diamonds. I was paid six thousand dollars a year [when I was coaching], but here I got a ring worth nine thousand dollars."

"We were treated royally," Clyde Lovellette agreed. "Shaq came up and I introduced myself. He said, 'I know who you are.' It was like, 'You don't need to introduce yourself.' It was a great night."

Mikan's health had deteriorated to the point where he couldn't stand for the ceremony, so he attended it in a wheelchair. Vern Mikkelsen, also diabetic, was sensitive to the possibility that Mikan might be embarrassed by not being to stand beside his old teammates during the ceremonies, so he arranged, through his son John, who knew members of the Laker organization, to have all of the Minneapolis Lakers seated for the ceremony. He needn't have worried. Mikan was thrilled by the honors, which, after all, were being bestowed for achievements that had taken place when he was young and strong.

During the halftime ceremonies, representatives of the Los Angeles Lakers gave Mikan, Mikkelsen, Martin, Kundla, Lovellette, and Arilee Pollard (standing in for her late husband) commemorative championship rings. Elgin Baylor, the last Hall of Famer to wear a Minneapolis Lakers uniform, presented Mikan with his ring.

The banners were raised, the ceremonies ended, and the game continued. The Lakers, wearing replicas of the old light blue and gold Minneapolis road uniforms, concluded the evening with a convincing 96–83 win over the Timberwolves. Mikan had to smile. Regardless of where the team played its games, he would always be a Laker.

Nineteen

A Final Campaign

MIKAN'S HEALTH DECLINED noticeably once diabetes had its grip on him. Fortunately, he had stayed in good enough physical shape throughout his life to slow down his decline, but he grew weaker with each passing year. He'd needed help to get to the platform in 1997, when he'd been honored as one of the NBA's fifty greatest players. He'd struggled when he lost his leg and was fit with a prosthetic one. In time, he found himself spending his days in a wheelchair.

An ESPN feature, aired in May 2005, showed in shocking detail just how far he'd fallen. For the segment, Mikan allowed himself to be filmed in a basketball uniform, without his prosthetic leg. The close-ups revealed his missing fingers on one hand, and his body succumbing to age. Viewers saw a man, at one time one of the biggest and most powerful players in professional sports, confined to a wheelchair, struggling with difficult physical therapy, needing assistance in day-to-day life, keeping up a brave front against the inevitable.

For those who knew him, it was excruciatingly painful to watch.

"I cried when I watched it," said Bobby Harrison. "It was sad. He might have died sooner, but some inner strength just kept him going. He was in really bad shape."

Mikan's former teammates were aware of his travails. They'd seen him at occasional Laker reunions, such as the statue dedication at the Target Center, and some had talked to him from time to time. Whenever they spoke to him, Mikan was surprisingly upbeat, given his situation—the same old George, taking on the latest setback with the same determination he'd shown on the court. On occasion, he'd become reflective and talk about the past, about the glory days of the Laker dynasty, the friendships and careers, the regrets and highlights. He rarely complained.

Vern Mikkelsen saw more of him than any of the other old Lakers. Mikan had moved to Scottsdale, Arizona, in 1999, and Mikkelsen would see him when he traveled to Phoenix to visit his son and his son's family.

"George and Pat had bought a nice place in Scottsdale because four of their six children lived there and he needed help," Mikkelsen remembered. "Every time I'd go down there to visit my kids, I'd get a phone call from George. 'Hey, when are you coming over?' He was treated by dialysis on Monday, Wednesday, and Friday, for four hours each time, for four and a half years, and he wasn't back to normal until Saturday and Sunday. That's when he'd call. I'd meet him and we'd call old friends and we'd talk about things. We'd laugh and we'd cry and do all the good stuff. Nobody thought he was going to die that quickly, but he did."

The ESPN segment was a stunner, even for Mikkelsen, who appeared in the segment. No one had ever seen Mikan looking so vulnerable.

Mikan had a strong reason for setting aside his pride and appearing the way he did on the segment. Like so many of basketball's pioneers, he found himself in dire financial straits in his old age, and he wanted to help direct attention to the fact that the present two-tiered pension setup was woefully inadequate and ultimately dismissive of the players most responsible for laying the groundwork for the league. Something had to be done.

Mikan's vulnerability was precisely the point. He'd earned and lost money after his playing days, but he'd never seriously worried that he wouldn't be able to take care of Pat and himself in their old age. Diabetes and kidney problems changed all that. Dialysis was expensive, and that, along with the costs of consultations with physicians and surgical procedures, ate up virtually every cent that he had. He received $1,700 per month from his NBA pension, but that money, along with his Social Security and earnings from autographings at sports-card and memorabilia shows, wasn't enough. In 1990, while he was still living in Minnesota, he decided that he would have to sell the memorabilia from his own playing days to supplement his income.

It was a bitter decision. It would have been even harder to take if he hadn't heard from David Kohler, a Laguna Niguel, California, collector of all things Lakers. Kohler owned Sports Cards Plus, a sports-card and memorabilia outlet that specialized in auctions of rare, game-used items and collections. His interest in Mikan's items, though, was strictly personal. Beside the store, Kohler had built a museum in his home to honor the Minneapolis and Los Angeles Lakers. Kohler had gathered the most comprehensive collection of Minneapolis Lakers memorabilia to be found anywhere. The Mikan items, which included a signed, game-worn Minneapolis Lakers uniform (one of three known to exist) and a pair of Mikan's game glasses, became centerpieces in his museum.

Although pleased that he'd found a good home for his cherished basketball memories, Mikan was disturbed that he was forced into selling them in the first place. He had money after the sale, but it was only a matter of time before that, too, would be gone. He started thinking about the players of his time, all growing old, many in worse condition than he was in. The more he thought about it, the more upset he became. It was bad enough that the older players' contributions to the league were being forgotten; that they were living under difficult circumstances in their old age was inexcusable.

As it was, the players retiring before 1965 had no pension until 1988, four decades after the founding of the NBA. Until 1965, there had been no pension for anyone, but that changed only when Lenny Wilkens, Oscar Robertson, and others threatened to boycott the 1964 All-Star Game unless a pension agreement with the NBA was reached. Unfortunately for many of the retired players, the Players Pension Plan, forged between the NBA and the National Basketball Players Association, applied only to players retiring in 1965 or afterward. Players who retired prior to 1965 still received nothing.

The pension eligibility requirements remained unchanged for the next twenty-three years, despite protests from the older, ineligible players. Bob Cousy, one of the founders of the Players Association, yet ineligible for pension benefits, got together with a former Celtics teammate, Gene Conley, and Katie Conley (Gene's wife), and founded the NBA Old Timers Association, a group of more than one hundred pre-65ers, whose main objective was to lobby the Players Association and pressure them into including them in the next collective bargaining agreement. George Mikan was part of this group, as were Hall of Famers Dolph Schayes, Paul Arizin, Red Holzman, Bob Pettit, and Bill Sharman. Finally, in 1988, in a new collective bargaining agreement between the NBA and the Players Association, the pre-65ers were brought in on the deal, although not on equal terms with the post-65ers. To be eligible, the pre-65ers had to have played in at least five seasons (as opposed to the three-year requirement of the post-65ers), and the monthly pension money given to the pre-65ers was substantially less than that paid out to the post-65ers.

Even so, this might have worked except for two major factors: first, there were eighty-eight three- and four-year players who weren't receiving pensions, even though they had contributed at least as much as the three- and four-year post-65ers receiving pensions; and, second, World War II and the Korean War had interrupted many careers, cutting back the number of seasons some players stayed in pro basketball. The agreement allowed a year of military service to count as a year of playing time, but there was a catch: the player must have joined the league immediately after his discharge from the service. He couldn't have gone back to school or taken any other employment prior to going back to basketball.

The excluded players found an advocate in Bill Tosheff, who had played for Indianapolis and Milwaukee during his three-year NBA career. Tosh, as he liked to be called, served three years in the Army Air Corps. After his honorable discharge in 1947, he'd attended Indiana University for four years. He was drafted by the Indianapolis Olympians in 1951, and co-shared (with Mel Hutchins) the Rookie of the Year award. None of this mattered as far as his pension was concerned. Because he had chosen to attend school, his military service didn't apply to his eligibility for an NBA pension, and his three years in the pros weren't sufficient to make him eligible either.

Angered by the inequities between the pre-1965 and post-1965 pensions, particularly the two-year discrepancy in the time-served requirements, Tosheff began a tireless campaign on behalf of the three- and four-year players—"my boys," as he liked to call them. Tosheff's passions were apparent the moment you started talking with him. He was straightforward and all business, disdaining chit-chat and moving to the point like a heat-seeking missile. He'd founded his organization—the Pre-1965 NBA Players Association, Pioneer Era—in 1988, after the three- and four-year players had been excluded from the pre-1965 pension agreement, and he minced no words when talking about his case. The NBA, he said, underscoring the statements of George Mikan and others, had no sense of history.

"One of the reasons the NBA is lacking in basic compassion," he maintained, "is the fact that you've got young people working there who don't know a damn thing about the guys from that era, the guys who set the table in that era. They've never researched the past. They know the names but they don't know a thing about how they got there."

According to Tosheff, the three- and four-year players were cut out of the pre-1965 pension agreement because Commissioner David Stern cut a "sweetheart deal" with the Old Timers Association. The deal, Tosheff said, involved the NBA's offering the pre-65ers a pension if they agreed to cut out the players who hadn't served a minimum of five years.

"The Old Timers Association approached David Stern, who was in his fourth year as commissioner," Tosheff explained. "He agreed to bring them in, but he told them, 'Do not go to the media for support. Keep it under wraps.' So nobody ever told anybody about what was going on back East. I found out and I asked Cousy, 'What's going on? You cannot do that. You're stiffing guys who were on your ball club, guys you played against, some of your friends.' "

Cousy bristled at the assertion that he and his group had made any such deal with the NBA. The Old Timers Association, he told the *Boston Globe*'s Peter May, was in no position to make demands.

"We had no legal standing whatsoever," he stated. "We basically had to beg. It never crossed my mind to get three or four [years]. We were told what was going to happen."

Friction developed between Tosheff's group and other groups, including the Old Timers Association and the Retired NBA Players Association. Tosheff claimed—and correctly so—that a pension for his three- and four-year players would amount to little more than peanuts in the NBA's pension fund.

The numbers bore him out. As of 2005, there were just over fifty known three- and four-year players not receiving pensions. If each of these players was given $300 per month (still less than the post-65ers were receiving in 2005) for every season played, and, for the sake of simple math, you gave each player an average of 3.5 years of service, it would have cost under a half million dollars per year to take care of the *entire* three- and four-year group.

Tosheff took his cause to Washington, D.C., in 1998, when he and several others, including former players John Ezersky and Walter Budko, and

NBA historian and University of Maryland professor Neil Isaacs, testified before a Congressional Subcommittee on Employer–Employee Relations. Significantly, David Stern declined an invitation to testify, as did representatives from the National Basketball Players Association.

Ezersky and Budko were excellent examples of the kind of injustices Tosheff was trying to correct. Ezersky, a native New Yorker who had served in the invasion of Normandy, had a brief, two-year career with pro teams, but he had to leave the game because he couldn't support his family on his basketball salary. His years in the service were not added to his time in pro ball because a year elapsed between his time in the service and his joining the NBA. After leaving basketball, Ezersky spent more than fifty years driving a cab, first in New York City, and later in San Francisco, retiring only when old age and poor eyesight demanded it.

Budko's case was even more compelling. Budko attended Columbia University for a year before serving in the navy between 1943 and 1946. After his discharge from the service, he returned to school under the GI Bill and earned his BS degree. In 1948, he joined professional basketball and split four years between the Baltimore Bullets and Philadelphia Warriors. The time he spent earning his degree wound up costing him his pension.

("And what's the NBA's slogan?" Tosheff would scoff over the years. "Stay in School.")

The men testified on June 15, 1998. The subcommittee, although expressing sympathy toward the plight of the pre-65ers not included in the current pension plan, did not take any action on it.

Tosheff would win a case here and there for his boys, securing them pensions that had been previously denied, and the NBA would occasionally send some money his way to distribute among his members, but nothing officially changed. A familiar mantra, offered by more than a few of the pre-65ers in Tosheff's group, probably cut closer to the bone than any of the powers-that-be would have admitted: "They're just waiting for all of us to die off. Then it won't be an issue."

Even the pre-65ers receiving benefits were sympathetic.

"The players today get a lot of credit for donating money to great causes," said John Kerr, who followed his long NBA career with a lengthy career as an announcer for the Chicago Bulls. "I think that's fine and good, but the NBA players today should be embarrassed for what they've given to the guys who made this league. They've not given money to the guys who really need it. They just forgot.

"They don't even know what they went through. These players today have brand-new training facilities, they've got team doctors, they got all this stuff. We used to rent a trainer when we went to different towns—five dollars a trainer. Today, our guys have a masseuse that goes with them. It just bugs me that they won't release a wallet to the guys who put basketball on the map."

George Mikan was an ideal candidate to speak for all of the pre-65ers, those receiving benefits and those left out. He and Cousy were the best-known names from that group, and both had enough clout to demand and receive an audience with the powers-that-be. Even so, it took one of Mikan's old Laker teammates to persuade him to join the cause. Vern Mikkelsen had become involved in some of the efforts to secure better pensions for the pre-65ers, and he badgered Mikan about jumping on board. Mikan was initially reluctant. He still maintained a good relationship with the NBA, and he wasn't interested in getting caught in the middle of a lot of fighting and politics.

"I almost had to force George to get into the deal," Mikkelsen remembered. "He didn't realize how important that stuff was. I said, 'Just come to the Hall of Fame. Meet all the guys. Be part of this thing. If we can just get our foot in the door, we can have our pension set.' Then he ended up being the best guy we ever had."

When Mikan did get involved, he did so with characteristic zeal. He lobbied for better pensions, wrote letters and made calls, gave interviews to the press. Rather than point fingers and engage in a lot of overheated rhetoric, Mikan maintained his good standing with the NBA offices while holding a firm stance in petitioning the league for a change. It wasn't always easy, especially as his health deteriorated and his energy flagged, and he began to wonder if there was ever going to be a payoff for his efforts.

The ESPN segment became his penultimate statement. A new collective bargaining agreement was in the works for 2005, and Mikan hoped that the new agreement, perhaps the last one he'd see in his lifetime, would reward the pre-65ers with a little more money. The current players, he insisted, owed basketball's pioneers more than meaningless lip service.

"What do they owe?" he posed on the ESPN segment. "The right to play. We gave 'em a league. We sacrificed. They're in collective bargaining right now, and we're hoping we're going to be listened to and we sure would like the . . . players of today to help us out a little bit."

The ESPN piece became Mikan's last public appearance. He was in a medical facility, battling a diabetic wound on his remaining leg, when ESPN aired the segment in May 2005. In all likelihood, he would be losing the leg, but he hoped to regain enough strength to begin a physical-therapy and rehabilitation program afterward. He tried to remain optimistic, but the truth wouldn't be denied. He'd finally run into an opponent too powerful to beat, regardless of his determination and effort. On June 1, just eighteen days before his eighty-first birthday, George Mikan passed away in his sleep.

In the days following his death, Mikan was eulogized in countless obituaries, newspaper and magazine appreciations and columns, and radio and television commentaries. All were glowing in their regard for the player and the man.

"George Mikan truly revolutionized the game and was the NBA's first true superstar," David Stern said in an official statement issued to the press. "He had the ability to be a fierce competitor on the court and a gentle giant off the court. We may never see one man impact the game of basketball as he did, and represent it with such warmth and grace."

Bob Cousy, in his statement to reporters, noted Mikan's importance to the early NBA.

"He literally carried the league," Cousy pointed out. "He gave us recognition and acceptance when we were at the bottom of the totem pole in professional sports. People came to see him as much as they came to see the game."

In Chicago, Ray Meyer mourned the passing of his first basketball pupil. Mikan, he said, had been like a son to him. Mikan, he said, had made him the coach he was.

"This is not a good day for me," he said when he received the news of Mikan's death. "He put DePaul basketball and pro basketball on the map. He put *me* on the map."

Bud Grant, who had remained a friend and hunting buddy to Mikan over the years, might have paid Mikan the compliment that Mikan would have appreciated the most, had he been around to hear it: "In the sports I've been involved in, and the people I've played with and against, and the people I've coached and coached against, he was the greatest competitor I've ever been involved with."

In Miami, where the Miami Heat were meeting the Detroit Pistons in the playoffs, Shaquille O'Neal interrupted a television interview he was giving to address the Mikan family directly.

"If the Mikan family is watching," he said, "please contact the Heat office because I'd like to pay for his funeral. I know who he was. I know what he did. Without George Mikan, there is no me."

Mikan's death, following so closely on the heels of his ESPN appearance, prompted sportswriters to weigh in on the pension issue and Mikan's role in trying to stir public awareness of the plights of his contemporaries.

In a *Newsday* commentary published four days after Mikan's death, Karl Vogel recapped the influence Mikan had on the NBA, as a player and, later, spokesman for better pension benefits. He praised Shaquille O'Neal's actions in recognizing Mikan's importance to the game and in paying his funeral expenses, but he chastised many of O'Neal's "spoiled, pampered peers," who seemed utterly clueless about the debt they owed their predecessors.

"Without No. 99 and the others of that era, there wouldn't be basketball as we know it," Vogel wrote pointedly. "Now is the time for the NBA and the players union to do right by the few of them who remain before they wind up like George Mikan."

Mike Bianchi, writing for the *Houston Chronicle*, ridiculed a situation in which one of the game's most important figures had to sell his memorabilia while current players, drafted as teenagers right out of high school, commanded and received ludicrously high salaries.

"Can you imagine seeing Tracy McGrady or Kobe Bryant having to beg for a few extra shekels during their dying years?" Bianchi challenged his readers. "Can you imagine Me-Mac having to sell off his championship rings just to pay his bill? Oh, that's right, Me-Mac doesn't have any championship rings. Mikan impacted the game more than any player ever."

Boston Globe columnist Bob Ryan was even harsher in his criticism of the way the NBA, its Players Association, and its players ignored the needs of the older, pre-65 players.

"Oh, sure, they'll say such nice things about George Mikan now that he is dead," Ryan declared, "but where were they when he really needed them? They should be utterly ashamed of themselves, and I mean all of them. I'm talking about David Stern and Players Association head Billy Hunter and anyone else who could have done something about the insipid exclusion of pre-1965 NBA players from any decent pension money. Did any of them see the eighty-year-old Mikan in that ESPN piece last month, his body ravaged by diabetes, sitting in a wheelchair (his right leg had been amputated in 2000), and making a plea for a decent pension, not just for himself, but for the other pre-1965 players who set the table for the bazillionaires of today? It is all a sick, pathetic joke."

For Pat Mikan, who had just lost her husband of fifty-eight years, the kind words directed toward George and the outrage over the inadequate pension given to players who had retired before 1965, although appreciated, couldn't lighten a very painful load: she would have to go on without George and, because of the terms of the present pension agreement, she would have to do so while living on one half of the pittance he'd been receiving from his pension.

The Mikan family took up Shaquille O'Neal on his offer to pay for Mikan's funeral expenses, and private services were held in Scottsdale.

On July 31, a public service was held in Minneapolis at the Target Center. Pat Mikan attended, along with other family members. They were joined by some of Mikan's Laker teammates, John Kundla, Bill Sharman, civic dignitaries, and an estimated four hundred fans, some wearing the old Lakers jersey with the "M.P.L.S" emblazoned on the front. The ceremony, a celebration rather than a solemn occasion, took place near the entrance to the arena, by the bronze statue of Mikan taking his famous hook shot.

One by one, friends and family members paid tribute to Mikan's gentle nature, to the way he smiled even when he was facing the latest medical crisis. Kundla spoke of his character, Vern Mikkelsen of the way he and Mikan had laughed and cried when they talked during the last years of Mikan's life. Shaquille O'Neal sent a statement thanking Mikan for paving the way for future NBA players, concluding that, for him, Mikan would always be "The Big Original."

Mikan would have loved it.

No one needed to cite his importance to the game, or tout his greatness as a player. That much could be found in the pages of basketball history books or encyclopedias, in statistics that would be bettered by modern players, but which were unparalleled during his brilliant career; that much could be found in the giant symbol in the lobby of the Target Center, reminding fans about who'd brought championships to Minneapolis long before the dynasties in Boston, Chicago, or Los Angeles.

In the final, most important analysis, the man had to be remembered for something else, for a standard that reached beyond the hardwood floors of basketball arenas, beyond wins and losses on the court or even in his adventures after basketball.

George Mikan had never been a complex individual. The man you saw was the man he was. He never suffered from pretense or hidden agendas; he lived and died a midwesterner at heart, adhering to the standard his father had given him about doing his best and being judged accordingly.

When talking to the press shortly after his father's death, Terry Mikan spoke about all the familiar characteristics associated with George Mikan—most notably, the competitiveness and drive to excel—but he also spoke of the side of his father that gave him the "gentle" part of his nickname.

"Whenever he would make a toast at a family function, Dad would ask us to raise our glass to kindness," Terry Mikan said. "That's the type of man he was."

ACKNOWLEDGMENTS

Any biography of George Mikan is bound to be an account of the early days of the National Basketball Association, and of the origins of the Lakers, one of the NBA's most enduring and storied franchises. I learned this early in my research, and it was repeatedly underscored when I conducted the many interviews that became the backbone of this book. Any research is a process of education, and that was certainly the case here. Rarely, if ever, have I enjoyed the process as much as I did with this book. In talking to the pioneers of the NBA, I was transported back to an era when pro basketball was played more for the love of the game than for fame and money, when players put up with the hardships of travel, inadequate playing conditions, backbreaking schedules, and very little in salary and benefits for their efforts. Still, there was a joy to their game that seems lost on so many playing the game today.

Learning about George Mikan was a matter of learning about the origins of the NBA—and vice-versa. Mikan would never be considered a terribly complex individual—what you saw was what you got, as the saying goes—but his dedication and passion for basketball could serve as a lesson to people in all walks of life. In talking to people for this book, I heard story after story about what a nice guy Mikan was off the court, and how fierce he was on the court; interviewees seemed to line up to tell me the stories. I also heard about George Mikan, husband and family man, and about how, regardless of the height of his success, he never got above his raisin', as the song goes.

While researching Mikan, the Lakers, and the early NBA, I spoke to a number of Mikan family members, as well as players and Mikan associates, often more than once. I'm grateful for the time they gave me. Each one had an interesting account, and I feel blessed to have heard it. My thanks, then, to: Paul Arizin, Ralph Beard, Carl Bennett, Bob Berger, Vince Boryla, Carl Braun, Price Brookfield, Charlie Butler, Bill Calhoun, Al Cervi, George Crowe, John Ezersky, Arnie Ferrin, Billy Gabor, Dick Garmaker, Nancy Goldstein, Harry "Bud" Grant, Bobby Harrison, Lew Hitch, Joe B. Holland Sr., Jim Holstein, Mel Hutchins, Joe Hutton Jr., Wallace "Wah Wah" Jones, Ed Kalafat, Bill Kenville, John "Red" Kerr, George King, David Kohler, Bob Kurland, Bob Lavoy, Andrew "Fuzzy" Levane, Earl Lloyd, Clyde Lovellette, Ray Lumpp, "Easy" Ed Macauley, John "Whitey" Macknowsky, Slater Martin, Al Masino, Chuck Mencel, Pat Mikan, Charles Mikan, Rich Mikan, Vern Mikkelsen, Irv Noren, John Oldham, Wally Osterkorn, Jack Phelan, Arilee Pollard, Bob Rensberger, Arnie Risen, Ephraim "Red" Rocha, Kenny Rollins, Mickey Rottner, Frank "Pep" Saul, Fred Schaus, Dolph Schayes, Dick Schnittker, Milt Schoon, Dennis Schulstad, Howie Schultz, Myer "Whitey" Skoog, Larry Staverman, Gene Stump, William "Blackie" Towery, Ernie Vandeweghe, Paul Walther, Bobby Wanzer, and Bob Wold.

I was very fortunate to have been able to talk to two of the most influential men in Mikan's basketball life: Coaches Ray Meyer and John Kundla. Both offered valuable insights on what it was like to work with Mikan and have him as a friend. Sadly, Ray Meyer passed away shortly after my interview. He will be missed by the entire DePaul basketball family, and by anyone who had the pleasure of listening to his many stories.

Dick Triptow, Mikan's teammate on DePaul and, later, the Chicago Gears, was an invaluable contributor to this book. A basketball historian and author, Triptow has kept meticulous records, scrapbooks, and photographs on pro basketball's pioneering days. He was generous in sharing them, and his time, with me. In addition, he helped enormously in my early days of researching by providing important contact information on players who otherwise might have been difficult to locate and reach. You don't find nicer guys, and I feel fortunate to have met him and spent time with him.

Bill "Tosh" Tosheff was extremely helpful in supplying me with information about the old NBA and the controversial pension issue, as well as providing me with contact information, press clippings on the Indianapolis Olympians, and, in general, all-around encouragement. Hopefully, he will succeed in his tireless crusade on behalf of the NBA veterans in need of pensions.

This book's notes and bibliography sections list many of the published sources consulted and cited in *Mr. Basketball*, but, in some cases, the books deserve greater recognition than a place on a list. Since it wasn't possible to interview George Mikan for this book, I relied heavily on his comments and observations in his two autobiographies, *Mr. Basketball* (written with Bill Carlson) and *Unstoppable* (written with Joseph Oberle). Both are currently out of print, but for fans of the game, they are well worth the search. Terry Pluto's oral history of the NBA's early days, *Tall Tales*, and of the ABA, *Loose Balls*, are both invaluable and delights to read, as is *The Show*, Roland Lazenby's history of the Lakers. Neil Isaac's *Vintage NBA* should be required reading for anyone interested in the pioneering days of the NBA—or, better yet, for today's players, many of whom seem to have forgotten that there was a time preceding sunrise the day before yesterday.

Thanks, also, to the fine basketball writers who spoke to me and offered tips or encouragement: Joe Oberle, Terry Pluto, Sam Smith (basketball writer extraordinaire for the *Chicago Tribune*), and John Christgau (author of *Tricksters in the Madhouse*, a great account of the first Lakers–Globetrotters game and all that it meant in terms of the eventual integration in the NBA).

I am grateful to the folks at Bloomsbury for their help in all aspects of getting this book in print. My thanks to Kathy Belden for ushering it along, and special thanks to Miles Doyle, who brought great enthusiasm and a lot of good ideas to the editing process.

Thanks, Susan. Always.

Finally, to my children—Adam, Emily Joy, and Jack Henry: I'm lucky to know and love you.

Michael Schumacher
March 1, 2007

George Mikan's Career Statistics

Season	Team	G	FG	FTM	FTA	TOT	AVG
1942–43	DePaul	24	97	77	111	271	11.3
1943–44	DePaul	26	188	110	169	486	18.7
1944–45	DePaul	24	218	122	199	558	23.3
1945–46	DePaul	24	206	143	186	555	23.1
College Totals		**98**	**709**	**452**	**665**	**1870**	**19.1**
1946–47	Chicago (NBL)	25	147	119	164	413	16.5
1947–48	Minneapolis (NBL)	56	406	383	509	1195	21.3
1948–49	Minneapolis (BAA)	60	583	532	689	1698	28.3
1949–50	Minneapolis (NBA)	68	649	567	728	1865	27.4
1950–51	Minneapolis (NBA)	68	678	576	717	1932	28.4
1951–52	Minneapolis (NBA)	64	545	433	555	1523	23.8
1952–53	Minneapolis (NBA)	70	500	442	567	1442	20.6
1953–54	Minneapolis (NBA)	72	441	424	546	1306	18.1
1955–56	Minneapolis (NBA)	37	148	94	122	390	10.5
Career Regular Season Totals		**520**	**4097**	**3570**	**4597**	**11764**	**22.6**

PLAYOFFS

Season	Team	G	FG	FTM	FTA	TOT	AVG
1947	Chicago (NBL)	11	72	73	100	217	19.7
1948	Minneapolis (NBL)	10	88	68	96	244	24.4
1949	Minneapolis (BAA)	10	103	97	121	303	30.3
1950	Minneapolis (NBA)	12	121	134	170	376	31.3
1951	Minneapolis (NBA)	7	62	44	55	168	24.0
1952	Minneapolis (NBA)	13	99	109	138	307	23.6
1953	Minneapolis (NBA)	12	78	82	112	238	19.8
1954	Minneapolis (NBA)	13	87	78	96	252	19.4
1956	Minneapolis (NBA)	3	13	10	13	36	12.0
Career Playoff Totals		**91**	**723**	**695**	**901**	**2141**	**23.5**

NBA ALL-STAR GAMES

Season	Team	G	FG	FTM	FTA	TOT	AVG
1951	Western Conference		4	4	6	12	
1952	Western Conference		9	8	9	26	
1953	Western Conference		9	4	4	22	
1954	Western Conference		6	6	8	18	
NBA All-Star Game Totals		**4**	**28**	**22**	**27**	**78**	**19.5**

Notes

Prologue

x   "George was good-natured . . ." Author interview with Bud Grant.

xi   "George, what in the heck . . ." Author interview with Vern Mikkelsen.

xi   "Pretend you're getting dressed . . ." *Ibid.* All other direct quotations in this section are from this source.

Chapter One

2   "Sparrows, as always . . ." Studs Terkel, *Chicago* (New York: Pantheon, 1986), p. 29.

4   "They were all Croatian . . ." Author interview with Gene Stump.

4   "It was an experience . . ." Author interview with Charlie Butler.

5   "Do the best . . ." Dan Barreiro, "A Century of Minnesota Sports," *Minneapolis Star Tribune*, November 28, 1999.

5   "The cab driver . . ." *Ibid.*

5   "dot the i . . ." George Mikan, as told to Bill Carlson, *Mr. Basketball: George Mikan's Own Story* (New York: Greenberg, 1951), p. 17.

6   "For a moment . . ." Dan Barreiro and Michael Rand, "George Mikan Dies: He Changed the Game, Built City's Pride," *Minneapolis Star Tribune,* June 3, 2005.

8   "What are you squinting at . . ." George L. Mikan, and Joseph Oberle, *Unstoppable* (Indianapolis: Masters Press, 1997), p. 19.

10   "We used to go . . ." Author interview with Charlie Butler.

11   "If you ever want . . ." Mikan, and Oberle, *Unstoppable,* p. 23.

11   "I never knew . . ." *Ibid.,* p. 24.

11   "guinea pigs" *Ibid.,* p. 22.

12   "George, why don't you go . . ." Mikan, *Mr. Basketball,* p. 31.

13   "We were going . . ." Sid Hartman, "A Great Career Had Rough Start," *Minneapolis Star Tribune,* April 8, 2001.

13   "Go to a school . . ." Jason Kelly, "Mikan Wanted to Play for ND," *South Bend Tribune*, June 5, 2005.

13   "You'd be wrong . . ." *Ibid.*

Chapter Two

15   "This big guy . . ." Author interview with Ray Meyer.

16   "There are no positions . . ." Mikan and Oberle, *Unstoppable*, p. 32.

16   "You see this . . ." Mike McGraw, "Fans, Friends, Players Pay Tribute to Ray Meyer," [Arlington Heights, IL] *Daily Herald*, May 19, 1998.

17   "George was a very intelligent . . ." Author interview with Ray Meyer.

17   "We even had a kid . . ." *Ibid.*

17   "Billy used to take him . . ." *Ibid.*

17   "He couldn't do anything . . ." *Ibid.*

18   "I saw George Mikan . . ." n.a., "George Mikan: A 'Gentle Giant' and NBA's First Superstar," *Sports Illustrated*, June 3, 2005.

18   "One of the luckiest . . ." Lindsey Willhite, "Ceremony Pays Tribute to Meyer," [Arlington Heights, IL] *Daily Herald*, October 1, 1999.

19   "I played with Paul . . ." Author interview with Ray Meyer.

20   "He [could] get a team . . ." Jim Enright, *Ray Meyer: America's #1 Basketball Coach* (Chicago: Follett, 1980), p. 52.

20   "I would have been . . ." Ray Meyer, with Ray Sons, *Coach* (Chicago: Contemporary Books, 1987), p. 46.

21   "He wasn't ready . . ." Author interview with Ray Meyer.

21   "This one's for you . . ." *Ibid.*

22   "farce" Meyer, *Coach*, p. 46.

22   "We'd get into the train station . . ." Author interview with Dick Triptow.

24   "the 9,000 spectators . . ." Wilfrid Smith, "Indiana Wins; Notre Dame Defeats DePaul," *Chicago Tribune*, January 31, 1943.

27   "Dartmouth was rarely . . ." n.a., "Georgetown and DePaul Win in N.Y. Tournament," *Galveston News*, March 25, 1943.

27   "Big Mike": Oscar Fraley, "6-8 Center in Cage Finals," *Hammond Times*, March 25, 1943.

27   "I can only say . . ." Jessica Lee, "Hyde Brings Towering Stature to House Inquiry," *USA Today*, September 11, 1998.

28   "I noticed a great change . . ." Meyer, *Coach*, p. 48.

Chapter Three

30   "I became round-shouldered . . ." Frank Litsky, "George Mikan, 80, Dies," *New York Times*, June 2, 2005.

30   "They were calling him . . ." Dean Spiros, "The Transformation from Awkward to Awesome," *Minneapolis Star Tribune*, June 3, 2005.

31   "It's raining": Author interview with Gene Stump.

31   " 'Goon' best describes . . ." n.a., "George Mikan . . . World's Greatest Basketball Player," *Look,* February 1, 1949.

31   "It was an embarrassing . . ." Author interview with Bob Kurland.

31   "He said, 'You know, Bob . . . ' " *Ibid.*

31   "If you go back . . ." Author interview with Arnie Risen.

32   "We did it in an organized . . ." Author interview with Bob Kurland.

33   "The changes just gave me . . ." Sam Smith, "Mikan Changed the NBA; Minnesota Will Honor Legend," *Chicago Tribune,* April 7, 2001.

33   "He showed the world . . ." Roscoe Nance, "Today's Stars Can Thank NBA Pioneer Mikan," *USA Today,* October 30, 1996.

33   "The first day . . ." Author interview with Gene Stump.

34   "We were the logical ones . . ." Author interview with Dick Triptow.

35   "Oh, man, we would battle . . ." Author interview with Milt Schoon.

35   "They had a different team . . ." Enright, *Ray Meyer,* p. 67.

37   "The game was on a Saturday . . ." Author interview with Jack Phelan.

37   "Ray was a very, very religious man . . ."Author interview with Gene Stump.

37   "He made the first nine points . . ." Author interview with Jack Phelan.

37   "Nobody ever did that to me before . . ." Author interview with Ray Meyer.

37   "If you look at his record . . ." *Ibid.*

38   "Even the last of the doubters . . ." Mikan and Oberle, *Unstoppable,* p. 47.

38   "We preferred the NIT . . ." Steve Jacobsen, "To NIT Greats, Game is Worse," *Newsday,* March 26, 1997.

40   "I couldn't make it much of a duel . . ." Mikan, *Mr. Basketball,* p. 37.

40   "We'd come up short . . ." Mikan, *Unstoppable,* p. 50.

Chapter Four

42   "Let him earn them . . ." Mikan, *Mr. Basketball,* p. 39.

42   "He knocked four of my teeth out . . ." Author interview with Jack Phelan.

43   "We were both hanging on . . ." Mickey Furfari, "Fan Fare: Mikan 'Toughest' Foe WVU Star Ever Faced," *Charleston Daily Mail,* July 6, 2005.

43   "He's never met anybody . . ." Meyer, *Coach,* p. 52.

43   "What you did was get him mad . . ." Author interview with Jack Phelan.

43   "Everybody roared . . ." Author interview with Gene Stump.

44   "Our guys rose up . . ." Lindsey Willhite, "How Mikan Became a Legend at DePaul," [Arlington Heights, IL] *Daily Herald,* June 3, 2005.

44   "When he got in the mid-30s . . ." Author interview with Ray Meyer.

44   "He was unstoppable . . ." Author interview with Gene Stump.

44   "I should have left him in . . ." Author interview with Ray Meyer.

45   "the battle of the giants" Joe Reichler, "College Cage Teams Start Title Week," [St. Joseph, MI] *Herald-Press,* March 26, 1945.

45   "They kept saying . . ." Author interview with Ray Meyer.

45 "I slipped the paper . . ." Spiros, "The Transformation from Awkward to Awesome."

45 "Coach, don't you worry a bit . . ." Author interview with Jack Phelan.

46 "We were all broke . . ." Enright, *Ray Meyer*, p. 68.

47 "The best defense . . ." Author interview with Bob Kurland.

47 "That's Bob Kurland . . ." Author interview with Gene Stump.

47 "He'd chase me . . ." *Ibid.*

48 "Just hold your arms up . . ." Meyer, *Coach*, p. 55.

48 "He killed himself . . ." Author interview with Bob Kurland.

48 "Coach Hank Iba . . ." Mikan, *Mr. Basketball*, p. 42.

48 "the only good thing . . ." Meyer, *Coach*, p. 55.

50 "You boys seem to have been misinformed . . ." n.a., "Oakie-DePaul Upset Starts Rumor Mongers' Field Day," U.P.I. wire story, printed in the *Oelwein Daily Register*, March 30, 1945.

50 "burned up" *Ibid.*

50 "We didn't have any restrictions . . ." Author interview with Dick Triptow.

50 "The bookies used to be . . ." Author interview with Jack Phelan.

51 "I used to sneak out . . ." Author interview with Gene Stump.

51 "the New York guys . . ." Author interview with Bill Calhoun.

Chapter Five

52 "DePaul maintains . . ." Wilfrid Smith, "Big Ten Ruling on Eligibility May Bar Mikan," *Chicago Tribune*, December 11, 1945.

53 "We landed in Ponca City . . ." Author interview with Gene Stump.

53 "They were a Baptist community . . ." *Ibid.*

54 "We were standing around . . ." Author interview with Bob Kurland.

56 "I tended to steer clear . . ." Mikan and Oberle, *Unstoppable*, p. 64.

56 "Somehow, he'd gotten my telephone number . . ." Author interview with Pat Mikan.

57 "My dad was about six-two . . ." *Ibid.*

57 "My mom and dad loved George . . ." *Ibid.*

57 "a beautiful girl . . ." *Ibid.*

57 "The friends George played with . . ." *Ibid.*

58 "If the Aggies win . . ." Wilfrid Smith, "Open Stadium 4 Team Basket Meet Tonight," *Chicago Tribune*, February 8, 1946.

59 "Did I learn a lesson . . ." Author interview with Vern Mikkelsen.

60 "Maybe my grumbling . . ." Meyer, *Coach*, p. 56.

Chapter Six

62 "He called me in . . ." Author interview with Dick Triptow.

62 "He was a very, very meticulous . . ." *Ibid.*

63 "He had another fellow . . ." Author interview with Bob Rensberger.

63 "He was a little offbeat . . ." Author interview with Dick Triptow.

63   "he was independent . . ." Author interview with Price Brookfield.

63   "He told us if we won . . ." *Ibid.*

65   "was actually a thinly veiled . . ." Mikan and Oberle, *Unstoppable*, p. 62.

65   "He was more or less a coach . . ." Author interview with Price Brookfield.

65   "He wasn't an assistant . . ." Author interview with Bob Rensberger.

66   "I felt sorry for them . . ." Dick Triptow, *The Dynasty that Never Was* (self-published, 1996), p. 150.

67   "Since I'd reached the pinnacle . . ." Mikan and Oberle, *Unstoppable,* p. 68.

67   "He was so eager to do well . . ." Author interview with Dick Triptow.

67   "We used to say that basketball . . ." *Ibid.*

69   "He was built . . ." Author interview with Milt Schoon.

69   "Coach Ray Meyer advised me . . ." Triptow, *The Dynasty that Never Was*, p. 153.

70   "When we played Sheboygan . . ." Author interview with Price Brookfield.

Chapter Seven

74   "I've been in lots . . ." Mikan, *Mr. Basketball*, p. 96.

74   "It was our first chance to fly . . ." Author interview with Dick Triptow.

75   "I had to pull on the bottom . . ." Author interview with Irv Noren.

75   "very unusual but memorable games . . ." Triptow, *The Dynasty that Never Was*, p. 68.

75   "As a player would dribble . . ." *Ibid.,* p. 69.

75   "We got paid off in singles . . ." Author interview with Dick Triptow.

76   "We played in a lot . . ." *Ibid.*

76   "The first point I made . . ." Author interview with Irv Noren.

77   "The biggest corner . . ." Mikan and Oberle, *Unstoppable*, p. 74.

77   "I do not like the way . . ." Maurice Shevlin, "Mikan Retires After Gears Lose, 44–41," *Chicago Tribune*, December 12, 1946.

78   "for peeking into the . . ." Mikan, *Mr. Basketball*, p. 48.

78   "I can't possibly have stability . . ." Triptow, *The Dynasty that Never Was*, p. 73.

79   "He wanted us all to shoot . . ." Author interview with Price Brookfield.

79   "the greatest player of all time . . ." Triptow, *The Dynasty that Never Was*, p. 76.

79   "He could hit that long shot . . ." Author interview with Price Brookfield.

79   "In my eyes, he was the greatest . . ." Author interview with Dick Triptow.

80   "I'd just gotten out of college . . ." Author interview with Gene Stump.

80   "I was a rookie . . ." Author interview with Billy Gabor.

80   "I was in my bunk . . ." Author interview with Carl Bennett.

80   "It was a sad day . . ." *Ibid.*

82   "We didn't know . . ." Author interview with Dick Triptow.

82   "I think it would have been . . ." Author interview with Charlie Butler.

84   "I just couldn't believe . . ." Mikan, *Mr. Basketball*, p. 48.

85 "My brother and I mortgaged . . ." Robert W. Peterson, *Cages to Jumpshots* (New York: Oxford University Press, 1990), p. 138.

85 "He thought I was Jewish . . ." Author interview with Fuzzy Levane.

85 "He said, 'We're going to get . . . '" *Ibid.*

86 "We had sort of a conservative team . . ." *Ibid.*

87 "We got together . . ." Ron Thomas, *They Cleared the Lane* (Lincoln: University of Nebraska Press, 2002), p. 14.

88 "It was a small building . . ." Author interview with Bobby Wanzer.

88 "On one end . . ." Author interview with Arnie Risen.

89 "Go in for me . . ." Triptow, *The Dynasty that Never Was*, p. 87.

89 "I walk out of the locker room . . ." *Ibid.*

90 "the dynasty that never was" *Ibid,* p. 128.

Chapter Eight

94 "He was in favor of anything . . ." Author interview with Bob Berger.

94 "I think that was absolutely . . ." *Ibid.*

95 "In those days, every newspaperman . . ." Sid Hartman, "Mikan Made Lakers Early NBA Dynasty," *Minneapolis Star Tribune*, April 6, 2001.

97 "I got six thousand dollars . . ." Author interview with John Kundla.

97 "He could make you look silly . . ." Author interview with Red Rocha.

98 "He was the first guy who played above the rim . . ." Author interview with Fuzzy Levane.

98 "Jim was the most graceful player . . ." Author interview with John Kundla.

98 "You never knew . . ." Sid Hartman, with Patrick Reusse, *Sid!* (Stillwater, MN: Voyageur Press, 1997), p. 70.

99 "I liked Sid . . ." Roland Lazenby, *The Lakers* (New York: St. Martin's Press, 1993), p. 69.

101 "He had the right idea . . ." Author interview with Charlie Butler.

102 "It reminded me of Siberia . . ." Curt Brown, "Present, Past to Have Day on Court," *Minneapolis Star Tribune*, May 21, 2004.

103 "That's when I knew I wasn't a center . . ." Lazenby, *The Lakers*, p. 74.

103 "My God . . ." John Christgau, *Tricksters in the Madhouse* (Lincoln: University of Nebraska Press, 2004), p. 70.

104 "Winter suggested in Hebrew . . ." Hartman, "Mikan Made Lakers Early NBA Dynasty."

104 "They were supposed to . . ." Dan Barreiro, "A Century of Minnesota Sports," *Minneapolis Star Tribune*, November 28, 1999.

104 "The route to the airport . . ." Sid Hartman, "My Memories of Max Winter," *Minneapolis Star Tribune*, July 28, 1996.

104 "I thought that was the biggest . . ." Roland Lazenby, *The NBA Finals* (Dallas: Taylor, 1990), p. 29.

106 "Mikan, you're a fool . . ." Mikan, *Mr. Basketball*, p. 50.

107 "George would set the pick . . ." Author interview with John Kundla.

107   "If George didn't get the ball . . ." *Ibid.*

107   "I'd still rather beat . . ." Mikan, *Mr. Basketball*, p. 46.

109   "The Lakers came down with the ball . . ." Author interview with George Crowe.

110   "In essence, we were two-handed . . ." Author interview with Bobby Wanzer.

110   "You had a diversification . . ." Author interview with Arnie Risen.

111   "Pollard sulked most of the night . . ." Bud Vanderveer, "Royals Beat Minneapolis in Surprise," *Syracuse Herald-Journal*, April 17, 1948.

112   "He was as good . . ." Author interview with Vern Mikkelsen.

112   "We always looked to Pollard . . ." Author interview with Howie Schultz.

113   "If it wasn't for Mikan . . ." Author interview with Fuzzy Levane.

Chapter Nine

115   "It was electric . . ." Jim Litke, "It Was the Best Game Nobody Remembers," *Charleston* [W.V.] *Daily Mail*, February 19, 2003.

116   "the toughest test of Mikan's brilliant career . . ." Ben Green, *Spinning the Globe: The Rise, Fall, and Return to Greatness of the Harlem Globetrotters* (New York: Amistad, 2005), p. 202.

116   "We said, 'If they're gonna . . . ' " *Ibid.*, p. 205.

117   "I tried to beat the Trotters . . ." Mikan, *Mr. Basketball*, p. 5.

118   "It just happened that we got the ball last . . ." Litke, "It Was the Best Game Nobody Remembers."

118   "The Globetrotters were known for comedy stunts . . ." John McGrath, "Globetrotters' Win Over Lakers Is a Forgotten Social Milestone," *Tacoma News Tribune*, February 19, 2003.

122   "I don't know how many teams . . ." Author interview with Arnie Ferrin.

123   "Marques Haynes could have played . . ." Author interview with John Kundla.

124   "He took them over . . ." *Ibid.*

124   "After the first game . . ." Bob Velin, "Globetrotters Helped Spur NBA to Integrate with '48 Win vs. Lakers," *USA Today*, February 21, 2003.

124   "I'll give the Trotters credit . . ." Mikan, *Mr. Basketball*, p. 55.

Chapter Ten

126   "barely noticed at the time . . ." Leonard Koppett, *24 Seconds to Shoot* (New York: Macmillan, 1968), p. 38.

126   "See what he wants" Author interview with Carl Bennett.

127   "You can have the greatest ideas . . ." *Ibid.*

128   "I had started this move . . ." Neil D. Isaacs, *Vintage NBA: The Pioneer Era (1946–1956)* (Indianapolis: Masters Press, 1996), p. 233.

129   "Fulks is slow . . ." Phil Pepe, *Greatest Stars of the NBA* (Englewood Cliffs, NJ: Prentice-Hall, 1970), p. 143.

129   "To win, you've got to have points . . ." Joe Jares, *Basketball: The American Game* (Chicago: Follett, 1971), p. 92.

130   "Max would honestly tell you . . ." Author interview with Carl Braun.

131   "He looked after Ed . . ." Author interview with Bud Grant.

132   "Georgie, how come . . ." Mikan and Oberle, *Unstoppable*, p. 103.

133   "I was the only player . . ." Author interview with Arnie Ferrin.

134   "When A. C. Green . . ." Author interview with John Kerr.

134   "We could not sleep comfortably . . ." Author interview with Clyde Lovellette.

134   "Can you imagine George Mikan . . ." Author interview with George King.

134   "We got up over the harbor . . ." Author interview with Bud Grant.

135   "Kundla just about passed out . . ." *Ibid.*

135   "If George had said we weren't . . ." *Ibid.*

135   "It got wild . . ." Author interview with George King.

135   "We had very hostile, nasty fans . . ." Author interview with Red Rocha.

135   "That fan got his name . . ." Terry Pluto, *Tall Tales* (Lincoln: University of Nebraska Press, 2000), p. 38.

135   "run up and down the sidelines . . ." *Ibid.*

135   "Boston was playing in Syracuse . . ." Charles Salzberg, *From Set Shot to Slam Dunk: The Glory Days of Basketball in the Words of Those Who Played It* (New York: E. P. Dutton, 1987), p. 181.

136   "I was walking in . . ." Author interview with Bill Calhoun.

136   "It was a bit distracting . . ." Mikan and Oberle, *Unstoppable,* p. 100.

136   "Luckily, it hit the floor . . ." Author interview with Bobby Harrison.

136   "We were warming up . . ." Author interview with Arnie Ferrin.

137   "If you went up in the stands . . ." Author interview with Gene Stump.

137   "A little old lady tripped me . . ." Author interview with Jack Phelan.

137   "I got into an altercation . . ." Author interview with Wally Osterkorn.

140   "That cast was hard . . ." Lazenby, *The NBA Finals*, p. 32.

140   "from my fingers up to my armpits . . ." Mikan, *Mr. Basketball*, p. 57.

Chapter Eleven

143   "We were playing Philadelphia . . ." Author interview with Bobby Harrison.

144   "George is going to retire . . ." Author interview with Vern Mikkelsen. All other quotations in this segment are from this source.

145   "Some guy, a professor at Hamline . . ." *Ibid.*

146   "That was a crazy night . . ." Peter Finney, "'Horns Martin Master in 1947," [New Orleans] *Times Picayune*, April 3, 2003.

146   "I'd been there about ten days . . ." Author interview with Slater Martin.

147   "All they expected out of me . . ." Salzberg, *From Set Shot to Slam Dunk*, p. 64.

147   "Hey, throw me that ball . . ." Mickey Hershowitz, "Mikan Left Big Imprint on Martin," *Houston Chronicle*, June 4, 2005.

148   "Don't be afraid to take your shots . . ." Roland Lazenby, *The Show: The Inside Story of the Spectacular Los Angeles Lakers in the Words of Those Who Lived it* (New York: McGraw-Hill, 2005), p. 37.

148   "I messed it up for George . . ." Author interview with Vern Mikkelsen.

149   "I spent two years learning that job . . ." *Ibid.*

150   "They said I invented the power forward . . ." Author interview with John Kundla.

150   "fat and lazy" Mikan, *Mr. Basketball*, p. 58.

150   "As it turned out . . ." *Ibid.*

150   "our strongest team" Author interview with John Kundla.

151   "I was lucky . . ." *Ibid.*

151   "A professional coach . . ." Author interview with Clyde Lovellette.

152   "To win championships . . ." Author interview with John Kundla.

152   "He's a hard guy to watch . . ." *Ibid.*

152   "Neil's got about twenty-five . . ." Author interview with Dick Schnittker.

153   "We'd already played four years . . ." Author interview with Ralph Beard.

153   "Babe Kimbrough, a sports editor . . ." Ibid.

153   "The two leagues were battling . . ." Author interview with Wah Wah Jones.

154   "We chose Indianapolis. . ." Author interview with Ralph Beard.

155   "I'm a Kentuckian . . ." Author interview with John Oldham.

155   "I always felt sorry for Pollard . . ." Author interview with Bill Calhoun.

155   "We used to come out of there . . ." Author interview with George King.

156   "At the time, we were winning . . ." Mikan and Oberle, *Unstoppable*, p. 85.

158   "We tried everything . . ." Author interview with Bobby Wanzer.

158   "We could never stop Mikan . . ." Author interview with Bill Calhoun.

158   "If you read about the rivalry . . ." Author interview with Arnie Risen.

159   "the roughest, toughest series . . ." Mikan, *Mr. Basketball*, p. 60.

159   "Al was a fiery guy . . ." Author interview with Red Rocha.

160   "He was able to put across . . ."Author interview with Dolph Schayes.

160   "Dolph was the only six-eight guy . . ." Author interview with Fuzzy Levane.

160   "If they'd had a three-point shot . . ." Author interview with Vern Mikkelsen.

160   "He was a good ballplayer . . ." Author interview with Whitey Macknowsky.

161   "We were going to run a double pick . . ." Author interview with Bud Grant.

162   "All of a sudden . . ." Author interview with Whitey Macknowsky.

162   "I don't know if everybody else knew . . ." Author interview with Bud Grant.

162   "I took two dribbles . . ." Author interview with Bobby Harrison.

162   "Harrison threw it from mid-court . . ." Author interview with Whitey Macknowsky.

162 "I was fouled on that play . . ." Author interview with Al Cervi.

162 "That locker room . . ." Author interview with Bud Grant.

162 "I told a reporter . . ." Author interview with John Kundla.

163 "Except for that big man . . ." Al Cervi, "We Can Run and Win, Says Nats' Coach," *Syracuse Herald-Journal*, April 10, 1950.

163 "The Nats do not seem capable . . ." Lawrence J. Skiddy, "Nats Fly Home for Back-to-Wall Fight," *Syracuse Herald-Journal*, April 17, 1950.

Chapter Twelve

168 "I felt determined . . ." Mikan and Oberle, *Unstoppable*, p. 125.

168 "They called him the Gentle Giant . . ." Author interview with Bobby Harrison.

168 "He could raise that left elbow . . ." Ron Fimrite, "Big George," *Sports Illustrated*, November 6, 1989.

169 "Without a doubt, he had the sharpest . . ." Author interview with Jack Phelan.

169 "I got more tattoos from him . . ." Author interview with Clyde Lovellette.

169 "He had a temper . . ." Author interview with John Oldham.

169 "He not only hated losing . . ." Author interview with Red Rocha.

169 "We had to stay out on the floor . . ." Author interview with Bobby Harrison.

170 "I threw the ball in to him . . ." Author interview with Paul Walther.

170 "I was a very aggressive . . ." Author interview with Billy Gabor.

170 "Mikan was a hard competitor . . ." Author interview with Whitey Skoog.

171 "Take a look at my body . . ." Roscoe Nance, "Today's Stars Can Thank NBA Pioneer George Mikan," *USA Today*, October 30, 1997.

171 "In my first couple of years . . ." Author interview with George King.

171 "We'd always kid George . . ." Author interview with Dick Schnittker.

171 "Boston takes Charles Cooper . . ." Thomas, *They Cleared the Lane*, p. 26.

172 "Walter, don't you know . . ." *Ibid.*, p. 27.

173 "It was delayed somewhat . . ." Author interview with Carl Bennett.

174 "Either I get Sweetwater . . ." Thomas, *They Cleared the Lane*, p. 24.

174 "Bennett, you just voted . . ." Author interview with Carl Bennett.

174 "Well, he was fifty percent right . . ." *Ibid.*

174 "Eddie Gottlieb was sitting next to me . . ." Dan Shaughnessy, *Seeing Red: The Red Auerbach Story* (New York: Crown, 1994), p. 88.

175 "As far as I'm concerned . . ." Green, *Spinning the Globe*, p. 229.

176 "I don't give a damn for sentiment . . ." Bill Reynolds, *Cousy* (New York: Simon & Schuster, 2005), p. 78.

177 "I had seen Cousy play . . ." Red Auerbach and John Feinstein, *Let Me Tell You a Story* (New York: Little, Brown, 2004), pp. 61–62.

179 "We're on the train to Minnesota . . ." Author interview with Carl Bennett.

179 "I don't think any of us felt comfortable . . ." Author interview with John Oldham.

180 "It was something we hadn't seen . . ." Author interview with Arnie Ferrin.

180 "Obviously, the early part of the game . . ." Mikan and Oberle, *Unstoppable*, p. 63.

180 "If you got a basket . . ." Author interview with Joe Hutton Jr.

180 "It was a terrible game . . ." Author interview with Vern Mikkelsen.

180 "This isn't basketball" Blake Sebring, "The Game that Changed the NBA Forever, [Fort Wayne] *News-Sentinel*, November 2, 2004."

181 "He was our leading scorer . . ." Author interview with Fred Schaus.

181 "Everybody was really upset . . ." Author interview with John Oldham.

181 "Our fans got all upset . . ." Author interview with Bobby Harrison.

182 "My grandson . . ." Author interview with John Oldham.

183 "Gamblers couldn't get at my boys . . ." Charley Rosen, *Scandals of '51* (New York: Seven Stories Press, 2001), p. 134.

184 "I don't think anybody got . . ." Author interview with Vince Boryla.

184 "It was at the time of the college scandals . . ." Zander Hollander and Alex Sachare, eds., *The Official NBA Basketball Encyclopedia* (New York: Villard, 1989), p. 203.

185 "It was a pleasure to play with fellows . . ." Mary Schmitt, "NBA's Crown Jewel, the All Star Game, Was Born 46 Years Ago Without Fanfare, But Early Stars Revel in Today's Hugely Popular Extravaganza," *Cleveland Plain Dealer*, February 7, 1997.

185 "I was scared . . ." *Ibid.*

185 "I know a lot of guys . . ." Steve Popper, "Macauley's '51 All-Star Honors Came Late (But He's Not Complaining)," *New York Times*, February 5, 1998.

187 "I didn't make a big stink . . ." Author interview with Vern Mikkelsen.

188 "I got off hot . . ." Red Holtzman and Harvey Frommer, *Red on Red* (New York: Bantam, 1987), p. 30.

188 "useless on the boards" Mikan and Oberle, *Unstoppable*, p. 141.

189 "We were friends . . ." Author interview with Bill Calhoun.

189 "We tried to take advantage . . ." Author interview with Arnie Risen.

190 "He still did a lot . . ." Author interview with Bobby Wanzer.

190 "I've always felt they stole . . ." Mikan and Oberle, *Unstoppable*, p. 142.

Chapter Thirteen

191 "He's just a monster . . ." Mikan and Oberle, *Unstoppable*, p. 149.

192 "See these gray hairs . . ." *Ibid.*, p. 147.

192 "If the lanes are widened . . ." Stew Thornley, *Basketball's Original Dynasty: The History of the Lakers* (Minneapolis: Nodin Press, 1989), p. 41.

192 "I got this tape . . ." Author interview with Carl Bennett.

193 "They tell me . . ." Michael Rand, "Rules for a Ruler," *Minneapolis Star Tribune*, June 3, 2005.

193 "They told Barker and me . . ." Author interview with Joe Holland Sr.

194   "The Chicago Black Sox . . ." Rosen, *Scandals of '51*, p. 194.

195   "The owner of the star threatened . . ." *Ibid.*, p. 193.

195   "Levy wasn't the only . . ." *Ibid,* p. 192.

196   "It all didn't come out . . ." Author interview with Ralph Beard.

197   "I got into Minneapolis . . ." Author interview with Pep Saul.

198   "The only time I remember . . ." Author interview with Whitey Skoog.

198   "We were destroying them . . ." Author interview with Lew Hitch.

199   "As the NBA was growing . . ." Mikan and Oberle, *Unstoppable*, p. 151.

199   "We'd play, and somebody would call . . ." Author interview with Carl Bennett.

199   "The first couple of years . . ." Author interview with Arnie Risen.

200   "We were going to play . . ." Author interview with Ed Kalafat.

200   "We were making more money . . ." Author interview with Fuzzy Levane.

206   "I always considered . . ." Author interview with Vince Boryla.

207   "They really had good talent . . ." Author interview with Whitey Skoog.

207   "Al drove the lane . . ." Author interview with Ernie Vandeweghe.

208   "Everybody in the arena saw . . ." Author interview with Ray Lumpp.

208   "If we'd won that game . . ." *Ibid.*

210   "It came down to a seventh game . . ." *Ibid.*

Chapter Fourteen

213   "We used to complain . . ." Salzberg, *From Set Shot to Slam Dunk*, p. 181.

213   "After a recent game . . ." Peterson, *Cages to Jump Shots*, p. 178.

217   "With ten seconds to go . . ." Author interview with Carl Braun.

217   "We were probably the cockiest . . ." Author interview with Vince Boryla.

217   "As we were walking out of the arena . . ." Author interview with Vern Mikkelsen.

217   "It wasn't Sweetwater . . ." Author interview with Vince Boryla.

218   "They were telling the newspapers . . ." Author interview with Jim Holstein.

218   "I can still see the clippings . . ." Lazenby, *The Lakers*, p. 93–94.

218   "Take that jump shot . . ." Author interview with Ray Meyer.

218   "We're not dead yet . . ." n.a., "Lakers Need One More Win Over Knicks for Title," *Syracuse Post-Standard*, April 10, 1953.

219   "when we won in New York . . ." Author interview with John Kundla.

219   "After we won the championship . . ." Author interview with Whitey Skoog.

219   "That was an evening to remember . . ." Lazenby, *The Lakers*, p. 95.

219   "We're going to win again . . ." Mikan and Oberle, *Unstoppable*, p. 164.

Chapter Fifteen

221   "Clyde, I've got a nucleus . . ." Author interview with Clyde Lovellette.

222   "Sometimes, when I was sitting . . ." *Ibid.*

223   "It was the finals of my first year . . ." Author interview with Arnie Ferrin.

224   "We didn't like to play . . ." Author interview with John Kundla.

224 "Playing on that floor . . ." Corky Simpson, "Olson's Still Rooting Hard for Lakers Rooter," *Tucson Citizen*, June 2, 2005.

224 "Marques Haynes told me a story . . ." Author interview with John Kundla.

225 "I remember we were playing Oshkosh . . ." *Ibid.*

225 "Well, Mr. Basketball . . ." *Ibid.*

226 "He never should have shot . . ." Author interview with Ed Macauley.

226 "The crowd was yelling . . ." Author interview with Carl Braun.

226 "I can't tell you what he said . . ." Author interview with Arnie Ferrin.

226 "George was hard on officials . . ." *Ibid.*

227 "It was a huge mistake . . ." Author interview with Vern Mikkelsen.

227 "The ball just came off . . ." Author interview with Pep Saul.

227 "George couldn't hit his ass . . ." Author interview with Dick Schnittker.

228 "It took away a lot . . ." Author interview with Bobby Harrison.

228 "The first time I jumped . . ." Author interview with Jim Holstein.

228 "a bust" Author interview with Bill Calhoun.

228 "It took the driving layup out . . ." *Ibid.*

228 "He was still closer to that basket . . ." Author interview with Clyde Lovellette.

229 "We were a small market . . ." Author interview with Dolph Schayes.

229 "The press supplied us with ammunition . . ." Author interview with Earl Lloyd.

230 "We were in bad shape . . ." Jack Andrews, "Nationals and Celtics to Open Semi-Final Round Tonight," [Syracuse] *Post-Standard*, March 25, 1954.

231 "Somebody tunneled Dolph . . ." Author interview with Bill Kenville.

231 "I punched out Macauley . . ." Author interview with Wally Osterkorn.

231 "I had played with Brannum . . ." *Ibid.*

232 "I think we came in with the wrong . . ." Author interview with Clyde Lovellette.

233 "those giants just wore . . ." Bud Vender Veer, "Nats in Special Drills for 2nd Laker Test," [Syracuse] *Post Standard*, April 1, 1954.

234 "My eight-plus years as a pro . . ." Mikan and Oberle, *Unstoppable*, p. 170.

234 "We were coming out at halftime . . ." Author interview with Bill Kenville.

235 "I was open" Lazenby, *The NBA Finals*, p. 50.

235 "We made 'em mad then . . ." *Ibid.*

235 "The doctor put a basketball in my hand . . ." Author interview with George King.

236 "To me, this was much more . . ." Author interview with Earl Lloyd.

Chapter Sixteen

239 "In my first year . . ." Author interview with Paul Arizin.

239 "The game was going down the tubes . . ." Author interview with Billy Gabor.

240   "Baseball has three outs . . ." Terry Pluto, *Tall Tales*, p. 29.

241   "I'm an old-timer . . ." Author interview with Carl Bennett.

241   "I thought it was going to be bad . . ." Author interview with Bill Calhoun.

241   "It was good for me . . ." Author interview with Dick Schnittker.

242   "The adoption of the clock . . ." Charles Paikert, "Timing Meant Everything for NBA: Biasone's Shot Clock Idea Saved the Floundering League," *Seattle Times*, May 21, 2000.

242   "You'd take one look at George . . ." Author interview with Ed Kalafat.

242   "I'm Croatian by nationality . . ." *Ibid.*

243   "He played well . . ." Author interview with Whitey Skoog.

244   "You just don't do that . . ." Author interview with Dick Schnittker.

244   "I was at the free-throw line . . ." Author interview with Jim Holstein.

244   "It changed the whole dynamic . . ." Author interview with Dick Schnittker.

244   "When he came back . . ." Author interview with Chuck Mencel.

245   "It bothered me . . ." Author interview with Clyde Lovellette.

245   "You can't start from where he was . . ." *Ibid.*

246   "Without Mikkelsen . . ." Hartman, *Sid!*, p. 76.

246   "I objected . . ." Matthew Kredell, "And at Center, Bill Russell . . . Former Minnesota Lakers Executive Recalls Working on Deal to Get His Draft Rights," *Los Angeles Daily News*, April 11, 2002.

248   "Politicians would start at the crack of dawn . . ." Author interview with Vern Mikkelsen.

248   "Except for one NBA title . . ." Mikan and Oberle, *Unstoppable*, p. 189.

250   "It was hard for George . . ." Author interview with Clyde Lovellette.

250   "Some people can be coaches . . ." Author interview with Vern Mikkelsen.

251   "George's coaching skills were good . . ." Author interview with Ed Kalafat.

251   "George was a good coach . . ." Author interview with Dick Schnittker.

Chapter Seventeen

254   "The young kids really liked it . . ." Kent McDill, "A Giant in His Game, Former DePaul, NBA Great Mikan Dead at 80," [Arlington Heights, IL] *Daily Herald*, June 3, 2005.

254   "I believe I was the first one to say . . ." Terry Pluto, *Loose Balls* (New York: Simon & Schuster, 1990), p. 45.

254   "People will stand and cheer . . ." Joe Davidson, "Mikan Changed the Rules, Wrote Own Course," [Salt Lake City] *Deseret News*, June 14, 2005.

255   "Guards get killed when they come inside . . ." John Leptich, "Mikan's Legacy Led to Changes in Game," [Mesa, AZ] *Tribune*, June 3, 2005.

256   "I thought the most significant contribution . . ." Brett Ballantini, "Dunking Out of Dire Straits," *Basketball Digest*, March 2001.

257   "This is all a bunch of crap . . ." Pluto, *Loose Balls*, p. 43.

257   "I'm convinced that we would have died . . ." *Ibid.*

258   "We called him the 'En Route Commissioner' . . ." Author interview with
       Vern Mikkelsen.

259   "I see the spirit of the ABA . . ." Mikan and Oberle, *Unstoppable*, p. 212.

Chapter Eighteen

260   "He's definitely a milestone . . ." Steve Aschburger, "Mikan Sets Tone for
       Garnett, O'Neal," *Minneapolis Star Tribune*, April 9, 2001.

260   "George Mikan was the first dominant big man . . ." *Ibid.*

261   "I'm feeling fine . . ." Oscar Dixon, "Mikan Statue Set to be Unveiled,"
       USA Today, April 6, 2001.

261   "Max tells me . . ." Curt Brown, "A Glorious Past . . . and a Promising Fu-
       ture," *Minneapolis Star Tribune*, March 30, 2001.

261   "I'm very happy that the NBA . . ." Dan Barreiro and Michael Rand,
       "George Mikan Dies: He Changed the Game, Built City's Pride," *Min-
       neapolis Star Tribune*, June 3, 2005.

263   "energized" Mikan and Oberle, *Unstoppable*, p. 219.

263   "The truth is . . ." *Ibid.*, p. 221.

264   "It's hard to imagine . . ." Michael Murphy, "Generation Gap," *Houston
       Chronicle*, February 8, 1997.

265   "I think today's kids . . ." Author interview with Bobby Wanzer.

265   "We had one pair of shoes . . ." Author interview with Ed Kalafat.

265   "I played in the NBA All-Star Game . . ." Author interview with Billy Ga-
       bor.

265   "For years, people have been saying . . ." Barbara Barker, "Ex-Stars Flare at
       Today's Pay," *Newsday*, July 18, 1996.

265   "The league is bigger today . . ." Lacy J. Banks, "Living Legends Want Re-
       spect," *Chicago Sun-Times*, October 31, 1996.

267   "These are the players who invented the game . . ." n.a., "Celtics Permeate
       NBA's Superteam," [Memphis, TN] *Commercial Appeal*, July 18, 1996.

267   "If you're making $400,000 . . ." *Ibid.*

268   "When we first started out . . ." Lacy J. Banks, "Real Dream Team Steals
       Show," *Chicago Sun-Times*, February 10, 1997.

269   "Jerry Buss, the team's . . ." Mike Downey, "Downey's 11: After Years of
       Coaxing, Lakers Honored Mikan," *Chicago Tribune*, June 3, 2005.

269   "Mikan was one of the true greats . . ." *Ibid.*

269   "This puts it all . . ." Steve Aschburner, "Wolves Notes: Lakes Pay Tribute
       to Minnesota Roots," *Minneapolis Star Tribune*, April 12, 2002.

270   "It's a history we're proud of . . ." Broderick Turner, "Two Eras in Har-
       mony," [Riverside, CA] *Press-Enterprise*, April 12, 2002.

270   "It was the first time I flew first class . . ." Author interview with John
       Kundla.

270   "We were treated royally . . ." Author interview with Clyde Lovellette.

Chapter Nineteen

271   "I cried when I watched it . . ." Author interview with Bobby Harrison.

272   "George and Pat had bought . . ." Author interview with Vern Mikkelsen.

274   "my boys" Author interview with Bill Tosheff.

275   "One of the reasons the NBA is lacking . . ." *Ibid.*

275   "The Old Timers Association approached . . ." *Ibid.*

275   "We had no legal standing . . ." Peter May, "Pension Deal in '88 Left Out a Select Few," *Boston Globe*, July 20, 2005.

276   "And what's the NBA's slogan . . ." Author interview with Bill Tosheff.

276   "The players today get a lot of credit . . ." Author interview with John Kerr.

277   "I almost had to force George . . ." Author interview with Vern Mikkelsen.

277   "What do they owe . . ." Joe Gergen, "Nation: George Mikan, 80, NBA's First Superstar," *Newsday*, June 3, 2005.

278   "George Mikan truly revolutionized . . ." n.a., "What Others Say About Mikan," *Minneapolis Star Tribune*, June 2, 2005.

278   "He literally carried the league . . ." Bill Jauss, "George Mikan, 1924–2005: NBA's Big Man Changed the Game," *Chicago Tribune*, June 3, 2005.

278   "This is not a good day . . ." Lacy J. Banks, "Former DePaul Standout Who Revolutionized Basketball as the True Big Man Dies of Kidney Failure, Diabetes, at 80," *Chicago Sun-Times*, June 3, 2005.

278   "In the sports I've been involved in . . ." Ray Richardson and Bob Sansevere, "NBA's First Dominant Big Man Dies at 80," *Seattle Times*, June 3, 2005.

279   "If the Mikan family is watching . . ." Michael Hunt, "Mikan Leaves Large Legacy," *Milwaukee Journal Sentinel*, June 4, 2005.

279   "spoiled, pampered peers" Karl Vogel, "NBA Players Union Needs to Do Right by Aging Former Players," *Lincoln* [NE] *Journal Star*, June 5, 2005.

279   "Can you imagine seeing Tracy McGrady . . ." Mike Bianchi, "Pioneers Merit Decent NBA Pension," *Houston Chronicle*, June 10, 2005.

279   "Oh, sure, they'll say such nice things . . ." Bob Ryan, "A Poor Effort by Those Getting Rich Via NBA," *Boston Globe*, June 6, 2005.

280   "The Big Original" Rich Alonzo, "Mikan's Life Celebrated," *St. Paul Pioneer Press*, August 1, 2005.

281   "Whenever he would make a toast . . ." n.a., "NBA Loses Giant of Player, Man in Mikan," *Augusta* [GA] *Chronicle*, June 3, 2005.

BIBLIOGRAPHY

Alfieri, Gus. *Lapchick*. Guilford, CT: Lyons Press, 2006.

Auerbach, Red, and John Feinstein. *Let Me Tell You a Story*. New York: Little, Brown & Company, 2004.

Bjarkman, Peter C. *The History of the NBA*. New York: Crescent Books, 2002.

Carlson, Stanley W. *The Minneapolis Lakers, World Champions of Professional Basketball, 1948–49–50: A Pictorial Album*. Minneapolis: Olympic Press, 1950.

Chamberlain, Wilt, and David Snow. *Wilt*. New York: Macmillan, 1973.

Christgau, John. *Tricksters in the Madhouse*. Lincoln: University of Nebraska Press, 2004.

Cohen, Stanley. *The Game They Played*. New York: Carroll & Graf, 1977.

Devaney, John. *The Story of Basketball*. New York: Random House, 1976.

Einhorn, Eddie, with Ron Rapoport. *How March Became Madness*. Chicago: Triumph Books, 2006.

Enright, Jim. *Ray Meyer: America's #1 Basketball Coach*. Chicago: Follett, 1980.

George, Nelson. *Elevating the Game: Black Men and Basketball*. New York: HarperCollins, 1992.

Green, Ben. *Spinning the Globe: The Rise, Fall, and Return to Greatness of the Harlem Globetrotters*. New York: Amistad, 2005.

Ham, Eldon L. *The Playmasters*. Chicago: Contemporary Books, 2000.

Hartman, Sid, with Patrick Reusse. *Sid!* Stillwater, MN: Voyageur Press, 1997.

Heisler, Mark. *Giants: The 25 Greatest Centers of All Time*. Chicago: Triumph Books, 2003.

Hill, Bob, and Randall Baron. *The Amazing Basketball Book: The First 100 Years*. Louisville: Fullcourt Press, 1988.

Hollander, Zander, and Alex Sachare. *The Official NBA Basketball Encyclopedia*. New York: Villard, 1989.

Holzman, Red, and Harvey Frommer. *Red on Red*. New York: Bantam Books, 1987.

Hubbard, Jan, ed. *The Official NBA Encyclopedia*. New York: Doubleday, 2000.

Isaacs, Neil D. *Vintage NBA: The Pioneer Era (1946–1956)*. Indianapolis: Masters Press, 1996.

Jares, Joe. *Basketball: The American Game*. Chicago: Follett, 1971.

Koppett, Leonard. *24 Seconds to Shoot: An Informal History of the National Basketball Association*. New York: Macmillan. 1968. Revised and expanded edition, 1970.

———. *Championship NBA*. New York: Dial Press, 1970.

Lazenby, Roland. *The Lakers: A Basketball Journey*. New York: St. Martin's Press, 1993.

———. *The NBA Finals*. Dallas: Taylor, 1990.

———. *The Show: The Inside Story of the Spectacular Los Angeles Lakers in the Words of Those Who Lived It*. New York: McGraw-Hill, 2005.

Liss, Howard. *The Winners*. New York: Delacorte Press, 1971.

Meyer, Ray, with Ray Sons. *Coach*. Chicago: Contemporary Books, 1987.

Mikan, George, as told to Bill Carlson. *Mr. Basketball: George Mikan's Own Story*. New York: Greenberg, 1951.

Mikan, George L., and Joseph Oberle. *Unstoppable*. Indianapolis: Masters Press, 1997.

Neft, David S., Roland T. Johnson, Richard M. Cohen, and Jordan A. Deutsch, eds. *The Sports Encyclopedia: Pro Basketball*. New York: Grosset and Dunlap, 1975.

Pepe, Phil. *Greatest Stars of the NBA*. Englewood Cliffs, NJ: Prentice-Hall, 1970.

Peterson, Robert W. *Cages to Jump Shots*. New York: Oxford University Press, 1990.

Pluto, Terry. *Falling from Grace*. New York: Simon & Schuster, 1995.

———. *Loose Balls*. New York: Simon & Schuster, 1990.

———. *Tall Tales*. Lincoln: University of Nebraska Press, 2000.

Reynolds, Bill. *Cousy*. New York: Simon & Schuster, 2005.

Rosen, Charley. *Scandals of '51*. New York: Seven Stories Press, 1999.

———. *The Wizard of Odds*. New York: Seven Stories Press, 2001.

Russell, Bill, as told to William McSweeny. *Go Up for Glory*. New York: Coward-McCann, 1966.

Salzberg, Charles. *From Set Shot to Slam Dunk*. New York: E. P. Dutton, 1987.

Shaughnessy, Dan. *Seeing Red: The Red Auerbach Story*. New York: Crown, 1994.

Smith, Seymour, with Jack Rimer and Dick Triptow. *A Tribute to Armed Forces Basketball*. Self-published, 2003.

Sullivan, George. *Wilt Chamberlain*. New York: Grosset & Dunlap, 1966.

Taylor, John. *The Rivalry*. New York: Random House, 2005.

Thomas, Ron. *They Cleared the Lane*. Lincoln: University of Nebraska Press, 2002.

Thornley, Stew. *Basketball's Original Dynasty: The History of the Lakers*. Minneapolis: Nodin Press, 1989.

Triptow, Richard F. *The Dynasty that Never Was*. Self-published, 1996.

Vancil, Mark, ed. *NBA at 50*. New York: Park Lane Press, 1996.

Vecsey, George. *Harlem Globetrotters*. New York: Scholastic Book Services, 1970.

INDEX

A Note on the Author

Michael Schumacher is the author of eight books, including *Family Business, Francis Ford Coppola, There But for Fortune, Crossroads, Dharma Lion,* and, most recently, *Mighty Fitz.* He lives in Wisconsin.